Simone De Beauvoir

Simone De Beauvoir

a life... a love story

*My life would be a beautiful story come true,
a story I would make up as I went along.*

SIMONE DE BEAUVOIR

CLAUDE FRANCIS
FERNANDE GONTIER

Translated from the French by Lisa Nesselson

ST. MARTIN'S PRESS
NEW YORK

Library of Congress Cataloging in Publication Data

Francis, Claude.
    Simone de Beauvoir: a life, a love story.

    Translated from French.
    Bibliography: p.
    Includes index.
    1. Beauvoir, Simone de, 1908–   —Biography.
2. Authors, French—20th century—Biography.
3. Feminists—France—Biography.   I. Gontier,
Fernande.   II. Title.
PQ2603.E362Z68313   1987   848'.91409   [B]   86-27908
ISBN 0-312-00189-4

First Edition
10 9 8 7 6 5 4 3 2 1

CONTENTS

ACKNOWLEDGMENTS

When one writes the biography of a controversial figure, it is not always possible to be certain that one has all the facts or is using the accurate version of events that have been recorded in different or contradictory ways. We did our best to obtain all the information currently available and to consult those witnesses who agreed to meet with us. Some of them asked not to be mentioned by name; those who authorized us to identify them are so identified in the course of the text.

We wish to express our gratitude to all those who have been directly or indirectly a source of information since we started to work on *Simone de Beauvoir* in 1975.

Raymond Aron, Tomiko Asabuki, Colette Audry, Hélène de Beauvoir, the marquis de Beauvoir, Elisabeth Badinter, Dierdre Bair, Mauricette Berne, Anna Boschetti, Jacques-Laurent Bost, Jean Cau, Madeleine Chapsal, Catherine Clément, Annie Cohen-Solal, Jeannette Colombel, Michel Contat, Catherine Chaine, Françoise d'Eaubonne, Josée Dayan, Françoise Ducout, Dominique Desanti, Sandra Elkin, Claire Etcherelli, Arlette Elkaim-Sartre, Sulamith Firestone, Betty Friedan, Gisèle Freund, Laurent Gagnebin, Geneviève Gennari, Françoise Giroud, John Gerassi, Madeleine Gobeil, Germaine Greer, Benoîte Groult, Paul Guth, Maurice de Gandillac, Gisèle Halimi, Sarah Hirschmann, Francis Jeanson, Serge Julienne Caffié, Olga Kosakievicz, Claude Lanzmann, Suzanne Lilar, Elaine Marks, Kate Millett, Andrée Michel, Caroline Moorehead, Jean Pouillon, Oreste Pucciani, Lauren H. Pringle, Pierrette Rosset, Malka Ribowska, Michel Rybalka, Madame le Ministre Yvette Roudy, Pierrette Sartin, Alice Schwarzer, Jean-Louis Servan-Schreiber, Gloria Steinem, Evelyne Sullerot, Nina Sutton, Michèle Vian, Catherine Valabrègue, Pierre Viansson-Ponté, Olivier Todd, Ellen Wright, Anne Zelinsky.

We wish to extend our special thanks to Mrs. Candida Donadio; Mr. W. J. Weatherby, who helped us in our search for Simone de Beauvoir's letters to Nelson Algren; Mr. Robert Tibbetts, curator of Special Collections of the Ohio State University Libraries, who gave us access to the Ohio State Nelson

Algren Archive, the largest repository of Algren's papers, with some 20,000 manuscript pages; and Madame Callu and Madame Berne, curators of Special Collections at the Bibliothèque Nationale.

We would like to thank the staffs of the libraries of Vassar University, Rice University, Tulane University, Smith College, Princeton University, Mills College, the University of Rochester, Oberlin College, Macon College, U.C.L.A., the University of California at Berkeley, Columbia University, Wellesley College, Harvard University, Yale University, Southern Illinois University, and the staff of St. Martin's Press and especially our editor, Toni Lopopolo.

NOTES AND
REFERENCES

The point of departure for this biography was our tracking down of the handwritten, unpublished letters that Simone de Beauvoir wrote to the American author Nelson Algren, with whom she had fallen in love. These 1,442 pages of delicate script recount, sometimes on a daily basis, Simone de Beauvoir's life as well as the lives of Jean-Paul Sartre and their friends. This correspondence, covering the years from 1947 to 1960, is a rich firsthand account of existentialism's golden hours, the turn of events in politics and literature, gossip among the intellectual set, and above all a love story.

Weeding through old regional newspapers from Lorraine, we also unearthed the tragic story of Simone de Beauvoir's maternal grandfather, whose financial ruin transformed the destiny of this "dutiful daughter."

We could not have written this biography without the benevolent welcome accorded us by its subject, Madame Simone de Beauvoir, who for ten years graciously invited us into her home and permitted us to tape more than sixty hours of interviews. She told us the names of the real persons who appear under pseudonyms in her memoirs. She told us the true story of Zaza's death and shared with us some facts that she had preferred to omit from her memoirs.

Under no circumstances is this an "authorized" biography. We alone are responsible for the manner in which we have made use of or interpreted the materials.

The first series of interviews with Simone de Beauvoir took place in her studio in 1975, 1976, and 1977; the second series took place in Paris in 1983, 1984, and the spring of 1985. The unnoted quotations and information about Simone de Beauvoir and her works not attributed to others are from our own interviews and correspondence. In September 1985 Simone de Beauvoir read the first set of proofs and made some comments, mainly on Chapters 1–3. We have included some of these annotations in the notes.

The correspondence with Nelson Algren is in the collections of the Ohio State University at Columbus. It is filed in folders lettered A to L, and a copy was most kindly made available to us by Mr. Tibbetts, the curator of Special Collections.

We have used our own archives on Simone de Beauvoir, some two thousand unpublished pages of manuscripts and notes from Simone de Beauvoir.

For the chronology of Simone de Beauvoir's life we used *Les Ecrits de Simone de Beauvoir,* which contains a chronology and a detailed bibliography of her books and articles, her lectures, interviews, prefaces, signed manifestos, and movie scripts.

In some cases we have substituted our own translations for the originals, and each time we have indicated why in a footnote. Sartre's quotes from *Les Carnets de la drôle de guerre* and *Les Lettres au Castor et à quelques autres* are translated by Lisa Nesselson.

For each chapter we have listed the sources used in that chapter.

INTRODUCTION

One morning in June 1982 our publisher called and asked us to write a biography of Simone de Beauvoir. We had just finished a book on the Icarians, a group of French settlers who had attempted to create a Utopian society in the United States in 1849, and we were starting our research for our next project. We asked to think it over.

We were staying at a hotel on the boulevard Raspail, five minutes away from Simone de Beauvoir's studio at 11 bis rue Schœlcher. It had become our landing point in Paris since that day in 1975 when we met de Beauvoir for the first time. We were then planning to write her biography-bibliography (a format devised by Michel Contat and Michel Rybalka in their *Ecrits de Sartre*). We knew that de Beauvoir liked this format, but we were still surprised when, even before we had time to sit down in her studio, she told us, "Let us get organized." For four years we worked on *Les Ecrits de Simone de Beauvoir*, spending every vacation, every sabbatical in Paris. She was very generous with her time and always eager to help. We came with our tape recorder, our notebooks, our stack of questions, and a bunch of flowers—usually tiger lilies, which reminded her of the Mississippi. She would greet us at the door, ready to work. We had gathered every bit of information we could find from Tamil to Finnish, and our original project was mushrooming into a mammoth five thousand pages of interviews, articles, and unpublished texts. After some soul searching on her part, and some encouragement from us, de Beauvoir decided to publish *When Things of the Spirit Come First* as a separate entity. In the preface she wrote, "It happens that two American professors of French origin, Claude Francis and Fernande Gontier, are going to publish *Les Ecrits de Simone de Beauvoir. . . . When Things of the Spirit Come First* was naturally to be part of this collection. But it was too voluminous to be integrated without throwing the work out of balance." Meanwhile we had come up with the idea that her articles and interviews on women, which spanned a period of forty years, could be published in a separate volume that would show the evolution of her feminism; we referred to it as *Les Ecrits féministes*. One day de Beauvoir, in her brusque voice, said, "Let us call it *Post-Scriptum to the Second Sex."* She was asked so many questions about her feminism that she thought it would be very practical to gather in a Post-Scriptum her views on the topic. Once she had accepted a project, de Beauvoir would move very quickly. So we signed two contracts with her, each of the three of us to receive an equal share of the royalties. *Les Ecrits de Simone de Beauvoir* satisfied her taste for academic research, and she was so pleased with it that she included it in the list of her works. But we discovered that she could say no as quickly as she could say yes. The Post-Scriptum was ready to go to press when de Beauvoir, reading the final set of proofs, had a change of heart. She found her articles and interviews "too repetitive" and told us, "We have to find a new format." The publication was postponed. Later she sent us a very businesslike letter saying she entrusted us with this publication, which should be done thematically.

That she could wield the ax after a manuscript had been completed and the work set in type was amazing. We heard so many different comments on her ability to make an abrupt turnabout, from people who hated her and from people who worshipped her, that we preferred to forget the incident and remember only the excitement of working with her.

There was always the unexpected, as on that evening in 1977 when, relaxing around the ritualized scotch on the rocks, one of us mentioned an album of photographs of Sartre that was to be published by Liliane Siegel, one of Sartre's young friends.

By the time we left we had in our briefcase all the snapshots that had covered an entire wall in de Beauvoir's studio. She had taken them down herself as we played with the idea of an album of her pictures that would tell the story of her life. *Simone de Beauvoir et le cours du monde* was published in 1978.

When it came to writing a biography of Simone de Beauvoir, we knew that it would not be an easy task. We were aware of twilight zones and topics that were taboo. We had discovered that she had willfully blurred some parts of her life or reconstructed the circumstances surrounding people who were dear to her. Several times while working on *Les Ecrits* she had said, "What I am telling you should not be printed, keep it off the record."

Disturbing questions sprung to our minds: Could we write an objective biography? De Beauvoir had written her autobiography in four big volumes; would she let us use facts she had intentionally omitted? Would we be free to give our own interpretation based on our research?

From the start we were reassured; de Beauvoir seemed eager to cooperate. As we had done for *Les Ecrits de Simone de Beauvoir,* we arrived with a list of prepared questions that de Beauvoir would answer methodically, often correcting herself and checking to see that we were taping the corrected version.

After two hours of work she would say, "We have worked enough." She would refill our glasses, and the conversation would turn to friendly talk. She would assail us with questions: Had we read that article? that book? seen that movie? Why did we stay at a hotel when there was a studio for sale in her building? We should go to Cabourg. "You don't know the Ile de Ré?" Her questions were often personal, and that was when she would speak of herself, her childhood, her life in an informal manner. Her voice would change completely, even her accent was not the same, the rapid, extremely precise diction giving way to a husky, hearty tone. Her carefully crafted phrases, her extremely proper and elegant French slipped into picturesque Parisian slang.

She laughed a lot and unleashed her sometimes abrasive sense of humor. It was fascinating to witness de Beauvoir's metamorphosis. We had wondered why Sartre accused her of indulging in schizophrenia; he had said there were two persons, the wonderful Castor and the rather unpleasant Mademoiselle de Beauvoir. On the one hand she was an extremely self-controlled, aggressive, self-demanding person; on the other hand she overflowed with vitality, sensuality, and a tremendous capacity to enjoy life. There was a carefully designed public image and a private one. Interested by the hidden side of her ambiguous personality, we prepared our interviews in order to entice her to be more open. She did not like to talk about politics or feminism—"Read my memoirs," she would say—but she loved to talk about herself, bouncing back and forth in time. She would speak at length about Sartre, his women, and "all that money he spent on them," about the grudges she held against old friends: One had become too involved in her political career, another had written something she had no business to publish, an American feminist had nothing to say but nonsense. Olga was so angry when de Beauvoir published *Thoughtful Passions: Jean-Paul Sartre's Intimate Letters to Simone de Beauvoir,* for she felt she had been slighted by Sartre and de Beauvoir, that after fifty years of friendship she refused to speak to Simone and died a few months later without having forgiven her. "But don't write that in your book."

Her favorite topics were her trips, the fine restaurants, the gourmet foods, the wines. With these seemingly unstructured interviews the trials of the biographers began. According to de Beauvoir's mood, we heard different versions of events. For instance, she said that her Uncle Hubert Brasseur had married against his father's will a woman who was socially inferior and had two children whom she hardly knew. "My sister and I were told they were just distant relatives." Later de Beauvoir told us that she had lunch with these first cousins every Thursday at her grandfather's apartment and that her aunt "was invited at home occasionally." One day her father, "who never amounted to anything," was ill-tempered, selfish, arrogant, and stingy; another day he was a charming, carefree, happy-go-lucky person. He never wrote a line; later we were told that he had written a play she remembered reading and some short stories.

We were wondering what to do with these contradictions. We agreed to show her the proofs of the manuscript. As she read them she presented us with more contradictions. In the course of our research we had gathered all the facts about the bankruptcy of her maternal grandfather and the ordeal it had been for his family. He was sentenced to fifteen months in jail on 132 counts of the fraudulent misuse of funds. Ruined and dishonored, he moved to Paris, to the slums neighboring the Montparnasse railroad station. Simone was one year old at the time of this misfortune that was to modify her entire life. Her mother's dowry was never paid, her father ("who once admitted to a friend that he was a failure") worked as the secretary to a famous Parisian lawyer until he went into business with his father-in-law and into a second bankruptcy in 1919–1920.

De Beauvoir had a theory: Each individual is shaped forever by the first months of his life. In *All Said and Done,* and in the interviews she gave to Francis Jeanson in 1966, she went into great detail to explain her point of view. If money may have little to do with an infant's happiness, it had an impact on the family and must have affected the environment of the child. This she denied. "I was happy; as far as I am concerned, this did not affect my happiness."

We asked, "Wasn't your mother upset? her personality affected by all that?"

"Yes. Yes, it did upset my mother, absolutely. She broke with all her friends. There was that shame; when I made an allusion to it in my memoirs, she became very upset. She was still upset after all those years" (Interview, September 17, 1980).

Describing de Beauvoir's parents' relationship, we had quoted from *A Very Easy Death* (p. 30): "Slaps, nagging, scenes not only in privacy but even when guests were there." As she read this, de Beauvoir exclaimed, "How could *you* write such a thing!" When we showed her the words in her own book, "How could I have written such a thing!" was her startling reaction. "I was completely mistaken." We remained unconvinced.

We had mentioned that her father kept in his office a photograph of his last mistress, who came sometimes with her husband to visit. Simone de Beauvoir, flushed suddenly with anger, denied it. "What gave you such an idea! This is fiction! I phoned my sister. I don't remember anything like this and neither does my sister!" So we read from *A Very Easy Death* (p. 34): "In his office my father kept the photograph of his last mistress, a pretty and brilliant woman who sometimes came to the house with her husband. Thirty years later he said to Mama, laughing, 'You did away with her photo!' She denied it, but he was not convinced."

De Beauvoir: "It is stupefying that I could write such a thing. It corresponds to none of my memories, to none of my sister's memories. I don't know what I wanted to hint. What is very clear is that I did meet that woman when I was twenty, and I was impressed by her beauty. She was brilliant." De Beauvoir continued, "For you it is easy, you just have to cross it out, but it creates a real problem for me, a problem concerning the errors you make when you write [a long silence] and yet I was in the heart of things."

We suggested, "Maybe you were too emotional."

De Beauvoir: "Emotion is no excuse for factual errors."

Reality does not always fit into molds. Ambiguities, contradictions, the unforeseen succession of events creates twilight zones. De Beauvoir gave a certain order to the story of her life; she structured her narrative and restructured her life. We came to realize that she could not accept easily and without pain the reality that her story would be retold by others and seen through eyes other than her own.

De Beauvoir's outlook on her life and the lives of others had changed over the years. The alcoholic Simone Jollivet she depicts in her letters to Nelson Algren had wiped out the image of the wild, successful young woman who had swept Sartre off his feet. "No, I was never jealous of Simone Jollivet, that second-rate actress!"

"But you say so in your memoirs."

"My memoirs are not the Bible!" And on that we agreed; in her autobiography, particularly in *Memoirs of a Dutiful Daughter* and *The Prime of Life,* de Beauvoir had taken license with aspects of her personality and her life and in fact created a work of art.

One small detail seemed to us extremely revealing. De Beauvoir wrote in the first sentence of *Memoirs of a Dutiful Daughter* that she was born in a room overlooking the boulevard Raspail, which was then an elegant bourgeois address. We asked her, "Why do you always mention the boulevard Raspail? Wasn't your address 103 boulevard du Montparnasse? Wasn't the entrance to the building between the Parnasse and Rotonde cafés?"

De Beauvoir: "Yes, but we had two windows overlooking the boulevard Raspail."

De Beauvoir chose to paint herself "the boulevard Raspail's way." We choose to enter her life by way of the boulevard Montparnasse. We are aware that truth is illusive and that, to quote Pirandello, *Everyone has his own truth.*

I knew that no harm could ever come
to me from him—unless he were to die
before I died.

The Prime of Life

Simone De Beauvoir

Isolde's Gesture

Friend Tristan, when I see you lying dead,
Reason forbids me to live . . .
She embraces him, lies down at his side,
Kisses his mouth and his face
And clasps him closely . . .
Chrétien de Troyes, Tristan et Iseult

*S*artre was dying. He held Simone de Beauvoir by the wrist and, without opening his eyes, told her, "I love you very much, my dear Castor."* He offered his lips to her and she kissed him. He fell asleep. She kept vigil for hours. At nine that evening, Sartre died. "I wanted to lie down beside him under the sheet. A nurse stopped me. 'No, beware . . . the gangrene.' It was then that I understood the real nature of the bedsores. I lay on top of the sheet and I slept a little. At 5 A.M. the male nurses came. They stretched a sheet and a kind of cover over Sartre and took him away."[1] It was April 15, 1980.

---

*Castor, the French word for "beaver," was Sartre's pet name for Simone de Beauvoir. When they were students at the Sorbonne, René Maheu, a friend of de Beauvoir, thought that "Beauvoir" sounded a bit like the English "beaver." It was customary to invent nicknames in their class, and since beavers "are constructive and live in groups," he affectionately called her the Castor, and the name stuck.

Three days later, twenty thousand people, perhaps as many as fifty thousand, turned out for Sartre's funeral. Friends and admirers, the curious, journalists, were a human wave breaking against the walls of the Montparnasse cemetery. People were everywhere, scrambling atop headstones, craning for a glimpse. That the ridiculous is never far removed from the sublime was demonstrated when an anonymous admirer perched in a tree came crashing down onto Sartre's coffin.

At twenty, Simone de Beauvoir had written, "I knew that he would never go out of my life again."[2] And now, aged seventy-five: "His death separates us. My death will not bring us together again. That is how things are. It is in itself splendid that we were able to live our lives in harmony for so long."[3]

Retold by Chrétien de Troyes or Béroul, this love story would sound like the stuff of legends. A pretty young girl, the most intelligent among her peers, meets the most brilliant boy around, and there you have it: the ideal couple. Ideal by virtue of being the most resolutely "modern" pair of their time. The couple through whom an entire era speaks to us and who gave half a century a tone, a lifestyle, a philosophy. A couple who intrigue as surely as they irritate. A partnership that inspired envy despite its being misunderstood and impossible to define, so original as to exceed our grasp.

Words have the power to bring us ideas, words hold the magic to tell us stories; whatever their intent, the words remain to capture and intrigue us, to hold us in their spell. They charge a body of work that has been in our midst, living alongside us for over fifty years. For a long time now we have carried on a sort of dialogue with these books and their authors, but above and beyond this enduring presence there remains that je ne sais quoi, that certain something by which we were more captivated, more provoked. For they were a couple, and above and beyond philosophy and fluctuating politics there remained this marvel: two human beings in absolute harmony. We are more taken with writers whose love lives weave their way through their work, and there are no stories more often told than those of the great enduring loves. Why would we remember Cosima and Richard Wagner, or Abélard and Héloïse, were it not that matters of the heart are the most enticing, that each heart has reasons of its own, and that the story of a couple whom life could not wear down and defeat moves us, intrigues us, and holds us a prisoner of its magic.

That Simone de Beauvoir and Jean-Paul Sartre were great writers, navigators who charted the ocean of a tumultuous half century, goes without saying. No amount of criticism, no animosity could obscure this overwhelming preeminence. But if this splendor has always had a special allure, it is that there was a double brilliance, a twofold fame.

"We were two of a kind and our harmony would last as long as we ourselves . . . and nothing could take precedence over this alliance," de Beauvoir wrote.[4] The world was their prize, reflected in a double mirror. Any separation was compensated for with nearly daily correspondence, their wills caught up in a sole objective, to write. This plan to live and to write heeding no voice save that of the other was a unique success. Their love overcame "the heart's intermittent vagaries" and "the casual loves" that occurred in the rhythm of the days and the years. This alliance, dominating all, was total and sufficient. "For me, his existence justified the world," she wrote.[5] To which he replied, "We understood ourselves to be very much alike . . . I never really spoke of my theories to anyone but her. . . . It marked the end of a solitude which I never felt again . . . the very deep and unique relationship which linked me to Simone de Beauvoir was the highest, the ultimate."[6]

They fascinate us because, of all the gifts exceptional people can give, they have presented us with something both rare and commonplace, the stuff that weaves its way through novels and binds them together: a love story that has been so long in the public domain that the two lovers seem real and at the same time fictional. They invented ways to live out their love, and in setting up freedom and honesty as its guidelines they conquered and maintained this harmony, sometimes in spite of themselves and always despite others.

Their love withstood the test of time, upholding a hard-won individuality, a romantic morality as complex as their individual temperaments. A privileged love, maintained through every stage of daily life by a choice unendingly renewed. For them it was enough to be what they were. It is an uncommon story to have remained sincerely interested in each other, day in and day out for more than fifty years.

Having accepted the challenge of living a life without compromise, Simone de Beauvoir now had to accept a loss whose significance defied all measure. "There is no such thing as a natural death: nothing that happens to a man is ever natural, since his very presence calls the world into question."[7]

To reach beyond the present toward a future even death itself will not undo is both the gesture of an existentialist and the practice of a philosophy that came naturally to Simone de Beauvoir. She proceeded to write a book devoted to the final ten years of Sartre's life, then published his letters that she had kept for fifty years, breathing youth back into their saga by returning to those spontaneous words scrawled for her from day to day.

She transcends the pain: "Nothing more than myself will ever be promised to me and that amounts to nothing if I don't make something of myself."[8] "The fact remains that I'm a writer . . . someone whose entire existence is ruled by writing."[9]

1

The Child and the Others

Any genius born a woman is lost to humanity.
Stendhal

THE VERDUN BANKER'S BANKRUPTCY

Simone Lucie Ernestine Marie Bertrand de Beauvoir was born in Paris on January 9, 1908, in the unimposing building at 103 boulevard du Montparnasse, at the corner of the boulevard Raspail. Two years later, a modest café, the Rotonde, opened its doors on the ground floor. It was there, in the carrefour Vavin, that legendary intersection presided over by the cafés of Montparnasse in its heyday—the Parnasse, the Dôme, the Rotonde, and the Café Baty—that Simone de Beauvoir spent her childhood unaware of her soon-to-be-illustrious neighbors Modigliani, Léonard Foujita, Moise Kisling, Ossip Zadkine, and Picasso. The intersection then was one big construction site. Drilling had been under way since 1905 to ford the last hundred yards separating the two boulevards. The junction would not finally be inaugurated until 1913, when President Raymond Poincaré arrived in a resplendent carriage with an escort of smartly uniformed Republican guards whose plumed helmets streamed in the wind. In his speech he did not miss the opportunity to draw attention to the slowness of the construction. Simone de Beauvoir grew up to the continual clatter of carts, steam-operated streetcars, and noisy demolitions. The shouts of masons during the day gave way to the joyous racket of the Parnasse and Rotonde cafés that filtered up to her bedroom at night.[1]

She came into the world smack in the middle of a family drama that would mark her early childhood and affect the course of her life—although de Beauvoir herself was loath to admit any such thing.[2] Her maternal grandfather, a banker in Verdun, was being forced to declare bankruptcy, and there was suspicion of fraud and gross mismanagement of funds. Everything he owned would soon be swallowed up in the encroaching debacle. This gentleman approaching fifty was going to be imprisoned, his honor and reputation ruined. A bankrupt! The very word "bankruptcy" weighed heavily; it denoted a crime punishable by law and a dishonor that reflected on one's entire family. Rejected by society, stripped of his possessions, a man whose fortunes had failed sometimes went so far as to commit suicide.

Gustave Brasseur loved life too much to come to that. Blessed with a solid constitution and a vigorous imagination, he had faith in his destiny. Originally from Belgium, he settled in Verdun in 1878, around the time a constitution was granted to Alsace-Lorraine, and proceeded to make his mark as a talented man of finance.* He set up a limited partnership under the name Gustave Brasseur and Company, which soon became the Bank of the Meuse, for the enterprise was an immediate success.

The nineteenth century was a grand time for financiers. Like any self-respecting financial baron, Gustave Brasseur thought big; soon he had opened branches of his bank. Dynamic and resolutely modern in his approach to business, he placed ads in the papers and ran full-blown publicity campaigns. The Bank of the Meuse, with a capital of two million francs—gold francs, that is—offered an ever diversifying array of services to the public: checking and savings accounts, foreign and domestic brokerage, loans, money orders, French and foreign dividend payments, and mouth-watering interest rates that began at 1 percent on deposit and rose to 2.5 percent in three months, 3.5 percent in six months, and a considerable 4 percent annually.

The money poured in and Gustave Brasseur became one of the region's great bankers. He had a knack for being both convincing and charming, and

---

*In 1871 France had lost the war with Prussia and ceded to it Alsace and a part of Lorraine. Further to the south, Verdun, in the Meuse, was restored to France.

he enjoyed a standard of living that, in his own estimation, was the best possible form of advertising. The local papers reported the lavish dinners he held for his shareholders, the balls to which he invited the cream of Verdun society, and the hunting parties he led with officers of the garrison. At election time he endeared himself to certain candidates by organizing receptions and galas that afforded his friends the opportunity to lead a discreet electoral campaign in the comfort of the Brasseur living room.

Gustave Brasseur was the product of an elite Jesuit education. He married a rich heiress who bore him three children: Françoise, a pretty brunette with hazel eyes (the future mother of Simone de Beauvoir); Hubert, christened in honor of the patron saint of hunters; and Lili, a rosy-faced blonde. Madame Brasseur was passionately devoted to her husband but not terribly maternal by nature, and she extended only a modicum of affection to her children. The family lived in a big house in the middle of a park in Verdun. Summers were spent at fashionable beaches, winters featured an occasional trip to Paris. Hubert boarded with the Jesuits, and his sisters were day students at the famous Couvent des Oiseaux, the institution to which the aristocracy and the upper middle class sent their daughters.* In 1895 the tuition there was 1000 francs and classes were taught by nuns from the congregation of Notre-Dame, themselves from the very best families. All her life Françoise de Beauvoir would look back on her years at the convent where she had been happy. There were only six students in her class, four boarders who dressed in black and two day students who wore white. She was a very good student and thrived on the attention of her teachers. Passionate by nature, Françoise suffered from her mother's coldness and her father's marked preference for her sister Lili, five years her junior. She would later give to her daughters— particularly to Simone, who bore a physical resemblance to her—the affection she had lacked in her own childhood.

Gustave Brasseur went in for all the innovations of the day with enthusiasm. He was an excellent tennis player, excelling at a sport then reserved for an avant-garde elite. An accomplished hunter, he combed the forests and countryside with the local aristocracy and was the proud owner of a three-shot rifle envied by all. Brasseur was a fan of the great outdoors and led his children on cycling expeditions through the Ardennes Forest. Before 1900,

---

*The Couvent des Oiseaux, or Convent of the Birds, located at the intersection of the rue de Sèvres and the boulevard des Invalides in Paris, was so named because its first proprietor, the sculptor Jean-Baptiste Pigalle, had an enormous aviary built on the premises. During the French Revolution it was converted into a prison. Later it served again as a convent where nuns from the Notre-Dame congregation taught young ladies. Branches of the convent throughout the nation saw to the education of the daughters of those who could afford it.

few had taken to the open road on bicycles, and their outfits were a source of amazement, especially those worn by the women: baggy bloomers and a boater hat held down by a scarf that trailed in the breeze. Humorists poked fun at them in the papers: "Who are those young men riding toward us? There they go . . . why, they're young ladies!"[3] One can imagine the impression Gustave Brasseur made as he and his daughters pedaled through country villages.

Françoise, the eldest, dreamed of being an explorer, but this was not to be; marriage was in order for her. Her father felt he had every right to hope for a match with one of the better families. Françoise was beautiful, a good musician with a charming voice, and her dowry was large enough to attract the heir to a good name or a substantial fortune. While plans were under way to marry her off, Françoise fell in love with her first cousin, Charles Champigneulles, heir to a stained glass window factory on the boulevard du Montparnasse. She was dreaming of an engagement when the luck that had smiled upon the Bank of the Meuse ran out.

The year 1906 marked a turning point in the banker's life. That year some of his investments proved disastrous, and for the first time Gustave Brasseur's intuition failed him. One of his best friends was not reelected to office, whereupon the banker lost the support of an influential politician. He embarked on several risky financial affairs which might have straightened out the situation had they succeeded, but they did not. This run of bad luck had one immediate consequence: Charles did not pursue his matrimonial plans with Françoise and eventually married one of their cousins, Germaine Fourrier. Since the question of money had dashed his daughter's plans, Gustave Brasseur maintained a tenacious bitterness toward his nephew for the rest of his life. When, ironically, Simone de Beauvoir, aged sixteen, fell in love with Charles' son Jacques, her grandfather thundered, "So long as I live, no granddaughter of mine will ever marry a Champigneulles!"

Among the subsequent candidates for his daughter's hand, Gustave Brasseur favored the cousin of a Parisian banker who was the protégé of a politician and who bore a handsome name: Georges Bertrand de Beauvoir.

THE BERTRAND DE BEAUVOIRS

*T*he Bertrand de Beauvoirs were a Parisian family of civil servants. Simone de Beauvoir's great-grandfather, François-Narcisse, born in 1795, spent his entire career with the Finance Ministry and was sent to

Argenton, in the Creuse region, as a tax inspector. Having amassed a comfortable fortune, in his forties he married Armande Rosalie Dransart, seventeen years his junior. They set up housekeeping at 64 rue Saint-Louis in the exclusive 8th arrondissement, where their first son, Ernest-Narcisse—Simone's grandfather—was born in 1838.

It is not known exactly when the Bertrand family took on the name "Beauvoir" and the nobiliary particule "de." Simone de Beauvoir's great-great-grandfather went by the name. We do know that Simone's grandfather's godfather, Philippe de Cellier, was a knight of Saint-Louis, a royal and military order founded in 1693 by Louis XIV to reward "virtue, merit and services rendered."

François-Narcisse Bertrand de Beauvoir had three sons, all of whom were educated by the Jesuits and to whom he bequeathed an estate which enabled the youngest to live off a private income. The eldest, Ernest-Narcisse, inherited, "among other properties," a large country house and five hundred acres of chestnut groves and woods in Meyrignac, in the Limousin region.[4] At twenty-one, Ernest Bertrand de Beauvoir entered the regional prefecture of the Seine as an assistant with a salary of 1200 francs. He spent his entire career in administration, retiring in 1897 with the honorary title of head clerk at a salary of 10,000 francs. He maintained a lifestyle more illustrious than his position. In 1870 he married Léontine Wartelle, the daughter of an opulent family from Arras. The couple moved into a handsome apartment at 110 boulevard Saint-Germain. Ernest de Beauvoir was lighthearted and gay by nature; he liked neither "arguments nor responsibilities" but was well aware of his rights and held a lofty idea of his rank in society. He played *la canne,* a sport that was all the rage during the Second Empire, and in it he rose to the rank of provost, or assistant master, a title of which he was extremely proud.*

The de Beauvoirs had three children, Hélène, Gaston, and Georges. Gaston, the eldest, hated to study and cared only for hunting; rowdy and robust, he bullied his younger brother, Georges, whose sensitive character must have exasperated him.

Georges de Beauvoir, born in Arras on June 25, 1878, was lively and intelligent. He proved to be his mother's favorite, and she kept close watch on his studies and encouraged his predilection for reading. He loathed his brother's violent games and involvement in sports.

Summers in Meyrignac, while Gaston ran wild in the woods, Georges imperiously summoned together the local farm children to instruct them in

---

La canne, literally "cane," known as singlestick in English, was a game of skill that, much like fencing, required considerable agility and grace. For sheer snob appeal, it compares roughly with polo today.

schoolwork. A photograph shows him in the midst of his "students," flanked by a servant girl in white cap and apron holding a tray loaded with glasses of orangeade.

Georges was consistently at the top of the honor roll at his school, the Collège Stanislas, and he seemed to have a fine future when, in 1892, his mother died. Deprived of his mother's encouragement and guidance, the gifted thirteen-year-old was left to his own devices. His sister, Hélène, married a Limousin country squire and left to live in a manor house, the Château de la Grillère. Between his bon vivant father and an older brother "devoted to complete inactivity," Georges' activities were limited to what he found amusing. An avid reader, he devoured anything and everything; possessed of an excellent memory, he passed his baccalaureate without difficulty. He could have followed in his father's and grandfather's footsteps and become a civil servant, but all his life he railed against "those budget-gobblers." His father, his uncle, his name, his family connections all served to convince him that he belonged to the aristocracy. He set himself above the commonplace and especially above any form of plebeian success that he considered vulgar. His concept of nobility was feudal and simplistic. For him it consisted of an escape from the bourgeois morality of hard work and domestic virtues. An aristocrat, according to him, lived on a private income, was received in salons and clubs, and kept mistresses.

Ernest de Beauvoir gave his son free rein. In 1897, in his sixtieth year, he had just retired, sporting the red ribbon of the Legion of Honor. He lived on his income. Robust, ever the bon vivant, he would be nearly one hundred at his death. Ernest de Beauvoir displayed total indulgence when it came to his nineteen-year-old son. Georges was a charmer; elegant, offhanded, frivolous, and ironical, he loved gallantry and style. Father and son laughed, carried on, sang, and partook of every amusement the *belle époque* had to offer.

Georges enrolled in law courses that he rarely attended. He spent his time in salons, cafés, at the racetrack, and, above all, hanging around backstage at the theatre. For he had discovered a passion for the stage. He took acting classes and later maintained that "if the attitude of the family had not made it impossible, he would have entered the Conservatoire and trained as an actor."[5]

He was a born charmer, but that ambiguous "de" in de Beauvoir did not automatically make him welcome in the faubourg Saint-German (where the aristocracy lived) or the clubs where meticulous attention was paid the degrees of noble lineage. His modest fortune did not permit him access to the salons of the haute bourgeoisie frequented by Marcel Proust. He frittered away the money left him by his mother as well as his share of his father's estate, which left Meyrignac to his older brother, Gaston. The country estate was in Limousin, one of the poorest regions of France. Chestnuts were not a moneymaking crop. Until his father's death Gaston owned Meyrignac in name only, for his father continued to live there, but Gaston, a gifted gambler, was able to live off the money he made at the racetrack.

Georges de Beauvoir might have risen above the mediocrity of his situation by becoming a writer or an artist. On more than one occasion he had vague impulses toward the idea of writing, but he found the stark reality of the blank page and the effort required to fill it discouraging.

No Guermantes or Swann, he was left with one area in which to shine: amateur theatre. To be an amateur actor was to be without status, but it did call upon one to be pleasing, charming, and entertaining, and it afforded the possibility of an entry into social circles that were otherwise inaccessible.

Georges de Beauvoir became a fanatical amateur actor. He brought the full force of his ambition and nostalgia to the theatre, where he reveled in the popular boulevard plays of Alfred Capus, Maurice Donnay, Vautel, Sacha Guitry, Robert de Flers, and Gaston Arman de Caillavet. He preferred comedy and pantomime, playing Pierrot or a soldier one day, cross-dressing as a cook the next. After the show he metamorphosed into a man of the world, imitating the elegance of actors of the Comédie-Française—Le Bargy or Féraudy—in their roles as aristocrats: the count in Musset's *Un Caprice,* Almaviva in *The Marriage of Figaro,* and the idle rich characters who abound in the plays of Dumas *fils.* Like them, he sported neither beard nor mustache, "that tragic constant on the face of man," as defined by his favorite author, Guy de Maupassant (who was quoting Nietzsche).

This handsome young man, frivolous and carefree, gave himself over entirely to his role as an entertainer. Hostesses gladly organized concerts, recitals, and plays in their living rooms. In the most brilliant salons one heard the most fashionable singers, musicians, and other performing artists: Sarah Bernhardt, Coquelin, Reynaldo Hahn, Harry Fragson, Julia Bartet, Feodor Chaliapin. Often high society itself took to the stage. Several enterprises, of which the Mondain Theatre at 23 rue Massé was best known, prospered in Paris by transforming living rooms into theatres—setting up scenery, building a stage, furnishing the costumes. Socialites such as Count Robert de Montesquiou and Prince de Polignac themselves designed the sets and costumes for their sumptuous fêtes. The world of the salon fascinated Georges de Beauvoir, and this charmer possessed the attributes that salon society valued above all: wit, good breeding, skill in the fine art of conversation, and a gift for public speaking. In those days, these were the talents essential to the success of a man of the world or a politician.

Like other men of his generation, Georges de Beauvoir had a taste for the lyrical, for words well spoken, for panache: he was the consummate boulevardier.* Persuaded that to work was to demean oneself, he lived without a care in the world. He frequented the racetrack, which ever since the 1830s had served as the place where everyone who was anyone in Parisian political, artistic, or literary circles gathered to see and be seen.

He passed the bar exam and, thanks to his connections, began working as a secretary in the law office of Alphonse Deville. Monsieur des Longchamps Deville was a thoroughly Parisian personality who held several municipal posts and wrote for numerous conservative papers.† He took his friend Ernest de Beauvoir's son under his wing, introducing him into the best journalistic milieus and allowing him to plead several cases. And there Georges de Beauvoir's professional ambition came to a halt. In order to become a well-known lawyer he would have had to work hard, and hard work bored him; only the theatre held his interest. On the threshold of thirty, he did as his father and grandfather had done before him: he married a young woman of means, or so he thought.

THE SCANDAL

*F*rançoise Brasseur and Georges de Beauvoir met at Houlgate, the elegant seaside resort to which shrewd family maneuvering had led them. Still melancholy and recovering from her unrequited first love, Françoise went without enthusiasm. Then the elegant Parisian dandy, who became the center of attention wherever he appeared, charmed her off her feet. In 1907, a few short months after meeting, they were married. Françoise was of an unyielding and passionate disposition, Georges was easygoing and carefree. From the moment they set out on their honeymoon he gave his egoism free rein. They left the Gare de Lyon in a sumptuously appointed first-class

---

*The *grand boulevards*, Boulevard de la Madeleine, des Capucines, des Italiens, Montmartre, Poissonnière, Bonne Nouvelle, were the center of the theatres, elegant cafés, and restaurants until World War I. The focal point of this fashionable quarter built in the nineteenth century was the Opéra, the masterpiece of the architect Charles Garnier. The theatres of the boulevards as opposed to the Comédie-Française were not subsidized by the state and depended only on ticket sales. They attracted the public with light plays, witty dialogue, and risqué plots. The most common topic of what became a genre known as the *théâtre du boulevard* was adultery. Elegant dandies who spent most of their time on the boulevards were dubbed "boulevardiers."

†The small square beside the Lutétia Hotel is named after him.

compartment with the Italian lakes as their destination. Then they stopped in Nice, where the racing season had just gotten under way, and Georges refused to leave. Françoise, who had dreamed of romantic strolls along the lakefront under the moonlight, spent her honeymoon amid the noisy excitement of the world's most chic and cosmopolitan season. There were kings, there were queens, there was a great assortment of other royal highnesses, and all the nobility of Europe, attracted to the crowned heads, were rubbing elbows with the demimonde. This was not what Françoise had hoped for. What was certain, Simone de Beauvoir would say later, was that "even at the time of her honeymoon she suffered both in her love and her pride."[6] Deep within herself she harbored a wound that never healed, a jealousy that never disappeared. Georges was in love with the wife whose beauty reflected well upon him, and all would have been for the best if, when they had barely settled in at 103 boulevard du Montparnasse in Paris, the business affairs of Gustave Brasseur had not taken a turn for the worse.

As soon as difficulties were suspected at the Bank of the Meuse, the affair took on political overtones, embittering and impassioning the people of Verdun. The newspapers seized on the story and heightened the controversy. Shareholders became worried, depositors took fright, clients began to withdraw their money. There was talk of questionable manipulations and unscrupulous record keeping. In 1907 the leftist press attacked: Gustave Brasseur, cleverly diplomatic, had "a foot in every door"—the state bank, the courts, the merchants, and the Church. His dealings were not altogether clear: On what complicity did he rely? From what influences was he profiting? Had funds been manipulated? Were special favors involved? Was there trafficking in influence? The papers claimed that their panicked readers demanded clarification and went on to say that "there has obviously been collusion and local complicities which must be brought to light since the victims wish to see things clearly."[7]

On July 28, 1909, a year and a half after Simone was born, the Bank of the Meuse was ordered into liquidation by the court. Not only were the bank fixtures to be sold, but the Brasseur family's personal belongings as well. The rush was on. A crowd pressed forward to watch as the banker's furniture, mirrors, rugs, tennis rackets, and bicycles were auctioned. A cynical journalist remarked that a large number of hunters showed up in hopes of acquiring the three-shot rifle that had been Gustave Brasseur's pride and joy on his great hunting expeditions, but the rifle was nowhere to be found.

Finally the scandal came to a head. Gustave Brasseur was arrested at noon and taken away while the curious massed along his path. A journalist pointed out that sandwiched between the two gendarmes one could see the man who had for so long "contemplated with a derisive pity we little folk who don't go off to play tennis."[8]

It became quite clear to the banker that he had enemies. The judge denied his release while the bank's accounts were examined, despite the efforts of Monsieur Vallée, a senator from the Marne and a former minister of justice who had taken on his friend's defense.

Gustave Brasseur's provisional detention lasted thirteen months. Each day Madame Brasseur could be seen at the prison, striding by with a basket for her husband, her head held high, armed with her faith in the banker's honesty and her confidence in God. All her life she displayed a fanatical devotion to her husband.

In Verdun one no longer spoke of anything but the bankruptcy, the scandalous collusion, the unscrupulous fleecing of the small investor. Even the Parisian press took an interest in the affair. On July 26, 1910, Gustave Brasseur appeared before the court. The bankruptcy receiver set out the statement of affairs: There was a deficit of one and a half million francs. The state prosecutor listed 132 counts of the fraudulent misuse of funds and asked for a stiff fine and the maximum prison sentence. Monsieur Vallée countered by bringing out the fact that his client's personal resources had sunk along with his bank. The lawyer pointed out that his client's financial operations had always been conducted in keeping with usual bank policy. True, in 1908, losses throughout the French savings system had been on the order of 400 million francs, and Brasseur's affairs had suffered from the general malaise. Many small banks were having difficulty.

Gustave Brasseur was sentenced to fifteen months in prison and fined 500 francs. He had already been in custody for thirteen months; two months later he was a free but ruined man.

He left for Paris with his wife and his daughter Lili. First they moved into a dismal apartment with soot-covered walls near the Montparnasse train station, facing a dead-end street.[9] At the start of the war, the family moved to a sixth-floor walk-up in the rue Denfert (later the avenue Denfert-Rochereau) that had a view of the sculpted Lion of Belfort in the square below. This apartment, more cluttered than "the backroom of an antique shop," was where Simone de Beauvoir and her sister, Hélène, two and a half years her junior, whom everyone called Poupette ("little doll"), went for lunch every Thursday during their childhood.

The banker's bankruptcy changed completely the entire family's social status: The Brasseurs were ostracized by their old acquaintances.[10]

Yet the resilient ex-banker had lost nothing of his imagination, his energy, or his love of outdoor exercise. At the first hint of spring, Papa Brasseur, an excellent walker, organized hiking trips in the Chaville woods. So it was that he instilled in his granddaughter a passion for long, challenging walks through the countryside.

Her father's bankruptcy and imprisonment had wounded Françoise de Beauvoir's affection and pride. She had broken off communication with her girl friends in Verdun and did her best to fit into the Parisian social circles in which her husband moved. The ethic of her Catholic upbringing in the Couvent des Oiseaux was not practiced in these circles. "Some of the women she met had had affairs with Papa." In his desk he kept a photo of his last mistress, a brilliant and seductive woman who sometimes came with her husband to pay a call.[11] Georges de Beauvoir took pleasure in this cruel teasing that was characteristic of a boulevard comedy. A great reader of Marcel Prévost, he declared that a man must not treat his spouse "with less ardor than a mistress." He would come home with a bouquet of flowers for Françoise, most often a bunch of violets," and the evenings were filled with laughter and kisses. Nevertheless he was convinced that the husband was entitled to make minor changes in the marriage contract, and he used that right quite freely.[12]

Deep in her heart Françoise harbored "an ardent and indelible" jealousy, all the while forcing herself not to appear affected by it. She hid her disappointments and humiliations and made a show of sharing everyone's opinion, particularly Georges'. But this constraint took its toll on her gay and affectionate temperament. She would undergo sudden changes of mood and launch into fits of anger that terrified Simone.[13] Thus her early days as a married woman were not easy ones.

The man she had married was fascinating yet surprising to a young woman raised in the strict bourgeois tradition. Georges, who frittered away his inheritance at the racetrack and at cards and had no professional ambition whatever, was a sterling example of the very thing that the bourgeoisie, firm believers in thrift and the work ethic, condemned. Françoise looked to her older daughter for a reflection of herself, for some sort of compensation. Simone bore a physical resemblance to her and displayed the same vitality, the same desire to learn. Françoise's own mother had shown her little affection, and her father had favored her blonde and rosy sister Lili. Françoise projected her own life experiences onto her daughters: Poupette was Lili, Simone was she. Françoise loved Simone dearly but imperiously. She latched onto her daughter with a somewhat bitter zeal, determined to impose upon Simone a destiny of her own choosing. "She was authoritarian to the point of rage."

HARLEQUIN'S CLOAK

Georges de Beauvoir did not give up his passion for the theatre after his marriage. While engaged to Françoise, he was rehearsing a play in which he performed the very night before his wedding. Returned from the honeymoon, he began to coach his wife; in the apartment on the boulevard du Montparnasse he gave Françoise diction lessons and taught her how to walk and how to apply makeup.[14] Leaning against the fireplace in the living room with its Louis XVI furnishings, he recited lines that his wife repeated until she had acquired enough confidence to go onstage. The house overflowed with laughter and song as friends came to rehearse, accompanied by Françoise at the piano. Georges recited long passages from *Cyrano de Bergerac,* which he adored, and plied his specialty, the comic monologue.[15]

In this playful environment, Simone grew and blossomed. She proved to be very gifted and began to read at the age of three. She quickly learned by heart the fables and poems that her father taught her to recite like a budding actress. Friends marveled at her talent and applauded her.[16] In her earliest childhood recollection, she remembers herself dressed as Little Red Riding Hood, carrying a basket with a pie and a pot of butter.[17] Georges de Beauvoir wrote revues, verse, short stories, even a play, *Le Chien.* Imitating her father, little Simone composed poems for her younger sister; her father read them to friends, who were amazed by the child's precocity.

In Georges and Françoise de Beauvoir's home, the theatre was everything. Conversation revolved around theatrical gossip and the theatrical magazine *Comœdia* was read regularly.[18] The visits of Alexandre Vargas, an actor at the Odéon and a close friend of Georges, transformed the living room into theatre wings full of backstage excitement. Dialogue sallied back and forth, as did gossip. Actors and plays were criticized, every detail of the latest success was debated and analyzed. The shadows of Sarah Bernhardt, Berthe Cerny, Coquelin, Paul Mounet, Mounet-Sully, Le Bargy, and Féraudy swept through the apartment.

Every summer, until the war began in 1914, Simone's parents traveled to Divonne-les-Bains with an amateur theatre troupe, performing for three weeks at the Grand Hotel, where they were also housed and fed. Georges' performances were quite well received, and his wife's beauty brought compliments his way.

The boulevard theatre, the café concerts, and the stage revues (the first Folies-Bergère revue was in 1908) fascinated all of Paris, yet in this rigidly stratified society, women who "went on the stage" were thought of as women of easy virtue. Performing in amateur productions did not carry the same stigma, but the fine line between the two was purposely ignored by those who enjoyed malicious gossip.

Even Grandma and Aunt Lili directed unpleasant remarks to Simone along the lines of, "So, your mom is still running around?" Louise Sarmadira, the maid, whispered, "Have you seen how Madame is all done up? A real eccentric!" The discreet dress of Verdun had given way to a more showy fashion; it was the era of tango dresses, and colorfully striped bayadere dresses were popular.

Certainly the combination of Gustave Brasseur's bankruptcy and Georges de Beauvoir's passion for the theatre slowly pushed this bourgeois family out of the mainstream and onto the fringe. "The de Beauvoirs have forsaken their social class," Simone's best friend's mother would later affirm, a pronouncement that Simone would not soon forget.[19] In her memoirs and novels she would paint a vitriolic portrait of this milieu to which nevertheless she belonged by virtue of her culture and manners.

THE VINES OF MONTPARNASSE

*T*he Montparnasse district was Simone de Beauvoir's village. Apart from a five-year hiatus from the autumn of 1931 to the summer of 1936, when she was "in exile" in Marseille and Rouen, she lived between the Lion of Belfort and the carrefour Vavin. As a child she loved to slide out onto the corbeled balcony off the dining room window, to perch there and watch the comings and goings in the street below. At seventeen, an authentic resident of Montparnasse with a baccalaureate, she dove into the neighborhood bars in revolt against the rigidity of her education. At twenty-one, having reached her majority and obtained her degree in philosophy, she settled in Montparnasse.

Before 1914 the quarter still had a country flavor. Many peaceful little corners had not changed since the days when Balzac lived there. Jean Cocteau recalled the vineyards, the alfalfa fields, and the grass that sprouted between the paving stones in the street. Yet Montparnasse was undergoing urbanization. Islands of new buildings were springing up in the midst of farmland and among the orchards that surrounded the farms and the numerous convents. The new structures were inhabited by journalists, teachers at the Ecole des Beaux-Arts, members of the French Institute, politicians, writers, and academics drawn by the proximity of the Sorbonne. This middle-class population preferred the streets near the Church of Notre-Dame-des-Champs. The building in which the de Beauvoir family lived was on the least fashionable part of the boulevard.

Theirs was a rounded edifice whose tiny French doors opened onto a stone projection that was encircled by an iron railing and pompously called a balcony. The entrance was situated between the Parnasse and Rotonde cafés on the boulevard du Montparnasse, and the dining room windows looked out on the boulevard Raspail; this structural ambiguity permitted the de Beauvoirs to assimilate with their bourgeois neighbors of the more affluent boulevard Raspail.

The de Beauvoir apartment was small by the standards of the day and could not compare with the handsome apartment on the boulevard Saint-Germain where Georges had grown up or with the large house in Verdun where Françoise had spent her childhood. There were only two bedrooms. Simone shared hers with the maid, a young native of Limousin, Louise Sarmadira. The room was summarily furnished, its sole decoration a reproduction of Murillo's *Assumption* that hung over the big sculpted "fake antique" wooden bed.

Simone's sister slept in a crib which at night was pushed into the narrow corridor that led to Georges' office. The office was a somber room with red velvet curtains and blackened pearwood furniture. The dining room with its heavy Henri II furnishings opened onto the entry hall and the living room through glass doors hung with crimped red silk curtains. The entire apartment was covered in red carpeting and heated by radiators. The only luxuries were a bathroom and a toilet. In the quarter's many new buildings a gas hookup and a sink equipped with hot and cold running water were considered sufficient conveniences; the full baths and elevators of the buildings constructed fifty years earlier by the architect Haussmann remained a luxury for the very privileged who lived in the vicinity of the Champs-Elysées.

Montparnasse then was still a humble district. Juglar, a wood and coal vendor, occupied the site where the Coupole now stands, and for Simone the workers black with coal dust and the dark entrance to the Vavin métro station were the very images of hell. Every day small herds of donkeys and goats proceeded down the boulevard on their way to the Luxembourg Gardens. On Sunday, Parisians liked to breathe fresh air on café terraces, surrounded by spindle-trees that filled with fireflies on summer nights. Hawkers, clowns, trained animals, and open-air orchestras had entertained in this quarter since the seventeenth century, when Parisians liked to flock to the windmills of Montparnasse to enjoy pancakes and a famous light wine.

Until World War I, a public horse-drawn omnibus operated through Montparnasse between Montsouris Park and the Palais-Royal. The neighborhood abounded in stables, which had attracted saddlers, coachbuilders, varnishers and glaziers, blacksmiths, and an array of craftsmen who gave the quarter its character. Little by little, as the automobile replaced the horse, the stables were converted cheaply into artists' studios, adding yet another picturesque element to the district. Milk and eggs could be bought from local farms. Roving vendors hawked flowers, vegetables, chickweed, panes of glass, birds. Simone de Beauvoir recalled a tumbler who sold the stuff of which children's dreams are made—Chinese parasols and tiny Japanese flowers that expanded and bloomed when dropped in a glass of water.

Before 1914, electricity was a luxury in this part of Paris. As soon as night fell, a darkness barely countered by the acetylene lamps of a few wine merchants took over. The neighborhood was not safe; there were knife fights, drunken indigents settled their scores, and couples made love furtively in darkened doorways and vestibules. After 6 P.M. a respectable woman would not risk venturing out into the street. Montparnasse was a twilight world, a mixture of misery and luxury, of fantasy and gestating talents.

Simone had few toys and rare distractions. Her parents took her to see George V and Queen Mary's carriage sweep down the Champs-Elysées; later she would attend General Joseph Gallieni's funeral. They also took her to see the Mardi Gras parades. Most of all she liked to watch from her balcony as the people came and went between the Rotonde, the Dôme, and the Restaurant Baty, the three poles of daily life for those whom the poet Apollinaire had dubbed the Montparnassiens, a special breed of artists, revolutionaries, rebels of all kinds, anarchists from all countries.

The wine merchant Baty had been George Sand's kitchen boy at Nohant. His restaurant, always crowded with Americans and Germans, was the most expensive on the boulevard, yet one could eat there for a few cents. Only one dish was served. The staff of *Soirées de Paris,* a newspaper founded by friends of Apollinaire, had met there monthly since 1912. At the Rotonde, whose regular customers included Modigliani, Picasso, and Kisling, one could—for an investment of 12 sous in a *café-crème*—while away the day reading the newspapers (in every conceivable language) that lay abandoned on the tables, listen to the stories of neighborhood painters or workmen, and go on conversing into infinity. Lenin, Trotsky, Zadkine, Léger, Brancusi, Modigliani; Spaniards, Italians, Bulgarians, Serbs, Chileans, Transylvanians, East Indians; there was even a bona fide redskin, a painter and poet who represented himself as "the direct descendant of the brother of Colbert, who colonized Canada"; all streamed in and out of the cafés. Some, due to poverty or sheer nonconformity, strode about in bizarre getups: One fellow would be draped in a kitchen curtain, another sported pajamas during the day, still another wore a Rembrandt-style bonnet, and the "barefoot mystic" wore a monocle without a lens. Some women draped themselves in Andalusian shawls, others wore leg-of-mutton-sleeved dresses they had picked up at the flea market.

One could spot Picasso, who would become a friend of Sartre and de Beauvoir, with a lock of black hair over his eye and a watch chain in his buttonhole, and there was the strange artist who had painted multicolored lozenges on his sleeves to conceal the threadbare places. There was also the man with blue glasses whose nose was painted red on one side and yellow on the other. One character always carried four umbrellas; from one he produced a terrified black kitten that he thrust into the faces of passersby when demanding spare change. No sooner had he taken a seat and ordered a drink than he would retrieve two bearskins from another of the umbrellas and slip them onto his feet. The artists mingled easily with the regular clientele of the Rotonde, who were masons, plasterers, house painters, drivers of wagons, and handlers of horses.

The cafés of the carrefour Vavin attracted street musicians and singers, high-spirited women who belted out repetitive old songs, with their audience joining in on the chorus. When the Rotonde changed owners just before World War I, this neighborhood café changed its style. A large dining room was built on the mezzanine, and a new clientele streamed in—the Parisians of the boulevards and foreigners in search of the picturesque. For it was in France, land of the good life, that the latter invested their money, while the French themselves held their nest eggs in Russian stocks. The franc was negotiable everywhere against the gold standard, and everyday transactions were still carried out with gold and silver coins. Checks and checkbooks were so stubbornly resisted among the populace that the term "checkwriter" was an insult. There was no checkwriter but there were many foreign accents to be found in the carrefour Vavin. Chauffeurs dropped off women in furs and men decked out in tails. The new proprietor of the Rotonde turned away former customers whose appearance was too raggedy. Jean Giraudoux would write with humor in his *Sketches from Provincial Life* that the Germans decided to declare war because of their *Sehnsucht nach Montparnasse*—their longing for Montparnasse—"except that instead of coming individually, by train, they all decided to come at the same time, on foot."

On her walk to school each day Simone passed the Rotonde regulars, an uncomfortable scene for a young girl raised according to bourgeois principles. From 10 A.M. the place was jam-packed. One drank seated, one drank standing, one drank while playing the piano. Drunken Americans sang, Russians punctuated their conversation by hurling glasses to the floor. Squeezed together in the booths, blond Scandinavians observed the frenetic tumult as though hypnotized. American women with bobbed hair, still clad in their evening gowns, lifted long-stemmed glasses of champagne or colorful liqueurs in their white-gloved hands.

When the lights went on around 5 P.M., a sort of craziness overtook the Rotonde. One dined in a deafening din shot through with "Negro rhythms" and punctuated by shouting in every language imaginable. The *tapeurs,* the pianists in the bars and dance halls, were often replaced by the customers themselves.

Roars and howls, squeals and wailing pierced the night. Modigliani, drunk, wove his way through the crowd, helping himself to the drinks of customers who were too busy laughing to protest. More than once he slumped in a heap, still clutching a bottle or a glass, and he was not alone. These were the sorts of extravagances one came to see, but there were also paintings on which to speculate. The Rotonde housed a veritable art exchange. The waiters had once known a certain penniless Picasso whose paintings were now commanding as much as 4000 francs, and they did quite well for themselves by promoting the work of their "protégés." They encouraged them to order drinks, loaned them money, and saw that they were reimbursed in canvases—which they then sold to Rotonde customers or the neighborhood businessmen. Georges de Beauvoir called the Rotonde "a den of foreigners." Voices flavored with the most extraordinary accents filtered up to Simone: "their faces, their silhouettes, the sound of their voices captivated me."[20] In her crow's nest, the unsuspected lookout recorded for herself this spectacle of humanity with its drama, its comedy, its enchantment.

Simone de Beauvoir said repeatedly that her earliest childhood was "very, very happy."

Early on she surprised her family with her intelligent and vivacious mind. She loved to learn and was encouraged to do so. She was given a stereo viewer, a toy kinetoscope, and, above all, carefully chosen books. Her father indulged her every question. She quickly became certain that she was different, unique. "It was understood that my first cousin Jeanne was too dumb for me." Simone took advantage of this exceptional situation. Poupette and Jeanne were subjected to her tyranny; in the country Simone would hitch them to a small wagon and make them pull it. She imperiously appointed herself teacher. Hélène de Beauvoir tells how she learned to read at the age of three because Simone, who loved "to be the teacher," would not stand for her sister's not being able to share all the same joys as she.

She could become violent. "If you so much as raise a finger to Simone, she turns purple in the face," her mother said, and her father took great delight in repeating, "This child is unsociable."[21] She knew what she wanted. It was also said, not without a touch of pride, "Simone is as stubborn as a mule." She pursued and would continue to pursue her desires to the point of obsession, her repugnance to the point of vomiting. She undertook everything—her games, her reading—passionately, plunging in with such intensity that the rest of the world ceased to exist. If her questions went unanswered, if one tried to impose "unjustified constraints" upon her, she rebelled and flew into such fits of anger that her "violence was intimidating." When she went too far and had to be shut up in a dark closet among the mops, brooms, and feather dusters, she would pound on the walls with her fists and her feet for an impressive length of time. She was not often punished. Well aware of this, she pulled pranks and stepped out of line "for the sheer pleasure of being disobedient." In family photos she stuck out her tongue or turned her back to the camera. She overflowed with vitality. Those around her were given to exclaiming, "Why, this child can't sit still for a second!" And yet, in the middle of a game, or laughter, or during rehearsals, amid pampering adults, without understanding the cause of her own outbursts, she would fling herself to the floor, "red in the face and convulsing." From time to time her parents argued violently. The first time she really became aware of this, her universe shattered: "I began to drown in the chaos which preceded creation."[22] Yet these scenes could not alter the solid joie de vivre that characterized her early childhood. She was already in the habit of forging ahead no matter what, and she had built herself an internal citadel wherein anything that might disturb her happiness was rejected. One of the most striking characteristics of her personality was the will to build her own happiness, to make the rules, to invent the forms and stick to them with a stubbornness that she herself would label schizophrenic. "This ability to pass over in silence events which I felt so keenly is one of the things which strike me most when I remember my childhood."[23]

Georges de Beauvoir continued to disdain the success that hard work and effort bring about. He said repeatedly that money was of no importance to him, that he was above such contingencies, "but threw a fit every time we asked him for money."[24] The style in which the family lived reflected his mediocre income. In the still stratified society of the years before 1914, the number of household servants one engaged and the duties they performed determined the social standing of the mistress of the house. The de Beauvoirs had only one all-purpose maid, while all their relatives employed numerous servants as well as governesses for the children.[25] At that same time, Jean-Paul Sartre's grandparents had no fewer than three servants, and Raymond Aron, a friend from their college years, said in his *Mémoires* that his mother, "whose lifestyle was modest," had a chambermaid and a cook. Modest businessmen and workers with a comfortable income all had a maid to do general housework. A government report on the living conditions of mine workers filed in 1909 indicates that 20 percent of miners' families employed a servant. Army and government administration regulations required that, above a certain rank, one must hire a domestic.

Françoise de Beauvoir felt responsible for their economic situation because her dowry would never be paid. She found it admirable that Georges did not hold her to it, "and she felt guilty toward him all her life."[26]

1914–1918

On August 1, 1914, at four in the afternoon, bells sounded a warning in every French city, village, and hamlet. General mobilization was decreed; the Germans had just declared war. The nation hoisted the tricolor, the Marseillaise rang out everywhere. To a man, France wanted to sign up. The rate of draft dodging was expected to be about 15 percent; the actual figure came to be just over 1 percent. In the train stations waves of men in bright red trousers, flowers in their rifles, enthusiastically boarded the troop trains that swept them away. Anything of German origin became an object of disgrace. Stores whose proprietors had German-sounding names were looted.

Carried away in the general patriotic fervor, Simone, age six, stamped on a celluloid baby doll "made in Germany" that happened to belong to her sister, and she wanted to toss out the window some silver knife rests stamped with the same infamous phrase. She made miniature allied flags and stuck them all around the apartment; she industriously wrote *Vive la France!* in blue, white, and red on a signboard. This restless little girl who had no gift for manual labor abandoned her books and games to knit ski masks and tear linen into strips. Her zeal garnered such compliments that she persevered. Her patriotism reflected that of her relatives, some of whom still lived in Lorraine.

Her uncle Hubert Brasseur was mobilized, and Georges de Beauvoir, who had been declared unfit when called up for compulsory military service, was assigned to the Zouaves. As a finishing touch to his uniform—especially flamboyant with its flared red bloomers, short jacket, and cap with a dangling pompom—and to prime himself for the part, Georges grew a mustache. Used to seeing him costumed for the theatre, Simone nevertheless thought him impressive. In October he left for the front. Like the rest of France, Françoise de Beauvoir thought the war would be brief. Paris was badly informed, the newspapers heavily censored. Clemenceau's paper, *L'Homme libre,* was banned for publishing a series of articles denouncing the use of cattle cars that had not been disinfected to transport the wounded—who contracted tetanus as a result. In spite of the advance of the Germans, communiqués became systematically optimistic when General Gallieni was named military governor of Paris. He had requisitioned all the taxis of Paris to transport an entire division to the front to reinforce the troops, who were fighting with desperate energy. Thus the Battle of the Marne was won, overturning the predictions of the top brass, who had not thought it possible that the men would have enough strength left to charge after their buglers in the wake of a two-week retreat. Gallieni's popularity among Parisians reached its peak.

Three months after his departure, Georges de Beauvoir suffered a heart attack and was evacuated to Coulommiers Hospital. There, with the popular singer Gabriello, he wrote a musical revue for the benefit of the wounded. He was then assigned as a clerk to the War Ministry. Having given up his Zouave uniform, Georges shaved his mustache. He plunged back into what Simone de Beauvoir called "that stubborn passion," the theatre, and continued performing in shows for the troops. Gabriello was one of the rare guests in the de Beauvoir household; he brought songs and gossip about the army theatre and did imitations that delighted Simone.

The war had given Simone a more attentive father. Forced to stay home, Georges de Beauvoir took pleasure in forming his daughter's taste. In a little imitation-leather notebook he compiled for her an anthology of poems that included François Coppée's "A Gospel," Théodore de Banville's "Little Jeanne's Jumping Jack," and Hégésippe Moreau's "Alas, If I Had Known." He gave her dictation from difficult passages of Victor Hugo. In the evenings he read aloud for his wife and daughters from the masterpieces of Racine, Corneille, and Molière, the plays of Edmond Rostand, *Hernani* and *Ruy Blas* by Victor Hugo, Eugène Labiche's comedies, the *History of French Literature* by Gustave Lanson, *The Origins of Contemporary France* by Taine, and the *Essay on the Inequality of the Human Races* by Count de Gobineau.

This was not only a literary education but a political one. Georges de

Beauvoir admired the ultraconservatives Charles Maurras and Léon Daudet and was opposed to universal suffrage; his opinion was that only educated men ought to be granted the right to vote. Fanatically devoted to the idea that he was a nobleman, he despised the Republic as heartily as he did "those foreigners" who had invaded the realm of arts and letters: Harry Fragson, a popular singer of the previous decade who had charmed Paris with his rendition of "La Chambrette d'amour," and Sergei Diaghilev, who had staged Oscar Wilde's *Salomé* to the music of Johann Strauss (whose name Willy, music critic and husband of Colette, insisted on pronouncing "Strass," as did all the French who grumbled about "those foreigners"). Nationalist, boulevardier, and xenophobe, Georges de Beauvoir was as convinced of the guilt of Alfred Dreyfus "as my mother was of the existence of God," Simone de Beauvoir would say. The day that Dreyfus, declared innocent, was reinstated in the army with the rank of major and awarded the Legion of Honor, Georges applauded the Nationalist deputy who, in protest, fought a duel with the undersecretary of the interior.

He maintained that any social advancement based on merit was vulgar, and he believed that an individual who rose from the lower strata of society could never rid himself of something that was inherently limiting. He asserted that the de Beauvoirs had a je ne sais quoi, a certain something which distinguished them from others. This pride instilled in Simone a self-confidence and inner strength that might otherwise have been lacking because the family was poor. She admired her father passionately; no one in her entourage was as widely read, as voluminous a reader as he, and no one else recited so dazzling an array of verse.

He had brought back from the front a number of interesting stories but, using his distaste for malicious and imbecilic critics as a pretext, never did anything with them—and thereby took after another would-be author, Colette's father, who had lined his library with blank notebooks destined to receive future works that never existed beyond their titles.

Georges instilled in Simone a worship of literature and put in her head the idea that "there was nothing in the world finer than to be an author."

Françoise de Beauvoir shared her husband's love of books. She encouraged a taste for writing in Simone, who at the age of seven wrote "The Misfortunes of Marguerite" and "The Pickle Family," in which she parodied her family and demonstrated the same sense of humor that runs through her memoirs. Françoise de Beauvoir had her sister Lili recopy the stories in her fine handwriting and later had them bound.[27] Encouraged by her parents, Simone continued to make up stories. One of her great-aunts, who wrote stories for children, portrayed Simone as the heroine in "The Perfect Doll."

Simone began attending school in 1913. At the age of five and a half she was enrolled in the beginners' class at the Cours Adeline Désir, a Catholic girls' school founded in 1853 and located at 39 rue Jacob in the former mansion of the Anspach family, the younger branch of the House of Brandebourg. The beatification of the institute's founder and namesake was currently under way in Rome.

The Cours Désir curriculum could not compete with that of the aristocratic boarding schools of Paris, the Oiseaux or the Dames de Sainte-Clotilde (the name of your school classified you socially). The junior classes with their small enrollments mostly accommodated children whose parents could not afford a private tutor. Simone's cousins—Jeanne de Beauvoir and her brothers, and Jacques and Thérèse ("Titite") Champigneulles—had governesses and tutors, as was the custom among the well-to-do bourgeoisie. Jean-Paul Sartre, then a boy of eight growing up on the other side of the Luxembourg Gardens, barely a mile away from Simone, had a private tutor named Marie-Louise until he entered the lycée. Going to school gave Simone the impression of being different, of having a life of her own.[28]

Françoise de Beauvoir watched over her gifted daughter's studies with a persistence that never let up for a day and came to weigh heavily on Simone. Françoise read numerous books on education, sought advice at the Christian Mothers' Association, and followed closely the curriculum at the Cours Désir. She accompanied Simone to school and sat in on her classes. The pressure parents brought to bear in parochial education was then far greater and more restricting than in secular education. Families supervised the programs, the teachers, the preparation of exams, and the discipline, and they actually attended classes. "Our mothers, installed on black imitation-leather settees, did their embroidery or their knitting."[29] To make up for the areas of instruction left wanting at the Cours Désir, Françoise de Beauvoir began to study Latin, gave Simone English and piano lessons, and dispensed an occasional slap in the interest of discipline. At eight, Simone could read English novels in the original language.

Everything interested and amazed Simone de Beauvoir; her curiosity was boundless. She was as passionate about plants and insects as she was about the illustrations in her atlas. Seizing with ardor upon anything knowable, her happiness never paled or lost its edge. Her duty as a student at the Cours Désir merged with her pleasure. She discovered that she could outdo herself in her scholarly triumphs; her activities were sorting themselves out, falling into place, and seemed to be leading somewhere. "I was responding ceaselessly to a necessity which spared me from asking: Why am I here? . . . From my studious armchair I listened to the harmony of the spheres."[30] She had only to look, to read, to think in order to attain the absolute. Soon she became conscious of what she called her mission, which was no more and no less than to unveil and decipher the world. "I had to call the past to life and illuminate every corner of the five continents, descend to the center of the earth, and orbit the moon. When I was compelled to do pointless exercises my mind cried out at the barren waste of my gifts . . . I was frustrated and filled with guilt."[31] She loved study and the rewards that knowledge brought her way, but from earliest childhood, behind the thirst to know, there lay a desire to conquer the world across time and across space. Looking at her textbooks—beautiful volumes filled with illustrations and maps—she wanted to bring the characters to life, to unfurl and activate the countryside. "The power I had over them intoxicated me as much as their silent presence."[32] Reading would always be a great pleasure for her, a grand harvest of images and ideas that surpassed all other pleasures. The day her mother took her to the reading room of which she was a member and announced to Simone that henceforth she too would belong, "I experienced one of the greatest joys I ever knew as a child. . . . 'All this belongs to me!' I said to myself, bewildered by such a profusion of wonders. The reality surpassed my wildest dreams: before me lay the entry to a rich and unknown paradise."[33] While still quite young she would discover that there was only one source of happiness greater than reading—that of writing.

During the war years, the closeness of the family clustered around the stove in the evening, listening to father's sonorous voice recite some poem, prompted the future writer to say, "How happy we four are!" only to add, "I remember one or two things which do not fit into this portrait and lead me to suppose that it wouldn't have taken very much to upset my self-assurance."[34]

As a second-class soldier, Georges de Beauvoir earned five sous a day, and the family was barely making ends meet. Françoise de Beauvoir no longer went out, and going on the stage was no longer an option. The Parisian salons of the *belle époque* had lost their habitués. The government had fled the capital during the night of September 3, 1914, trailing journalists, theatre people, courtesans, businessmen, and the idle rich in its wake.

Simone's mother meticulously organized her time and meager resources. Every centime that passed through her fingers was noted in a big black book. As France settled deeper into the interminable war, finding food became more difficult. Françoise strove to come up with Jerusalem artichokes, beets, Chinese artichokes, and horsemeat to feed her family. She concocted soups from flours and eggless omelets. "Suspect margarines" replaced butter and oil; a bitter saccharine substituted for sugar. They drank *figuette,* a homemade wine made from fermented dried figs. Signs of war were everywhere. The games that children play reflect the world around them, and Simone and Poupette embarked on veritable psychodramas: In a city under siege, they withstood famine and deployed treasure troves of ingenuity "to do the most with the least resources."

Borrowing from stories of the day, Simone set out to write a saga recounting the adventures of a heroic Alsatian orphan girl who led her numerous brothers and sisters across the Rhine to France. The geographical obstacles of the enterprise put a halt to this early literary attempt. She then invented games appropriate to the circumstances: her sister was the czar and she was the president of France.

Every school curriculum was linked to the war. Students read "The Little Seven-Year-Old Soldier," "A Girl of Lorraine Writes to Her Brother," or "Letters to the French"—all burning with patriotism—and recited "Dead for the Fatherland" by Victor Hugo or "A Soldier Speaks to His Son" by Victor de Laprade. Classroom discussions and composition topics reflected the concern that children be shown that they too were working for their country in working for themselves. Making sure that you did your best was your patriotic duty as well as a gesture of thanks to those who were fighting for you. Throughout the four years of the war, schoolchildren participated in all the public collection days, soliciting donations for Soldier at the Front Day, Belgian Refugees Day, Day of the 75 (a famous cannon), Christmas for the Army, Day of the Poilu, Tubercular Soldiers Day. The little badge sellers outdid each other in their patriotic zeal. In Montparnasse the children of Paul the hatmaker, dressed up as Alsatians, scored a big hit. Simone (seven) and Hélène (five) were the star attraction, sporting sky-blue military greatcoats, perfect in every detail, that their mother had had sewn from a length of woolen cloth someone had given her. Yet Simone could not help noting that some of her "mother's friends find that utterly ridiculous."

The 14th topped all the other arrondissements of Paris in the proceeds collected from the sale of badges in the street—after all, potential donors galore packed the cafés of the boulevard du Montparnasse. If people were still playing dominoes at the Dôme, the Rotonde welcomed a new clientele: soldiers on leave who came to forget the horrors of the trenches, foreigners stranded by the war who discussed the news from home—be it true or false—for hours on end. There were "painted" women, their hair cut short in the style launched by Hélène Perdriat, a very fashionable avant-garde artist of the day, and, as always, artists in surprising getups. "It's a den of defeatists," Georges de Beauvoir was given to saying. And when Simone asked, "What's a defeatist?" he replied, "A bad Frenchman who believes that France will be defeated."[35]

The deprivations of the war worked against Simone's normally good health. By the age of eight she had become "sickly and timid," and a doctor prescribed gymnastics lessons. A leotard was found that fitted so tightly that one of her aunts, laying eyes on Simone, exclaimed, "She looks just like a little monkey!" The cruel words took on the full force of their meaning when she found herself in gymnastics class surrounded by girls who "wore outfits of pale blue jersey with short, elegantly pleated skirts." These children ran, jumped, somersaulted, and laughed with "the freedom and daring which I had always associated with street urchins. I suddenly felt awkward and ugly: a little monkey."[36]

In *Memoirs of a Dutiful Daughter* she returned to this fact again and again: "My shapeless dresses accentuated my awkwardness . . . I was sadly aware of what the photos later confirmed: badly dressed, ungainly."[37] Or, "My cousin Annie often made me a present of her hand-me-downs."

In *When Things of the Spirit Come First,* the collection of stories in which Simone de Beauvoir tried to put her past to rest once and for all, she described herself in this way: "I always had on my dark purple dress, cotton stockings often full of holes, clunky shoes, no makeup, and dirty nails."[38] Thinking back on her trip to visit her childhood friend Elisabeth L. ("Zara"), she sees "the cotton stockings, the summer dress that the sun had eaten away in large spots." Zara was obliged to lend her something to wear when people came to visit, "and the children sniggered" behind her back. Simone de Beauvoir remembered: "My sister and I wore our clothes until they were threadbare and even after that."[39] Sometimes, at Christmas, they were invited to "children's parties on a staggeringly lavish scale," where the other little girls wore dresses of silk and lace while "we wore woollen dresses the color of mold or mud."[40]

THE ALCHEMIST'S DREAM

Gustave Brasseur had not resigned himself to his ruin. The war came to the rescue when his son was drafted, and he found himself in charge of a small shoe factory. Thanks to the orders from the army, business was fairly good. A dreamer and an optimist, he cooked up projects to restore his fortune, a goal that was an obsession with him. In his opinion the shoe factory was slim pickings. The neighborhood was not lacking in dreamers; in Montparnasse one bought and sold anything and everything. In his memoirs, Roland Dorgelès tells of the strange enterprises of the day and the ventures in which he took part.* The Spanish sculptor Manuel-Martínez Huiguë, known as Manolo, shamelessly exploited the habitués of the neighborhood. He organized a lottery in which the prize was a bust he himself had sculpted, claiming it was a relic of antiquity and showing a document to that effect bearing illegible signatures. The ticket buyer who later inquired about the date of the prize drawing was told, "The lottery is over with. André Salmon won the bust." It goes without saying that André Salmon was in on it from the start.

In this environment Gustave Brasseur came upon a scheme that suited him. He had met an alchemist who, before his very eyes, had transformed lead into gold. One day he showed up at the de Beauvoir household and took a small gold nugget from his pocket with a flourish. With this tangible proof of the transmutation of metals, Gustave Brasseur imagined boundless wealth for the entire family—one need only finance the alchemist. In his throaty voice he tried to persuade his wife, his daughters, his son-in-law. (Having been declared bankrupt, he had lost the right to dispose of funds without the agreement of his wife and children.) Conversation degenerated into argument; Simone and her sister were scolded and slapped in the general family edginess. From her bed at night, the child could hear "the cries of hatred and anger," and she hid beneath the sheets "with a heavy heart."[41] Constant quarrels over money, difficulties with money, lack of money were part of her daily life.

Prices were on the rise in Paris. On March 15, 1917, Nicholas II of Russia abdicated. All the major Russian cities were in the hands of revolutionaries and the army was no longer taking orders. The czar's fall was cause for rejoicing in Paris, where he had been suspected of wanting to sign a separate peace treaty with Germany. People imagined that the revolutionary army was going to attack the Austro-Hungarian Empire with increased energy. In France, morale was at its lowest. The great April offensive had been a failure. The Battle of Verdun had been a mass slaughter, with 700,000 soldiers massacred on both sides. Troops had mutinied or simply refused to fight. Workers in seventy-one industries were on strike. Violent demonstrations made their way through the streets of Paris with cries of "Down with the war!" People imagined that spies were everywhere. Convinced that the Germans would soon lay siege to the capital, Gustave Brasseur arranged his family's escape route. A diligent walker, he had laid out a plan to reach Longjumeau in the Yvette Valley, about fifty miles from Paris, on foot.

---

*Roland Dorgelès was a French writer famous for his book on World War I, *The Wooden Crosses*.

Sleep became increasingly difficult for Simone. Each night her mother brewed her a cup of orange blossom tea to ward off the nightmares peopled with refugees and the wounded.[42] It was colder than ever in the apartment; Simone's and Poupette's hands were chilblained, itchy, and inflamed from the constant damp. German planes bombed Paris nightly, and Georges de Beauvoir refused to take shelter in the basement. Françoise took her daughters to the cellar two or three times, then decided to follow her husband's example. That way they would either survive together or die together, and Simone was reinforced in her belief that the de Beauvoirs were of a different kind.

Throughout the war, Simone never missed a day of class. Often she found herself alone with the teacher and one other girl, "a simpleton of twelve." The Cours Désir had lost most of its pupils because the children of the elegant 7th arrondissement had generally been sent to the country for safety's sake. Most school buildings were serving as hospitals. "One day when I arrived with my sister and Mother, we found the building empty: everyone had dashed down into the cellars. We were highly amused. Our own courage and spirit in the face of danger showed plainly that we were beings apart."[43]

When victory came in 1918, all France celebrated in a general bout of enthusiasm. The returning soldiers were acclaimed. Galas gave way to galas, patriotic demonstrations led to further patriotic demonstrations, and commemorative ceremonies paved the way for yet more commemorative ceremonies. People flocked to the theatres, to the cabarets, to the movies, dance halls, and nightclubs. In the carrefour Vavin, the Rotonde was packed to the rafters night and day. The uproar did not let up; people kissed, wept, shouted *Vive la France!* The nightmare had lasted four long years, the toll in human life had been enormous: 1,400,000 soldiers killed at the front, another three million wounded.

From her balcony Simone could watch the hearses make their way up the boulevard Raspail to the Montparnasse cemetery, for after the trenches came the ravages of the Spanish influenza: 100,000 deaths in 1918. Simone's young uncle, Hubert Brasseur, barely back from the front, succumbed to the disease, and all Montparnasse mourned the passing of Apollinaire.

The war's end did not alleviate the family's financial difficulties. In the spring of 1919 the franc weakened and the rate of inflation soared. The high cost of living was on everyone's mind. Freshly demobilized, Georges de Beauvoir let his father-in-law talk him into joining him as a director at the shoe factory. A few months later, the insolvent enterprise was forced to close its doors. Under French law, Gustave Brasseur was barred from any commercial enterprise. After the death of his son, he had coaxed his son-in-law to

become the director of the factory. Georges de Beauvoir was legally responsible for the bankrupcy.

Gustave Brasseur had one last card to play. His son had invented "a
prototype for a tin can which could be opened with a small coin." They would
mass-produce it, and finally they would be rich. The last of the jewels were
sold, money was borrowed. In the meantime, a competitor stole the patent
out from under them. In desperation they took the man to court, and the
competitor won.

Somehow they had to live. Madame Brasseur spent her days knitting
children's clothes. Gustave Brasseur, his face flushed, his head bald, his chin
"daubed with a prickly, frothy grey scum," lived in a perpetual state of
anxiety.[44] He never stopped talking about money—bills, mortgages, debts—
and on Thursdays, when Simone and Hélène lunched at their grandparents'
apartment, if someone rang the bell, "he would put his finger to his lips and
we held our breath."[45]

2

71 RUE dE RENNES

My life is going to lead somewhere.
Memoirs of a Dutiful Daughter

"THE DARKEST DAYS"

"Nothing went to waste at our house: not a crust of bread, or a bit of string, not a complimentary ticket or an opportunity for a free meal."[1] The need to economize was so constant that Simone carried over into her games her thoughts of rigor, deprivation, and economy. Waste of any kind had become an obsessive fear. At school she wrote in minuscule, barely legible letters and filled in every blank space in her notebooks. Her teachers were alarmed by what they interpreted as premature signs of miserliness.

During the war years, personal deprivation and the broader national plight conveniently blended together. After the second bankruptcy (the shoe factory) and the impossibility of Georges' working again as a lawyer, poverty, quite distinct from wartime sacrifice, weighed upon the family. In the autumn

of 1919 they were obliged to leave the apartment above the Rotonde and
moved into a sixth-floor walk-up at 71 rue de Rennes. Upon learning that she
would never again observe the spectacle of her boulevard from the vantage
point of her balcony, Simone felt overcome with despair. "I was being cut off
from life, condemned to exile."[2]

The kitchen and office looked out on a firehouse wall.[3] There was nothing to see but rooftops, with the sky reduced to a geometric outline. The
rooms were somber. There was no running water; water had to be carried up
in pitchers, and dirty water was drained into a heavy slop pail under the sink
that Georges had to empty.

Simone and Hélène shared a room so narrow that there was room for no
piece of furniture other than their beds. Only one room, the "office," was
heated with an open wood fire, and that was where the family most often
gathered. Françoise de Beauvoir put all her energy and ingenuity into econo-
mizing. She reheated leftovers, recycled clothing by letting out hems and
turning old coats inside out. She never took a bus or the métro without
working on her knitting or some unelaborate lacework for her daughters'
petticoats as she rode. She took on the burden of a penniless household alone.
There were heavy kettles and basins to move, coal and wood to be carried
upstairs, floors to be scrubbed on hands and knees. In a letter to Nelson
Algren in 1950, Simone de Beauvoir described the rundown stairway and the
dark and dirty apartment where she had grown up.

> The flat was sad, nearly dirty, I loathed it. I lived with my sister in a
> very cheap room, very little and unconvenient, two beds could hardly
> stand in it; and when we were up, there was no place to stay, so we had
> . . . to spend the day in my father's bureau where everybody gathered;
> in winter, it was the only place where there was a fire. I loathed the
> people, I hated to read or study in this dull place. I enjoyed it only in
> the afternoons when nobody was at home; then I could sit in the deep
> leather armchair, and read forbidden books such as Musset, Victor
> Hugo, and I felt a queen. But coming back in the evening by the dirty
> staircase to stand the whole night in the cold grim house with my
> parents arguing together, no privacy, no peace, I hated it. Maybe it is
> the reason why I am such a poor housewife; everything concerning the
> house and a good wife's life, such as my mother's, scared me to death.[4]

The strenuous housework exhausted her mother. Revolted by the constraint, the chores, and the drudgery, she had the feeling that she was de-
meaning herself. Françoise gave up taking care of her appearance and soon
began to look like an overworked matron. When one day she put on a veiled

velvet hat, a charmed Poupette exclaimed, "Mommy! You look like a chic lady!" Françoise laughed without reservation, for "she no longer cared about elegance. She pushed contempt of the body, for herself and for her daughters, to the point of uncleanliness."[5]

Convinced that their studies were the sole road to salvation, Françoise asked only the absolute minimum of help with the housework from Simone and Poupette. Simone's tasks included grinding the coffee and taking out the garbage. The trash can was much too small, and stray peels and greasy scraps of paper were always falling out. She retrieved them with disgust and crammed the mess into the already overflowing bins, all the time trying to avoid a scolding from the concierge. It also fell upon Simone to cut old newspapers into square pieces and thread them onto a string for use as toilet paper.

Françoise de Beauvoir taught her girls that virtue and culture counted far more than wealth; in lieu of *La Semaine de Suzette,* a lay journal for children, she had them read *L'Etoile noëliste,* a Catholic publication that reminded its readers of the virtues of poverty. She shared her husband's certainty that, in view of their breeding and education, they belonged to the elite. Despite the state of near deprivation in which the family struggled, Simone was convinced that "morally, therefore absolutely," they ranked far above the rest of society.[6] As for Georges de Beauvoir, he quoted Edmond Rostand: "My elegance is anchored in my morality."[7]

After the shoe factory went under, one of Georges' cousins, Choppin de Janvry, a wealthy banker, got him a job with the newspaper *Le Gaulois.* It was up to him to find new companies that were in the process of issuing stock and persuade them to take out paid advertising in *Le Gaulois.* When turned down, Georges discreetly made it clear that the paper would not present its readers with an altogether flattering description of the enterprise in question. This form of blackmail barely enabled him to get by. The refined man-about-town, who had once placed good manners above all else, demonstrated in outbursts his rage at being déclassé. His profession was always given as "lawyer" in the *Bottin mondain,* the official directory of professions; he bore an elegant-sounding name; his father and brother "owned property." He would not stand for being mixed in with a class he considered inferior, and he made this clear with his loud and aggressive behavior. When forced to ride the bus, he insulted the other passengers; in public he arrogantly criticized everything. He made a point of affecting the language of the lower classes, going their vulgarity one better. "He worked so hard at appearing coarse and common that in the end, no one but he believed he wasn't." He gave Simone the impression of having "deliberately neglected" prosperity and success. He

fancied himself misunderstood, "a victim of obscure cataclysms." The men
he cited as examples to his children were the most fabulous geniuses on the
face of the earth, but "their very overabundance of genius destined them to
err."[8] In the apartment with the threadbare carpeting, Victor Hugo, Emile
Zola, and Anatole France were the butt of his sarcasm. He weighed their style
and their thoughts and "looked upon their aberrations with a serene impar-
tiality." He enjoyed the sound of his own words. His wife and daughters,
utterly captivated, followed his evolving train of thought, which was "ungraspable and infinite. People and things were summoned before him: he was
the sovereign judge."[9]

His politics were of the extreme right. In Georges de Beauvoir's considered opinion, French civilization was dying because of foreigners and Jews
and because of the intellectuals and their assorted nonsense: human rights,
pacifism, internationalism, socialism. All the world was fair game for his
contemptuous outbursts and abusive remarks.

His love for the theatre lingered. He had lost most of his connections and
now performed in the suburban clubs run by Monsieur Jeannot, a great
promoter of religious theatre, where he appeared along with a ravishing
Poupette.[10] Simone had played the role of the young Madame de Sévigné at
the Cours Désir, but she would refuse to "take to the stage" again after a
party given by some wealthy cousins. A friend had written a revue in verse
for the occasion, and Simone, dressed as a Spanish dancer, had to strut back
and forth, making eyes and fluttering a fan, while Poupette, the main attraction, clad in a grand tulle dress brocaded with stars, sang to the tune of
"Funiculi-Funicula":

> There comes our way a lovely señorita
> Whose stride's adept, whose stride's adept
> The chic and stately style of Barcelona
> The Spanish step, the Spanish step.[11]

Simone had felt awkward, put upon, ill at ease. From then on she preferred
to watch her father and sister from the audience.

Thanks to Alexandre Vargas, the family continued to hear the latest
backstage gossip and to receive complimentary tickets. It was then that
Georges de Beauvoir became courteous and glib once again. "On rare occasions—when we went to the theatre and his friend from the Odéon introduced him to a well-known actress—he rediscovered all his worldly
graciousness."[12] As for Simone, who cried at *Cyrano,* sobbed over *l'Aiglon,*
thrilled to *Britannicus,* she gave herself up body and soul to the spell of the
stage.

MEYRIGNAC

Summer brought a welcome respite to Simone's life. The constraints and frustrations of the cramped apartment in the rue de Rennes, which was glacial in winter and offered views only of rooftops and a tiny patch of sky, faded away when summer vacation time arrived and the family headed for Meyrignac in the Limousin region of west-central France, where Ernest de Beauvoir had retired. They left Paris in a bustle of voices and edgy excitement. In 1914 they had had to give up traveling first class. Unable to afford even the comforts of second-class train travel, they consigned themselves to third class. In this highly compartmentalized society, there was a world of difference between third and second class that in turn had nothing in common with the privileged passengers in first class. At the station, the porters needed a great deal of persuading to carry anything for third-class passengers, and Françoise lost her temper when faced with their stubborn refusal. "We wore ourselves out carrying luggage, registering it, keeping an eye on it." In the train compartment Georges swore, bumped into and insulted the other passengers, and alluded to the sort of people he generally socialized with. The other passengers talked back, their tone mounting. This aggressive exhibitionism made Simone uncomfortable. She dreamed of the moment when the train would arrive at the Uzerche station and they would pile their trunks onto a mule-drawn cart and set off on foot through the chestnut groves past Meyrignac, a four-farm hamlet buried in one of the poorest regions of France. For the space of a summer, the de Beauvoirs became lords and ladies of the manor, living on the family property.

Settled in their country surroundings, Françoise relaxed immediately and Georges began to feel like his old self. His older brother Gaston, the owner of Meyrignac, was there with his entire family, but it was Grandfather de Beauvoir who set the tone. This octogenarian bon vivant hummed away from morning to night. He came down from his bedroom around noon, his chin freshly shaved, his white side-whiskers carefully brushed, the Legion of Honor ribbon pinned to the lapel of his jacket, and he would comment on news items in *L'Echo de Paris* until lunchtime.

Simone's love of food was proverbial. All morning she did her vacation chores breathing in the odor of caramel and other aromas from the kitchen that promised delicacies to come. She was never disappointed. Partridge with cabbage, chicken vol-au-vent, duck with olives, saddle of hare, pâtés, tarts, pies, frangipane, clafouti (fruit, especially cherries, cooked in batter), and other dishes followed one another, accompanied by the tune of "Les Cloches de Corneville," which came from a lazy susan fitted with a music box that played the air from the operetta when spun. Throughout the meal they laughed and carried on, singing, declaiming, stepping on one another's words, jumbling memories, anecdotes, and quotations, countering bon mots with silly jokes. After the feast the children were free to explore the countryside, to run wild in the chestnut groves and dash across the fields. Like a squirrel, Simone filled her secret stashes: two apples here, three there. Later, book in hand, she would munch on them, dreaming all the while of the toast and chocolate that would be hers come snacktime. Sometimes she set off with her grandfather, who taught her the names of trees, flowers, mushrooms, plants, and the exotic birds he raised in his aviary.

He had had a miniature waterway built on the property. Two bridges led to a tiny island of greenery, a fake waterfall fell onto a bed of water lilies, goldfish swam in tiny ponds, and peacocks strutted in a park where rare foliage grew.

Evenings in the living room with the green plush armchairs and yellow muslin curtains, Françoise de Beauvoir played Ernest de Beauvoir's favorite songs on the piano and everyone sang along. Then it was time to retire. The old house resonated awhile longer with the sounds of preparations for slumber, then settled into silence.

It was then that Simone reveled in the luxury of having a room to herself. She had been dazzled when her friend Zaza had shown Simone her bedroom in the enormous apartment where her family lived in the rue de Varenne. At Meyrignac her dreams of space were fulfilled. The whole world came to her through the window: the whispers of the night, the scent of cherry laurel, the burbling of the spring, the grunts and grumblings of animals in the stable. She told herself that one day she would explore the entire world, leaving no meadow uncharted, no stone unturned. She found the solitude exalting.

About ten miles distant, in the Château de la Grillère, lived Aunt Hélène de Bishop, Georges de Beauvoir's older sister. The Grillère manor, built around 1870, was a vast dwelling ornamented with hunting horns, mounted animal heads, and peacock feathers. Only one room, the billiard room, was in general use; the rest of the estate lay dormant. Aunt Hélène, who had a cook, Maria, and a chambermaid, Anna, spent her days rummaging through her cabinets and closets. Uncle Maurice de Bishop rode back and forth on horseback, exploring his woods. At midday he ceremoniously prepared the luncheon salad in accordance with the tradition that reserved this privilege for the master of the household. Their two children, Robert and Madeleine, were educated by private tutors and grew up free of restraints. Robert hunted and fished for crayfish; Madeleine, an avid reader of novels, dreamed of passionate romances. Madeleine was free to read whatever she liked, while Simone's fare was carefully chosen and censored, the forbidden pages pinned together.

Each year the de Beauvoirs spent a few days at La Grillère, where the meals were copious. Come evening, Aunt Hélène would wait until the very end of the sunset to place an oil lamp on the table in the billiard room. Uncle Maurice and Robert, ensconced in their easy chairs, leafed through the hunting magazine *Le Chasseur français,* silently awaiting the bedtime hour. Occasionally Aunt Hélène sat herself down at the piano to sing turn-of-the-century romantic ditties whose racy couplets enchanted Simone and Poupette, who did not let on that they understood.[13] The two and a half months in the Limousin enabled the children to store up a measure of health and happiness. They were free; Simone read and wrote stretched out on her stomach, Poupette sketched and drew. They made up scenarios of their lives to come, imagining they would one day be famous. They set off to explore the area known as the Landes, the chestnut groves and the fields that stretched for miles around, sampling berries off the bush, munching on hazelnuts, wild strawberries, and apples, skinning their arms and legs along dense trails in the midst of bees and birds, in the fragrance of honeysuckle and hay. Simone felt herself becoming one with the "odors of undulating buckwheat, the intimate scent of the heather, the heavy noon heat or the shiver of sunset; I weighed a fair amount and yet I evaporated into the blue sky, without a care in the world."[14]

ELISABETH L.

*B*efore she met Sartre, Simone de Beauvoir's most passionate attachment was for a classmate, Elisabeth L.* Simone was ten years old when Elisabeth arrived at the Cours Désir, radiating an aura of romanticism. She had spent a full year flat on her back in severe pain, the victim of an accident in which she had been seriously burned. With her short hair and her boyish look, Elisabeth's ease and casualness surprised Simone. Zaza, as she was called, did cartwheels and splits, hung upside down from branches, rode

---

*Zaza Mabille in the memoirs.

horseback, played tennis. She was allowed to go shopping alone. She had been to Italy, she read poems Simone was forbidden to read, and she caused a scandal at school by writing that she preferred the rebel Alceste to the socially acceptable Philinte, and Napoléon to Pasteur. She wrote and ran off copies of a newspaper, "The Family Chronicle," that she dispatched to members of her family—a substantial readership that included eight brothers and sisters and an army of aunts, uncles, and cousins.

Zaza had a biting wit and scoffed at anyone, herself included. She scorned a humanity that in her opinion was not very respectable, and she displayed a violent cynicism toward people who valued only money and social niceties. All hypocrisy revolted her.

Simone listened in fascination. Finally here was someone who said aloud what she had been thinking secretly! She became passionately devoted to Zaza, and when on one occasion the object of her affection was absent from school for two weeks, Simone languished, her drive and spirit gone.

> The blue of heaven had been dimmed. The classes bored me . . .
> my life was dull and monotonous . . . it was as if without any warning,
> the whole world had died . . . when Zaza came back, we began to talk,
> to relate various things that had happened to us, and to comment on
> them; my tongue was suddenly loosened, and a thousand bright suns
> began blazing in my breast; radiant with happiness, I told myself: 'I
> needed Zaza!' So total had been my ignorance of the workings of the
> heart that I hadn't thought of telling myself: 'I miss her.' I needed her
> presence to realize how much I needed her. This was a blinding revela-
> tion. All at once, conventions, routines, and the careful categorizing of
> emotions were swept away and I was overwhelmed by a flood of feeling
> that had not been foreseen in any code. I allowed myself to be uplifted
> by that wave of joy which went on mounting inside me, as violent and
> fresh as a waterfalling cataract.[15]

Every morning when Simone was ten years old, she read a chapter of *L'Imitation de Jésus-Christ,* a training book on religious meditation for adults. Both her confessor and her mother encouraged her penchant for asceticism. Her intelligence set her apart from her classmates; she was not arrogant, but her insatiable curiosity about people and things could not be quenched. "I liked to make people talk on and on. The other students in class did not satisfy my eagerness to learn." Romantic and passionate, her seething imagi-nation never openly expressed, she was already living like a special being—the heroine of the books she would someday write. She hoped that someone would recognize and discover her, that she would no longer be alone. Eli-sabeth L.'s arrival was all her dreams come true; the rest of the world no longer existed. Hélène de Beauvoir admits that Simone's friendship with Zaza was the major development of her own childhood, since her older sister brutally abandoned her for a new playmate. Simone gave herself utterly and fanatically to this friendship that for years would torture her in ways she did not understand, without Zaza's ever suspecting the intensity of her feelings. For, at the age of Romeo and Juliet, Zaza's heart yearned for her cousin André. But their families, in the throes of a vendetta worthy of the Capulets and the Montagues, were enemies, and the two adolescents were forbidden to see each other. Much later Simone learned her friend's secret with considerable surprise. As for her, throughout her adolescence she loved no one but Zaza. Timid and reserved, Simone never let anyone catch a glimpse of the upheaval in her heart. She consoled herself by carrying on an imaginary dialogue with Zaza. Reading André Laurie's novel *The Schoolboy of Athens,* she identified with the serious schoolboy subjugated by the handsome Euphorion, an impertinent young aristocrat who reminded her of Zaza.

Simone's view of the world changed as she came into contact with Elisabeth and her family. Madame L. raised her nine children in a style that was both liberal and God-fearing. Simone could not help but compare the easygoing authority of this calm and smiling grande bourgeoise with her own mother's rigorous conformism.

Maurice L., a graduate of the Polytechnic Institute, had worked as chief engineer for the Orléans railroad before becoming director of the Citroën automobile factory. A Catholic and a liberal, he had been a member of the democratic Catholic group le Sillon, a political and social movement that saw itself as the voice of the "democratic international." Their founder, Marc Sangnier, organized meetings of pacifists and antiracists and established a network of youth hostels. Maurice L., a Christian Democrat, spoke in defense of Sangnier's ideas at public meetings. Dragged along by Zaza, Simone attended a debate between Maurice L. and a militant representative of Action Française, Henri Massis. The struggle between these two factions was often brutal; on one occasion a group of people from Action Française cornered a few of Marc Sangnier's supporters and forced them to swallow castor oil by the glassful. Georges de Beauvoir could not have been more pleased. He continued to staunchly support the extreme right-wing views espoused by Charles Maurras, the editor of *L'Action française,* the royalist daily paper.

Christian involvement in political life was a concept completely foreign to Simone. Her father was a nonbeliever and her mother had taken refuge from her husband's infidelities in religion, where she found consolation for the family's poverty in the Gospel. In Françoise de Beauvoir's eyes, religion was an intellectual process, not a political struggle; she read countless works of piety, the lives of the saints and books dealing with Christian education,

which she carefully annotated. She encouraged Simone's tendencies toward
mysticism. Françoise de Beauvoir had compelled her daughter to read stacks
of novels whose hero was Christ, and it was "with a lover's eyes" that Simone
in her imagination looked upon his handsome, tender face and bleeding body
and wept rivers of tears. Simone often slipped into the Cours Désir chapel
and immersed herself in a profound religious meditation. Secretly she considered entering the Carmelite convent and devoting her life to the contempla-
tion of the glory of God.

As the years went by, Simone's faith deepened and her mysticism grew.
Unlike Saint Bernard, Simone was in no position to throw herself into the icy
torrents, and she settled instead for locking herself in the bathroom, where
she mortified her flesh by scraping her thighs with a pumice stone or whip-
ping herself with a gold necklace until she drew blood. At about thirteen, her
desire to be swept up in the path of true knowledge was so strong that her
spiritual advisor lent her a copy of the *Précis de théologie ascétique et mystique,* a
manual of ascetic and mystic theology for the use of young men aspiring to
the priesthood. Since earliest childhood Simone had issued herself strict and
imperious orders; she enjoyed forcing herself to excel through the variations
on self-denial she invented. From the age of six she had hoped to bring on
fits of ecstasy, to partake of visions, but nothing of the sort came to pass. The
games she played reflected her desires, and she spent hours lost in heroic
reveries. One day she would be Joan of Arc at the stake, expiring in flames;
another episode would find her cast as Mary Magdalene drying Christ's feet
with her long tresses; in yet another variation Simone was a martyr imprisoned in a dungeon, challenging the heathens with religious hymns. She and
her sister played "martyr" for years. Simone was always the heroic saint, her
sister locking her in an imaginary tower and depriving her of everything—
even her mass book, which she tore to shreds. They invented a technique for
pinching themselves with sugar tongs until they bled or flaying themselves
with the sticks of miniature flags. In her quest for the absolute at the age of
fifteen, Simone was indignant that immediately after the mysteries of the
mass and communion one could jump right back into the daily routine. For
her it was all or nothing. "I was too much of an extremist," she would write,
"to be able to live under the eye of God and at the same time say both yes
and no to life."[16]

More secret fantasies haunted her. She identified with Saint Blandine,
whose blood-soaked shirt afforded glimpses of her flesh as the lions sank
their teeth into her before the gaze of an admiring crowd. She was Geneviève
de Brabant, naked beneath her cascading hair and "thrilled to repent at the
feet of a handsome man, terrible and pure."[17] Elaborating on this theme, she
sank into and foundered in remorse until the hero, moved by her anguish,

placed his hand upon her head, at which point Simone was ready to swoon. She had read that a sultan used a conquered enemy as a step stool to mount his horse, and she cast herself in the role of the step stool: "trembling and half-naked," she felt "the tyrant's sharp spurs tearing her back."[18]

Early on, Simone discovered what was called a "forbidden pleasure." While on vacation in Meyrignac, having done her chores like a good girl, she repaired to the woods where supervising eyes would not intrude and sought out the shadow of the trees in order to partake of "that joy." Opening a bootleg volume of Balzac, she read of the strange idyll of a man and a panther. At night she told herself "peculiar stories which put her into a queer state of mind."[19] In the first version of *She Came to Stay,* de Beauvoir described at length the discovery of her body in the woods of Meyrignac, but her editor asked her to cut the first chapter, which was thought to be too shocking for the reading public of 1943.

Back in Paris she came across, and read in the bathroom, part of a serialized novel in which the hero ardently kisses the heroine's milky white breasts. "This kiss seared me—male, female, and voyeur rolled into one, I gave and received it and feasted my eyes upon it until I'd had my fill." Before drifting off to sleep she told herself burning tales of fiery passion. At the age of twelve she conjured up "a man's body pressed against my own," a man's hands upon her, stroking her flesh, and she despaired that one could not marry before the age of fifteen.[20]

On the sly she eagerly read Paul Bourget, Alphonse Daudet, Marcel Prévost, Maupassant, and Pierre Loti. She hid *Les Demi-Vierges* and *La Femme et le Pantin* under her mattress and was thrilled by the homosexual characters of Colette's "Claudine" books and Claude Farrère's *Mademoiselle Dax*. This violent sensuality sent prohibitions, proprieties, and soon religion itself flying to pieces in her head.

At school she became insolent and restless. Poupette, even more openly impudent, started a newspaper, "The Cours Désir Gazette," for which Simone wrote several "cruel lampoons."[21] She thought her teachers ignorant and stupid and let them know it. In the twenties the demoiselles of the Cours Désir still wore long skirts that swept the floor and leg-of-mutton-sleeved blouses in moiré-patterned taffeta. Georges de Beauvoir "made no secret of the fact that he found these pious old frauds a little backward."[22] Himself a great reader of Voltaire, Beaumarchais, and Hugo, he resented the gaps in the education his daughters were receiving and would have liked to send them to the lycée. Simone fought this idea because she did not want to be separated from Zaza. Instead, with support from her father, who laughed along with her childish pranks, she became increasingly insubordinate. Nor were her teachers about to let her go unpunished, and so it was that in 1922 the best student at the Cours Désir failed to receive the *prix d'excellence* that would have recognized her academic standing. The awards ceremony in the Wagram Auditorium was a pompous occasion that for several years had been Simone's hour of glory. This year she was demoted to "special mention," and she endured the affront with rebellion in her heart.

She came to the conclusion that her sustained and systematic disobedience, the impure reveries in which she delighted, and the reading in which she secretly indulged were in contradiction with her religious principles. Too unyielding to go on fooling herself, she was struck one day by the evidence: Either the things of this world mattered not and the reward lay in eternity, or eternity would have to be sacrificed in order to partake of earthly pleasures. She sensed that nothing was about to make her give up the joys of this world. Yet it disgusted her to live in bad faith, to quibble with her conscience. She realized that she no longer believed in God, and she shouldered the burden of her loss of faith. At fourteen she came to understand fully the terrible meaning of solitude: "the earth was rolling through space that was unseen by any eye."[23] She discovered an anxiety that she had never known. One afternoon, alone in the apartment, panic seized her; death, no longer the threshold to eternal life, meant an end to all existence. She rolled on the floor shrieking and clawing at the carpet.

There was no one with whom she could talk about this anguish that gnawed at her heart. For three long years she hid her loss of faith from her mother and from Zaza. She no longer went to confession but continued to take communion when her mother was with her. Her father's skepticism offered no real comfort, and she dared not confide in him. Accustomed to compelling and constraining herself, she learned to live a life split in two. Literature came to her rescue. She began to keep a journal in which she declared herself and her feelings truthfully. All the major crises of her life— her mother's death, World War II, the Occupation, the war in Algeria, Sartre's death—Simone de Beauvoir would tackle pen in hand.

"MY FATHER LET ME DOWN"

*H*er relationship with Georges de Beauvoir became strained. Between the ages of ten and thirteen, Simone's feelings for her father were exalted. He impressed her with his culture, his intelligence, his "gift of gab"; she saw him as a remarkable being, a hero, a victim of his destiny. As she grew older, the contradictions in his character did not go unnoticed. Bitter and disenchanted, he directed a sort of hostility toward his daughters, reproaching them for the money they cost him. "We had the impression that we had indiscreetly imposed ourselves upon his charity." With Simone he became verbally brutal. By the age of fourteen, the pretty child had been transformed into an unattractive adolescent. Clad in hand-me-downs from her cousins, she felt ill at ease.* Her father did not help matters with such remarks as, "My poor daughter, how ugly can you be!" He reminded her that she had no dowry and concluded bitterly, "You'll never marry—you'll have to work for a living." Simone was upset by her father's frequent observation that "Simone has a man's brain; she thinks like a man; she *is* a man."[24] She took her sister aside to ask in great secrecy whether she might not stand a chance of appealing to someone, someday. But the reassurance she expected was not forthcoming; Poupette misunderstood the question. Since their father was forever saying that "Simone was a man," well, of course, sure enough—she must have a man's brain!

The atmosphere in the household was a heavy one. Quarrels could start for no reason. Françoise dared not ask her husband for money; any request above and beyond the miserable sum he reluctantly allowed for household expenses led to an outburst. She grew impatient, and voices rose with tempers. Simone recalled "slaps and smacks, grumbling and grousing, scenes not only in private but in front of guests."

Georges de Beauvoir strayed from home more and more often. He went out to play bridge nightly, and he spent Sunday at the track though "he didn't have enough money for a real debauch." Sometimes he would slink in at 8 A.M., smelling of alcohol. He was spotted at the Café de Versailles, known for its prostitutes, and seen coming out of the Sphinx, the famous brothel on the boulevard Edgar-Quinet.

A steady volley of reproaches, disputes, and recriminations made life difficult indeed in the narrow little apartment in the rue de Rennes. Poupette became insufferable with her arguing and grumbling, and Simone withdrew into silence. The stress and tension were not without repercussions. Simone became a walking collection of nervous tics: her nose twitched constantly, and an involuntary movement made her shrug her shoulders. She was scrawny and riddled with phobias.

---

*Simone de Beauvoir told us: "For my sister's holy communion I had a suit from my cousin Annie, who often gave me her used clothes. This time my mother had taken the trouble to alter the outfit to my size and to wash my hair. I was clean for once, and the other students at the Cours Désir were surprised." When Annie later became a nun in the Convent of the Sacred Heart, she gave her entire wardrobe to Simone.

There was one haven from the frequent storm: Georges de Beauvoir's worship of literature. For him, money, power, and worldly success vaporized in the face of creative genius. Simone knew that this was one domain where women could rise to glory instead of vegetating like her mother. In *The Second Sex* she would write of woman: "Stuck in her role as housekeeper, she stops the expansion of existence, she is obstacle and negation. . . . She appears as the one who waits, who obeys, who carries on." Describing the adolescent girl, she continued: "Imaginary accomplishments save her from her mother's influence by enabling her to compensate for the mediocrity of her environment."[25] At the age of fifteen Simone de Beauvoir responded to the question "And what do you want to be when you grow up?" without hesitation: "A famous writer."[26]

This certainty gave her great inner strength. Her career would depend entirely on her studies and her intelligence. On that much her parents were agreed; they wanted her to read, to study, to be a success. They suggested no other path, and from this she derived the reassuring conviction that she was what she was meant to be. Her future was all laid out; she would never vacillate, never waver. Her family's difficulties would not modify the course of her life, and one day she would break through to economic independence and glory.[27]

Monsieur L. wanted Elisabeth to study mathematics, as her older sister had done. And Simone wanted to do whatever Zaza did. Through this little gesture of independence she opposed the wishes of her father, who prized only the study of literature and the law. Because the Cours Désir offered preparatory classes leading only to the baccalaureate in Latin and languages, a special teacher had to be hired to instruct the two pioneers in the mysteries of basic mathematics, algebra, trigonometry, and physics. Simone undertook the study of Italian and three months later could decipher the original texts of the Italian poets. Her days had to be filled to the brim. "I would not tolerate boredom, for it quickly turned to anxiety." Slowly she regained her self-confidence; the awkward age was over.

An international golf champion enrolled at the Cours Désir and passed her first baccalaureate at the age of fifteen and a half. Suddenly Simone caught a glimpse of an unknown world. A young lady whose style was utterly 1925 had burst into the cozy cocoon of a school where everything was going on just as it had before the war. The newcomer wore her hair short in the flapper style and sported pleated skirts and practical blouses. She had traveled widely, she was muscular, solid, brimming with self-assurance. Although younger than her classmates, she was more in tune with life than they and knew more about the world and current trends. She seemed to have dropped in from another planet where everything went faster and farther, where life could be lived in a new and different way.

1925

*I*n 1925 France, along with the rest of Europe, sought a new view of life. All along the Seine, from the place de la Concorde to the Palais de Chaillot, the International Exhibition of Modern Decorative Arts had set up shop, synthesizing the latest word in design and heralding a new style of living. Out with the ponderous Napoleon III furnishings, the clutter of knick-knacks and cumbersome trim—the pompoms, the fringe, the overstuffed and overplush. Bring on the bright, lively colors, the striking geometric forms, plenty of light and space and air. Women were dispensing with the dust-collecting bric-a-brac that surrounded them; many would no longer tolerate the rigors of housekeeping when the delights of tennis, golf, aviation, skiing, and motoring beckoned. Art was stepping out of the museums and into the streets.

The change in manners was apparent everywhere. Like all the young girls of the day, Simone dreamed of having a "cozy-corner," a thickly padded divan covered with the vibrantly colored throw pillows launched by Sonia Delaunay. Chests of drawers and armoires were banished; only shelving would do. Indirect lighting was the last word in modernity. Practicality was the watchword.

Olympic athletes inspired the great decorators. Garlands of nude bodies adorned Lalique vases and ornamented the pediments of modern buildings. Contemporary design was a hymn to health and the beauty of the human body. Corsets and whalebone stays were dismissed as instruments of torture. The movies helped to spread the new vision of womanhood and decor, of sex appeal and dynamism. Hollywood created the prototypes and the gestures that were soon to be emulated by the secretaries, clerks, and blue-collar workers of Paris.

Women had their hair clipped above the ears like boys, and their skirts now stopped above the knee. They wore ties with their man-tailored shirts. In the evening they draped themselves in asymmetrical dresses emblazoned with clashing, joyful, provocative colors.

Speed, comfort, color, and light were the order of the day. Paul Morand made stylish the man-in-a-hurry who drives his roadster like a rocket across the face of Europe, sampling every pleasure haunt the night has to offer. Victor Margueritte's novel *La Garçonne* was an enormous success. Published in 1923, this novel depicts in a very crude manner the sexual mores after World War I. The main character, Monique, discovers on the eve of her marriage that her fiancé has a mistress. Outraged, she seeks revenge by going to bed with a stranger. She is rejected by her family, who want her to marry —at any cost—her fiancé, who rejects her now. She starts to work as an interior decorator and mingles with artists, noncomformists of all kinds, and wealthy drug addicts. She decides to live as freely as a man. She indulges in sexual experiences using her partners as sex objects. At the end, she will discover happiness with a man who understands her. In *La Garçonne,* Victor Margueritte challenged all the bourgeois traditions.

Women took to wearing low-heeled shoes *à la garçonne,* button-down shirts and bow ties *à la garçonne,* cufflinks *à la garçonne,* and ladies did their smoking with the help of long cigarette holders—how else but *à la garçonne?* The expression was everywhere, and the words "liberated" and "emancipated" were on everyone's lips. André Gide published *The Counterfeiters* and *Corydon,* Paul Morand published *L'Europe galante,* and Victor Margueritte was drummed out of the Legion of Honor for having given the outside world a false impression of young Frenchwomen.

In 1925, when the world tumbled into modernity, Simone de Beauvoir was seventeen years old. She had passed her baccalaureate in Latin and literature with honors and in basic mathematics with highest honors. She decided to become a lycée teacher while waiting to become a writer. Madame de Beauvoir distrusted secular education and feared for Simone's soul. Georges de Beauvoir was not opposed to a teaching position, for it represented financial security, but he felt humiliated; he saw his daughter as the incarnation of his own failure. Had she been a boy she would have gone on to the Polytechnic Institute, but since she was a girl she could be nothing better than a bluestocking. He reiterated that a professor was a priggish pedant, that an intellectual was a Dreyfusard, a shameless good-for-nothing, a troublemaker bent on torching the true values—race, class, and family—in favor of a raging idiocy that fell under the headings of pacifism, socialism, and internationalism.

Then Georges de Beauvoir conceived the notion that his dishonor would be erased if his daughter accomplished something truly extraordinary. Merely passing exams in order to qualify for a profession would reflect badly on Monsieur de Beauvoir, but if Simone could rack up degrees for the sheer virtuosity of collecting them, she would be something of an artist and a phenomenon. Now *there* were possibilities! He pushed his daughter into pursuing not one, not two, but three *licences,* in literature, philosophy, and mathematics.* He also advised her to take up law, "which could always come in handy." Collecting diplomas—now there was something delightfully feminine, charmingly baroque, and above all, useless.

So it was that Simone enrolled in courses at the Catholic Institute that would lead to a *certificat* in general mathematics. She took her advanced literature classes at the Ecole Normale Libre in the Paris suburb of Neuilly, a private institute of higher education founded in 1907 by Madame Charles Daniélou for the training of private-school teachers. Madame Daniélou was a pioneer. She became the first woman *agrégée,* in literature, in 1903. With her husband, the legislative deputy Charles Daniélou, she fought the Combes laws, which provided for the total separation of church and education. Thinking realistically, she reasoned that private—that is, religious—education could survive only if its instructors benefited from training similar to that given to teachers destined for the official state-run institutions. She founded the *collèges* Sainte-Marie and the elementary schools named after Charles Péguy.

Simone inaugurated her new life as a college student with a tartan plaid dress, made to order in her size, spanking new and never before worn by anyone else. She climbed the steps of the Sainte-Geneviève Library telling herself proudly that she had finally leapt into "the hurly-burly of real life."[28]

"EVERYTHING IN MY LIFE MUST SERVE A PURPOSE"

*S*he made herself a solemn vow: Everything will serve. That much established, she proceeded to make up the rules for her very own religion. From now on, time would be sacred; she had to get her studies over with as quickly as possible so as to embark on real life. She organized her time with a jealous intensity that she herself described as schizophrenic.

First, she would have to sleep less: She deprived herself systematically

*Until 1968, a *licence* (roughly the equivalent of a master's degree in the United States) was composed of four *certificats.* Ordinarily a student earned one *certificat* a year, but a very intelligent and determined student might earn two in one year. After the *licence* came the *Diplôme d'Etudes Supérieures.* The students who wanted to become tenured lycée professors took a highly competitive national exam called *l'agrégation.*

of sleep. Then there was the matter of preparing to meet the day. Washing up in the cramped, unheated washroom without benefit of running water had always been a major project; now she would barely take the time to brush her teeth, and she would give up cleaning her nails altogether. She banished extraneous reading matter and no longer engaged in frivolous conversation. And she no longer intended to play tennis in the rue Boulard on Saturday mornings. But there Madame de Beauvoir put her foot down. Not play tennis! Why, that was one of the elegant sporting pursuits that served to distinguish high society from the common mass! Saturday-morning tennis was an indispensable social activity and an important opportunity for respectable encounters between young men and young ladies, a fertile territory for nourishing the social ties that pave the way to marriage!

Simone had to sacrifice her Saturday mornings to fresh air and exercise. Yet no amount of angry protest from her father could persuade her to give up memorizing Greek verbs or solving math problems while seated at the dinner table. She appeared at meals with grammar book in hand and mumbled Greek conjugations between bites. Or, setting a notebook beside her plate, she would fill it with equations without lifting her head. The family was astonished by her "slovenliness."

Without the slightest regard for anyone else, caught up completely in her project, she adopted heroism as the remedy for mediocrity. Rather than regret pleasures she could not have, she pushed herself further into asceticism. She outdid herself, taking on a punishing workload with the express purpose of seeing how far she could go, only to push her limits just a bit further each day. Hopefulness had been forged into willpower; liberty was a challenge in itself. Joy sprang from an excess of hard work and the surpassing of herself. Simone practiced the discipline of saints and conquerors.

Nothing could deter her in her quest for the vessel from which all happiness would pour. She would go willingly by way of the Brocéliande Forest, cross the Sword Bridge, and enter the accursed castle where the oppressed maidens bemoaned the fate of the working class:

Toujours draps de soie tisserons	We will always weave silken sheets
Et n'en serons pas mieux vêtues	And will not be better clad for all our labor
Toujours serons pauvres et nues	We will remain poor and unprotected
Et toujours faim et soif aurons.	And will always be hungry and thirsty.[29]

One day she would come to their rescue, but in order to do that she had to be wary of falling under the horrible spell of ease and indulgence.

That autumn her grandfather Gustave Brasseur died after a long illness. To the very last he had kept his dreams of making a fortune. From time to time, as he lay paralyzed in bed, he would tell his wife, "I have an idea, we'll all be rich." He died with this obstinate hope in his heart and nothing in the bank. His wife took in boarders to survive.

Simone wore black from head to toe, but she did not experience her grandfather's passing with any particular grief. He had bounced from failure to failure, taking Georges de Beauvoir down with him. All his life he had been the victim of swindlers and con men, and with them, blackmail, lawsuits, court proceedings, and creditors had come into Simone's life. This Balzacian patriarch had never accepted the fact that his son Hubert had married for love, "beneath his station," and the old man treated his two Brasseur grandchildren like distant relations. "We were told that they were indeterminate cousins."

Two teachers made a big impression on Simone at the Ecole Normale Libre in Neuilly. Mademoiselle Mercier,* aged thirty-five, was an *agrégée* in philosophy. You could count on the fingers of one hand the number of women who had passed the philosophy *agrégation.* So rare was this honor that the pioneering recipients had their portraits in the photo weekly *Illustration,* often accompanied by a second photo of the distinguished laureate surrounded by her proud family. Mademoiselle Mercier, a rare example of intellectual success among the ranks of women, encouraged Simone to devote herself to philosophy.

Robert Garric taught literature.[30] He was a leftist Catholic who organized groups of student volunteers to teach workers in the poorer quarters. This marked Simone's first exposure to the idea that the knowledge of the elite should be made available to the common man. Garric was young, only thirty, and his enthusiasm proved contagious.

Simone signed up for Garric's social work program and was put in charge of a team that taught once a week in a big building in the Belleville quarter, a low-income district of Paris. Simone taught French literature to young women workers and apprentices while the two other members of her group held classes in gymnastics and English. She liked the lively atmosphere at the center, but what she appreciated most was the freedom this benevolent activity brought her: Under the pretense of setting off to do good works, she might go walking with her sister or go to the movies. She quickly found Garric's well-intentioned project disappointing. The young women workers

---

*Mlle Lambert in the memoirs.

came to the center to talk and gossip among themselves and to flirt at the dances the center organized. The friendship between the social classes that Garric touted so highly did not take hold. "We killed time together, but we never understood each other." From her two-year involvement with the program she reached the conclusion that militant action does not pay off, and she would stick to that opinion for some time. For her, suitable action for intellectuals lay in the realm of ideas, not in the street.

At the same time, Garric's literature courses opened up new horizons for her. She began haunting the bookstores in the Latin quarter, standing for hours on end, reading everything she could get her hands on. She took out a membership at the lending library of the Maison des Amis du Livre, where Adrienne Monnier, clad in a homespun dress, welcomed everyone who mattered in the world of literature.*

Across the street at 12 rue de l'Odéon, Adrienne's friend Sylvia Beach tended her shop, Shakespeare & Co., a celebrated crossroads of the American bohemian literary community. In the two bookshops, pillars of intellectual life between the wars, Simone de Beauvoir initiated herself into modern literature and lent new meaning to the term "wholesale borrowing" by slipping into her satchel four or five volumes more than the two permitted by her membership.

She read until she felt light-headed and could read no more. She read Gide, Claudel, Mauriac, Radiguet, Jammes, Proust, Vildrac, Jacob, Léautaud, Reverdy, and a proliferation of ephemeral avant-garde reviews. Reading was her only entertainment.

At 71 rue de Rennes, discussions of literature became increasingly bitter. Georges de Beauvoir was working for the magazine *La Revue française,* under the direction of Antoine Redier, who zealously promoted the virtues of women in his novels *Léone* and *Pierrette.* In 1918 he had published *Le Mariage de Lison à l'usage des combattants et des jeunes filles sans dot,* a handbook on marriage for soldiers and young ladies without dowries. Redier, along with his colleagues and contributors, admired the Academicians and the style of Anatole France. In Redier's opinion, contemporary authors were pretentious, decadent, and immoral. Georges de Beauvoir and his friends chimed in to de-

---

*La Maison des Amis du Livre ("the house of the friends of books") at 7 rue de l'Odéon was a combination salon and bookstore where authors often read from their work. Joyce read passages from *Ulysses,* and Claudel, Jammes, Gide, Valéry, and Jules Romains were frequently on hand. Adrienne Monnier received the first dadaïst texts from Zurich. Aragon, Philippe Soupault, and Breton founded the magazine *Littérature* in her store. Fargue, Léautaud, Cendrars, Jacob, Reverdy, Vildrac, Duhamel, Satie, Milhaud, Auric, Katherine Mansfield, André Chamson, Maurois, and Martin du Gard were among the visitors of note. Young people flocked there to meet their seniors.

nounce the charlatanism of modern artists. "During these indictments," all eyes were fixed on Simone, who counterattacked by denouncing the aestheticism of "those barbarians" the Academicians.[31]

The theatre was another subject for disagreement. Georges de Beauvoir did not look kindly on the revolution then under way on the stage. Baty, Jouvet, and "those foreigners" the Pitoëffs were in the process of obliterating French culture; the works of such foreign playwrights as Pirandello and Ibsen demoralized the public. When a young actor from the Comédie-Française with whom Georges de Beauvoir found himself rehearsing pointed out that one could no longer ignore Ibsen, Georges replied superbly, "I can."

Simone thought her parents incredibly stubborn, and they in turn bemoaned the path their daughter was taking. No longer in a position to prohibit her reading a particular book or seeing a play, they tried instead to convince Simone that her tastes and opinions would lead to her downfall and, above all, that hers were worthless beliefs because they were not the beliefs of her milieu.

Repeated discussions and quarrels led nowhere, for each party only maintained its position. Yet these running debates were not a complete waste of time for Simone; they obliged her to go to the bases of her beliefs and to define her convictions, and in doing this she learned to avoid what was hazy, vague, or evasive and to prepare a brutally solid defense of her opinions. At eighteen she felt "marked, cursed, separate." But did not all her favorite authors say that a writer owed it to himself to be damned? She recognized their restlessness in herself, and she put no less ardor than they had into embracing immorality.

Simone began to question the very foundations of her education: the religion, the femininity, and the politics. Her rebellion exploded in endless arguments with her father. "Our disputes soon took on an acrid tone. If he had shown himself to be tolerant, I could have accepted my father for what he was. But I myself was still nobody. I decided what I was going to be by adopting opinions and tastes that were at variance with his own."[32] In particular she rejected her father's ideas on marriage. Like most men of his generation, he believed that a husband was entitled to a certain amount of leeway in the marriage contract, while it was the wife's strict duty to remain chaste and faithful. Simone could not accept a right of one spouse to be unfaithful to the other. She declared that man and woman were equal and demanded total reciprocity and absolute equality between the two partners in a relationship. She was already of the opinion that abortion should not be a crime, that her body was hers alone, and that what she chose to do with it was nobody's business but hers. It was inconceivably bold for a young woman of Catholic upbringing to talk that way about something one simply did not discuss. If ever there were a taboo, this was it. That Simone was capable of even uttering the word "abortion" demonstrated the force of her provocation.

In the first quarter of this century there existed a small feminist movement that supported the right of women to have the number of children they wanted or to refuse maternity altogether. Nelly Roussel, a mother of three, married to a sculptor, led the fight. She had gotten her start in neo-Malthusian propaganda working beside her brother-in-law, Paul Robin, a graduate of the Ecole Normale Supérieure who had been banished from teaching for conducting an experiment in "coeducation of the sexes." Starting in 1895, he ran a dispensary where information about contraceptives was available to poor women. Nelly wrote for the publication *Régénération*. The courts denied her the right to respond when her views were attacked, maintaining that no publication should be obliged to print a response that was inconsistent with the law and morality. When this judgment was handed down against her, she was reproached for recommending sterility to women without at the same time advising chastity. The neo-Malthusian movement differed from that of Malthus in that in lieu of suggesting that its followers refrain from enjoying sex, it encouraged them to do so, while taking the necessary precautions to prevent procreation. The judgment's preamble stated that this amoral and antisocial theory would halt the progress of humanity and lead to decadence, and the court accused Nelly Roussel of undermining the patriotic principles on which the lives of all civilized peoples depend.

Nelly Roussel continued her struggle against the National Alliance for the Increase of the French Population—an uphill battle in a nation where the president himself crowned prolific mothers to the rousingly patriotic strains of the Marseillaise. In *La Voix des femmes* in 1920 she wrote, "Let's put our wombs on strike! No more babies in the service of a capitalism that turns them into work-flesh to be exploited or pleasure-flesh to be defiled.[33] But in the wake of the deaths of 1,400,000 men in World War I, politicians wanted to repopulate France, and they passed the "law of 1920," making abortion a crime. Repopulation was seen as a moral imperative, and women were all but ordered to have children. Mayors throughout France awarded medals to the largest local families, and the largest of all were honored by the president of France in a ceremony at the Elysée Palace. The tradition continues today. Nelly Roussel died in 1922, still clamoring in vain for women's independence and a new conception of the relationship between the sexes.

Simone de Beauvoir would contribute to changing the law of 1920 when, twenty-five years later, she rocked the foundations of society with her succinct pronouncement, "One is not born a woman, one becomes one."[34]

At the age of seventeen her argumentative audacity already led her to stubbornly defy her parents and to reject majority opinion in favor of the dictates of her conscience. For her the individual, the human entity, became the sole reality; class and social distinctions struck her more and more as artificial cultural constructs.

In bitterly opposing her father's opinions and defending her own, Simone discovered how alone she was in her views. She had believed that she was putting into practice the virtues she had been taught, first by being the best student, then by going on to prepare for a teaching career. Yet she realized that her family and the others around her looked upon her activities as a last resort. She did not understand the views on which this contempt for work was based; all she knew was that everything she had been taught was being turned against her and used to criticize her. She sensed injustice and revolted against it. It seemed to her that everything varied according to preconceived notions: One day it was her solemn and virtuous duty to study hard; the following day her studies made her a social outcast and an inferior being. One day work was sacred, the next day it was the idleness of the elite that distinguished it from the dregs of society.

One day her brain was worthy of a man, the next day she was nothing more than a bluestocking. Since she was not a member of the sex whose intelligence led to everything, her intelligence would apparently lead to her downfall. They did not approve of her intelligence, they did not like it, and they were the ones who had mystified her all these years. Now that they treated her like a rebel, to whom could she talk? The only sane thing to do was to start talking to herself. She began to write and, pen in hand, found herself in excellent company. She extricated herself from the trap of disapproval simply by rising above the trap. She had begun keeping a journal in a spirit of defiance, and unexpectedly she found herself in a world whose novelty stunned her and left her giddy. She was on to something; she had set out on the path of her vocation, she had entered the realm of writing. "I was both the landscape and its beholder; I existed only through myself and for myself."[35] She was overjoyed; she felt both saved and justified. "I congratulated myself on an exile which had chased me to such heights of joy."[36] From now on she knew she would be happy facing a blank page that reflected none other than herself. The business of living furnished the basis for the business of writing. She began to put her experience into words in the tale of Eliane, who expressed Simone's revolt against being taken in and her desire to stand up for herself in the face of others. Simone did not finish this story, but in the summer of the same year, at Meyrignac, she began and completed her first novel.

JACQUES CHAMPIGNEULLES AND SURREALISM

She knew now what she wanted. That young women were attending the university was newsworthy; in 1929 there were 2,560 women enrolled in the liberal arts and 1,080 in the sciences. Yet only a few in this first wave of pioneers felt independent enough to go out alone for a walk or to shop.

Simone longed to escape the austerity of her life and join the company of people carrying on lively discussions on café terraces. She wanted to go out, to be an active part of the changing society to which she felt she belonged. Right there in Montparnasse there were artists, intellectuals, foreigners, and women who painted or wrote, proving that there were more liberated ways to live.

At seventeen she told herself it was time she fell in love, and conscientiously she deepened her affection for her nineteen-year-old cousin Jacques Champigneulles,* a handsome lad who paraded in and out of Montparnasse cafés nurturing emotional uncertainties befitting a wealthy adolescent. Jacques' paternal grandfather, Ernest Champigneulles, had married Madame Brasseur's sister, Simone's great-aunt Alice, who wrote children's stories. Like his brother-in-law Gustave Brasseur, Ernest Champigneulles had entered into risky financial ventures. His son Charles, who had been Françoise de Beauvoir's first love, was on the verge of bankruptcy when he was killed in an automobile accident, leaving a daughter, Titite, and an eight-year-old son, Jacques, who inherited the stained glass window factory on the boulevard du Montparnasse. When she was eleven, Simone admired her cousin, who at thirteen already possessed the manners of a young gentleman. He treated Simone as a precocious child and spoke man-to-man with Georges de Beauvoir. Jacques lived with his sister and an elderly maid in their big house on the boulevard du Montparnasse. (His mother, who had remarried, lived principally in the country.) Jacques was a frequent visitor to the de Beauvoir household, stopping by in the evenings to help Simone with her Latin translation. One evening, on the balcony, he recited Hugo's "La Tristesse d'Olympio" for Simone, but above all he preferred Mallarmé's hermeticism.

Jacques had a gift for drawing and painting. He dreamed of transforming

---

*Jacques Laiguillon in the memoirs.

the stained glass factory—which had survived solely because of his tutor's prudent management—into a center that would renew the art of stained glass making throughout the world. He had discovered the newly hatched surrealism and diligently followed all the avant-garde movements. On his advice, Simone and Hélène went to the local galleries to see shows of Braque, Matisse, Picasso, and the other young painters. "I made the rounds of all the exhibitions . . . I walked all over Paris . . . looking at absolutely everything."

Jacques sent her to every mecca of the avant-garde between the wars: the Studio des Ursulines (a cinema), the Vieux-Colombier Theatre, the Ciné-Latin, and Charles Dullin's controversial revolutionary theatre, the Atelier. Jacques' best friend knew Jean Cocteau and had submitted a play to Dullin.

The Champigneulles house on the boulevard du Montparnasse was a place of refuge for Simone. She loved the glassed-in gallery where she spent hours listening to her cousin talk about the world of art and his own plans as a writer, for he too intended to write. Jacques and his sister Titite liked Simone, and in their company she never felt as though she had become a monster, which seemed to be the prevailing sentiment among her other cousins. Jacques vacillated between bourgeois morality and the lure of debauchery. He frequented the bars of Montparnasse, "those magical places where anything could happen."

In 1925 the surrealist painters, sculptors, and writers made their presence known. The two phalansteries they had set up in the quarter attracted all the young people who wanted to change their lives. Jacques Prévert and Marcel Duhamel had just rented a sort of pavilion from a rabbit pelt dealer; the house, surrounded by a small garden, was in the rue du Château, a timeworn street lined with houses that truck farmers and carriage rental establishments had abandoned. Duhamel, who would one day edit detective novels for Gallimard, was then the director of the Grosvenor, a fine hotel on the right bank, where his uncle, a hotel magnate, had placed him. Duhamel saw to it that the pavilion was made habitable. He had gas and electricity lines—amenities that did not yet exist in the rue du Château—brought in. Yves Tanguy, Raymond Queneau, Michel Leiris, Robert Desnos, Roland Tual, Max Morisse, and their friends could be found there at all hours of the day and night. The Grosvenor's kitchens fed the gang who came to the new hangout to read poetry or listen to jazz on the phonograph. The group took home tramps and prostitutes in order to shock their neighbors. Aragon lived there for a time and organized a reception in honor of Elsa Triolet's brother-in-law, the Russian poet Vladimir Mayakovsky.

The surrealist outpost in the rue Blomet, a rundown house surrounded by lilacs, was less provocative. Joan Miró and André Masson had their studios

there, and Georges Limbour, Michel Leiris, Antonin Artaud, Alberto Giacometti, Armand Salacrou, Francis Picabia, Max Ernst, Joseph Delteil, and Pierre
Naville were frequent visitors.

For Simone, Jacques reeled off tales of the high-water marks in surrealist
achievement. On the occasion of Joan Miró's first gallery exhibition in 1925,
the guests gathered in front of the Pierre Gallery, where the opening was
scheduled for midnight. Miró greeted them clad in white spats, striped trousers, black tailcoat, his monocle in place—the picture of Proustian elegance.
Taking the gathering for a political demonstration, the police intervened. Of
course the police were used to surrealist pranks and hijinks. Not long before,
people had come to blows at a banquet given at the Closerie des Lilas by the
Mercure de France in honor of the poet Saint-Pol Roux. It all started because
André Breton, the pope of surrealism, did not care for the novelist Rachilde,
who happened to be the wife of Alfred Valette, the director of the *Mercure
de France*. During the banquet the young writer Aragon declared that the
surrealists, being revolutionaries, would always shake hands with the enemy.
Madame Rachilde responded that a Frenchwoman could never marry a German. Breton stood up to protest that these remarks were insulting to his
friend the German painter Max Ernst, who was seated next to him, adding,
"Madame Rachilde has been boring us stiff for twenty-five years now, but
no one has dared to tell her so." A fight ensued—fruit went flying, glasses
crashed to the floor, Breton yanked a window off its hinges. The poet Philippe
Soupault swung from a drape, knocking over tables with his feet. Passersby
formed a crowd and protested furiously upon hearing the writer Michel Leiris
shout, "Down with France!" followed by Max Ernst's reply, "Down with
Germany!" The fight became a free-for-all, and Leiris was nearly lynched; the
police hauled him in to the station, and he got a good beating. All of the
following day's newspapers covered the episode.

The surrealists replied to an attack by the already famous playwright
Paul Claudel, then serving as an ambassador of France, in an open letter:
"With all our might we sincerely hope that war, revolution, and colonial
insurrection come to annihilate this Occidental civilization whose vermin you
defend all the way to the Orient."[37]

Breton, Aragon, and other surrealists attacked two of their number at the
premiere of Diaghilev's staging of the ballet *Romeo and Juliet*. The surrealists
maintained that Max Ernst and Joan Miró had committed treason in designing
the sets for this capitalist enterprise. As soon as the curtain went up, the
surrealists began hooting and whistling and dropping red pamphlets from the
balcony. One man flung himself at the English ambassador's wife, Lady
Abdy, and began ripping off her dress. Members of the audience threw the

surrealists out one by one, and at the door Diaghilev's formidable secretary delivered a good punch to each offender.[38]

The rough stuff was an inherent part of surrealist activity; they routinely barged into bars that displeased them just to smash windows, shatter glasses, and break bottles. The displays of excess delighted Simone, who was fed up with halfway measures and complacency. Over the past two years her likes and dislikes had firmly taken hold, and she had adopted the surrealist doctrines. These enfants terribles of the twenties were conspicuously anti-Catholic. *The New York Times* reported that they insulted nuns and spat on priests, that they had announced the destruction of language and systematically robbed everything of its original meaning, pushing their despair even to the point of suicide. Of the surrealists, Michel Leiris and Raymond Queneau would one day be among Simone de Beauvoir's best friends. They gave her, at eighteen, the words with which to define her revolt, enabling her to take her own position of opposition.

In March 1926 Simone passed her *certificat* in literature summa cum laude. This was an unusual feat, and she was roundly congratulated. Jacques, who had just bought a car, took her for a drive in the Bois de Boulogne. With her hair streaming in the wind, Simone could feel her heart beating—Jacques had just told her that a woman could be okay even if she had a degree. He spoke to her of his favorite hero, in Alain-Fournier's *Le Grand Meaulnes,* and recited for her one of Cocteau's poems.

During the June session she went on to pass her exams in general mathematics and Latin. Neither math nor classical languages really interested Simone, and Mademoiselle Mercier encouraged her to pursue her interest in philosophy and to attempt the *agrégation*. It was a long summer. Simone felt an overwhelming sadness, a boredom that left her weeping uncontrollably. One night during an anxiety attack at the Château de la Grillère, she had the impression that nothing existed beyond the present moment. Suddenly conscious of this unequivocal nothingness, she was so terror-stricken that she wanted to call out for her mother's help but was unable to. A few days later she set to work in the attic at Meyrignac and by the light of a portable oil lamp began to write her first fictionalized autobiography.

In 1926, Simone became immersed in philosophy. She read Plato, Schopenhauer, Leibnitz, Hamelin, and Bergson. She planned to earn two *certificats,* one in the history of philosophy and one in logic. The study of philosophy reinforced her tendency to take in the world as a whole. Haunted, like Chateaubriand, by the finite limits to her lifespan, she was obsessed by the idea of succeeding quickly. That spring in the Sorbonne library, she began writing a new novel. Simone felt very much alone. She had made friends at the Institut Sainte-Marie in Neuilly, but only Zaza and Jacques really counted. And Jacques had let her down: He was not writing, he never would write, and his plans to revive the art of stained glass would remain an elusive dream. His life was taking the same turn as those of Gustave Brasseur and Georges de Beauvoir.* Years later, in a letter to Nelson Algren, she wrote, "I saw this cousin of mine whom I was in love with when I was 16. I told you he drank himself from a big fortune and a rich marriage to misery. . . . He inspects the lands of the Seine and gets about 60 dollars a month. Now he is getting blind and drinks and can hardly speak and hear."

Every Sunday morning Simone met Zaza in the Tuileries or on the Champs-Elysées. The L. family had moved to the exclusive rue de Berri. They went out a great deal and entertained at home even more. Elisabeth/Zaza could not bear this fashionable society life. She was extremely gifted, particularly in music, and might have had a career as a soloist had her mother not been opposed to the idea. Zaza went on for a liberal arts degree with little enthusiasm. As Simone witnessed her friend's passage from revolt to submission, she grew indignant at the waste of Zaza's talent. Occasionally Zaza, who actively read the writings of the Catholic priest Lamennais, stood up for the idea that nothing was of greater importance in a woman's life than having children. In her journal Simone asked herself how anyone could possibly prefer children over literature or art.

For as long as they had known each other, Simone de Beauvoir had been filled with love and admiration for her friend, placing herself "in a state of humility" vis-à-vis Zaza. At eighteen, the depth of her feelings for Zaza no longer tormented her, but at the same time they no longer sufficed. Now it was a need for something new that gnawed at her. She was responsible for her own future, and it was time she threw herself into the real world. Claiming that she was going to work at a charity mission with a volunteer group from school, Simone extorted twenty francs from her mother, along with permission to stay out until midnight. She went straight to the Sarah Bernhardt Theatre and bought a gallery seat for the Ballets Russes. It was a symbolic gesture in the face of her family's chauvinism; for the first time she had taken charge of a situation. She wanted to be cosmopolitan, and here she was basking in the glorious late-night festivities. Simone was intoxicated by the sight of silks and furs and diamonds, but unlike her dreamy vigils on the balcony above the Rotonde, this time she was a part of it all—she had insinuated herself without anyone's realizing it. And she had not felt such

---

*After bounding from failure to failure, Jacques Champigneulles died a homeless alcoholic at the age of forty-six.

fascination since the age of five. Until now her parents had formed a screen between her and the world, but here she felt once again like the gay and independent little girl her father had called unsociable.

Now she would feel she was perfectly justified in lying in order to have such enriching experiences. The charitable assistance groups furnished a handy alibi; she went back to the Ballets Russes, and she ventured to the Bobino music hall to hear Maurice Chevalier. The age of obedience had passed.

3

THE AGE
of FRIENDSHIP

I pictured life as a happy adventure.
Memoirs of a Dutiful Daughter

STUDENTS OF THE RIGHT

Simone set out in life at a most extraordinary time of change for women. The traditional definition of femininity was in jeopardy, and a brand new Eve, a prototype whose evolution would mark the twentieth century, had been born. The writers Paul Morand and Victor Margueritte had sung her praises. Schiaparelli and Chanel had dressed her. Bugatti built the convertible so that her short hair and long scarves might fly in the wind. The painter Giovanni Boldini drew her flying her own plane. A thrilling new eroticism had taken hold of the young. Simone, almost five foot three, with blue eyes and a crown of short brown hair, was the personification of the new Eve. She streaked through her studies like a meteor, accumulating honors in transit. She was pleasing, fascinating, attractive.[1] She found herself surrounded by a group of young male students some of whom commuted across

Paris for the simple pleasure of a few hours of conversation in her company. Her girl friends were plentiful as well. Her husky voice and sharp delivery seduced them as surely as the boldness of her thinking and the brutality of her opinions, though the latter contrasted oddly with her elegant manners. Simone de Beauvoir was neither a vamp nor a distant princess; she was the ideal modern young woman, beautiful, intelligent, independent, and ambitious. New friendships blossomed in her wake, and foremost among them was that of Maurice Merleau-Ponty.*

In June 1927 Simone's name figured among the top three recipients of the *certificat* in general philosophy, preceded by Simone Weil and followed by Maurice Merleau-Ponty, all three destined for fame. Merleau-Ponty, intrigued that two women had beaten him, had himself introduced to Simone. She took an immediate liking to his "limpid, rather beautiful face," his "thick, dark lashes," and his "schoolboy laugh."[2] They began meeting daily in the Luxembourg Gardens. Simone was always scrupulously punctual at the appointed place beneath the statue of some French queen, anticipating Maurice's approach as he cheerfully ran toward her, "pretending to be embarrassed about being late."[3] Merleau-Ponty attended the Ecole Normale Supérieure and showed Simone around the former convent it occupied in the rue d'Ulm. The ENS was the summit of prestige, a breeding ground for talent. It trained its students for careers as University professors but was also an important stepping-stone to government positions and careers in finance and diplomacy, for future directors of major corporations and for political aspirants. The students of the ENS were divided into two groups: On the one side were the socialists and socialist sympathizers, among them Raymond Aron, Paul Nizan, Jean-Paul Sartre, Georges Lefranc, and Simone Weil; on the other were the right-wing students, or *talas*, † including Pierre-Henri Simon, Robert Brasillach, and Merleau-Ponty and his friend Maurice de Gandillac.‡[4]

Maurice Merleau-Ponty was the same age as de Beauvoir. He had an older brother and a sister. His father had died when he was three, and he grew up in La Rochelle in the care of his mother and a loving sister. In 1947 he confided to Sartre that he had never gotten over his incomparable childhood. Succeeding brilliantly at the Lycée de La Rochelle, he continued his studies at Janson-de-Sailly and Louis-le-Grand and then entered the Ecole Normale Supérieure. He was still living with his mother in the rue de la Tour, in the fashionable 16th arrondissement.

---

*Jean Pradelle in the memoirs.

†The *talas* were the Catholics, or those who go to mass *(Ils vont à la messe)*; the atheists were called *patalas*, those who do not go to mass.

‡Clairaut in the memoirs.

Simone de Beauvoir bared her soul to Maurice, who listened attentively and seriously. He saw some good and some evil in everyone, and he disapproved of the way in which she reduced everything to black and white. At school he was seen as one of the *talas,* but he had lost his faith and continued to practice religion only to spare his mother's feelings. In his opinion, Catholicism's claims needed to be reexamined in depth before one could reject them entirely. Simone's reply was that they knew even less about Buddhism, so why show favoritism toward the religion their families happened to follow? He accused her of preferring the search for truth to the truth itself. Simone argued that all the systems were lacking, and she demolished them one after the other. Maurice reluctantly gave in on every point "but retained his confidence in rational humanity.[5]

Like Simone, Maurice hated obscene songs, tasteless jokes, and brutality of any kind. Strangely enough, this was what won him Sartre's friendship. One day a group of ENS students singing particularly crude antimilitary songs prompted Merleau-Ponty and Maurice de Gandillac to begin whistling and hissing in protest. No sooner had the rowdy singers jumped their critics than Sartre had stepped in and mediated a solution in which neither side lost face. Merleau-Ponty liked Claudel, was indifferent to Proust, and was anxiously in search of the truth. De Beauvoir thought he was too Gide-like. Maurice's unease was purely cerebral, while hers was a gut-wrenching, all-out commitment to moral discomfort.

As she roamed the paths of the Luxembourg Gardens waiting for Maurice, Simone told herself that if he had wanted to marry her, he would not have suited her requirements any more than had Jacques. She weighed and compared Maurice's smiling optimism against Jacques' nihilism, concluding that her own violent nature separated her as much from the one as from the other. This reinforced her feeling that she would end up living alone. "I'm so sure that the one who would really be all to me, who would understand the whole of me, and be fundamentally the brother and the equal of myself, simply doesn't exist," she wrote in her journal.[6]

Merleau-Ponty never confused feelings with ideas. Simone feared that she sometimes let her own moods and states of mind take the place of rational thought. She asked Maurice to lend his impartial lucidity to her struggle to "guard against all falsehood." He would serve as her "living conscience" and sounding board, and she assured him with the full force of her natural conviction that she would work and slave "like a beast" until she got at the truth.

In Maurice's company everything became light. He taught Simone to be cheerful, and under his tutelage she set aside some of her metaphysical anguish. He was surprised by her and wrote her, "Despite your fanaticism . which upsets me as if it were a lack of consideration for others and which is so contrary to my own way of thinking, I have the greatest and most inexplicable affection for you."[7]

That summer in Meyrignac, a nineteen-year-old Simone settled in under the attic skylight and began a prolific correspondence with Maurice. With her sister's support, Simone dared to ask her mother to refrain from reading and censoring her mail—a gesture that further loosened her family's control over her.

Simone's relationship with Merleau-Ponty gave her the push and the assurance she needed to begin another novel. Alone in the attic, by the light of an oil lamp, she wrote the saga of a young girl who, finding herself in conflict with friends and family, bitterly sets out to sample action, love, and knowledge.

In September, Zaza invited Simone to visit Gagnepain, the L. family estate near Aire-sur-l'Adour. The family also owned the Château de Haubardin,* near Dax. Simone's parents allowed her to travel alone by train for the first time, an exhilarating freedom.† She stopped off in Bordeaux to visit the settings of François Mauriac's novels. As we often end up hating the very things we once loved most, twenty years later these two novelists would clash on the very nature of the novel. But on that September 10, 1927, Simone strolled up and down the streets along the quais, reciting whole pages from Mauriac's *L'Adieu à l'adolescence.* She drank a cup of hot chocolate at Tourny's and then sat down to lunch at the Petit Marguery, a restaurant near the train station, without troubling her head about the question "What will people say?" that ruled every move Mauriac's characters ever made. Yet it was unusual to see a young woman dining alone. Simone pursued her interior monologue, thinking about Zaza, whom she would soon see. Simone had finally understood that under Zaza's veneer of resignation and good manners there dwelled a passionate being. After all, had she not slashed her own foot with an ax just to escape the summer's endless social obligations and have some time to herself? Simone would never have found the courage to do anything like that, and the hidden violence that simmered inside her friend both frightened and fascinated her.

From the minute she arrived in the Basque country Simone felt completely out of touch, more than ever the poor relation. "Badly dressed, and caring little about my personal appearance," her clothes did not begin to

---

*The Laubardon estate in the memoirs.
†She described this trip and her stay in *When Things of the Spirit Come First.*

compare with the finery around her, and she felt ill at ease.[8] She was so tense that she could not seem to control her gestures or her laughter or what popped out of her mouth. The conversation inevitably turned to the conflict between Action Française and the Church, which had just condemned the Maurras doctrines. (A royalist and an avowed atheist, Charles Maurras favored an alliance with the Catholic Church, which he regarded as being closely connected with the monarchy. His nationalist ideas bordered on fascism, and they triumphed in Italy.) No opportunity was missed to attack state education and intellectuals in general. "For generations these people had been fighting a losing battle against nondenominational education; in their eyes I was heading for an ignominious future."[9] Simone felt like an exile. Her educational triumphs would never make up for the fact that her family was practically penniless. Some weeks earlier, at the Château de la Grillère, her cousins Robert and Madeleine had organized several picnics and parties for their friends. Because Simone had played a few sets of tennis with the same partner, the boy's mother was upset and warned Françoise de Beauvoir that her son would not marry a girl without a dowry. Simone, still vaguely enamored of her cousin Jacques, had laughed at the episode, but it was a rude reminder that the de Beauvoirs no longer belonged to the bourgeoisie. They were still invited out only because of family ties. The business got on Georges de Beauvoir's nerves, and he blamed his daughters for his disappointments. He swore only by his niece Jeanne, the paragon of a perfect young lady and the heir to Meyrignac.

The words "solitude," "exile," and "rejection" appear frequently in Simone's journal. "I'm not like other people; I'll have to try to accept that." And, "Always this never-ending conflict! A ready acknowledgement of my own powers, of my superiority to all of *them;* keenly aware of all I could do; but this feeling of complete futility in everything! No, it can't go on like this."[10]

That fall, in order to gain a measure of financial independence, she agreed to take over Mademoiselle Mercier's philosophy class at the Institut Sainte-Marie. Simone had resolved to finish her *licence* in philosophy in March and her *licence* in literature in June. She planned her assault on the University, meticulously organizing her studies and her time down to the last second.

A strange period in Simone's life was beginning—a period so strange that she sometimes told herself, fearfully but not without a touch of pride, that she was going mad. None of her friends seemed to have any difficulty conforming to what was expected of them by their families and their milieu. Even Merleau-Ponty, whom she cared about most, felt no more anguish than the others. He had regained his faith that summer when Maurice de Gandillac convinced him to go on a religious retreat to Solesmes Abbey, where Merleau-Ponty went to confession and received communion. Simone listened to his account with a lump in her throat and felt left out. At Maurice's insistence she read Plotinus and a series of studies on mystical psychology, asking herself whether some form of mystical experience might not serve her needs. She reached the startling conclusion, "I want to touch God or become God."[11] Now and then what she referred to as her deliriums took hold, and she vacillated between apathy and wild happiness without apparent reason. She wandered around Paris in the middle of the night, climbed the stairs leading to Sacré-Coeur, and wept at the sight of Paris lit up at her feet "because it was so beautiful and because it was useless."[12]

Simone abruptly shut herself away and went back to work on her novel. That year she was taking a course taught by Jean Baruzzi, the author of a thesis on Saint John of the Cross. Simone undertook to write an enormous dissertation on "the personality." "A real summing up," Baruzzi said when he returned her paper; he congratulated her publicly and announced that he saw in it the seeds of a major work.

Baruzzi's students included the surrealist poet René Daumal, who was trying to transcribe the mind's experiences directly onto paper, and Roger Vailland, a writer who enjoyed shocking his readers. A piece he had written for the magazine *Le Grand Jeu* claimed that all men had the right to practice bestiality. Simone de Beauvoir avoided both men; even if her imagination was bold and unafraid, she was easily shocked and disgusted by certain aspects of reality. Where literature was concerned she was inured to every conceivable form of depravity, but in actuality she was still extremely prudish. The moral standards of some of her fellow students made her uncomfortable. She tensed up as soon as anyone began talking about her classmates' private lives and morals. "Coarse jokes, rude words, free and easy behavior, and bad manners disgusted me."[13] She grew bored quickly with the boys from good families who invited her to tea in bakeries or pastry shops because cafés were off limits for ladies.

In this prudish environment where voices were lowered and treads were muffled, Simone de Beauvoir's strong personality and forceful opinions evoked surprise. Michel Pontrémoli,* son of the famous archaeologist Emmanuel Pontrémoli, had no interest in women, but came all the way from the porte Dauphine several times a week to talk with Simone. He admired Gide, she admired the surrealists, and they agreed to disagree. Michel was writing a novel, and he encouraged Simone to continue working on hers.

---

*Michel Riesman in the memoirs.

Her discussions with Maurice Merleau-Ponty, Maurice de Gandillac, and Michel Pontrémoli did not bring Simone what she sought. Utterly true to her own brand of stubbornness, she searched elsewhere for inspiration, subjecting her classmates at the Sorbonne to a battery of questions. Yet in general, their casual approach disappointed her; Simone de Beauvoir did not take anything lightly.

STUDENTS OF THE LEFT

Simone passed her examinations in the history of philosophy with flying colors. A group of left-wing students whom she had gotten to know asked her to sign a petition. The magazine *Europe* had launched a protest campaign against a proposed bill decreeing the mobilization of women. Simone was all for the equality of the sexes and thought it only proper for women to defend their country, so she handed back the petition saying, "But this is very patriotic!" Her remark was met with snickering, for the leftist students had nothing but contempt for patriotism. They explained to her that if the new law were enacted, it would have nothing whatever to do with equality between the sexes but "would result in a general mobilization of freedom of conscience." Freedom of thought was sacred to Simone de Beauvoir; she signed the petition.

When the Italian-born American political activists Sacco and Vanzetti were sentenced to death after their conviction on insufficient evidence in a controversial trial for a double murder, the affair provoked great protest around the globe. Simone, who opposed the death penalty, signed a petition in favor of their reprieve. But political activities did not interest her. Literature was her sole future. In her diary she went on analyzing the works she read, the people she met, and the things that happened to her. She disliked all labels, detested all conformity, and asked only that reason govern men's conduct. She was wary of the socialists, who, according to her, "were pursuing ends that were both secular and limited."[14] Their moderation irritated her; the Communists' extremism attracted her much more. In the library she had noticed a young man, older than she, dressed entirely in black. Pierre Nodier spoke to no one, but Simone managed to strike up a conversation with him. Nodier was on the editorial committee of the leftist magazine *L'Esprit*. "My conversations with Nodier were beginning to broaden my mind. I used to ask him lots of questions."[15] Nodier belonged to the Philosophies, a group of young left-wing intellectuals, and he introduced Simone to fellow members Pierre Morhange, Georges Friedmann, Henri Lefebvre, and Georges Politzer.

Georges Politzer was interested in the still unexplored domains of scientific psychology and psychoanalysis. At the request of the Communist Party he was going to specialize in political economy. In 1928 he published the criticism of the foundations of psychology. He rejected Freud's definition of the unconscious. For Politzer the unconscious was simply *le vécu,* or that which has been lived.* We take in far more information than we realize. Psychoanalysis enables the patient to find a new meaning for this or that attitude, but—contrary to Freud—Politzer thought that this secondary meaning was not subconscious and was not preexistent within the subject. Simone de Beauvoir, trying to clarify her own ideas, agreed with Politzer's theory of the primacy of *le vécu,* which pointed in the same direction as her own feelings. "What is lived" was her major concern, what she tried to unearth and track down from her earliest works onward.

Young Politzer, with his flamboyant red hair, came up with definitions that quickly got around and caused a furor at the Sorbonne. His definition of "life" created a sensation: "The triumphant, brutal life of the sailor who stubs out his cigarette on the Gobelins tapestries in the Kremlin terrifies you, and you don't want to hear about it: and yet *that* is life."[16]

Henri Lefebvre was a Cartesian and a rationalist, like the French left itself. He referred willingly to the philosophy of the Enlightenment, a philosophy of progress and happiness and freedom in all its forms. In 1947 he would publish an essay supporting the idea that Descartes' *Discours de la méthode* was objectively revolutionary. For Lefebvre, Cartesian idealism was the precursor to dialectical materialism. Years later, in 1951, the French Communist Party would define itself as Descartes' legitimate heir.

These young intellectuals challenged the official philosophy based on idealism in the manner of Kant or Bergson. They were looking for a doctrine that would give the world meaning and justify their rebellion. The recent past continued to weigh heavily on French society and political beliefs. On one side was the France of the elite with its powerful executive boards or, as the philosopher Alain put it, "the France of the bigwigs." On the other side was a democratic France that put its faith in talent and individual merit. Although World War I had transformed society to an enormous extent, this sharp division between the right and the left had not disappeared. The debate continued between the followers of Maurice Barrès, who put stock in the elite heritage of family dynasties, and the partisans of Edouard Herriot, who

*The term is used here, and later on, by the existentialists in its philosophical sense.

believed that it was legitimate to climb the social ladder through personal merit, hard work and accomplishment, competitions and scholarships.

Part of Communism's attraction stemmed from the fact that Marxism remained to be discovered and explored. Until 1939 it seemed as though the party leaders were much better acquainted with the writings of Lenin and Trotsky than with those of Karl Marx. Communist intellectuals were the first to undertake serious studies of Marx's writings, which were just beginning to become known in France. Small groups such as the Philosophies boned up on Marxism and joined the party in 1928–1929. These young Marxist philosophers had arrived at Marx through Hegel, and theirs was a humanist interpretation of Marx. Marxism was not recognized by the University, and it remained largely ignored in intellectual circles.

The first group to be won over to the Communist Party was that of the surrealist writers—André Breton, Louis Aragon, Paul Eluard, Benjamin Péret —in 1927. They saw in Communism an organized form of total revolt against society. Breton would be bounced from the party in 1933; Aragon would become its intellectual leader.

Simone de Beauvoir struck up a friendship with Jean Miquel,* a young Communist and one of Alain's former students. Jean Miquel took a lively interest in everything—movies, the theatre, painting, the music hall. Thanks to him, Simone discovered the realist chanteuse Damia, who performed at the Bobino and other popular music halls, dressed always in black. Jean also acquainted Simone with Romain Rolland, whom he admired, and he had no trouble rallying Simone to the cause of pacifism.

He introduced her to Alain's disciples, who formed a regular sort of club at the Sorbonne. They read and ardently discussed everything the master wrote for *L'Ecole libératrice* and *La Nouvelle Revue française,* and they were all attracted to Communism. Most interesting among them was Simone Weil, the future author of *Gravity and Grace,* who was taking the same classes as the future author of *The Second Sex.* Simone Weil dressed oddly and always carried copies of *Libres Propos* and the Communist newspaper *L'Humanité* that spilled from her pockets. She was extremely committed politically, and she took the world's sorrows personally. The strength of her convictions prompted her to become a worker at the Renault auto factory, to join the international brigades at the time of the Spanish civil war, and later to work at the Free French headquarters in London during World War II. Simone de Beauvoir wanted to get to know her fellow student and managed to start a conversation that soured abruptly when Weil declared flatly that the only thing that mattered was "the Revolution which will feed all the starving people of the earth." De

---

*Jean Mallet in the memoirs.

Beauvoir shot back that the only thing that counted was to make sense of the reason for human existence. Weil lashed out, "It's easy to see you've never gone hungry!" and this effectively ended the exchange. Yet there was much common ground between this doctor's daughter who had never lacked for anything and a Simone de Beauvoir who was always just a few steps ahead of privation.

If her conversation with Simone Weil was cut short, those that she pursued with her new comrades went on for days, sometimes weeks, until one of them finally gave in. For she was ready to welcome left-wing thought. She had real Vaulabelle's seven-volume *History of the Two Restorations* at the age of fourteen, which had given her a liberal sway of which her father strongly disapproved. Now, much to her mother's dismay, she was reading the work of Jean-Richard Bloch, whose Jewish messianism had led him to Marxism.[17]

In March 1928, her degree in philosophy completed, Simone decided to write her thesis and to prepare for the *agrégation* competition at the same time, a feat that was then technically possible, if physically and mentally daunting. If everything went according to plan, she would have her diploma by June of the following year. This undertaking posed a major challenge to a woman student at the Sorbonne because nine out of ten recipients of the *agrégation* had attended the more selective (and all-male) Ecole Normale Supérieure. Her friends predicted that she would probably have to present herself for the *agrégation* five or six times before succeeding, if then. De Beauvoir had participated in one of Professor Léon Brunschvicg's seminars, and she approached him about being her thesis advisor.

Léon Brunschvicg and Henri Bergson, who had received the Nobel Prize for Literature in 1927, were the dominant figures in French philosophy. Brunschvicg reigned at the Sorbonne, where his interpretation of Kantianism would leave its mark on minds as diverse as those of Paul Nizan, Jean-Paul Sartre, Raymond Aron, Maurice Merleau-Ponty, and Simone de Beauvoir. He taught that "we only know . . . the world our mind constructs and there is no means of apprehending the world which would enable us to go beyond the physical. In this sense, there is no 'metaphysical.' Science leaves philosophy no real object aside from science itself."[18] According to his teachings, philosophy reflects upon all human activities. Brunschvicg's neo-Kantianism was an attractive construction for the young writer who wanted to "tell all." Another aspect of Brunschvicg's view entailed idealism and moral attitude. Brunschvicg accepted Einstein's theories that were modifying notions of time and space: "The mind constructs reality through science which does not primarily consist of elaborating upon concepts or deducing their results, but in judging." For him, moral progress was expressed through self-detachment —putting oneself in the other's place. He told his students that thinking was judging and that concepts were not absolute givens but provisional steps along the way toward the conquest of truth and the construction of reality. In his preface to Georges Gurvitch's *The Trends of Contemporary German Philosophy*, Brunschvicg drew attention to the German philosophers who were not well known in France.

He agreed to be de Beauvoir's thesis advisor and suggested "The Concept in Leibnitz" as a topic. From that moment on she spent her days at the Victor Cousin Library, alternately reading Leibnitz and writing her novel.

ONE DECEPTIVE EVENING

*E*venings at 71 rue de Rennes were so suffocating for Simone that she felt like banging her head against the walls. She was overworked with her demanding studies, and there was nothing relaxing about this particular household. "I'm not like the others," she kept telling herself, thinking all the while that there was not that much distance between tenacious solitude and outright lunacy. Tired of asking questions that went unanswered, she returned to the greener pastures of childhood romance. Her cousin Jacques was about to do his military service in Algeria, and in the meantime he was spending his evenings in the bars. He justified his behavior by quoting Marc Chadourne, whose recently published best seller *Vasco* championed adventure for adventure's sake, and Philippe Soupault, who confirmed that adventure lurked around every corner in Paris. A generation of novelists followed Paul Morand in celebrating the overwhelming poetry of the bars and the bittersweet magic of doomed encounters. Simone sat on a red divan in the stained-glass factory gallery and listened to Jacques, who spoke to her through clouds of blue smoke about these unknown places filled with people who radiated an ineffable strangeness. She slipped back into the nebulous romance that, while it had never been defined, had never been forgotten. Jacques, seductive and charming, amused himself by gently stirring up his cousin's feelings, but he never said he loved her.[19]

Françoise de Beauvoir encouraged this imaginary sentimental arrangement. When she was Simone's age, she had been in love with Jacques' father, Charles. "At times she entertained the idea that Jacques was in love with her, and she would tell me, 'Jacques came to see *me,*' or 'Jacques has not come to see you in a long time!' She had a mean streak." For Françoise, a marriage between hers and Charles' respective children would have a romantic touch, and it would reward Simone with a return to her rightful place in society.

Simone and her parents attended a farewell dinner given by Jacques' mother a week before his departure. Françoise de Beauvoir waited all evening for a marriage proposal that never came. Jacques wanted to take Simone to the movies after dinner, but the de Beauvoirs refused; the future soldier's mother insisted, and Simone's parents gave in. She was to be home by midnight.

In 1928 the lively boulevard du Montparnasse was busy day and night. On this particular evening Simone sampled for herself the poetry of the bars, and for her their magic would never wear out. At the Stryx she had her first cocktail, a dry martini. She felt good in this Swedish bar with its painted enamel walls, art-deco decor, and elegant clientele who came in search of a bit of exoticism. Perched on a bar stool, Simone quickly adopted the behavior of the customers, addressing the bartender by his first name and breaking a glass or two with aplomb. After the Stryx, Jacques took her to the bar of the elegant Scandinavian restaurant the Vikings, where she discovered the gin fizz. When 2 A.M. arrived, Simone was getting acquainted with a crème de menthe at the bar of the Rotonde. She had come full circle to the very building in which she was born. It is always a somewhat artificial exercise to single out one event as a turning point in someone's life, but that evening, in a bar in Montparnasse, Simone de Beauvoir cast off the last ballast of her social upbringing and discovered freedom. From then on, such admonitions as "It simply isn't done" and "But what will people say?" would no longer stand in her way.

At 71 rue de Rennes, Simone's parents were waiting in the office. They had just returned from the boulevard du Montparnasse, where they had pounded on the door and rung the bell, demanding the return of their daughter whom Jacques had dishonored. Simone tried to lie, saying that she and Jacques had gone to the movies and then dallied over a cup of coffee. But this was 1928, and young ladies did not go out at night. Only easy women on the prowl went around without chaperones. Simone was repudiating her class and turning her back on her upbringing! The momentous evening concluded with a round of hysterics.

THE BARS

*T*he following day Simone met her cousin at the Select, a bar with a dubious reputation frequented by foreigners, homosexuals, and drug addicts. Jacques gave Simone his best friend's address and told her to look him up if ever she felt bored. Simone interpreted this conspiratorial gesture and the previous evening's activity as a veiled declaration of love. Jacques left.

Simone grew daring, venturing alone into the Rotonde or the Vikings to order cocktails. When her cousin Madeleine came to visit, she took her to a café in the rue Lepic in Montmartre where male prostitutes hung out. But the fashionable Jockey Bar on the boulevard du Montparnasse, which had replaced the Académie du Caméléon in 1923, was her favorite watering hole, and it was there that she spent the money she earned at the Institut Sainte-Marie. The Jockey's proprietor, the American painter Hillary Hiler, had decorated the place himself, painting stylized Indians against a black background on the outside and hanging posters of movie actors and music hall entertainers on the walls and ceiling inside. Small signs bearing raunchy verse in American slang also adorned the walls. A saxophonist played jazz, alternating with two Hawaiian guitarists or the phonograph. Sometimes the thoroughly bizarre painter Jules Pascin, clad entirely in black and eternally drunk, would sit in on drums, surrounded by his court of models, gypsies, and blacks. The Jockey attracted celebrities: Cocteau, Aragon, René Crevel, Moïse Kisling, Hemingway, F. Scott Fitzgerald, movie stars, women artists—everybody knew everybody else, and the atmosphere was good-natured and relaxed. In the evening the most magnificent vechicles in the history of the automobile pulled up to the door and out stepped men in tuxedos, their white silk scarves draped around their necks with a studied negligence, in the company of women glittering in sequins and pearls. They were in flight from the banal luxury of the Right Bank clubs, and they sighed with emotion when the saxophone played "The St. Louis Blues." Among the clientele there were also students from the Beaux-Arts, medical students, and intellectuals in search of adventure. The wealthiest arrived in two-seater convertibles packed with as many as six or eight passengers. There were elegant prostitutes on the premises, artfully made up and clad in magnificent silk dresses trimmed with sequins and fringe. These women fascinated Simone, who had always been sensitive to feminine beauty, and she listened as they bargained with clients for their services.

Perched on a bar stool before her trusty gin fizz, Simone told herself she was gathering material for her novel, researching "the many faces of vice." But no sooner had she begun her second gin fizz than the search for material gave way to the search for thrills. The bars were truly magical places where anything could happen; you had only to do whatever popped into your head. Simone tried her hand at casting spells—she smashed glasses, she snatched the hats from other customer's heads and flung them in the air, shouting hoarsely, "Chapeau!"* Nothing was considered shocking. Jean Oberlé tells of the night a girl danced at the Jockey stark naked without eliciting the slightest surprise. Cocaine was readily available in all the bars of Montparnasse, and the washroom attendants did not bother to try to hide the fact that they were selling it. Numerous artists, writers, and intellectuals were known to use drugs.

Kiki—the most famous model in Montparnasse, thanks to the paintings of Foujita, Modigliani, Derain, Soutine, Friesz, and Picasso—appeared twice nightly, belting out guardroom songs in her stentorian voice, then passing someone's hat for contributions. She and Man Ray had a mad affair in which pistol shots had expressed their feelings for one another. Kiki performed in the first surrealist film, *L'Etoile de mer.* Man Ray photographed her with a rose clenched between her teeth, and the picture sold three hundred thousand copies.

Simone lived out her fantasies in the smoke-filled air of the Jockey, stopping by often enough to become known among the regulars. Her loneliness melted away with the first cocktail, and she mingled with the other customers, sharing her imaginary life. Some days she passed herself off as a painters' model; on others she claimed to be a hooker. No one was fooled, and men tried to shock Simone with obscene gestures or sexually explicit drawings. Nothing penetrated to her imaginary world. Complete strangers casually swept her along to dance the Charleston, the shimmy, or the fox-trot on the tiny dance floor. Simone enjoyed the embrace of an anonymous partner, took pleasure in a hand's caressing her neck for the length of a song. "My body would have presentiments of escapes and abandonments that were easier and more satisfying than my mystical spasms." She "merrily defied convention" and delighted in the satisfaction of knowing that she was "so totally at odds with authority."[20]

In those heady early days of female emancipation, the women who worked in offices and department stores were discovering the pleasure of earning a salary, and they could be seen in the innumerable bars and dance halls of Montparnasse spending it as they pleased. The clientele was an incongruous mix of American tourists attracted to Paris by a strong dollar, students, hoodlums, and simple working girls, all out for a good time. It was the custom to dance with a stranger on condition that you parted without having exchanged a word. A girl who spoke to her partner was immediately pegged as someone looking for more than just a dance.

---

*Generations of French students have shouted "Chapeau!" to make fun of a man or a woman wearing a hat. At the movies they would do it every time they saw a hat on the screen.

The daughters of the bourgeoisie did not "go out." They socialized in the apartments of friends and family at little get-togethers called matinées. Invitations would be sent, worded along the lines of: "Monsieur and Madame X request the company of their children's friends on such and such a date from 5 to 9. There will be dancing. R.S.V.P." The dancing was done to the sound of a phonograph or perhaps a piano. For special occasions an amateur orchestra was summoned. In 1927 several lycée students—Ray Ventura, Coco Aslan, and Paul Misraki—formed the first French jazz orchestra. It was out of the question for Simone and Hélène de Beauvoir to host a matinée at their house. And there was nothing to do for distraction apart from the rare play or film that the family saw together. Simone de Beauvoir, worked up to an intellectual white heat, put just as much energy into letting off steam and giving her imagination free rein as she gave to her studies.

LIVING DANGEROUSLY

Simone introduced her sister to the mysteries of bar life. Hélène had just passed her baccalaureate in philosophy cum laude, and she wanted to become a painter. Her childhood had been less happy than Simone's; she had felt the family's poverty more strongly and had rebelled more openly against the constraints of her upbringing. She was taking drawing lessons at the Grande Chaumière,* practically next door to the Jockey, and she shared her sister's belief that the artist must rid herself of the influence of propriety and authority.

The two sisters, one blonde, the other brunette, revived their favorite childhood games, inventing characters and situations, this time with a bar as the setting. They delighted in attracting attention to themselves. They would enter separately, pretend not to know each other, then pick a fight that would degenerate into a wrestling match accompanied with much tugging of hair and shrieking of insults. They were pleased beyond measure when one of their little scenes created a stir.

Soon the Jockey became too familiar, losing its aura of adventure, risk,

---

*A famous academy of painting where students, particularly foreigners, prepared to enter the Ecole des Beaux-Arts. Every Monday, at the corner where the rue de la Grande-Chaumière meets the boulevard du Montparnasse, would-be models vied for sittings. In 1930 a model earned 15 francs for a three-hour sketching session (and a decent meal cost roughly 5 francs).

and bravado. Further exploration was in order. Simone began to allow men to approach her in the street. She went drinking with strangers in bars and small cafés. One night a car followed her down the street, and when the driver suggested that they take a spin to suburban Le Plessis–Robinson, she accepted. After stopping for a few drinks at the place de la Bastille the driver tried to kiss her. Simone hopped out of the car and ran off, pleased that she had "performed a truly gratuitous act."[21]

This little adventure left Simone with a good bit of self-confidence. She spent an evening at a street carnival on the avenue de Clichy with a young thug who had a recent scar across his cheek. They drank *cafés-crème* and tried their luck in the shooting gallery. Another thug joined them. Simone made a valiant effort to ditch her two companions as the last bus was about to leave, but they caught her before she had a chance to board it. They argued for some time and insisted on accompanying Simone home—despite the considerable distance between the avenue de Clichy and the rue de Rennes—on foot. When they arrived, the boy with the scar tried to kiss Simone, but she extricated herself from his embrace when a group of policemen went by. Furious, the boy threatened to teach her a lesson but settled for the money Simone offered him, insulting her as he took it. It had been a close call, and she had been frightened.

Nobody knew about these strange escapades. Simone's mother would never have set foot in a bar, and her father looked upon a woman who frequented bars as being totally corrupt. Zaza and Merleau-Ponty would never have understood what demon had gotten into her. She continued to live on several levels at once, her actions entirely justified in her own mind.

From the first spring day a deep-seated longing for fresh air and greenery always took hold of her. When a nostalgia for vacations in Meyrignac overtook her, she headed for the Bois de Boulogne with Hélène, Zaza, Merleau-Ponty, and Gandillac. Then, as a sort of rehearsal for the following year, they all attended the oral examinations for the *agrégation* in philosophy. There was an overflow crowd in the amphitheatre to hear Raymond Aron, who was awarded first place in the competition. The star of the class of 1928 should have been Jean-Paul Sartre, but to his classmates' utter stupefaction, he had failed the written exam, having taken the unwise step of expressing his own original ideas in lieu of expounding on the required themes. In his *Mémoires* Raymond Aron tells how receiving Sartre's and Nizan's congratulations meant more to him than those of Brunschvicg himself—a good indication of the extent to which the two were esteemed by their peers. De Beauvoir and Sartre crossed paths at that time, but it was not until the following academic year that they met.

STÉPHA

*T*he de Beauvoirs left for Meyrignac as they did every summer, and Simone leaped into the pleasures of country life without reservation. Since she did not own a bathing suit, she went swimming in her camisole and petticoat, then stretched out in the grass to read and dry off. She explored the woods and went out with her cousin Madeleine, who was often invited to neighboring manors.

At the end of the summer Simone returned to the Landes region, having stopped along the way to spend a day with Merleau-Ponty in Bordeaux. As soon as Simone arrived at the Château de Gagnepain she sensed that she was not entirely welcome. Instead of being allowed to share Zaza's room, Simone found herself sharing accommodations with the children's new governess. Simone knew full well that Zaza's parents thought her a bad influence on their daughter, particularly for encouraging her friend to go on for an advanced degree, against their wishes.

Zaza was demoralized. During the summer she had written, "I feel such utter indifference for the whole of creation that I already seem to be dead."[22] Each time Simone thought she was about to talk with Zaza alone, some member of the family turned up to frustrate their exchange of confidences. Since Simone was stuck with the governess, she struck up a friendship with her. Stépha was Simone's age; she had come from Poland, where her father owned a large candy factory, to take classes at the Sorbonne. In Poland she had demonstrated for Ukrainian independence, gotten arrested in a raid, and spent a few nights in jail. Her parents had shipped her off to Berlin to continue her studies, then to Paris. Wanting to observe the daily life of a French family, Stépha had accepted the post of governess for the summer vacation.

Stépha always came down to dinner wearing a bare-shouldered evening dress, and this scandalized the puritanical L. family. Moreover, Madame L. felt that their foreign governess was not keeping her place when she sat down at the piano to sing nostalgic Ukrainian folk songs. Stépha's natural elegance was out of keeping with the prevailing atmosphere. Simone formed what would be an enduring friendship with Stépha, and they began seeing each other when they returned to Paris. Stépha led a freewheeling life in the company of the artists and intellectuals who gathered in Montparnasse. She spent countless hours at the Closerie des Lilas talking politics with exiled Ukrainians. In Berlin, Stépha had met a young Spanish painter in exile for his radical opinions, and they now lived in the same hotel in the rue Saint-Sulpice. These sophisticated foreigners were thoroughly acquainted with the French language and French literature. They were pacifists, internationalists, and revolutionaries.

Simone was quickly accepted as part of the crowd, which also soon adopted Hélène de Beauvoir and her inseparable friend and fellow aspiring artist, Gégé.* Merleau-Ponty found the lot of them too bohemian for his taste and refused to be seen with them.

This crowd's political and sexual maturity prompted Simone to reevaluate her own attitudes. She continued to share Zaza and Merleau-Ponty's belief that boys and girls alike should be virgins on their wedding day, which was one way of maintaining a certain equality between the sexes. She detested the notion that boys should sow their wild oats before settling down and looked upon it, traditional though it might be, as cheating. So it came as a rude awakening when, one night at the Stryx, she overheard an elegant young woman complaining that Jacques Champigneulles had dropped her. Simone had attributed every virtue to her cousin, and this hero had turned out to be an ordinary boy like any other. The irrepressible Stépha, who was overseeing Simone's sentimental education, did her best to shatter her myth about physical love. "But Simone, that's life!" was her matter-of-fact response to Simone's squeamishness. Taking care not to traumatize her less experienced peer, Stépha steered Simone toward a reconsideration of her naïvely headstrong view of the world.

Simone loved Paul Claudel because his work glorified the soul's presence in the body and represented physical pleasure as an expression of the spirit. Stépha had no special consideration for the so-called spiritual aspect of romance, and she did not glorify mind over body or particularly admire scholarly achievement.

Simone vacillated between the two avenues of accomplishment: On the one hand were her friends and acquaintances at the Sorbonne, whose futures were clearly laid out in the prescribed order of career, family, and success; on the other hand was the virtually rootless creative life to which Stépha belonged. Simone saw the ultimate truth neither in work nor in debauchery. "Without a doubt I saw no salvation except in literature." On that much her friends were all agreed.

---

*Germaine Pardo. Her son, Frédéric Pardo, Sartre's godson, painted François Mitterrand's official presidential portrait.

At the Rotonde and the Jockey the young people, some of whom intended to be famous one day, took part in interminable discussions devoted
to politics, art, and literature. Stépha had read several passages from Simone's
novel and, like Zaza, encouraged her to continue working on it. Simone was
right at home in this casual, open, cosmopolitan group. Gone were the feelings of being a rejected presence on the fringe of bourgeois society that she
had with Zaza's parents and others like them; here she was at ease, in a new
circle to whom the future belonged.

She took up again her taste for jazz and alcohol, for the light touch of
strange bodies and the promise of adventure. Four francs bought her way into
the Européen, a popular music hall where comedians and singers made coarse
jokes. Simone felt fine among the loosely dressed necking couples, and she
walked the length of the boulevard Barbès contemplating the whores and
pimps "with a sort of envy."[23] On her own or as part of a group, Simone
ventured to the Jungle, a fashionable new nightclub that had recently opened
across the street from the Jockey. The entertainment included Chiffon, a
dwarf who sang obscene songs while kicking up her skirts.

Where did this passion for disreputable haunts come from? In her journal
she wrote, "There is within me I know not what yearning—maybe a monstrous lust—ever-present, for noise, fighting, savage violence, and above all
for the gutter."[24] On Tuesdays and Saturdays, at the Salpêtrière Hospital,
Simone attended lectures by Georges Dumas, author of the celebrated *Studies
in Psychology.* * The study of madness was gradually entering the philosophy
curriculum. Psychology was beginning to be looked upon as an objective
science founded on biology and independent from metaphysics. This new
approach to the mental processes fascinated Simone because it seemed to her
that a very fine line separated normality from abnormality. She sometimes
had the impression that she herself floated in the twilight zone between the
two. She saw herself like a modern Janus, attracted to the clarity of knowledge in one direction and fascinated by the disorder of the senses in the other.
Merleau-Ponty had accused her of putting life on a pedestal and exaggerating
its nobility, yet here she was, writing in her journal, "I want life, the whole
of life. I feel an avid curiosity; I desperately want to burn myself away, more
brightly than any other person, and no matter with what kind of a flame."[25]

---

*Georges Dumas, philosopher, physician, and psychologist, founded, along with P. Janet,
the *Journal de psychologie normale et pathologique*.

THE CASTOR

*W*hen courses resumed at the Sorbonne in November 1928, Simone faced her last, pivotal year of studies. She was not yet twenty-one. Among the candidates for the *agrégation* in philosophy that year was a small group of students from the Ecole Normale Supérieure who were known for their intellectual audacity, their aggressiveness, and their drinking bouts. This band was made up of Paul Nizan, Jean-Paul Sartre, and René Maheu.* Sartre had caused a scandal at an ENS gala by showing up completely nude, followed by a scantily clad Nizan. These boisterous student pranks shocked Simone de Beauvoir, and she struck up a friendship with the least rowdy of the three, René Maheu. He had written numerous poems and articles, wanted to be a writer, was married, and was known at school as the Lama. Nicknames were a tradition at the ENS, and it was Maheu who now dubbed Simone the Castor, the French word for "beaver."[26] Sartre and other friends from those days called her the Castor for the rest of their lives. Simone knew everybody without belonging to any one group. She was constantly in conversation with someone, and she kept up with all the gossip with the help of a friend who was a "regular Proustian concierge." Maheu despised dilettantism in friendship and complained, "You're wasting your time on people who aren't worth a second look. You must be a psychologist to like it, otherwise there's no excuse for you!"[27] In her autobiographical novel *The Mandarins,* de Beauvoir, ever fascinated by the inner mechanisms of the self, portrayed her heroine, Anne, as a successful psychologist.

With Maheu she had a sense of finding herself. She saw in him a full, undivided human being. "Maheu wanted to become somebody and was very clear about his goal." Unlike the majority of Simone's friends, he was not torn between the spiritual, the intellectual, and the pleasures of the flesh. Maheu had no complex whatever about his "unmistakable body." "How proud he was of the young red blood pulsing in his veins!"[28]

Although Simone's sexuality had not tormented her since the onset of puberty, her angelic behavior was beginning to weigh a little heavily. Maheu was living proof that you could be an intellectual without being a pure spirit and that there was nothing to be ashamed of in acknowledging one's flesh.

---

*André Herbaud in the memoirs.

Of course their understanding hit an obstacle when Maheu added that this particular freedom applied only to men. Simone, who had long claimed the freedom to use her body as she wished, at least in theory, saw no reason why a double standard should apply. After all, she was a contemporary of *La Garçonne,* and she "would not admit that there should be a law for one sex and a different one for the other . . . women should be as free to dispose of their bodies as men were."[29] Maheu responded that a man ceases to respect a woman once he has "had" her and that no woman could surrender herself with impunity to a man. Simone stubbornly held her ground: Every human being existed as an individual, and if society respected only married women, then society had to be changed. Antireligious, anticlerical, antinationalist, and antimilitarist, Maheu pushed Simone into wiping out the last traces of her Catholic education.

In the spring of 1929 three candidates for the *agrégation,* all born in the same year, did their apprenticeship at the Lycée Janson-de-Sailly: Claude Lévi-Strauss, Maurice Merleau-Ponty, and Simone de Beauvoir. A woman in a boys' lycée? Coeducation was then highly suspect, and the separation of the sexes was rigorously enforced in all the lycées. Simone de Beauvoir was the first woman to teach philosophy in a boys' lycée. Today we might say she was a token woman, but at the time she was considered a pioneer. De Beauvoir related with humor how one of her professors told her, in an overwhelmingly damning tone, "You'll make it." It was commonly said in the hallways of the Sorbonne that a woman had to attempt the *agrégation* at least four or five times before succeeding. Arriving at Janson-de-Sailly, Simone recalled with emotion the times she had walked alongside the walls of the Collège Stanislas, where her father, her uncles, and Jacques had studied—a "boys' school" had seemed so utterly unattainable to her then.

Life was smiling upon her. According to her friends at the Sorbonne and the crowd in Montparnasse, she had what it took: beauty, intelligence, the will to suceed. She made up her mind.

> Even if I flunked, I would leave home; and if I passed, I wouldn't take a teaching post, but would stay in Paris: in either case, I would take a place of my own and earn my living by giving private lessons . . . I would earn my own living, and be free to come and go, to have people in and to write . . . I made my sister a part of this future. At nightfall, on the banks of the Seine, we would talk and talk about our triumphant tomorrows: my books, her pictures, our travels, the world. . . . In the flowing river waters trembled the reflected columns, and shadows went gliding

over the inverted bridges; we would pull down our crêpe veils* in order to make the sight even more fantastic.[30]

The year which had begun in such happiness would finish with two events of paramount importance in Simone de Beauvoir's life: Sartre's love and Zaza's death.

LOVE AND DEATH

Simone introduced Maurice Merleau-Ponty to Zaza and noticed that they hit it off from the start. The two laughed and giggled often and teased Simone, whom they called "the amoral woman." That spring, when Simone and Maurice passed their oral exams brilliantly, Zaza was in the auditorium, flushed with pride and emotion. She took them out for a snack at a bistro, the Yvelines, to celebrate. They got together on several occasions to go rowing in the Bois de Boulogne. Maurice was on cloud nine, Zaza talked of no one else; it was obvious they had fallen in love. Simone was delighted for her childhood friend and ardently hoped that Zaza would marry for love and escape her mother's tyranny. After all, Madame L. had sent her daughter off to Berlin in the fall to stop her from going on for a degree, to get her away from Simone and the Sorbonne, and to encourage her to accept the idea of an arranged marriage. Inevitably, in the Berlin of the twenties, Zaza had found a freedom unimaginable in Paris. Entrusted to the care of the French ambassador, she had met all sorts of important people. At the University she had struck up friendships with students from around the world and had taken to dining with them in small restaurants frequented by workers. The radiant and confident Zaza who returned from Germany was in the process of translating a work by Stefan Zweig and making plans to write a novel.

Zaza and Maurice decided secretly to get married in two years, after Maurice had passed the *agrégation* and fulfilled his military service. But Madame L. detested the "freedom from morals" prevalent among students at the Sorbonne and forbade her daughter to go rowing in the Bois de Boulogne in their dubious company. Zaza did not have the strength to openly disobey her mother; she would tell her all about Maurice after the summer, and in the

---

*Simone and Hélène were wearing mourning for Grandfather de Beauvoir, who had just died in Meyrignac.

meantime they would write one another. Knowing Zaza's parents, Simone thought this was a reasonable precaution.

A long letter from Zaza left Simone perplexed. Zaza implied that things were not going well at all. Madame L. had decided to marry her off to someone she had chosen, and she was campaigning hard for Zaza to accept the arrangement. Zaza had announced that although she had nothing against the boy in question, she would never marry without love. "My dear, it's the man who loves, not the woman" was Madame L.'s authoritative reply.[31] An aunt backed her up with the wisdom that the sacrament of marriage invariably unleashes the love of one's spouse. Then matters seemed to quiet down. Zaza described for Simone the nearly unbearable joy Maurice's letters brought her. "Life is marvelous," she wrote. Toward the end of summer another letter from Zaza made it clear to Simone that the difficulties had resurfaced. Maurice's letters had suddenly become ambiguous, and they threw Zaza into fits of despair. She no longer understood what he was really thinking. Did he love her enough to wait two years for her? Confused and desperate, she confided in her mother, who then forbade her daughter to write to Maurice because for her the situation was clear: He had no intention of marrying Zaza.

Zaza appealed to Simone for help, sending her passages from Maurice's last letter that revealed a deep confusion. A worried Simone confronted Maurice and asked him if he still loved Zaza. Yes, he loved her. Had he given up the idea of marrying her? No. Then, in Simone's opinion, the matter was simple: He had only to ask the L.s for Zaza's hand in marriage; then they would see that he was sincere. Maurice refused to do any such thing. Simone tried to her hardest to convince him and got nowhere. He loved Zaza, but it was necessary to wait. His sister had just gotten engaged, his older brother would be leaving shortly for Togo; if he were to tell his mother that he too would soon be leaving to get married, it would be the death of her. This ridiculous rationale left Simone unconvinced. She kept at him, describing the depth of Zaza's despair, but to no avail.

Each party was sticking stubbornly to its own version of the story, and the assorted truths did not match up. What in the world could the L.s have against Maurice Merleau-Ponty? He was a practicing Catholic, the son of a naval officer, and a brilliant student at the ENS; his future could only be a success. The L.s should have been congratulating themselves on their daughter's fortuitous choice and rejoicing in her happiness.

Simone met with Zaza, who was extremely unhappy, was unable to understand her mother, and was in a confused state of mind. She could not bring herself to stand up to her parents, whom she loved. Yet their endless discussions and arguments, restrictions and advice, orders and supplications were wearing her out. She was losing weight, she had violent headaches. She did not know whether she should go on struggling to save her love or simply give in to despair. Simone endeavored to approach the matter logically in order to help Zaza find an appropriate course of action. It was obvious that the L.s did not like intellectuals, nonbelievers, and the Sorbonne and the ENS, which were secular institutions. No doubt they feared that a student from the ENS would lead their daughter down the error-ridden path of modern ideologies. Yet Maurice was far from being a revolutionary; he had even been on retreat at Solesmes Abbey, where he had recaptured the faith and religious convictions of his childhood. If Zaza would only explain all this to her mother, clearly and reasonably, surely the misunderstanding would be cleared up.

But the L.s and Merleau-Ponty stubbornly held to their respective positions. And the incessant conflict and uncertainty were affecting Zaza more deeply than anyone cared to admit. Simone, trying to save her, came up with another solution: Maurice could ask the L.s for Zaza's hand *without* consulting his own mother, and the matter could be kept secret from her until after Maurice had completed his military service. This would give Madame Merleau-Ponty plenty of time to recover from her eldest son's departure for Togo and her daughter's imminent marriage—if only Maurice would announce his intentions to those most directly concerned! Madame L. "was in a state of rage"; anything that stood in her way was a challenge. Fed up with Simone's persistent meddling in the affair, she forbade her to set foot in the L. home in the rue de Berri.

The L.s finally found their own solution: Zaza would spend a year in Germany, and afterward they would see. In the meantime, they relaxed their restrictions and gave Zaza permission to have Maurice as a guest. On the day he was to arrive, Zaza received a last-minute *pneumatique** from Maurice: An uncle had just died, and the requisite mourning would be incompatible with the joy he would feel at seeing her again. He put off another rendezvous on the pretext that his brother had just set sail. He wrote to assure Zaza of his feelings for her, but Zaza felt more and more defeated. Simone tried to steer her into revolting against the hold her parents had on her, but nothing seemed to reach her anymore—she forgave everyone.

Leaving the National Library one day, Simone met Zaza for the last time. She was bubbling over with gaiety, gushing optimism, and Simone accom-

---

*The express letter service within Paris, which utilized a network of pneumatic tubes running alongside the city sewers and compensated for the scarcity of private telephones, was discontinued by the French postal authorities in 1984.

panied her while she did some shopping. Zaza talked about the books she was rediscovering and her love for Maurice, a love whose intensity she felt she was only just beginning to fathom. When they parted, Zaza left Simone with an impression of uneasiness. Four days later a note from Madame L. informed Simone that Zaza had been rushed to a clinic, critically ill, running an extremely high fever. Over the next few days she was delirious, calling out for "my violin, Maurice, Simone, and champagne." The fever was fatal; Zaza died at the age of twenty-one.

What was behind this tragedy? Why had Zaza been tormented to such an extent? Madame L. sobbed and Monsieur L. spoke of God's will, but Simone saw only the behavior of an upper-middle-class Catholic family whose senseless oppression had tyrannized and suffocated her friend, provoking a despair so intense that it could only culminate in death. For a long time to come she felt a deep bitterness toward Maurice Merleau-Ponty, who because of his unbending attitude had to share the responsibility for the tragedy.

Simone de Beauvoir would try repeatedly to recreate this tale of love and death in her early attempts at novel writing, conjuring up protagonists whose lives evolved in a twilight of doubt. Zaza inspired a series of characters, all of them called Anne. Sartre, who declared that "the family is a pocketful of *merde,*" wanted to make her the heroine of his first novel, a work that remained unfinished.[32] She is the other heroine of *Memoirs of a Dutiful Daughter,* which de Beauvoir concludes with the sentence, "We had fought together against the revolting fate that had lain ahead of us, and for a long time I believed that I had paid for my own freedom with her death."

When *Memoirs of a Dutiful Daughter* appeared, thirty years had gone by and one of Zaza's sisters came to tell Simone what had really happened. When Elisabeth and Maurice met it was love at first sight. They had immediately begun making plans for their future, and Elisabeth introduced Maurice to her parents. Everything seemed to speak in his favor. The L.s had nine children and were not at all displeased to see their third daughter perfectly happy and ready to marry.

At that time the good bourgeoisie was very particular about the matches it made. One could marry into a family with little wealth on condition that the family had an honorable name. The L.s proceeded to make the premarital investigation that was customary in their milieu.

The Merleau-Pontys had lived in La Rochelle for some time; they had three children; the father, a naval officer, was often at sea. What a shock it was when the L.s' routine investigation revealed that Madame Merleau-Ponty was the recognized mistress of a University professor and her two youngest children were the result of a double adultery, insofar as the professor was also married!

Jean-Paul Sartre's mother, Madame Mancy, who had lived in La Rochelle with her second husband, confirmed the story to Simone de Beauvoir. The liaison was one of public notoriety. At gala dinner receptions in La Rochelle, the professor would be seated between his wife and his mistress. Maurice and his sister bore their mother's husband's name and were legally his children; their natural father treated them with tenderness, and they looked upon him as a friend of the family. When she was widowed, Madame Merleau-Ponty moved to Paris. Maurice and his sister were very attached to each other and passionately devoted to their mother. Raised in a protective environment, Maurice had no knowledge of his true parentage until the day Monsieur L. took him to the Bois de Boulogne for a man-to-man talk. There he informed Maurice of his mother's scandalous past, adding that because Maurice was illegitimate and a child of sin, he could not possibly allow him his daughter's hand in marriage.

Maurice was thunderstruck by the revelations. His sister had just become engaged—it was critical that her fiancé's family not discover the truth. The investigation had created serious problems for the Merleau-Pontys. Brother and sister closed ranks on their mother's side. Maurice agreed to give Elisabeth up in order to prevent the scandal from affecting his sister's future happiness. But he loved Zaza, and she could not understand why he suddenly seemed to be running away, why his letters had become vague. Maurice wrenched himself away from his love, anguishing over his beloved's having to suffer because he was unable to reveal the real reason behind his new reticence. His feeble excuses left her unconvinced. When Madame L. saw how deeply her daughter was torturing herself, she clumsily tried to substitute another fiancé for Maurice. The L. family had always made practical marriages.

Everyone conspired against Zaza's love, and each party concealed a truth that she was unable to grasp. Her depression became so serious that her parents decided to tell her the whole truth. For this deeply religious family —a family who visited Lourdes every year to serve as volunteers and stretcher bearers—Catholic morality was sacred. In their eyes, adultery was a mortal sin. One made sacrifices to the extent of kissing a leper, but one did not marry a man born in sin.

Zaza's love for Maurice was so deep, so passionate, that to destroy it was to destroy her as well. She understood her parents' reasoning, but she refused to submit to the suicide of the heart that was being asked of her.

Maurice had no idea that Zaza knew the full story. She did not want him to know that she was aware of his mother's disgrace. Unable to give Maurice up and incapable of disobeying her parents, she remembered reading in the writings of the Jansenist philosopher Pierre Nicole that in certain cases obedience could be a sin. Elisabeth felt less and less capable of reasoning and making a decision. As for Simone, Zaza shared only false confidences with her.

Zaza became the victim of such extreme confusion and irreconcilable contradictions that she gradually slid into madness. The night before the crisis came to a head, Elisabeth ripped off her clothes and came down the stairway of the family apartment entirely nude. Her father took her back to her room. Had she cast off her clothing as a symbolic gesture, refusing the lies and secrecy, intending to shine at last in the pure light of her own true vision? The following day she appeared at Madame Merleau-Ponty's door and asked her whether Maurice was already in heaven and why Madame Merleau-Ponty hated her. Maurice's mother, upset by the appearance of this young woman flushed with fever and wearing no hat, tried to comfort Zaza and said she had no objection whatever to the marriage. Maurice, in a panic, took her home in a taxi. The doctor had her transferred to a clinic in Neuilly. The L.s assured Maurice that they were no longer opposed to the marriage. But by then it was too late; Elisabeth was delirious and dying.

Simone de Beauvoir was the only person concerned to whom nothing had been said, and she had participated in anguish as the tragedy played itself out. Virtue had led to despair and death.[33]

4

Jean-Paul Sartre

*Sartre was the double in whom I found all my
burning aspiration raised to the pitch of incandescence.*
Memoirs of a Dutiful Daughter

JEAN-PAUL

*W*hile Zaza's tragic love affair took its fatal course, Simone was
busy preparing for exams. Her paternal grandfather died in May 1929 at the
age of ninety-one, and his passing brought an end to the long, happy vacations at Meyrignac, now the property of Simone's uncle. On the train that
carried the family to the Limousin to pay their final respects, Simone mulled
over the degree to which circumstances had deprived her of the life to which
a young de Beauvoir should have been entitled. The *agrégation* and the realities
it represented were as foreign to her assembled aunts and cousins as the rites
of passage of the American Indians. Simone felt like an exile among her
relatives.[1] Her past was unraveling, stranding her with no choice but the
future. Looking around at her extended family, Simone realized that every
other person there had his or her path in life all laid out. What would hers
be?

"In this future life, which I began to feel was imminent, the essential thing would still be writing. I felt I had been right not to bring out anything too despairing while I was still so young: at present I wanted to express both the tragic sense of life, and its beauty. . . . I was all expectancy, and in the violence of this feeling all regrets were swept away."[2] In her journal that May she described her sheer joy at being alive. Her senses were heightened, and she was overwhelmed by the simple fact of existing, at being able to feel the sun's warmth on her skin and to hear the rustling of chestnut trees in the wind.

Her burgeoning relationship with René Maheu was not entirely incidental to this delight at being alive. "I had a loving friendship with Maheu," Simone de Beauvoir told us, "but there was never a kiss or the slightest caress between us." In *Memoirs of a Dutiful Daughter* she wrote, "I like him more and more, and the pleasant thing about it all was that he made me like myself more."[3]

They studied together, and René cautiously expressed his jealousy for Simone's other friends and would-be suitors. There was Maurice de Gandillac, who had just given Simone his first novel to read; Heveshi Bandi, the Hungarian journalist who courted Simone in the rarefied air of the National Library; and Stépha, whose freewheeling manners René found shocking. For Maheu the sight of Simone engaged in conversation with classmates was too seductive, and he disdainfully kept his distance.[4] He discreetly spirited Simone away from the other young men who paid her court, particularly Sartre, who had made overtures, one of them (sent via Maheu) a drawing, "Leibnitz Bathing with the Monads."* Without a doubt, Simone left hearts beating wildly in her wake. Her friendship with Maheu overwhelmed her with joy, even if she sensed their relationship's "fragility, with distress" now and then. After all, Maheu was married and Simone had no desire to be "the other woman." In love with love, she found it indecent that married couples "should be inseparably bound by material cares: the only link between two people who loved one another should be love."[5] Her feelings for Maheu resembled those she had held for her cousin Jacques. As her heart overflowed with emotion, she called upon herself "to live out her own story from day to day, without either hopes or fear, as it brought only happiness."[6]

The essay topic for the philosophy *agrégation* in 1929 was "freedom and contingency," a dissertation subject made to order for the future existentialists. Sartre, Nizan, Maheu, and de Beauvoir hunched over their pens and

---

*In the philosophy of Leibnitz, the monad was a fundamental unit of substance that was seen as the basic constituent element of physical reality.

attacked their papers. Simone had supplied herself with a Thermos of coffee and a box of butter cookies. After the two days of written exams, Georges de Beauvoir took his daughter out to celebrate at the Lune Rousse, a cabaret noted for its monologuists and comedians. It was just another contradiction among many that this father who sang the praises of women who remained at home like good housewives and who glorified "true young ladies" saw nothing odd in rewarding his daughter with a night out at a club, as though she were a boy! As for Simone, being treated like a boy was not unusual. On numerous occasions when mixed gatherings had split into menfolk and womenfolk, as was the custom, Simone had quite naturally remained with the men since it was their conversation that interested her.

Her father invited her to have fried eggs at the Brasserie Lipp after the show. This was Georges de Beauvoir's way of showing off his daughter's beauty and intelligence, for the Brasserie Lipp was, and is, a showplace for the cognoscenti and the power brokers of Paris.

The oral portion of the competition remained. Using Maheu as intermediary, Sartre invited Simone to study with him. De Beauvoir and Sartre often described the scene: Sartre's dormitory room, the ever-present cigarette smoke, Nizan, Maheu, and de Beauvoir boning up on the material, the late afternoons spent roaming around amusement parks. The gang is joined by Rirette Nizan and they all pile into her car for a run around Paris, stopping here and there for a beer. During these little excursions Sartre sang the latest jazz tunes in a pleasant light tenor voice. They stopped at the Nizans, who lived in the rue Vavin in a new building covered entirely with white tile. Their bedroom wall sported an enormous portrait of Lenin. Nizan was acquainted with many of the authors published by the NRF, and he took his little band of friends to the Café de Flore, where Gallimard's stable of brash young hopefuls passed the time of day.*

On the day that the results of the written examination were posted, Simone de Beauvoir arrived at the Sorbonne just as Jean-Paul Sartre was leaving. "You passed," he told her, adding in the same breath, "I'll take you under my wing."[7] Maheu had failed.

During the two-week study period before the orals, they parted only to sleep. They went out with the Nizans, with Raymond Aron, and with Georges Politzer. Sartre, "whose munificence was legendary," treated them to endless cocktails until the early-morning hours. He recommended an assortment of comics and pulp magazines to Simone, including the Pardaillan and Fantômas series, and he spoke highly of westerns. His new companion

*The *Nouvelle Revue française* was published then as now by Gallimard.

frequented the art cinemas and liked abstract art and hermetic poetry. With Sartre she discovered how full life could be: Everything was of interest. They went on talking for hours, mutually stimulated and enthralled. Each possessed the same "calm and yet almost frenzied passion" that prodded them to write.[8] Sartre told her that she must at all costs preserve her taste for freedom, her love of life, her curiosity, and her determination to be a writer. And he offered to help her. He showed her "Er l'Arménien," which he had just written. She read him her novel about the twenties in which she "said it all." They were frank, pitiless, constructive in their criticism. She found outmoded the gods and titans that Sartre used to expound his theories. He told her that the novel presented "countless problems." From the very beginning their relationship was built on a true foundation: an intellectual understanding that would endure as long as they themselves. Nothing would put a stop to the conversation they began while studying for the *agrégation* orals.

When the results were announced, Sartre was ranked first and de Beauvoir second. Georges Davy and Jean Wahl, the two professors on their jury, had discussed at length which of the two gifted candidates should be ranked first. "For although Sartre demonstrated obvious qualities, great intelligence, a strong culture be it in some ways sketchy, everyone agreed that *she* was the true philosopher." Her friend Maurice de Gandillac said she was "rigorous, demanding, precise, very technical, at twenty-one the youngest of her class."[9]

France's youngest *agrégée* boarded the train for her final vacation at the Château de la Grillère in the Limousin. Sartre was supposed to join her, on the pretext that they would be writing together. René Maheu, the first to arrive, awaited Simone at Uzerche, where she planned to meet him. Simone's parents, shocked, refused to finance the trip; they did not approve of a friendship, however innocent it might be, with a married man. But Simone no longer permitted anything to stand in the way of her projects. She borrowed the money she needed from her cousin Madeleine and set out for Uzerche, where she spent three days. Maheu, passionately interested in prehistory and paleontology, spoke of the dolmens and menhirs in the Landes region, and peopled the forests with Druids. The past left Simone cold. She was surprised by Maheu's aestheticism and his respect for certain conventions. The nature of their relationship is open to interpretation. They became "occasional lovers years later, but not before I met Sartre."

Sartre arrived in August and checked into the Boule d'Or Hotel in Saint-Germain-les-Belles. They resumed the conversation they had begun in Paris, and Simone soon realized "that even though we went on talking till Judgment Day, I would still find the time all too short." Early in the morning, Simone set off across the fields to join Sartre and, lost in discussion, it seemed like no time before the bell of the manor summoned her back to lunch. "Sartre lunched on cheese or gingerbread, deposited by my cousin Madeleine in an abandoned dovecote." At nightfall he returned to his hotel. After their chaste intellectual trysts in the fields had been going on for four days, Georges and Françoise de Beauvoir appeared and politely asked Sartre to leave the district because people were gossiping about Simone's "visibly scandalous behavior." Sartre retorted that they were working with the most honorable of intentions and that he would not cut short his stay. The two writers hid themselves more deeply in the chestnut groves. The most singular love story of the twentieth century had begun.[10]

THE SARTRES AND THE SCHWEITZERS

*T*he young man who had just entered Simone de Beauvoir's life sporting a loud pink shirt was born in Paris in the well-to-do 16th arrondissement, at the intersection of the rue Mignard and the rue Guy-de-Maupassant, a stone's throw from the Bois de Boulogne, in one of those opulent-looking buildings in which the comfortable bourgeoisie lived before World War I. His father, Jean-Baptiste Sartre, had attended the Naval Academy and upon graduation was posted to Indochina with the rank of second lieutenant. France had governed the Indochinese union, which grouped together Cambodia, Laos, and Vietnam, since 1897. Paul Doumer, the governor general, had ordered the army to intervene on several occasions in order to quell local rebellions. The French army discovered the sundry charms and illicit pleasures of Asia, and many an officer never made a move without his opium pipe. The men were also given to contracting a variety of tropical fevers. Jean-Baptiste Sartre left Indochina with his health shattered.

In May 1904, at the age of thirty-four, he married Anne-Marie Schweitzer in Cherbourg. Anne-Marie, the youngest of three children, was twenty. Her older brother, Georges, a graduate of the Polytechnic, pursued a comfortable career. The middle child, Emile, was somewhat eccentric. He taught German, he never married, and upon his death in 1927 a revolver was found under his pillow and his trunks turned out to contain a hundred pairs of completely worn-out socks. The Schweitzers were all excellent musicians, even if they were not quite so illustrious as their famous first cousin, Albert Schweitzer, the Alsatian doctor and musician who received the Nobel Prize for his work in Africa.

Jean-Baptiste Sartre and Anne-Marie Schweitzer settled in Paris. On June 21, 1905, Jean-Paul Sartre was born. Several months later father and son both came down with a potentially lethal intestinal ailment. Jean-Baptiste's father, a doctor in the town of Thiviers, treated both patients but suceeded only in saving his grandson; his son died on September 17, 1905.

Dr. Sartre was a taciturn individual. He had wed the daughter of a wealthy property owner from the Périgord region, Marie-Marguerite Chavois. Shortly after the marriage he learned that his father-in-law had met with financial ruin. Outraged by what he considered to be a breach of trust, he did not speak to his wife for forty years, communicating with her exclusively by sign language. She called her husband "my lodger." Three children were born of this bizarre union: Jean-Baptiste; Joseph, a stutterer who never left home; and Hélène, who married a cavalry officer who eventually went mad.[11]

After her husband's death, Anne-Marie Sartre could not imagine living with her in-laws in their bizarre household in Thiviers, and she returned to live with her own parents. Her father, Chrétien-Charles Schweitzer, was an Alsatian bon vivant and a womanizer, as his grandson Jean-Paul would later prove to be. This vigorous man who had no use for idleness enjoyed drawing attention to the longevity of the Schweitzers. He had written his doctoral thesis on the German poet Hans Sachs in 1887.* Schweitzer's specialty was the methodology of living languages (one of his students published the notes he had taken at Schweitzer's lectures at the Sorbonne). He was a member of the Society for the Propagation of Foreign Languages in France, and, in collaboration with the great Anglicist Louis Cazamian, published a history of English civilization that would long remain in use in secondary schools.

He had written a series of German and English textbooks that were widely used in junior high schools and teachers' institutes, and he had developed an original method for teaching languages. Generations of schoolchildren grew up with his *Direct Method for the Teaching of German* or his *Direct Method for the Teaching of English.*

Jean-Paul Sartre was five years old when his grandfather founded the Institute of Living Languages at 1 rue Le Goff in Paris. His students included many foreigners who learned French with the help of his *Direct Method for the Teaching of French.* [12] Chrétien-Charles Schweitzer had been awarded the Legion of Honor, and had received numerous academic honors.[13]

The Schweitzers lived well. They employed a cook, a housekeeper, and,

---

*His secondary thesis, *De Poemate Latino Walthario thesim proponebat Facultati Literarium parisiensi ad gradum doctoris promovendus,* was published in Paris in 1889 by Berger-Levrault.

for their country house in Meudon, a gardener. The family spent two months each summer in Arcachon and often visited Alsace. All the Schweitzers were bilingual, and little Jean-Paul learned German at the same time he learned French. His grandfather supervised his education, and his mother saw to his recreation, taking him on daily excursions to the Luxembourg Gardens, the circus, the theatre, or—her personal favorite—the movies. At a very early age he began making up little stories, "For a Butterfly" and "The Banana Merchant." He was not yet ten when he reworked La Fontaine's fables into alexandrine verses and corresponded with his grandfather entirely in verse throughout one summer. None of the scholars around him doubted that this precocious youngster would one day be "a prince of letters." A governess looked after Jean-Paul until, at the age of eight, he entered the Lycée Montaigne.

Sartre was eleven years old when, in 1916, his mother married a Monsieur Mancy, a graduate of the Polytechnic who had been courting her for several years. He directed the Delaunay-Belleville naval shipyard in La Rochelle. Later Sartre would say, "He made a good living and as a result we lived quite well."[14] Sartre continued his studies at the Lycée de La Rochelle; his stepfather paid careful attention to his progress and helped him with his math homework. Sartre was obviously destined to attend one of the major colleges, and consequently he was sent to Paris to prepare for his baccalaureate at the Lycée Henri-IV. In 1921 his teachers entered him in the national prize competition for secondary school students. In 1924 he was admitted to the Ecole Normale Supérieure along with Raymond Aron, Daniel Lagache, and Paul Nizan. The latter had been his inseparable friend since their days at the Lycée Henri-IV.

Nizan and Sartre discussed their future during long walks together across Paris. Nizan was nervous, tormented, withdrawn; Sartre was an extrovert. At the lycée they had shown off for the amusement of their classmates, who had nicknamed them Nitre and Sarzan. Among other distinctions, Sartre had earned the title S.O., or *Satire Officiel*, for his habit of making scathing comments and speaking with cynical authority. Together the two friends perfected little scenarios that put their professors, their peers, and the world at large on trial. "They were hysterical," says Sartre's friend Robert Wagner, the son of a banker, in describing the night he invited Sartre and Nizan to dinner at his father's house. "Until then, only Charlie Chaplin films had suceeded in cracking up my father, who was as Protestant as they come. Nizan and Sartre shot remarks back and forth; it was irresistible."[15]

At the ENS Sartre and Nizan shared a room. Nizan was the very incarnation of Meaulnes, the romantic and elusive central character in the popular novel by Alain-Fournier, *Le Grand Meaulnes*. Nizan mysteriously disappeared for days on end, only to return with bloodshot eyes and rumpled clothing. He set off for Aden and ended up spending a year there. He judged his classmates harshly: "their sinister thoughtlessness, their aggressive futility, stem from the fact that they have no obligations and are by nature irresponsible."[16] He viewed their membership in extremist political parties as distractions without real impact or consequence because, as he wrote, "these sons of bankers and industrialists can always return to the fold of their class." With his customary honesty, Sartre would reveal in *Situations IV* that Nizan's anger toward the world during their college years was sincere, while his own was a mere soap bubble, a "counterfeit currency." Nizan came from a working-class background. His father had become a railway engineer by rising painstakingly through the ranks, only to have his career shattered because of professional mistakes. He had never recovered, and he spoke often of suicide. Nizan had been deeply affected by his father's social reversal. For Sartre, who could not fully understand the reasons for his friend's wanderings any more than he understood his disdain for the ENS, Nizan was restlessness personified. That Sartre suffered in silence over the breach between them is apparent in one of his manuscripts, *La Semence et le scaphandre (The Tin-Tacks and the Diving Suit)*. [17]

Sartre could not have been more certain of himself. As he strolled along the boulevard Saint-Germain with Raymond Aron, he spoke of the measure of his genius without vanity, without hypocrisy:

> Attain Hegel's level? There, of course, the ascension wouldn't be too difficult or take too long. To get beyond it might require a little effort. I see ambition in two images. One is of a young man in white flannel trousers, shirt collar open, gliding catlike from one group to another on a beach filled with young girls in the flower of womanhood. The other image is that of a writer who raises his glass to acknowledge a toast from men in formal attire standing around a table.[18]

Sartre liked the atmosphere at the ENS and gladly led the hazing of new students, sometimes with surprising brutality. He was admired for the extraordinary richness of his ready wit and was often kidded about the incredible ease with which he cranked out the written word. "What's this? A mere 350 pages in two weeks?" Raymond Aron chided him, bowled over by the wealth of his friend's imagination.[19]

Sartre wanted to live his youth as though it were the youth of a great man. "I was very conscious of being the young Sartre in the same way one says 'the young Berlioz' or 'the young Goethe.' "[20] It followed that he could not understand Nizan's marriage or his membership in the Communist Party. Following André Gide's principle, Sartre believed that the great man should leave himself open and available. Gide, a major influence on this generation, was the very image of the free man because he was opposed to everything: family, Church, political parties, nationalism, dogmatism, the proprieties, authority, and fanaticism. Nizan saw this negativity as a purely bourgeois attitude; he believed a writer should play an active role. Nevertheless Nizan supported Sartre's various enterprises. For the college newspaper Sartre had written several violent and abusive articles opposing the French army and the obligation of ENS students to undergo compulsory military training. The press took up the affair, and Sartre and several others were summoned to appear before a disciplinary committee presided over by the director of the ENS, Gustave Lanson. Nizan, who was still in Arabia when the affair blew up, swore that he had instigated the articles.

Sartre and his gang—Péron, Larroutis, Baillou, Catan, Nizan—were renowned for their gags and stunts. Sartre played a part in every hoax. He was one of those who spread the rumor that Charles Lindbergh had been awarded an honorary doctorate by the ENS for his first solo transatlantic flight. Never at a loss for ideas, Sartre amused his classmates with a parody of the defense he had presented for his thesis on "the image in the physical existence." He had already rejected psychoanalysis; for him, the concept of the unconscious was equivalent to a squared circle. The psyche and consciousness could not be separated. Sartre had evoked his vision of the world in one of Brunschvicg's seminars, outlining the opposition between the *en-soi* (in-itself) and the *pour-soi* (for-itself). "These tables," he explained, "signify absolutely nothing. They are here for no particular reason, make no point, and receive no reward. At each instant consciousness signifies and gives meaning to these blind realities which deny it although they exist and are rendered significant only by virtue of consciousness."

Sartre was generous and extravagant. As a youngster he helped himself to money from his mother's purse in order to treat his friends to pastries. Simone de Beauvoir, who in 1981 still vividly remembered the meticulous care with which her mother had kept track of every little expenditure in her ledger, asked Sartre with surprise, "You mean your mother didn't count? She didn't know how much she had in her purse?" "No," replied Sartre, who would maintain a privileged relationship with money throughout his life.[21] As a student he never ate in the school cafeteria; called to military duty in 1939, he refused to take his meals in the army mess hall. His mother bailed him out as often as necessary. Every financial transaction between mother and son was as involved and convoluted as those between Proust and his mother. Sartre's mother took infinite care to pay, without her son's knowledge, the income taxes he neglected to pay—and which were considerable—once he became famous. All his life he gave without counting. He liked to walk around with his pockets stuffed with bills, handing out generous tips wherever he went. He displayed a complete lack of interest in obtaining articles of clothing for himself and left it to his mother or Simone or one friend or another to get him a coat, a tie, a pair of socks, or a suit as the need arose. Sartre wrote of his relationship with money: "Money has a sort of perishability that I like. I love to see it slip through my fingers and vanish. But it must not be replaced by some solid, comfortable object. It must escape in an ungraspable burst of fireworks. In one soirée, for example. Go dancing somewhere, spend a lot of money, drive around in taxis, etc. Everywhere I go people are scandalized by the way I spend money—and this is true even among the most generous people."[22]

Studied negligence was the prevailing style of dress at the ENS, and Sartre carried the look a bit farther than most. But the legend has been exaggerated. As a young man Sartre paid attention to his appearance, even though he never approached the dandyism of Nizan with his monocle and rattan cane. Sartre spoke freely of his ugliness, an ugliness that vanished as soon as he came to life. He watched his figure carefully and worked out regularly. The speed with which he hoisted himself up the rope at the gym, his legs held rigidly at a right angle, astonished his classmates. He was also an excellent swimmer who effortlessly knocked off a kilometer in the pool. Later he took up boxing, and he coached his students at the Lycée du Havre, where he organized boxing tournaments.

Sartre was a seducer. At the age of six he was already dreaming of the prestige accorded the *homme fatal* in the books he had read. While Sartre's classmates at the Lycée de La Rochelle bragged about their conquests, the eleven-year-old Sartre outdid them. He told them he took his mistress to a hotel, and he even asked his mother's maid to write what he thought was a love letter, addressed "Dear M. Sartre." While still a schoolboy he rejected the notion of "the beautiful soul," replacing it with that of "the body victimized by desire." He perfected his moves in the Luxembourg Gardens, where the shrubbery concealed his fleeting romances. The will to seduce was colored by an urge for power. He wanted "to conquer a woman almost like you'd conquer a wild animal," but, he added, "this was only in order to shift her from her wild state to one of equality with man." Sartre's Pygmalion tendencies were already apparent; he always encouraged his conquests to express themselves, be it through writing or performing. As an adolescent his head was filled with notions about the romantic *homme fatal*. His models were the stormy lives of Shelley, Byron, and Wagner. If he shared many of the ideas of his generation, including Marxism, internationalism, and pacifism, his basic romantic framework was straight out of *Hernani* and *Antony*. From the heroes of Hugo he got "an unhappy soul fashioned from shadows," from the heroes of Alexandre Dumas, a character that was crazy and sublime.

At nineteen Sartre discovered passion. Simone Jollivet*was twenty-three years old, a self-described disciple of Nietzsche and a writer. Her confidences and nonconformity fascinated Sartre. Jollivet had been nursed by the mother of a gypsy named Zina, who was passionately devoted to her and never left her side. Jollivet had taken charge of Zina's sexual initiation by deflowering her herself. She also told the story of how she had been raped by a family friend as a child. As an adolescent she would kiss her parents good night, then sneak out through her bedroom window to spend the night in the town's elegant brothel, the faithful Zina ever at her side. She liked to receive her admirers in the nude, standing before the fireplace, her long blonde hair cascading onto her shoulders, reading Michelet's *History of the French Revolution.* In 1925 her lovers wept with admiration and showered her with jewels. Sartre and Simone Jollivet met in Thiviers at the funeral of a mutual cousin, Annie Lannes, Sartre's first love, who had died of tuberculosis at nineteen. According to Jollivet, Sartre, wearing a borrowed hat that was several sizes too big and appearing incredibly slim in his black suit, looked a great deal like the eighteenth-century revolutionary Mirabeau, whose intelligent ugliness he shared. It was love at first sight. The couple disappeared from Thiviers for four days and four nights. Uncles and cousins scoured the countryside in search of the runaways, found them, and brought them back to the fold. Jollivet returned to Toulouse, where her father was a pharmacist, and Sartre regained his room at the ENS, where he wrote her, "Tell me if you prefer your Jean-Paul to this Percy Bysshe Shelley the ladies love so . . . I love you in every way you could possibly wish for, my dear love."[23]

At the first vacation break, Sartre took the train to Toulouse and, penniless as a result of his habitual inability to hold on to money, wandered the streets until midnight waiting for Simone Jollivet's window above the pharmacy to light up. At dawn he departed and spent the day roaming the town. Completely exhausted after four days of this routine, he fell asleep in Jollivet's bed. When he awoke she read to him from *Thus Spoke Zarathustra*, with emphasis on the passages in which Nietzsche deals with the will, which permits man to conquer his instincts.

---

*Camille in the memoirs. Her real name was Simone-Camille Sans; later her stage name would be Simone Jollivet.

For two years Sartre took the train to Toulouse whenever Jollivet bid him come. He rambled through the streets between trysts and wrote his beloved, "I want to be not your first but your *only* love."[24]

To be able to invite her to Paris, Sartre did translations and borrowed money. When Jollivet attended the ENS ball, the eccentricity of her appearance and her bizarre manners surprised and impressed Sartre's classmates. Sartre did not have the means to keep her in Paris, and the following year she returned at the expense of an old lover. Whereupon she fell in love with the actor Charles Dullin, whom she had seen in the movie *The Miracle of the Wolves* and had decided to seduce. To accomplish this, she attended the theatre every night, always taking the same seat in the front row. Dullin noticed her. She became his companion and remained with him until his death. Sartre exorcised the demon of his passion for her in *A Defeat*, a novel that recounted his romances.* He also wrote "Empedocles," a story in which he identified with the philosopher, physician, prophet, and magician whose cosmology based on the four elements was ruled by love and hate. In 430 B.C. Empedocles threw himself into the crater of Mount Etna in order to prove to himself that he was God; Sartre would not go quite so far, but in his letters to Simone Jollivet he outlined his concepts of contingency and of consciousness as a vacuum. In his first successful novel, *Nausea,* he gave his heroine the name of his dead young cousin Annie and the ambiguous and volcanic personality of Simone Jollivet.

His stormy, intermittent romance with Jollivet did not prevent Sartre from pursuing his role as a seducer. In 1927 this Don Juan fell in love with the daughter of a wealthy produce wholesaler (he would later refer to her as "a grocer's daughter"). He proposed marriage, but the young lady's parents were far from thrilled at the prospect. The preliminary inquiries were not reassuring: Their would-be son-in-law had a mistress and, far worse, espoused subversive ideas. When Sartre failed the *agrégation* in 1928, the engagement was broken.

Sartre rediscovered "the freedom of the great man—the freedom to fulfill his destiny."[25] Fickle and carefree, he could still be seen trying to charm some student off her feet at the Sorbonne. Like Chateaubriand, he wanted to be the Enchanter, the one whose presence gives things their true meaning and reveals the juncture of art and love. Seduction and writing followed from the same intellectual reasoning. Later he would wonder at "the depth of imperialism there was in all that."[26]

Une défaite, inspired by the love between Nietzsche and Cosima Wagner, was rejected by the publishing house of Gallimard.

Following their sojourn in the Limousin in the summer of 1929, Sartre and de Beauvoir wrote each other daily. In September Simone moved into the building in the rue Denfert where her grandmother still lived in the sixth-floor walk-up, paying her rent for a room with a view of the Lion of Belfort in the square below. At last she had a room of her own, and she set about decorating it with orange wallpaper. She was finished with drab colors, she would no longer wear dull, lackluster clothing; from now on it would be silky fabrics, shimmering velvets, and patent leather shoes. She made herself up with flair and dazzled her students at the lycée where she had obtained a temporary position teaching Latin to ten-year-old girls.[27] These pupils were quite unlike the well-behaved and disciplined students she had taught at the Institut Sainte-Marie in Neuilly. Her charges quickly realized that their new teacher, elegant and smiling and obviously just starting out, would not be a strict disciplinarian. They marched right up to the rostrum to look at her necklaces, touch her clothing, and chat and carry on. Strict measures were called for; she gave a demerit to the least disciplined of the bunch—who immediately began banging her head against the wall, shrieking, "My father will kill me!"[28] The entire class interceded loudly on behalf of their classmate, and Simone decided that the only thing to do was to outshout the whole bunch and let those listen who wanted to listen. The headmistress summoned Simone to her office more than once and at the end of the school year refused to renew her contract. This was the first of many run-ins with the educational administration; they culminated in de Beauvoir's dismissal from the University altogether in 1943, which ended her career in public education.

Scheduled to leave for his compulsory military service in November, Sartre returned to Paris in mid-October and was living with his grandparents at 200 rue Saint-Jacques. He was in no hurry to become, as his grandfather put it, "that prince, a professor of letters."[29] He dreamed of grand upheavals, of long voyages; he wanted to bear witness to everything. "Neither the pariahs of India nor the monks of Mount Athos nor the fishermen of New-foundland would have any secrets from him."[30] With Tibetan lamas in short supply, Sartre made do with mead cocktails at the Vikings or the apricot cocktails of the Bec de Gaz for his share of high adventure.

In Simone de Beauvoir Sartre had found a playfellow. They launched into comedies, parodies, apologues, laments, nursery rhymes, epigrams, madrigals, poems, and fables—composed on the spot. Their inexhaustible train of thought sped on, they could not be shut up. Their playful temperaments ran wild. Simone had rediscovered in heightened form the frivolity of her childhood and the gaiety that had reigned in the apartment over the Rotonde. She would become so carried away that Sartre was prompted to say, "Look at the Castor in one of her trances again!" Sartre enjoyed the comic pastimes, which were as good a way as any of winning others over, but he was not inclined toward wild beatings of the heart. He had invented the theory of "emotional abstracts" and wanted to put emotions into words, a task that required detachment and constant self-mastery. He did not want to sacrifice lucidity to a disorderly state of mind.

THE CAROUSEL OATH

For Simone the meeting with Sartre was an explosion of joy and torment. He "corresponded exactly to the dream companion I had longed for since I was fifteen: he was the double in whom I found all my burning aspiration raised to the pitch of incandescence. I should always be able to share everything with him."[31] In her eyes, Sartre's existence justified the world, as her parents, or God, once had. He guaranteed her permanent security. There was nothing left to wish for "except that this state of triumphant bliss might continue unwaveringly forever."[32]

The happiness was not a simple one. Sartre at twenty-four wanted to know everything without losing any of the love that had just come his way. He wanted the essential and the contingent,* the timeless and the ephemeral, the best and the worst—in short, variety—in his relationships with women. He had not given up his dream of "ruling over a gracious and idle community through love."

"I gladly think back on the succession of women," he would say in 1976. "Each one meant everything to me at a given moment. It's due to Simone de Beauvoir's qualities that she's taken the place in my life which she has and which no one else could take . . . we understood what we were for each other."[33]

Sartre was not cut out for monogamy. He explained that the form that sexual relations traditionally took did not stem from any particular social organization; monogamy was a rule thought up by the Church to enforce its concept of marriage. Sartre acknowledged that what had sprung up between them was a unique relationship, an understanding that would endure as long as they did, but it did not mean that they should forgo the riches to be found

---

*Contingent: a thing that may change and that is not of primary importance—which is not to say that it is unimportant.

in encounters and relationships with other people. It had always been more or less understood that a man should experience relationships with several women; what was new about their arrangement was the implication that the woman as well should enjoy relationships with other men. Before becoming lovers they were writers, and their works should benefit from their combined experiences. "What we have," Sartre said, "is an essential love; but it is a good idea for us also to experience contingent love affairs."[34] These would be true loves, not fleeting romances that by their nature would not be taken into account. Contingent loves could last a long time, they might even be veritable passions, without in any way altering the essential bond that held the two of them together.

Simone agreed to this plan because it corresponded to her own convictions. Two events, the disintegration of her parents' marriage and Zaza's death, had left a deep and lasting impression on her. She rejected the rules, habits, and customs of a society that had led Zaza to her death. She denied the institution of marriage, which inevitably led to cheating, deceit, and extramarital affairs. The individual could remain genuine only in a relationship whose form had yet to be invented, and that was what she intended to do with Sartre. Her attitude was a courageous one; to reject marriage in 1929 was to relegate oneself to the fringes of society. Even the fiery and tantalizing Stépha had chosen to marry Fernando Gerassi. Simone saw herself living her life with the same independence as a man. Economically, she was dependent on no one. Her love for Sartre would be the guarantee of her freedom as well as the most perfect possible expression of happiness. If a revolutionary act consists of going up against societal structures, her attitude was revolutionary, while that of Don Juan Sartre was not. The speech he had given Simone on the freedom of the great man was one he had spoken before. What changed, he wrote later, was that "I got caught at my own game. The Castor accepted this freedom and held on to it . . . I was dumb enough to be worried by it instead of realizing what extraordinary luck I'd had. I fell into a sort of melancholy."[35]

One evening as they were strolling through the Tuileries gardens near the Carousel arch, Sartre suggested that they sign a sort of two-year contract, agreeing that they would spend the two years living in Paris in "the closest possible intimacy" without actually sharing the same roof. He would then set off for two or three years in Japan, and he advised Simone too to find a post abroad. After a few years they would reconvene somewhere in the world and resume their more or less communal life where they had left off.

The separation that Sartre envisioned scared de Beauvoir, but she saw no point in worrying about it before the time came. Each fear was a weakness that had to be combated. Simone had confidence in Sartre. Their love-admiration bound them together with the certainty of a knight's solemn oath.

They sealed a second pact: They would never lie to each other and above all never conceal anything from each other. They would have everything in common, their work, their plans, their experiences. Each would scrupulously inform the other of any and all contingent loves. It was an agreement that could be reached only between two beings who regarded themselves as equals, two people who were transparent to one another.

It was the strangest and riskiest oath of love that the two lovers swore on a stone bench near the Carousel arch, their backs against the balustrade of one wing of the Louvre as night fell on the city that fifteen years later would resound with their combined names. What was most surprising was that they won their wager. Speaking in 1975 of his concept of the seducer who never settles down with one person and his relationship with de Beauvoir, Sartre said, "I had to hold the two ideas together. It was fairly difficult and all the while I wanted to keep them and I did keep them."[36]

For Simone de Beauvoir the matter could not have been clearer: Sartre was the great love of her life, she had hit the jackpot of happiness, and nothing short of Sartre's death could take that away from her. In *The Prime of Life* she explained, "I have never met anyone in the whole of my life who was so well equipped for happiness as I was, or who labored so stubbornly to achieve it. No sooner had I caught a glimpse of it than I concentrated upon nothing else. If I had been promised renown and glory at the price of happiness, I would have refused. It was not merely this effervescent sensation in my heart, but also the belief that here lay the truth about my existence, indeed about the world."[37]

They made a two-year commitment, during which neither would engage in contingent loves. Sartre would spend eighteen of the twenty-four months on military duty in the meteorological service in Tours.

They commuted back and forth between Tours and Paris. No sooner had they been reunited on the station platform than Sartre would seize de Beauvoir by the arm. "I have a new theory," he would tell her. Despite his warm, outgoing exterior, Sartre did not excel at the sensual subtleties of romance. "I am cold," he wrote in 1939.[38] Throughout his youth his sexuality had not bothered him much, "not to say that at twenty-five I was ignorant of the matter, but that the whole thing seemed to me a scandal of unreasonable proportion."[39] Sartre despised all physical disorders. In the course of a voyage, de Beauvoir, her stomach ravaged by seasickness, heard Sartre explain that she had simply not exercised sufficient willpower, that she had failed to maintain a good grip on herself. On occasion, in the middle of an attack of nephritis, Sartre replied to his amazed physician that no, he was experiencing no discomfort. After all, pain was nothing more than a word!

Beneath her cool exterior, de Beauvoir was a passionate being. Sartre was greatly surprised by her violent outbursts in the face of persons and things. Through her he discovered bursting into tears, crying jags, and other expressions of anguish and anxiety. He admired her ability to get to the heart of things and recounted with tenderness the Castor at eighteen, seated on a metal chair in the Luxembourg Gardens, concentrating on the passing of time with such intensity that "she was time itself." Her imagination and powers of abstraction were so great that she became the desert, the sky, the trees. As for Sartre, he never lost his lucidity. He defined his spirit as being like "an antiseptic operating room." "I treat my sentiments as I do my ideas," he wrote.[40]

De Beauvoir had made an effort to dominate her body, for she believed that the physical should never prevail over the spiritual. What surprised her most about her love for Sartre was the discovery of her own sensuality. She realized that her physical appetites were greater than she wanted them to be. "To inhabit one's body is cause for celebration," yet this celebration, this joy, threatened to become an obstacle in her understanding with Sartre, to whom she dared not speak of the full force of her desire. Physical love was no longer a privileged link. She sensed that she was the victim of a need as elementary as those for food, water, and sleep, yet she had a difficult time learning to accept it as such. Her desire had become an ever-present ache, and she hated to suffer. She thought she was the only person alive to undergo "this torture." She wondered at having never come across a description of it in any book. Each night her obsession overtook her, her need so insistent, so difficult to control that the slightest touch on the street, in the métro, aroused shudders of desire. In her reading she found countless reasons to accept her sensuality with elation, feeling deeply as she did that her mind and body were not two separate entities. The Claudelian sublimation of physical love had seemed to her satisfactory until she met Sartre; now she was alarmed to discover that her sexuality was gaining supremacy over her reason. Through the demands of the flesh she discovered "that humanity does *not* subsist in the calm light of the Good; men suffer the dumb, futile, cruel agonies of defenseless beasts."[41]

She did not manage to pull herself together. Her passion for Sartre having wrenched her away from her very self, she was no longer the center of her own life. With her equilibrium compromised, de Beauvoir tried to regain control of herself, to put an end to the destructive torment. "I tossed and turned in an abyss of death, the infinite, nothingness. I was never sure, when the sky calmed, if I had awakened from a nightmare or if I was falling back into a long blue dream."[42]

THE OTHER SIMONE

Sartre had trained himself to live in complete transparency with his friends, "without a veil, completely nude," and he continued this practice with de Beauvoir.* Had they not agreed that they would be transparent to each other, that they would pool their experiences, tell each other everything, analyze people and events, enrich their lives as writers, bear witness to mankind, and unmask the world? The transparency they accepted and sought had to be as strong between Sartre and the Castor as it had been between Sartre and Nizan, but for the Castor, the crystal at the heart of their love was not without its cutting edge.

Sartre was still seeing Simone Jollivet, and the portrait he painted of her horrified de Beauvoir.[43] Sartre's conquests had garnered him considerable prestige at the University. After all, Simone Jollivet was no ordinary woman. She dressed magnificently, looking to her favorite paintings for fashion inspiration. She threw parties at home in Toulouse in a cellar decorated by turns as a Renaissance palace, a medieval castle, and a Roman villa—as the spirit moved her. Some of Sartre's friends had been invited to these gala events. René Maheu, for one, knew the provocative young woman and spoke kindly of her. He told Simone all about the Roman orgy he had attended where the other Simone, clad as Messalina, presided half-reclining on a sofa, her faithful Zina at her feet, while Maheu in Roman garb portrayed an emperor of decadence.

As soon as she had discovered how joyful and fulfilling a tailor-made love could be, Simone de Beauvoir discovered the torments of jealousy.

Sartre admitted that he admired the other Simone's audacity, her intelligence and ambition, her contempt for taboos, her extravagant manner of dress. He had been ardently in love with this young woman who was both passionate and cold, capable of using her body to trap wealthy lovers or to grant herself the luxury of an affair with Sartre for the sheer fun of it. She was feisty and high-spirited, prone to quarrels, and versed in the pleasures of making up.

---

*Sartre's concept of transparency called for utter sincerity between two people striving to keep each other informed of everything they say, do, and feel in every circumstance and in all situations. It therefore implied an effort to be totally lucid vis-à-vis oneself.

Simone de Beauvoir endeavored to give an objective ear to the spicy anecdotes Sartre shared with her. Had not she herself gone slumming in bars, impelled by the dictates of surrealism in the search for adventure? But she had not anticipated these feelings of frustration and jealousy and found it difficult to deal with them. She did not want to feel this way, but she could not maintain her serenity.[44] And there was another worry. She had written novels, but only her friends had read them; she had published nothing, not a single article or story. Sartre had confidence in her and encouraged her, but for the present all she had to her credit was an *agrégation* in philosophy and the promise it held for financial independence. She was nothing more than an intellectual who dreamed of being somebody.

At the same time, she saw Simone Jollivet's name on posters for the Atelier Theatre mounted on Morris columns* and affixed to the tile walls of the métro. Jollivet was beginning to make a name for herself as an actress, and her relationship with Charles Dullin, founder of the Atelier Theatre, put one of Paris' most talked-about theatres at her feet. The Atelier, devoted to the avant-garde, doubled as an acting academy whose students, in search of new modes of expression, challenged the traditional methods taught at the Conservatory and the Comédie-Française. De Beauvoir did not underestimate the prospects of a young woman carried along by such propitious currents. Sartre told Simone that Jollivet intended to mount her own productions of several plays in order to assure herself of made-to-measure roles.† She saw herself as a young Sarah Bernhardt. Under her real name, Simone-Camille Sans, she wrote for the magazine *Correspondance,* founded by Charles Dullin in 1927. She sat on the editorial board along with four young authors, Armand Salacrou, André de Richaud, P.-A. Bréal, and Morvan-Lebesque.[45] How could Simone withstand being compared to a rival who would soon be a celebrity?

De Beauvoir knew her own worth and what she was capable of achieving. One day soon she would have written a great novel, then she would be a celebrated young author, and in no time at all she would have nothing to fear. But in the meantime?

Dullin being married had set Simone Jollivet up in a ground-floor apartment in the rue Gabrielle, not far from his theatre. She in turn had sent for Zina. Whenever she was bored she picked up a man on the street or in a bar, brought him home, and had her way with him, much as a boy hiring a

---

*Morris columns are the cylindrical billboards that are specially devoted to posters for performing arts events.

†Simone Jollivet triumphed in two of her stage adaptations, Shakespeare's *Julius Caesar* in 1937 and Aristophanes' *Plutus* in 1938. In 1941 her play *La Princesse des Urains* was a flop. Her adaptation of Balzac's *La Marâtre* in 1949 would be the last play produced by Charles Dullin.

prostitute for the night. Zina did the same. Not all their choices were wise ones; two characters chosen at random beat them up and took jewelry and other valuables. Simone de Beauvoir listened to Sartre's accounts of the other Simone's adventures and noted with dismay that he was fascinated by them.

Jollivet was a disturbing young woman. Nothing seemed to satisfy her, not the classes she took at the Atelier, not the roles she portrayed, not the stories she wrote at night, not her liaison with Charles Dullin. She returned to Toulouse, where an old admirer showered her with gifts and generously replenished her finances. Dullin chose to behave as though nothing had happened. Upon her return, she was seized with an urge to reawaken her passion for Sartre, whose intelligence she admired. She invited him over and entertained him with backstage stories from the theatre world. She took him to rehearsals at the Atelier, and Sartre found Dullin's work fascinating. He studied the great director's techniques in action as he blocked actors' movements, changed decors, and devised lighting, makeup, and costume designs. Sartre enjoyed himself backstage and in the wings, for the tension, the temper tantrums, the quarrels and displays of friendship, and the emotional hyperactivity were much to his liking.

Simone de Beauvoir, obsessed with her love for Sartre, was frightened to feel her own ambitions deadened, her independence lost. She tried to summon up willpower and motivation, but it was no use; she thought about Sartre constantly. Of course she found an excuse: She had to live every precious romantic moment because her happiness was in imminent danger, Sartre having applied for a position as lecturer in Japan. Once he had left she would have no choice but to get a grip on herself, and then she could get down to work without distractions. This austere vision of the future without Sartre justified for her the avidity with which she experienced every moment of her present happiness—and brought her back to square one, her wild love for Sartre and her fear of somehow failing in his eyes.

Japan was the future but Simone Jollivet was the present, and Jollivet constituted an intolerable menace. In addition to her talents, was there not a fascinating touch of madness about her? This bewitching woman was in league with Lucifer. According to her, her shocking behavior was her way of rendering homage to the Prince of Darkness. She declared that great writers and artists made her mysterious propositions in the night and that these friendships from beyond the tomb held a privileged place among her relationships. Above all, she exchanged ideas with "the only equals she acknowledged," Dürer, Nietzsche, and Emily Brontë.[46]

Dullin, utterly spellbound by Jollivet, forgave her everything, including being drunk onstage and making an exit on all fours with her skirt hiked up over her head. This unprecedented weakness on the part of so great a man convinced de Beauvoir that she could never hope to triumph over this femme fatale. She was horror-stricken at the realization.

She had met freedom, love, and death in one autumn. One must try to be heroic, she told herself, one is no less human. But the force of her emotions shattered her concentration. She could no longer write. Sartre, alarmed by this unforeseen laziness, tried to stimulate his alter ego by holding up the prolific Jollivet as an example—which did little to allay de Beauvoir's considerable doubts. Was it possible that Sartre had a greater affinity for the other Simone? De Beauvoir despised the manner in which Jollivet made use of her body for venal ends one day and for purely physical pleasure the next. Realizing that she felt this way gave her yet another reason for self-doubt. Was she not in fact a puritan, conditioned by her upbringing? "I am no longer certain of what I think or even if I think," she wrote, nonplussed, in her journal.[47]

These internal dialogues led nowhere; each feeling of hopelessness gave birth to another. It was time to end the torture and face up to the situation: She would have to meet Simone Jollivet. "It got on my nerves that she did not seem to pay any attention to me."

While Sartre had been telling de Beauvoir about Jollivet, he had also been telling Jollivet about de Beauvoir. Simone Jollivet, curious to meet this Simone de Beauvoir, invited her to the rue Gabrielle. Jolivet greeted her guest in a theatrical costume: a white tunic that swept the floor opened on a long dress of scarlet silk. Jewels glittered at her wrists, waist, and ears. Long coils of blonde hair encircled her head before cascading down onto her shoulders. She looked like someone straight out of a Renaissance painting. De Beauvoir examined her hostess, noting her round, slightly childish face, her flutelike voice and attractive gestures. She spoke with an obvious desire to please and stole an occasional glance at her own reflection in the mirror. She was charming, slightly fluttery in her manner. She spoke competently about the classic Spanish drama *La Celestina*; she was preparing an adaptation of it and Dullin had entrusted her with the direction. She had recently seen a Japanese Noh drama. Was de Beauvoir familiar with the Noh theatre? Jollivet described it for her, miming and imitating the Japanese actors with considerable grace. She reviewed her own ideas concerning the theatre and elaborated on Dullin's with simplicity and assurance. She did not resemble the femme fatale Simone had conjured up from the accounts of Sartre and his friends. She could not picture Jollivet nude, leaning against a fireplace mantel, reading Nietzsche to her lovers in an elegant brothel. The image and the reality seemed not to coincide.

In the course of the visit, de Beauvoir felt a growing sense of defeat.

"Nothing but a really rousing counterblast of egocentricity could have restored the balance."[48] But what self-affirmation, without completed works at
hand, could possibly salvage her sinking pride?

When she took her leave of Jollivet it was night. In order to calm herself
down she began walking the streets aimlessly and, as if bewitched, her steps
kept bringing her back toward the Atelier, to the square that today is named
after Charles Dullin. She was the victim of one of the most disagreeable
emotions that had ever come over her: jealousy. Jollivet was the very model
of the liberated, creative woman, and Simone could not stop admiring this
provincial pharmacist's daughter who had dropped out to the fringes of
bourgeois society only to triumph in the very milieu that de Beauvoir hoped
to conquer with her pen. She could not shake the dark uneasy feeling of
jealousy. She paced up and down the Butte Montmartre for hours, disgusted
with herself, unable to get the other Simone off her mind.

"*A* WE *THAT IS NOT TWO* YOUS"[49]

*S*artre was worried to see Simone working without conviction.
"Watch out," he told her, "that you don't turn into a housewife." He compared her to the heroines of contemporary literature who, having conquered
their independence, were happy to lean back and be some man's companion.
Until his death Sartre said repeatedly, "The wonderful thing about Simone
de Beauvoir is that she has the intelligence of a man . . . and the sensitivity
of a woman. . . . That is to say that in her I found everything that I could
possibly desire."[50] She was the Lover, she was the Friend, and Sartre had no
intention of losing the woman he called his "little everything," his "sweet
little one," his "dear, dear love," his "sweet little flower."[51] Even so, with
respect to de Beauvoir's capacity as lover, Sartre, for lack of another point of
reference, compared her to a man when describing the nature of their alliance.

> I have had three "intimate friends," and each one corresponded to a
> specific period in my life: Nizan, Guille, the Castor (since the Castor was
> *also* my friend and still is). What friendship brought me, much more
> than affection (such as it could be), was *a federative world* where my friend
> and I pooled all our values, all our thoughts, and all our tastes. And this
> world was constantly renewed through incessant invention. At the same
> time, each of us supported the other, and the consequence was a *couple*

of considerable strength. . . . The result of this federation, when it reached its culmination with the Castor, was an overpowering happiness, similar to summer.[52]

In his *Mémoires* Raymond Aron bears witness to this understanding. From the day de Beauvoir walked into Sartre's life, all his friends—and what friends!—were relegated to second place. It was with her that he would elaborate his entire body of philosophical work in a common sharing of ideas. The long love song to Sartre that is de Beauvoir's memoirs does not really bring this out.

In an interview with Madeleine Gobeil in the French *Vogue* of July 1966, Sartre, asked what de Beauvoir represented for him, replied, "In a certain way, if you like, I owe her everything. . . . Once she gives me in a way the green light, I put complete trust in her, and the criticisms of others have never made me change my opinion about something I've done. You could say that I write for her, or more accurately, for her to filter through the thing.[53]

There is not one page that he did not submit to her scrutiny, not one page of hers that she did not show him. Not a single feeling or act came to pass without one of them presenting it to the other for judgment. They successfully accomplished the tour de force of living their two lives as if they were one dual life. "Together we make one," de Beauvoir said, and in 1977 Sartre explained that "there exists a relationship of depth which sometimes manages to create almost one individual, a *we* that is not two *yous* and is really and truly a *we*. I've had this *we* all my life with Simone de Beauvoir."[54]

Such an understanding does not just happen; it must be carefully constructed. "We were extremely attentive to one another right from the start." The Castor and he whom their friends nicknamed the Kobra recognized and loved each other in their difference.

De Beauvoir was romantic, passionate, irrepressible. She went into raptures over rustlings of the wind through chestnut groves, rays of sunshine, and wide open spaces; she was tortured by anxieties about death and capable of going into a trance before an expanse of countryside. An operatic air, a painting, a moment of beauty brought tears to her eyes. She pushed her likes and dislikes to the limit. "You're a schizophrenic," Sartre told her. "It is true," de Beauvoir said; "when I had a project, nothing could stop me. Sartre would tell me, 'You prefer your project to the realities of the world.' "

Sartre admired the turbulence and agitation of a personality so unlike his own. He detested greenery, open fields, nature in general. "He never stops thinking," his classmates proclaimed. Raymond Aron wrote that, "faced with an object, in lieu of evading the issue or skirting it in favor of a myth, a word, an impression, or a preconceived notion, he looked at it; he wouldn't let it go before having understood its ins and outs, the multiple meanings. . . . Obstinate, naïve, his attention seized things in their profusion and entirety."[55] This process often tried his friends' patience, but it fascinated Simone: "Only those madmen who would discover an entanglement of intrigues in a rose petal inspired the same sort of humility in me."[56] She and Sartre had in common their vocation as writers, each of them encouraged by parents from an early age. They shared the same desire to build the man of the future through the medium of their books. They held the same distain for hierarchies, routine, careers, prerogatives, and duties—all the serious trappings of life.

From the start the two lovers granted one another total independence. They did not live together and never would. Sartre lived with his parents and Simone rented the room from her grandmother, who treated her with the same discretion she accorded her other lodgers. This room became a rallying point for Sartre's and de Beauvoir's friends. There were others, including the Closerie des Lilas, the Falstaff, and the apartment of Madame Morel,* a wealthy Argentinian who hosted young writers in her salon.

From 1929 to 1931 Simone de Beauvoir was the living antithesis of a dutiful daughter—a designation that was fraught with irony. Freedom went to her head: She went entire nights without sleeping, smoked English cigarettes, dined in the restaurants of Montparnasse. Paris was a feast programmed according to her whims. When Georges de Beauvoir was asked what his daughter was doing, he would reply, "She's living it up." A future George Sand? A future Colette? It was certain that she would follow in their footsteps.

Fernando Gerassi often took Simone to the Café des Arts at the corner of the boulevard Edgar-Quinet and the boulevard du Montparnasse, where painters, musicians, and avant-garde artists, most of them foreigners, gathered. The regulars included Vicente Huidobro, a Chilean poet and friend of Apollinaire and Tristan Tzara, who had founded the creationism movement, the painter Cossio, the Franco-American composer Edgar Varèse, whose work provoked scandals, and the two enfants terribles of painting, Robert and Sonia Delaunay.

Robert was tall, blond, handsome, and passionately interested in theories. Sonia had been one of the most famous women in Paris ever since her dress designs, realized by Jacques Heim and displayed at the International

---

*Madame Lemaire in the memoirs.

Exhibition of Modern Decorative Arts, had deposed the emperor of fashion, Paul Poiret. Her fabrics and tapestries were shipped to London and New York by the truckload. In 1927, invited to lecture to the philosophy students at the Sorbonne, she spoke about painting's influence on the art of fashion design. Excerpts from her speech were quoted in the press, and the actor-director Louis Jouvet included whole passages of it in the season's program at the Comédie des Champs-Elysées. The Delaunays set the tone in design for the theatre as well as the cinema. They drove around town in a convertible that had been painted like one of their canvases, sometimes accompanied by their old friend Blaise Cendrars. Cendrars, a modern adventurer, had lost an arm while serving in the Foreign Legion during the war. He advocated complete freedom and every possible boldness of expression in literature.

This group drank heavily. During their get-togethers they questioned the nature of art, literature, and society. One of their number wanted to rent the Eiffel Tower and hang *Merde* in neon letters on it as a response to Citroën, who had similarly emblazoned his trademark in the Parisian sky; others wanted to set fire to oil wells and scorch the earth. A Futurist wind blew in from Russia—did not Mayakovsky and Sergei Yesenin want to wipe the slate clean of ancient art and start over from scratch? De Beauvoir liked hermetic poetry, surrealist films, abstract art, African masks. She listened, observed, reflected. She was looking for a suitable means of expressing herself. Virginia Woolf, in her reflections on language and the novel, paralleled de Beauvoir's preoccupations. Like Woolf, de Beauvoir sought a way to reduce the distance between words and reality. Sartre found their research pointless; he believed that the writer should play with this distance, not try to eliminate it. De Beauvoir was not attracted by realism, thinking "that words retain reality only after having murdered it." Sartre maintained that the writer must not let himself be carried away by the pounding of hearts, giddiness, the uncoordinated movement of bodies, the turmoil of passion, that he must dominate such feelings if he hopes to express them. For a long time to come de Beauvoir would oppose her notions to those of Sartre. Certainly in 1930 she had far greater artistic affinities with the Café des Arts group, and she often attended their gatherings.

One night the gang decided to finish up the evening at the Sphinx, the not yet famous brothel that had just opened at 31 boulevard Edgar-Quinet, on the site of a stoneyard for marble headstones. The otherwise undistinguished façade of the building was decorated with a sphinx. The madam, who had spent several years in a New York speakeasy and returned to France just before the market crash of 1929, had an avant-garde conception of what was suitable architecture for a brothel. The large reception room on the main floor opened onto a bar and dance floor. The bedrooms were elaborately flashy. Swathed in luxury, the Sphinx was the sole air-conditioned building in all Paris. Henry Miller, who had written the advertising brochure for the establishment, received a commission on any American compatriot he induced to visit the premises. The journalist Albert Londres and the writer Georges Simenon benefited from the same arrangement when they brought along their friends. As many as a thousand bottles of champagne were consumed nightly. The girls, many of whom worked at the Folies-Bergères and the Paris Casino, were not all prostitutes but served as part of the decor, contributing to the atmosphere. Painters took them on as models. Writers and actors met at the Sphinx as they would at a private club. The city's finest journalists came to round up the news and sniff out the latest scandals, which proved to be plentiful. There was the Hanau Bank scandal (its founder and president was the first woman banker), the Oustric scandal, the Aéropostal scandal, and the kidnapping of the White Russian General Koutiepov. Rumor had it that the Sphinx itself had been financed by several banks and important politicians. No one was surprised when, of the two members of a couple, it was the woman who went upstairs with a girl. Simone de Beauvoir, carried away by her literary remembrances of Toulouse-Lautrec and Van Gogh, found the place a highly poetic outpost. Later, in Marseille, she would enjoy strolling on the rue Bouterie and looking in through the half-open doors at the gaudy posters hung above the iron beds. In her extensive travels she never failed to investigate the quarters of ill repute. The novelists and journalists of the years between the wars affirmed that it was there, in the sleazier locales, that the truth about a culture could be found. In Africa as in America, in Madrid as in Naples, the poetry of the lower depths would long hold a strange fascination for de Beauvoir.

She struck up a friendship with a young jewelry clerk who sold the Burma line of fake gemstones and was the mistress of one of Sartre's students. Together they frequented the dance halls in the rue de Lappe, one of the sleazy streets where Apache dancing was the rage. They applied stark white makeup with blood-red lips and had a *succès fou*. Simone's favorite dance partner was a young butcher's assistant. She continued to visit the Jockey and the Jungle with her sister and Gégé. Simone always agreed to any rendezvous, no matter who proposed it, and more than once she congratulated herself on having made a narrow escape.

Sartre had his own friends. After passing the *agrégation,* Paul Nizan had taken a job with Editions du Carrefour, a publishing firm in the rue du Cherche-Midi. His responsibilities included the magazine *Bifur,* of which he would soon be solely in charge. Like de Beauvoir, Nizan had not wanted to get bogged down in a teaching position; for them teaching was something to fall back on if they failed to make their mark quickly in the world of literature. Nizan had joined the Communist Party, which in the early thirties had instituted a policy of infiltrating publishing houses. Jean Servet, director of the agitprop section, had given the party's intellectuals the responsibility of combating psychological literature in favor of Marxist, Russian, or German writing. At the publishing firm of Gallimard, the essayist and philosopher Bernard Groethuysen and Brice Parrain, who would publish Sartre's *Nausea* in 1938, accomplished quite a bit along these clandestine lines. They had tried to get Nizan hired at Gallimard, but Gallimard was opposed. So it was that Paul Nizan was put in charge of *Bifur,* a splendid magazine that reflected all the aesthetic tendencies of the twenties. Nizan made a virulent attack on the Sorbonne's brand of philosophy. "I say: in philosophy 'indifferent' means 'satisfied.' 'Without party' means 'exploiter.' French philosophy is indifferent. . . . It is time to demand a reckoning from this philosophy." He opened up his magazine to his "little comrades" from the ENS, including Georges Friedmann, Georges Politzer, and Sartre, whose first published piece, "La Légende de la vérité"—which said that only the artist, the writer, and the philosopher can claim the privilege of grasping reality from life as it is—appeared in *Bifur.* The content of this article illustrated what Sartre would later call his neurosis, that is, the certainty of having been *chosen* to save the world through literature. In *Memoirs of a Dutiful Daughter* de Beauvoir explains that her conception of the writer's role and of literature was identical to Sartre's.

Sartre and de Beauvoir sometimes went to Grandchamp, near Saint-Germain-en-Laye, where Paul Nizan lived with his in-laws, the Alphens, in the modern house they had recently had built. Monsieur Alphen, whose career as a musician had been cut short as the result of a war wound, knew quite a few of Paris' literary figures. Literature and revolution were frequent topics of conversation, and everyone made short films under the direction of Rirette Nizan's brother, who worked as an assistant director. One of the films was *The Vulture of the Sierra.* Another starred Sartre, de Beauvoir, Emmanuel Berl and his wife, Nizan and his wife; in this surrealist venture Sartre is a pious young man corrupted by girls (Simone and Rirette). When they take off his shirt, an enormous scapular is revealed glistening on his chest. Nizan appears dressed as a priest and representing Christ. "Do you smoke?" he asks, pulling from his chest a heart-shaped cigarette lighter.

Sartre and de Beauvoir visited the annual Communist celebration in Garches with the Nizans. They amused themselves by taking aim with bean-bags and toppling puppet effigies of the great bankers and generals of the Third Republic.

Raymond Aron was finishing his military service in the meteorology bureau at Saint-Cyr. He had pulled strings to see that Sartre was assigned to that branch of the service. Aron had a car and occasionally drove Sartre and de Beauvoir to dinner in Versailles, where his parents lived in a large house with a tennis court. Much more politicized than Sartre, Aron had joined the Young Socialists. In 1925 he spent two weeks in Geneva as a delegate to the general assembly of the League of Nations. He had published an article in *Libres Propos* criticizing Julian Benda's *La Trahison des clercs,* a book which had attacked the engagement of intellectuals in the political arena, denouncing the partisan nature of their works. In Benda's view, poets, novelists, philosophers, and critics had become political eulogists, singing the praises of one political system or another. "Zola," Benda explained, "was within his role as a scholar in recalling the world to a respect for justice. Anatole France was not, in making himself the daily advisor to Minister Combes." The book had caused a storm of controversy. Raymond Aron defended the right of intellectuals to involve themselves in debating even issues of dubious merit. Sartre and de Beauvoir, extremely idealistic, would more likely have defended Renan's "Even as the Empire crumbles, one must go on philosophizing."

At this time the two had anarchic leanings and believed that society could change only through violent upheaval. The political platform of the Socialist Party struck them as so many halfway measures. Léon Blum challenged historical materialism, economic determinism, and the Leninist conception of the dictatorship of the proletariat. Sartre and de Beauvoir tended to avoid talking politics with Raymond Aron and instead discussed philosophy. De Beauvoir was then on Aron's side as he tried to send "Sartre's rash syntheses" flying into pieces. Each habitually maintained his own opinion. Sartre was wary of Raymond Aron's *logicisme,* * René Maheu's aestheticism, and Paul Nizan's Marxism. Sartre's closest friend, Pierre Guille,† a graduate of the ENS and an *agrégé* in literature, would serve as secretary, first in the Chamber of Deputies and later in the National Assembly. Sartre and Guille had both gotten assigned to the meteorological service to satisfy their military obligation, and during their training at Saint-Cyr they attended Aron's classes, at times exasperating him by launching paper airplanes during his lectures.

"Neither philosopher nor politician," Raymond Aron would write, "Pierre Guille charmed us all because he was likable."[57] He was a refined

---

*The *Larousse Encyclopedia* defines *logicisme* as "a philosophical doctrine that reduces all the sciences to mathematical form."

†Pagniez in the memoirs.

epicurean who believed in a golden age for the bourgeoisie, had no literary ambitions whatever, and was interested in everything. He and Sartre could dissect and analyze a voice or a gesture in minute detail for hours on end. De Beauvoir shared their passion for understanding people. She believed that reality had to be seized as it presented itself in real-life situations. Pierre Guille enjoyed life; sampling intelligently what the world had to offer and living happily satisfied him. Sartre, who often became irritated with other people's ideas, appreciated Guille's sense of nuance, which balanced the tendency of his own imagination to get carried away. Thanks to Pierre Guille, de Beauvoir and Sartre became friendly with Madame Morel, the friendship lasting until the time of the Algerian war, when their political differences shattered it.

Madame Morel, born in Argentina, the daughter of French colonists, was the very image of the wealthy foreign woman made fashionable by literature. Her father, a physician and freethinker, had raised his two daughters as if they were boys, letting them romp and hunt across the pampas of his vast domain. A private tutor had taught them Latin and mathematics, and they had lived in isolation until the age of eighteen, when their father sent them to Paris to complete their education, as was the custom in Argentine high society. After the total liberty of their youth, Parisian society seemed an odd set indeed. Both girls married; the elder died in childbirth, the younger sister wed a Doctor Morel. Madame Morel was an attractively petite and elegant brunette. People surprised her, and she spoke of them with "an ethnographer's detachment." Guille, then Sartre, gave lessons to her son, the Tapir,* and became regular visitors in her home, Madame Morel having put a room at their disposal. The friendships formed and the conversations conducted in her salon took on a delicate, almost turn-of-the century tone. She received friends of friends, and then the quartet—Madame Morel, Guille, Sartre, and de Beauvoir—would closely examine each one's life, reading and criticizing their letters and manuscripts. The group took regular vacations together on the property their hostess owned near Angers or at her villa in Juan-les-Pins. They traveled together to Spain. Madame Morel's friendship would long remain an anchor in Simone de Beauvoir's life. Raymond Aron said Madame Morel "was charming in a sense in which the word's meaning has been lost. She charmed by virtue of her intelligence and her spontaneity." How unfortunate that *cette dame,* as Guille and Sartre referred to her, kept no diary, for she was one of the privileged witnesses of the life Sartre and de Beauvoir led.

Among their friends there was yet another *agrégé* in literature, originally

*The nickname ENS students gave to students who took private lessons.

from Bône, Algeria, and in everyone's opinion quite handsome. "Dark-haired, with an amber complexion and burning eyes, his face evoked both Greek statues and the paintings of El Greco." Marc Zuorro* wanted to join the Opera, and he studied voice with the best teachers "with a fanatical assiduity."[58] He loved boys and never went anywhere without a cortège of admiring young men. Life was an elaborate string of intrigues, half-truths, and indiscretions for Zuorro. In Madame Morel's salon he summoned up a world worthy of Proust. Zuorro had not the slightest doubt about his imminent glory; he spoke freely of his life to come, to be spent socializing in palaces, driving an enormous white automobile, indulging in adventures and affairs, and taking exotic journeys. De Beauvoir laughed at all this, for she had no interest whatever in the glaring and unmistakable material indications of success. Once famous herself, de Beauvoir was often accused of "not playing the game." The old anarchic spirit had not died.

For two full years de Beauvoir steered clear of everything that bored her and embarked on an orgy of pleasure: the cinema, the theatre, the music hall, books. She denied herself nothing. In spending time with her friends, all older than she, she woke up to the gaps in her knowledge and began reading pell-mell German, American, Russian, and English novelists. On weekends she joined Sartre in Tours, returning on the 5 A.M. train in order to be at the lycée by 8:30 A.M. She slept so little that it was not unheard of for her to nod off for a few seconds in the middle of teaching a class. She ate in haste, wolfing down chocolate or cookies, having an occasional bowl of borscht at Dominique's in Montparnasse, where the Russian colony gathered. She spent long hours at the Rotonde, bringing back to life on paper the little girl who had grown up in the carrefour Vavin, as she worked on a novel inspired by Alain-Fournier, Virginia Woolf, and Rosamond Lehmann.

In 1930 Sartre's grandmother left him 80,000 francs.† With the windfall in hand, Private Sartre hired taxis and treated Simone to dinner at the finest inns in Touraine or at Pierre's on the avenue d'Italie. "Without batting an eyelid I downed sausages, a fish in sauce, jugged hare, crêpes flambées." Gastronomic pleasures she would always value highly.

The time when Simone would have to accept a tenured teaching position was rapidly and inescapably approaching. Being obliged to leave Paris seemed an ordeal to her, and she began to look for a way to avoid the dreaded exile. She had her cousin Choppin de Janvry recommend her to Madame Le Verrier,‡ who with Louise Weiss codirected the publication L'Europe nouvelle.

---

*Marco in the memoirs.
†The salary of a *professeur agrégé* was then 2500 francs a month. Thus the inheritance represented more than Sartre could expect to earn in two and a half years as a teacher.
‡Madame Poirier in the memoirs.

Founded in 1918, this magazine was a forum for those who, after the armistice, had continued working for the causes of freedom, pacifism, and equality for all peoples and for both sexes. Louise Weiss' positions, seen then as being extremist, should have appealed to the future author of *The Second Sex.*

In 1921 Louise Weiss, as a correspondent for *Le Petit Parisien,* filed a special report on conditions in Soviet Russia. The civil war raging between Trotsky's Red Army and the White Russians aided by France, England, and America was ravaging the country. Millions were starving. Weiss revealed the fate that had befallen the "demoiselles," the French governesses who had been employed by noble Russian families who had long since emigrated, been sent to Siberia, or been shot. These Frenchwomen, completely forgotten in the revolutionary chaos, were hanging on in abject misery, and Weiss succeeded in repatriating 125 of them. She then became an apostle of the recently created League of Nations and a champion of political rights for women.

Louise Weiss considered the suffragist leagues insufficient to rouse parliamentary representatives from their apathy on the issue of women's right to vote. She set up an Association for the Equality of Political Rights of French Men and Women. When de Beauvoir came knocking on the door at *L'Europe nouvelle* she was asked for her views on politics and women's rights and for any ideas she had to contribute. Simone answered vaguely. Her participation in Garric's social work teams had convinced her that political engagement was as futile as religion. That young working mothers had in 1928 obtained the right to work one hour less so as to have time to nurse their infants, and that those in public service were now entitled to two months' paid maternity leave, were not essential issues to her. According to Simone, a woman who wanted to succeed just went ahead and succeeded. Her girl friends had acquired economic independence and were living as they saw fit. Her sister, Stépha, Gégé, and Simone Jollivet were all concerned more with art and creativity than with their daily bread, even when putting those interests first sometimes called for a certain frugality.

The atmosphere at *L'Europe nouvelle* seemed to her to be terribly fashionable and bourgeois. She was invited to a cocktail party where all the other women were clad in designer dresses, while she wore a red wool dress with a machine-stitched white collar that was "far too modest for the occasion."[59] Once again she felt the discomfort that had plagued her as a child at her rich cousins' parties or when Zaza discreetly lent her a dress at the Château de Gagnepain to avoid the giggles of her friends and younger sisters.

The *Europe nouvelle* crowd was intimidating. There was Louise Weiss, an *agrégée* in literature, tall, lovely, imposing, and the dominant figure of her day in Parisian feminism. There were Cécile Brunschvicg, future secretary of state for the Popular Front, Madame Paul Valéry, a painter, Hélène Vacaresco, delegate to the League of Nations, and Yvonne Sarcey, founder of *Annales,* a lecture club and a journal. Together they comprised a formidable group of worldly intellectual women.

Louise Weiss and Cécile Brunschvicg launched publicity stunts to call attention to the cause. They chained themselves to the gates of a public garden while the police dispersed demonstrators before the cameras of duly notified photographers. At Christmastime a squad of young and elegant feminists climbed atop the streetlights surrounding the major department stores and chanted rhymed slogans protesting the sale of war toys. This militancy did not appeal to de Beauvoir.

Nor was she greatly tempted by a post in Budapest that the Hungarian journalist Heveshi Bandi offered, or another in Morocco, especially now that she knew that Sartre had not gotten the lecturing position he had hoped for in Japan. Disappointed, he decided to replace an instructor in Le Havre who had suffered a nervous breakdown. Simone de Beauvoir requested her placement for fall 1931 and was assigned to Marseille. To live five hundred miles from Paris! Her distress was so overwhelming that Sartre suggested they get married, for then they could obtain a joint assignment. He maintained that it was stupid to make such a sacrifice on principle, that marriage would not change the style of life they had agreed upon. De Beauvoir declined. Marriage was nothing more than one of society's intrusions into private life; to marry would be to begin to fit the mold of familial and social obligations and alter their personal relationship, whose character she considered priceless. "Sartre is sufficient unto himself, he suffices for me. And I suffice for myself." At twenty-three she chose Sartre not in matrimony but in freedom.

Sartre and de Beauvoir decided to revise the commitment they had made at the Carousel arch. They abandoned the idea of a contract along with the clause concerning long solitary trips. Their understanding would endure as long as they themselves, and their mutual transparency was their guarantee of love. They did not swear eternal fidelity because neither of them wished for that.

That summer, invited by Fernando Gerassi and encouraged by Hélène de Beauvoir, who also found herself there, Sartre and de Beauvoir left for Spain. For the first time the lovers lived together, and Sartre did not spend the entire summer with his parents. They traveled first class, the sole luxury permitted them by the remains of Sartre's inheritance. That fine sum had melted away in the space of a year.

Travel abroad! Since she had been old enough to dream before the pages of her atlas, foreign travel had been one of Simone's burning desires. Remembering the expeditions to Meyrignac, their heavy baggage in tow and her mother's losing her temper with the porters, Simone swore she would reduce the aggravations of travel to an absolute minimum: "Our luggage will not be heavy!" Today one must stop and recall the style in which people traveled in 1930. The bourgeoisie set out armed with trunks, suitcases, crates, and boxes carted by porters in braided caps. Alexandra David-Néel, the explorer who reached Lhasa, crossed the Himalayas with evening dresses and a portable bathtub in her luggage. Simone de Beauvoir inaugurated the concept of traveling light that would be taken up some thirty years later by student campers and the flower children of the sixties who backpacked around the globe in jeans and sandals.

De Beauvoir was not enticed by luxury hotel accommodations and swank neighborhoods.[60] She wanted to observe and share life as it was actually lived in the places she visited, and thus she chose modest pensions, working-class restaurants, regional foods. She sought to grasp the culture of a country through its food. "Each day I forced myself to swallow cupfuls of a black sauce heavily laced with cinnamon. I ate almond and hazelnut pastries, quince jellies, and cakes that were gritty between my teeth and tasted like old dust."[61] In her travels she would always make a point of sampling every local delicatessen.

Spain had become a republic in April and "was still surprised by her triumph. You might have said that she celebrated it each day." Fernando Gerassi showed Sartre and de Beauvoir around Madrid and introduced them to the Spanish left. At the Plaza del Sol they saw Ramón Valle-Inclán, who was to Spanish youth in 1930 what Sartre would be to French youth in 1945. The brutal realism of his work, the audacity of his style, and his anticlericalism made him a hero of the day; people still point out the brasserie where he often sat. "Bearded, one-armed, glorious, he told anyone who cared to listen, and each time in a different way, the story of how he lost his arm."[62]

Accustomed to the ways of Montparnasse, de Beauvoir did nothing more than follow the habitués of the carrefour Vavin, particularly the American writers and artists who were discovering Hispanic culture and taking advantage of the extremely favorable exchange rate for the peseta. The bodegas were crowded with shoppers and everyone attended the bullfights where Ortega and El Estudiante reigned triumphant. Simone, and Sartre, who followed her, the eternal pipe clenched between his teeth, made the most of this celebration of love and death glorified by Ernest Hemingway. They went to the bullfights every Sunday.

September came, time for them to part. Sartre left for Paris, and Simone, awash in her own tears, turned toward Marseille.

5

THE TEACHERS

What a pleasure it was to live without orders, without constraint!

The Woman Destroyed

PROFESSOR OF PHILOSOPHY

*I*n 1931 Simone de Beauvoir became a member of the academic establishment, a teacher at the age of twenty-three. Her situation was not lacking in prestige. The teaching of philosophy in the lycée was the glory of the national educational system; France was the only country in the world where secondary studies concluded with a year of philosophy. The quality of its schooling was the Third Republic's triumph, much as Versailles had been in another era. The *agrégation* in philosophy was widely considered to be the most difficult, and the philosophy teachers formed an intellectual aristocracy. Many among them—Jules Lagneau, Henri Bergson, Alain, André Bellessort, Jean Grenier, Gustave Monod—had become famous, and most of them worked for the triumph of secular ethics and disseminated republican ideas. They were feared by right-wing bourgeois families, who paid particular attention to the content of this instruction and especially that given their daughters. When it came time for de Beauvoir to instruct her class at the Lycée Montgrand on ethics, a general outcry resulted. The young, well-bred anarchist did not mince words in sharing her opinions about labor, capital, justice, and colonialism. She deliberately challenged her students by talking about Gide and Proust—not exactly approved reading matter in a provincial lycée—and assigning the complete text of Lucretius' *De Rerum Natura* along with a section from George Dumas' *Traité de psychologie.* Her former teacher's ideas were far from being universally accepted, and his chapters on sexuality and sexual pleasure shocked many. Simone rigorously demolished the arguments her students had picked up from their parents. One of her best students, a doctor's daughter, ostentatiously traded her front-row seat for one at the very back, crossed her arms in defiance, and refused to take notes. The complaints poured in; Simone was summoned before the headmistress, who advised her to stick to the curriculum. The matter went no further.

De Beauvoir's casual lifestyle was also considered shocking. She had chosen to serve out this year of solitude to prove to herself that she was not dependent on contingencies. She also wanted to prove that she was capable of depolarizing herself intellectually from Sartre. On her arrival in Marseille, at the top of the main staircase of the Saint-Charles station, looking out over the city, her cry was not Rastignac's "Marseille, I challenge you!" but "Simone, I challenge you!" She had sworn to herself that she would be revealed to herself.

Every Sunday and Thursday, clad in an old dress and espadrilles and carrying a string bag with a few bananas and brioches, Simone set off on ever-longer hikes through the countryside. Systematically she combed the region, getting lost in a ravine in Lubéron, struggling into the wind as she climbed Sainte-Victoire, exploring the customs routes that followed the rocky inlets. Sometimes, completely exhausted, she would lie down and fall asleep on the ground. Hiking became a passion that only advancing age would lessen.

"Each walk was a work of art." Like an athlete, she mapped out elaborately detailed routes which she forced herself to follow to the end. She imposed the same discipline on her body that she had applied to her brain. By attempting continually more demanding itineraries, she lifted her walking expeditions to the level of sacred duty and came to experience the same joy from her exertions as a marathon runner crossing the finish line or an alpinist conquering a peak. She was soon capable of covering twenty-five miles in a day.

Simone's solo hikes invited criticism at the Lycée Montgrand. It was thought scandalous for a woman to ramble through the countryside on her own. Of course it was hardly less scandalous for her to go to cafés, dine in restaurants, attend movies, and roam the seedier dock quarters alone. Her colleagues warned her about the inherent dangers of such behavior: She could get herself raped! De Beauvoir was fearless. Nothing could shake her tranquil self-assurance. She thought nothing of flagging down trucks for a lift, and on one occasion she jumped from a moving car in the middle of nowhere when the driver proved to have dishonorable intentions. Simone de Beauvoir hitch-hiked even before the word was known.

During the Easter break in 1932, she took Sartre with her for long hikes through Brittany. In June she walked from Nice to San Remo wearing sandals and carrying a rucksack. In July she left Marseille on foot to rejoin Sartre in Narbonne for their second trip to Spain and the Balearic Islands.

In the spring she shook up the tiny lycée population by going to class straight from the tennis court, still sporting her white tussore tennis dress, her racket in hand. Not everyone disapproved of her demeanor, and some found her aristocratic independence impressive. Her students developed crushes on her, her tennis partners were taken with her, and one fellow teacher, a married woman, made passionate advances that Simone rejected.

Although she disapproved of all narcissism while in Sartre's company, in Marseille she took stock of the life she was leading and found the figure she cut as a single woman rather dashing and romantic. She began a new novel, roaming Marseille's worst neighborhoods in search of detail and inspiration. She took in the docks, the port of Aix, where tramps and winos sold rags, and the red-light district, where she peeked in through doors left ajar for a glimpse of the prostitutes. "Because of my private mythology I found the rue Bouterie an enchanting street."[1] She wrote the novel at the Cintra bar in the old port of Marseille, rounding out the plot to herself as she walked around the lake at Berre. She pursued her creative dialogue during her long solitary hikes. Novelist and critic in one, her own company was all she required. The challenge and beauty of a work being born transformed the countryside, making it seem unreal, and she experienced a surge of elation at giving her imagination free play. She had already touched upon the theme that would be central to *She Came to Stay* (*L'Invitée*), the mirage of the Other. An existentialist before existentialism, for her, "hell was other people."[2] You plunged into this hell when you eliminated yourself except for your image reflected in another's eyes. In her novel de Beauvoir wanted to avoid equivocation: The reader must not think this a mere love story when what the book offers was a completely new analysis of human interaction, describing an emotion whose sources had not been explored by other novelists. The mirage of the Other has since, through existentialism, become a familiar concept in the psychology of novels, but de Beauvoir was the first to use it. "I made both my protagonists women, thinking, somewhat naïvely, that this would preserve their relationship from all equivocal undertones of sex."[3] She assigned two of her own principal characteristics, her zest for life and her urge for literary achievement, to her two main characters, thereby enabling her to see herself in a double mirror. One of the characters, Madame de Préliane, forty, possessed multiple charms, innate elegance, and creative talent, as demonstrated by her direction of a puppet theatre. De Beauvoir liked puppets for their "nonhuman purity."[4] When visiting Japan years later, she would take a lively interest in Bunraku.

The other woman, Geneviève, was twenty and looked up to Madame de Préliane "with passionate intensity."[5] To make the tale more complex, de Beauvoir interwove the tragic story of Zaza, whose fate then remained inexplicable for her. Simone imagined Zaza as Anne, married to a "conventional-minded bourgeois" and languishing in the closed society to which she belonged.[6] Anne meets Madame de Préliane, who encourages her to develop her musical gifts. Torn between her duty and her need to escape, Anne dies. At the funeral, Geneviève realizes how alone she is and understands that every human being must create a life for herself and shoulder the weight of her own freedom.

The novel did not satisfy Simone. The only part of the work she considered truly valuable was the way in which the characters were presented from the Other's point of view. Madame de Préliane and Anne were seen as Geneviève saw them, and she in turn was observed through Anne's eyes.

The separation from Sartre was offset by their meetings in Paris during school vacation and on days off cadged through the ruse of imaginary flu attacks and liver upsets. They corresponded almost daily, which kept matters vivid and clear between them. Sartre had launched upon "a pamphlet on contingency."[7] In a letter to de Beauvoir he told of having come across and intimately understood the tree that would later become the famous chestnut tree in *Nausea*. De Beauvoir tried to persuade Sartre to add "fictional depth" to his text, spicing the narrative with some of the suspense one found in the detective novels they both enjoyed. The pamphlet on contingency would indeed become *Nausea*.

ROUEN

*I*n 1932, thanks to Madame Lemaire, who knew the minister of education, de Beauvoir obtained a teaching assignment at the Lycée Jeanne-d'Arc in Rouen, one hour from Le Havre by train. Even before she had found a place to stay she bought a railroad pass to Paris. She took a room at the Rochefoucauld Hotel near the train station. Trains, platforms, and station waiting rooms were the myths of an entire generation, reflected in the films and novels of the era. Simone de Beauvoir was well acquainted with travel imagery and made it her own. "I was always itching to go somewhere." For four years the Rouen train station was at the center of her existence; each day she had breakfast opposite the departure hall. A routine was soon established: Sartre went to Rouen on Thursdays, and they spent weekends together in Paris.

Colette Audry,* who was then teaching literature at the lycée in Rouen, remembers the young woman of twenty-four, "slender, with a very light complexion," who shook her hand one chilly October morning, mentioning Paul Nizan as a reference. "She struck us as being excessively well mannered, except for her husky and headlong, rapid speech, which hardly went along with the rest. . . . From that moment on, you noticed nothing more than her expression, inseparable from her voice and what her voice was saying, the sharp assertiveness of her affirmations, her naïve attentiveness when asking a question, her slightly angular shyness when sharing a secret."[8]

Audry goes on to describe her "dry and pitiless humor in relating anecdotes" that concluded with a great burst of "hearty laughter." "So it was that she appeared, happily growing and evolving, blessed with solid appetites, exceptionally ardent both at work and at play, transforming each minute into a moment of happiness, happy even in her fits of hopelessness and bitterness, which were as sudden and brief as a July storm. . . . She would be a writer, there was no doubt about that, not for her, not for us."[9]

In Rouen, de Beauvoir's daily life was very different from what she had known in Marseille. There were no more long solo expeditions of rambling over scrubland and scrambling across rocky inlets. The Brasserie Paul became

---

*Colette Audry would be a writer and a journalist and would oversee a collection at the publishing house of Denoël, serve as president of the Women's Democratic Movement, and participate in compiling material for *The Woman of the Twentieth Century*.

her headquarters. The place was a sort of long corridor, "its imitation-leather banquettes spilling their horsehair."[10] The waiters wore white aprons that came to their ankles over black dress suits that were as old and dusty as the four walls. There were few customers, for the food was mediocre, but Simone liked the peace and quiet. For two years she went there to work on an enormous novel, the pages of which became scattered among the student compositions she neglected to correct. This novel, a panorama of society after the war, had two heroes; a brother and sister. Pierre and Madeleine Labrousse were modern versions of Julien Sorel and Lamiel, providing a double outlook —masculine and feminine—on their time. In *The Mandarins* de Beauvoir would also divide her point of view among Anne, Dubreuil, and Henri. Her characters' physical and intellectual characteristics were copied from de Beauvoir's circle of friends. She borrowed the tender platonic friendship shared by Madame Morel and Pierre Guille. She made use of the manner in which Simone Jollivet fleeced her lovers before turning from the world's oldest profession to the second oldest profession. The hero, like Charles Dullin, wants to recreate the theatre and asks himself, What *is* artistic truth and at what point does it become a betrayal of one's principles? It was a question that de Beauvoir asked herself. Paul Nizan and the young Communist intellectual crowd lent their traits to Laborde and his friends. The hero joined them but rejected their determinist vision of the world, which they placed over and above all individualistic values. The tragic love story lived by Merleau-Ponty and Zaza was transposed so that "bourgeois spiritual values were made to look not merely ridiculous but lethal."[11]

The small Morel clan encouraged Simone to continue, as did Sartre. Pierre Guille thought the first few chapters had the charm and qualities of an English novel. After two year's work, Simone de Beauvoir would abandon this novel that prefigured *The Mandarins.* It was the fifth novel she had written and rejected, telling herself that it was not what she was after. Perhaps it is unfortunate that Sartre did not push her to rework this novel as she had pushed him to continue revising *Nausea*—which he rewrote four times, incorporating her suggestions.

Sartre was bubbling with ideas. He was writing "The Transcendence of the Ego," and his philosophical work in progress was undergoing constant fusion and change. He led de Beauvoir into the heart of his cogitations, confiding "his new theories" to her pell-mell, that she might help him untangle and clarify them. She demolished a theory on comedy that was based on a plausible but fallacious argument. She urged Sartre to follow his reasoning, pointed out contradictions, and went through each of his ideas with an intellectual fine-tooth comb, thereby contributing constantly to his work.

Sartre would dedicate his entire body of philosophical work to Simone de Beauvoir. In Rouen, Le Havre, or Paris their joint efforts continued in their conversations, their letters, their notebooks—a barrage of communication. Be it on man, society, or art, the point of view they had arrived at the night before would be discarded the next day. Given the ever-changing recipe of this intellectual primeval soup, it was difficult for de Beauvoir to pin down in a novel the essence of a story that negated itself from one moment to the next.

In their quest for material to fuel their respective writing projects, Sartre and de Beauvoir devoted entire days to analyzing, scrutinizing, and dissecting the lives of their friends and colleagues. They made up backgrounds for people they spotted in cafés, on trains, in the streets. Each new encounter or acquaintance inspired pages of spoken novelization. They tried to second-guess other people's relationships with love, politics, money. They set themselves up as the center of the world, leaving others to orbit around them like so much dust in the cosmos, "pleasant, odious, or ridiculous."[12] De Beauvoir, who could not have cared less about public opinion, refused to admit that society's rules might apply to her. One day, having dressed in haste and sporting a gaping hole in one of her stockings, she wanted to go into a luxury hotel for a drink and Sartre refused to accompany her. She insisted that what others thought had no hold over their behavior; Sartre maintained that the unflattering opinion others might form reflected poorly on him. With her customary flair she blithely continued to raise eyebrows in Rouen as she had in Marseille. She found it practically impossible to imagine the people around her as individuals like herself, with consciences to match. Along with Sartre she was looking for a system that would explain human behavior. "We distrusted classical French psychology; we did not believe in behaviorism; and we had only a very limited faith in psychoanalysis." Freudian psychoanalysis was beginning to be fashionable. Their friends, with Politzer in the forefront, interpreted every little thing according to Freud or Adler. But Sartre and de Beauvoir were on the lookout for an entirely new method of evaluating the world and the people in it, and this exploration constituted the bulk of their daily work for four years. From this common effort sprang Sartre's concept of bad faith, which "embraced all those phenomena that other people attributed to the unconscious mind."[13]

Tracking down instances of bad faith—dishonesty and deception in their various manifestations—became an ongoing exercise. De Beauvoir discovered what she dubbed the "mirage" effect: "We applied this term to anyone who feigned convictions or feelings they did not in fact possess."[14] These "mirages" are plentiful in de Beauvoir's novels and Sartre's plays.

To extend the range of their investigation, they took an avid interest in the sensationalist press and the offbeat. Monstrous or abnormal behavior fascinated them, for in it they found the passions of normal people amplified to extremes. Sensational crimes and the subsequent trials called into question the relationship between the individual and the community. Sartre and de Beauvoir's anarchic instincts reveled in the unmasking of flaws in the social system that created murderers. They had the notion that the society of 1933 was "no more enlightened than the so-called primitive ones." They undertook to collect "all the examples of prerational mentality that abound in this civilized world of ours."[15]

The crime committed by the Papin sisters on February 2, 1933, illustrated their theory. In their eyes it was a perfect example of the bourgeoisie's faults carried to extremes. The two sisters, household servants to a lawyer in the city of Le Mans, gave entirely satisfactory service for six years. When their employers were out, they released their frustrations in genuine psychodrama, taking turns acting out the role of lady of the household. Caught in the act one night when the lawyer's wife and daughter returned earlier than expected, the startled servants were seized by some murderous impulse and went on a rampage. They tortured, killed, and mutilated mother and daughter and thus "became both the instruments and the martyrs of justice in its grimmest disguise." Sartre and de Beauvoir looked upon the Papins' actions as cause and effect, enslavement and retribution. Another crime that de Beauvoir and Sartre subjected to analysis was Violette Nozières' murder of her father. He had certainly molested her, but the press responded to the girl's accusations of rape with evocations of "the sacred character of Fatherhood."[16]

To change this alienating society, de Beauvoir believed that the ruling class had to be overthrown. She could not tolerate "its lies, stupidity, prejudices, and false virtues." Sartre asked himself whether he should not have joined the Marxists, who were working for revolution. De Beauvoir responded that the struggle was not theirs because they were not members of the proletariat. She remained convinced that their own contribution to transforming society would be made through their writings. They had to remain free of specific political commitment because only "freedom is an inexhaustible source of discovery."[17] Joining a political party and agitating for causes meant conforming to a political mold, and this would have deprived them of their independence. The path that Nizan, a disciplined and active militant, had chosen to follow was not encouraging. His *Aden Arabie* (1931) and *Watchdogs* (1932), books that ridiculed the teaching of philosophy at the Sorbonne and bourgeois society, were not well received. "Simplistic childishness" was Gide's assessment, while a critic from the Communist newspaper *L'Humanité* accused Nizan of giving "more of a showy literary exercise, a superficial argument having no real bearing on the class struggle," instead of making a useful contribution to the study of the proletariat.[18]

The party was wary of intellectuals, of the vague and generous romantic idealism that had inspired them to swell its ranks en masse. It now asked them to join a rigid organization and to adhere to a rigorous doctrine.

De Beauvoir wanted nothing to do with such a commitment. Nizan flashed one of his most mocking smiles when she told him about her novel. "A story you made up?" he inquired. Neither she nor Sartre would have written *Watchdogs.*

The Trotskyite dissidents she knew were wondering about the possibilities for a new revolution. This path interested her no more than the others. As we have already seen, while at the lycée in Rouen, de Beauvoir got along well with Colette Audry, whose friends included Nizan, Simone Weil, and Boris Souvarine,* but all the options for engagement seemed limited to her because the world remained to be invented.

"I HAVE BEEN FAITHFUL TO THEE, CYNARA, IN MY FASHION"†

*I*n September 1933, Sartre left to accept a lectureship at the French Institute in Berlin. De Beauvoir was twenty-five years old. In order to extend the range of her reading and in order to read German philosophers in the original, she began taking German lessons two or three times a week with a German Communist who had fled to France. Teaching bored her. With her friends Marc Zuorro, Colette Audry, and Simone Jahan,‡ she formed a sort of avant-garde group at the lycée. They shocked by virtue of their freewheeling manners, the elegant nonconformity of their dress and their hairstyles, their disdain for the establishment at the University and in Rouen. For them, teaching in Rouen was the purgatory before Paris. The political activities of some of their number prompted complaints to the school administration. Nizan, who taught in Bourg-en-Bresse, had been called to order and

---

*Boris Souvarine, expelled from the Communist Party, director of the magazine *Est-Quest,* specialized in anti-Communism.

†"This line of dialogue from the film *Cynara* was to become a sort of password for us over the years" (*The Prime of Life*).

‡Simone Labourdin in the memoirs.

consequently quit his job and became director of the *Humanité* bookshop.

Simone de Beauvoir was once again on the lycée blacklist. She had been seen with Sartre, she was seen in the company of Pierre Guille, who came to visit or waited for her at the station, she was seen with Zuorro, who lived with a beautiful blond young man and occasionally with a colleague, Simone Jahan. In class de Beauvoir had a habit of making scandal-provoking remarks. The teaching staff had received copies of a flyer urging them to campaign in favor of raising the birthrate. Simone addressed the issue with irony and told her charges that woman was destined for better things than bringing children into the world. A rumor quickly spread through the school that Mademoiselle de Beauvoir had encouraged her students to behave as she did, to free themselves and take lovers. She was accused of having asked each of her students for their personal approval—and only the most virtuous had protested!

The Departmental Commission for the Birthrate and the Protection of Children sent the prefect a report denouncing "the instruction which an unworthy teacher is directing against the family."[19] Simone defended herself in a long letter written with Pierre Guille's help. She counterattacked by accusing the students' parents of supporting Hitlerian doctrines. The minister of education, Madame Lemaire's friend, chose to drop the matter, but at school many of the other teachers heartily denounced de Beauvoir to their classes. Confrontations between right and left became more frequent. De Beauvoir did not go on strike or urge her students to join the Communist Youth League, as Colette Audry did.

De Beauvoir detested all forms of power and refused to exercise that which she held over her students, in much the same way as she would refuse stardom later on. She treated those students for whom she had a personal liking as companions. Because she rejected a hierarchy in human relationships, she was touched by the sight of young men from the Military Academy at La Flèche sweating in their heavy blue wool uniforms among those students taking the baccalaureate examinations that she was proctoring. They looked like hunted animals, and she had the impression of participating in "a brutal ritual."[20] She gave everyone a passing grade.

Sartre wrote her from Berlin. Nazism was on the rise; there were gigantic parades, enthusiastic demonstrations, and flags everywhere. Hitler, in power since January, had had himself invested with special powers and had imposed a series of special measures: dissolution of the Reichstag, censorship of the press, a ban on public meetings. In order to quell resistence to his regime, he used the burning of the Reichstag as a pretext for sending thousands of Communists to concentration camps.

Against this backdrop Sartre wrote the second draft of *Nausea* and his essay "The Transcendence of the Ego." And he fell in love with the wife of one of his colleagues, a woman he had known since his days at the ENS. He called her "the lunar woman" and was attracted to her personality, which included a lack of belief in happiness and a tendency to lock herself away for days on end to smoke and daydream. This was Sartre's first *amour passionnel** since he had known de Beauvoir, and she was worried. Was Marie Ville† another Simone Jollivet? Would Sartre drift from her, carried away by a tumultuous romance in the land of Nietzsche? Jealousy gnawed again at her heart. Their understanding was based on the immediate exchange of ideas and projects, but now someone else would have first crack at the theories Sartre was working out during this particularly creative period.[21]

In February 1934 Simone de Beauvoir made up her mind to see Sartre in Berlin. She obtained a medical certificate declaring that she was suffering from nervous exhaustion and promptly left for two weeks. True to herself, she met the problem head on, unwilling to sink into a morass of doubt, questions, and anxiety.

Sartre's welcome reassured her. He lived in the French graduate student residence at 14 Landhaustrasse, where he could not have women visitors. A postdoctoral student, Henri Brunschwig, gave up his room to accommodate Sartre and de Beauvoir. But he was afraid that his landlady would refuse to accept an unmarried couple, so Sartre and Brunschwig decided that wedding rings were mandatory. When Simone arrived, Sartre took the ring from his pocket and slipped it on her finger. No sooner had she arrived than he took her by the arm and began explaining, "My ego, like the ego of any other person, is by its nature a recognizable phenomenon."[22] She happily joined in their customary dialogue; she had gotten off with a fright. Simone met her rival, liked her well enough, and saw that Marie Ville was no threat to her fundamental understanding with Sartre. Each of their actions and all of their worries always featured what Sartre called "a heady aroma of ideas."[23]

The ostensible danger posed by Marie Ville having passed, de Beauvoir gave herself to discovering Berlin. During the three years she had known Sartre, her passionate curiosity had led them to visit Spain twice, Spanish Morocco, London, and fascist Italy. A companion of Sartre, the journalist Pascal Copeau, who was the son of Jacques Copeau, the director of the avant-garde Vieux-Colombier Theatre and a cofounder of the *Nouvelle Revue française,* took them on a tour of Berlin on Simone's first night there. The Nazis

---

*Sartre's own term for the loves that counted in his life.
†Marie Girard in the memoirs.

had closed down certain pleasure haunts, but those that remained were a far cry from general respectability. Their guide stopped to chat with a tall, elegant transvestite in silk stockings who steered them to "some incredibly debauched nightspots."[24] Certain cabarets were done entirely in black from floor to ceiling, even to the black glasses that contained the drinks served by grotesque dwarfs. Drugs were everywhere. The painter Kisling, who was in Berlin in 1934, tells how customers were served cocaine in matchboxes along with their drinks. Every imaginable sort of trafficking was secretly under way somewhere. Black market currency transactions were commonplace among foreign students.

Most of Sartre's friends were antifascist intellectuals who were convinced of the imminent collapse of Hitlerism. They were not particularly worried about anti-Semitism, which they considered "too egregiously stupid an attitude to merit serious concern."[25]

Colette Audry wrote from Rouen that Simone's absence from the lycée was not going well with the administration. Concerned, Sartre suggested that she cut short her trip to avoid serious trouble. She was far from being a saint in the administration's opinion; why aggravate matters further? De Beauvoir shook with rage at the very idea that some will other than her own might prevail upon her life. She refused to alter her plans. To defy the world was one of her basic rules of conduct, one from which she would never deviate. A touchy and rebellious Simone took her time returning to Rouen—and nothing came of her absence.

At the first hint of fine weather she set off again for Germany. The political situation had degenerated, and her optimism followed suit. Nazism seemed less and less a flash in the pan. Nuremberg was decked with swastika flags, battalions of Brownshirts made the old stones resonate with their cheering. For the first time, de Beauvoir was frightened. The day she and Sartre had planned to go to Vienna, the Austrian chancellor, Dollfuss, was assassinated. At the University, Nazis were throwing Jewish students and teachers out of windows. Terror was the order of the day, and Sartre and de Beauvoir were relieved to be leaving Germany.

They crossed Alsace on foot, taking along hardly more than what they carried in their pockets. Sartre made up songs about the world situation, one of which, "Street of the White Cloaks," would one day be on everyone's lips. Sartre stopped at Mulhouse to visit his uncles; Simone left for Corsica with Pierre Guille and his sisters and discovered the joys of camping. As a child she had dreamed of living in a trailer or a caravan; at the age of twenty-six, living with her house on her back struck her as one of the most delectable forms of liberty. A movement had been launched to prompt young people to take to the open road, and once more de Beauvoir was among the pioneers in the revolution in leisure-time activity. In 1936 the concept of "leisure for all" would become law in France, but in 1934 campers still stirred angry reactions. Everyone, regardless of social standing, found it scandalous that coed groups of young people should flaunt long-established traditions of sex segregation by spending the night under the same roof or in the same tent. Rocks were often thrown at campers, and the mayor of Fontainebleau issued a decree that said much about what was considered right and proper in the 1930s. "For the public good and in the interest of decency," it forbade the wearing of shorts because "sunbathing along the Seine must not serve as an excuse for unsuitable exhibitionism, or in any way encourage the taking of liberties of a nature likely to offend general morality and, often, aesthetic principles."[26]

The greeting *Salut les copains,* which hikers and campers hurled at one another, became a rallying cry, an affirmation that they were entitled to a different way of life. Simone de Beauvoir understood well this desire for fresh air, sunshine, and freedom. The seaside? As a child of eight she had spent several days on the beach in Normandy after an illness. The mountains? When she was nineteen she had made a short visit to Cauterets at an uncle's invitation. She wanted to sample everything nature had to offer. So it was that she dragged Sartre to the snowy slopes to try their hand at skiing. With edgeless wooden skis, no ski lift, no ski instructor, no groomed trails, they were on their own, well ahead of the special snow trains that in 1936 would transport fifty thousand novice skiers. De Beauvoir skied regularly for more than twenty years during the heroic era of the snowplow, the parallel Christiania, and *l'arrêt Briançon,* a maneuver for stopping in which the skier plops down on his backside.

CHARLES DULLIN

*I*n the wake of the evening when she had wandered the streets near the Atelier, lost in the somber depths of depression and jealousy, a solid friendship had sprung up between Simone de Beauvoir and Charles Dullin and Simone Jollivet. While Sartre was in Berlin, Simone frequently visited them at their country home in Férolles, near Crécy-en-Brie. Dullin would meet Simone at the station in an old horse-drawn cart and drive her out to the restored farmhouse with its exposed beam ceilings, rustic open hearth, and choice furnishings, where the other Simone awaited, artistically garbed. Jollivet outdid herself in the kitchen, regaling de Beauvoir—whose love for food amused her friends—with thrush pies, terrines, foie gras, and an array of "the most complicated and delicious dishes."[27] Meanwhile Dullin told stories about the theatre and sang songs that he had performed at the Lapin Agile before the war. The carefree feeling of these days, marked by Dullin's kindness, Jollivet's incredible stories, de Beauvoir's sharp humor, and great outbursts of laughter, enabled them all to forget the direction history was then taking. That summer the little group whiled away many happy hours in the garden, and de Beauvoir was reminded of the song and laughter of bygone days in Meyrignac or at 103 boulevard du Montparnasse. Their friendship would never falter. When Dullin was threatened with the loss of his position as director of the Sarah Bernhardt Theatre in 1945, because of alleged collaboration with the Nazis, he asked her to come to the defense of his adaptation of *King Lear,* which the critics had violently attacked. She would take up the counterattack in *Action,* defending Dullin and Jollivet's direction and accusing the critics of dishonesty: "They speak of nothing but themselves, for them an article is an exercise in style, they try to show themselves as spiritual, scathing, they have no goal other than to demonstrate their qualities as polemicists." She concluded, "It's Shakespeare they don't like."[28]

ANDRÉ MALRAUX'S AFFAIR

*I*n Rouen, de Beauvoir struck up a friendship with Renée Ballon,* writer, journalist, secondary school teacher, and Trotskyite. Ballon knew the whole NRF intelligentsia and had been invited to a prestigious cultural congress, the Decades of Pontigny Abbey, where writers and artists debated a subject each summer. André Chamson and André Malraux† faced off in verbal combat before the stars of Pontigny, Gide, Martin du Gard, and Schlumberger. André Malraux won people over by virtue of "his ardor, his eloquence, his excitability." As a womanizer, he pretended to read women's hands, revealing what he had observed about them in the process.

Renée Ballon was a tall woman "with an elegant body, sparkling eyes,

*Louise Péron in the memoirs. De Beauvoir tells her story in *The Prime of Life,* pp. 167–179.
†J.B. in the memoirs.

and an ugly face."[29] An idyll had its start in the gardens of Pontigny Abbey, where she claimed to have bitten Malraux on the shoulder. Upon learning that he was her first lover, he exclaimed, "My God! They're all virgins around here!" Ballon fell hopelessly in love with the writer and convinced herself that he would divorce his wife in order to marry her. Some time later Malraux, who had just become the father of a baby girl, sent Ballon a letter intended to put an end to her fantasizing; it ended with the words "If we meet in future, let it be by chance rather than by arrangement."[30]

Simone de Beauvoir watched Ballon sink ever more deeply into paranoia. She had a very slender grip on reality, and she read bizarre meanings into the most innocent or unintentional gestures and symbols. She "had plastered her room with reproductions of his favorite pictures" and no longer read any books but his. "She tried to guess what he would say, think, or feel in any given circumstances."[31] In pursuit of her mirage, she badgered him with telegrams, express letters, and phone calls. After an evening at the theatre with the writer André Philip* she got it into her head that Philip suspected her of wanting to seduce him and had reported these suspicions to Malraux. She wrote Malraux yet again to set the record straight. But the letterhead she used was imprinted with a little golden basin and, according to her, Malraux must have thought she was defiantly telling him that she had a lover, for the basin, she explained, has a clearly defined implication as a psychoanalytic symbol. Ballon's reasoning moved more and more in this direction; everything was laden with hidden meaning. In *The Mandarins* de Beauvoir would attribute this interpretive lunacy to Paule when Henri leaves her. She would also make use of a dinner scene that took place when Renée Ballon set a table for twelve guests even though she had sent only two invitations, one to the former director of *Libres Propos,* who had moved to London, and the other to Colette Audry, who found herself alone with Ballon. And there was nothing to eat.

In a moment of lucidity, Renée Ballon, grasping the fact that it was all over with Malraux, wrote to a fifty-year-old Socialist who had showed an interest in her at Pontigny. He took her to spend the night in a hotel near the Gare du Nord. This incident was the basis of Sartre's short story "The Room."

One morning Ballon showed up on Clara Malraux's doorstep, and Madame Malraux managed to convince her to enter a clinic. Cured, she joined the Communist Party and distinguished herself in the Resistance during the war. Renée haunted de Beauvoir's dreams for some time, appearing in her room foaming at the mouth. Simone managed to shut her up in a violin case

---

*"A friend of J.B." in the memoirs.

on the mantel, then awoke with anxiety at the thought that "inside it there was a living thing, all twisted up with hatred and horror."[32]

THE LITTLE RUSSIAN GIRL

*S*imone de Beauvoir had taken special notice of one of her students, Olga Kosakiewicz.* The teachers, who were unanimously agreed that she possessed "personality," called her *la petite Russe.* She was a boarder, and de Beauvoir sometimes offered to take her out on Sundays after having seen her cry during an exam at which she handed in a blank sheet of paper. Olga, with her pale face and long blonde hair, could be quite charming. When she passed her baccalaureate, her parents sent her, against her wishes, to study medicine in Rouen. There she lived in a boardinghouse for young ladies.

There was something original and undefinable about Olga that interested de Beauvoir. Olga's friends were Rumanian and Polish Jews who had been forced out of Central Europe by the Nazis. Many exiles studied and scraped by as best they could in Rouen, where the cost of living was lower than it was in Paris.

Simone listened as Olga told of her childhood. Her father, a member of the imperial nobility, had married a young Frenchwoman. During the revolution they had managed to escape to France, where they felt as though they had somehow been demoted from their rightful station in life. The household retained an atmosphere of nostalgia. Olga and her sister, Wanda, two years her junior, were boarding students at the lycée, aware that they would have been educated at an institute for young ladies of the nobility if the revolution had not stripped them of their rank and thrown them into a milieu that was foreign to them. From their parents they learned to scorn superstition, prejudice, and bourgeois ethics. During vacations they basked in the fabulous atmosphere their parents created in recounting the last years of the Russian court and reading from the works of Pushkin, Turgenev, Chekhov, and the occasional melancholy Russian folk tale. Their mother "introduced them to mythology, and the Old Testament, and the Gospels, and the legends concerning the Buddha, all in such a way that they were enchanted, yet felt no need to believe what they heard."[33]

*Her stage name would be Olga Domenique. In Sartre's letters to de Beauvoir she is Zazoulich. (Vera Zasulich was one of the first Marxist revolutionaries in Russia.)

Olga was prone to the same violent temper tantrums that de Beauvoir had displayed as a child, "and even now she was liable to fits of rage so fierce that they almost knocked her unconscious."[34] De Beauvoir held fury in high esteem. And Olga possessed the virtue that she and Sartre prized above all, genuineness.

With utter confidence, Olga gave herself up to the affection she felt for Simone. Little by little the attachment deepened to the point of virtual bewitchment. De Beauvoir wrote that from the first moment they met she "savored the special charm of her features and gestures, her voice, speech, and special way of talking. . . . There was an impetuous, whole-hogging streak in her that I found most disarming." Olga lived in permanent defiance of all forms of tyranny. She would dance until she fainted. "There was a fresh, childlike quality about her enthusiasms . . . I enjoyed talking to her, because she listened with passionate intensity to all I said."[35] Olga occupied an widening place in de Beauvoir's time and affections. There was something exotic and charming about her, a je ne sais quoi that Sartre would later call, for lack of a subtler term, "class."

Perhaps a nostalgia for lost elegance that time had snuffed out stirred in Simone's unconscious. Georges de Beauvoir had considered himself an aristocrat, fallen from the heights of distinction and refinement to the lower middle class, whose "vulgarity" angered him. Face to face with Olga, a very young Simone reawakened to find her reflection in a living mirror.

TAKING STOCK IN LE HAVRE

*U*pon his return from Germany, Sartre was depressed to find himself still in the role of teacher. He had the feeling that the biography of the great writer had come to a standstill. He and de Beauvoir dwelled long and hard on their progress, or lack of it, and detected a decided slant toward the latter: They were not famous and they had not published anything. The epic novel of the era between the wars and *Melancholia* (the forerunner of *Nausea*) had been abandoned. De Beauvoir made up her mind to write nothing, at least for a while. Awaiting his daughter's success, George de Beauvoir announced brutally, "If she's got something to say, out with it!"

All that winter the two writers sat in the cafés of Le Havre, bemoaning the fact that monotony would henceforth be their lot. Their friends and comrades from the ENS were involved in politics, writing, publishing, creating, producing. Nizan, Aron, Politzer, Lévi-Strauss, Merleau-Ponty, Audry, and Jollivet were making progress. Hélène de Beauvoir knew her way around young painting circles and was preparing to exhibit her work. Fernando Gerassi's work was being shown at the Bonjean Gallery.[36] Everything was in motion around them, but their own fortunes were at lowest ebb. Stranded in the calm eye of the storm, they had no idea what book would rescue them. Sartre was battling the specter of boredom, and de Beauvoir tended to burst into tears as soon as she had a drop too much to drink. He was thirty, she was twenty-seven; both began to worry about old age, foreshadowed by the departure of a few strands of hair from Sartre's head. De Beauvoir tottered between "the joy of being and the horror of being no more."[37]

The teaching profession, which Sartre looked upon as swallowing his freedom, still meant liberation to de Beauvoir. If their destinies ran parallel, the raw material was different: "Sartre was 'his own heaven,' and consequently always doubtful, always surrounded by uncertainties. But for me there was no doubt at all where he was concerned; for me his mere existence justified the world—though there was nothing that could perform the same service for him."[38] The exercises in psychological analysis that had occupied so many of their hours no longer interested either of them.

> We were tired of our precise intellectual examinations of conscience, tired of the virtuous and orderly lives we were leading, tired of what we called "the construct." Because we had "constructed" our relationship on the basis of total sincerity, total mutual devotion, and we were sacrificing our moods and any possible inkling of trouble to this permanent and "directed" love that we had constructed. At the heart of the matter, what we were nostalgic for was a disorderly life, one where we'd let ourselves go in imperious turmoil and agitation.[39]

Sartre gets to the root of the problem a little further on: "We needed outrageousness in order to counteract having been moderate for so long. The whole thing culminated in that episode of black humor which turned into near madness around the month of March—and ended up with my encounter with O., which was precisely what we desired and which we made a point of letting her know."[40]

Despite their nearly debilitating boredom, Sartre and de Beauvoir continued to work. De Beauvoir read Edmund Husserl in the original German. Her trips to Spain, Italy, and Germany had made her aware of gaps in her knowledge of history. In her last novel she had stumbled over the passages requiring descriptions of military situations and settings; now she embarked on the vast project of catching up. Sartre worked on *The Psychology of the Imagination,* formulating his ideas on the conscious mind and its capacity for annihilation.

Out of curiosity, Sartre asked one of his former classmates who practiced medicine to give him an injection of mescaline. He wanted to see what a hallucination was. Because Sartre was suffering from near exhaustion at the time, the mescaline affected him with unexpected ferocity: He had disconcerting visions of rabid, jaw-gnashing buildings and vicious crustaceans, visions he would later give to a character in his play *The Condemned of Altona.* One day a lobster pursued him for hours through the streets of Venice. De Beauvoir looked upon this pseudolunacy as an evasion, but Sartre's depression was real enough. As soon as he was alone, his anxieties mounted a full-scale attack. De Beauvoir invited over some students he had coached for the baccalaureate to distract him. Among them, Jacques-Laurent Bost and Lionel de Roulet, who were preparing for a *licence* in philosophy, had become friends. They, with Olga Kosakiewicz, were the kernel of what Sartre and de Beauvoir called the Family, a group of young people who were dear to them. Most had been their students at one lycée or another, and there had been sentimental and sexual involvement among members of the Family. Sartre and de Beauvoir felt responsible for their careers and their financial wellbeing; they paid for their vacations, their doctor bills, and their taxes. In return, the Family members would defend Sartre and de Beauvoir's work and their political positions.

Jacques-Laurent Bost, whom Sartre nicknamed his disciple, was the brother of Pierre Bost, the famous novelist and screenwriter who worked as a reader for Gallimard. He was descended from a family of Protestant pastors; his grandfather, Pastor Jean Bost, had founded charitable organizations to see to the needs of abandoned young girls, rest and retirement homes for the crippled and the elderly, facilities for epilectics, and Bethesda, a center for retarded and disabled young girls. He had published numerous volumes of Protestant thought, including the works of Laforce. Jacques-Laurent Bost, nineteen, boasted a radiant smile, "a most princely ease of bearing," and a great deal of good humor and spontaniety.[41] He would be the inspiration for Gerbert in *She Came to Stay* and for Boris in Sartre's *The Age of Reason.* Jacques-Laurent made friends and gathered admirers wherever he went. They called him Little Bost to distinguish him from his older brother, in whose footsteps he followed. Novelist, journalist, and screenwriter by turn, he worked until recently on the staff of *Les Temps modernes.*

Lionel de Roulet, a Swiss Protestant, was an excellent skier who had a lively, fun-loving outlook on life. He had founded a pseudopolitical party, the Mérovingiens, which claimed the French throne for the descendants of Chilpéric. No doubt he had heard of a play by Hervé that had been a big hit before the war, in which Marcelle Lender (the actress so often painted by Toulouse-Lautrec) sang:

Il est dix heures, c'est l'instant	'Tis 10 o'clock as time is spent
C'est l'heure où Chilpéric se lève	The hour when Chilpéric arises
Espérons qu'il a fait un rêve	Let's hope his dreams held good surprises
Qui le rende heureux et content.	To make him happy and content.

Lionel de Roulet followed a career in the cultural services and was later with the Council of Europe. He would marry Hélène de Beauvoir during the war.

And then there was Olga, a Slav to the very ends of her long blonde hair. Extreme, generous, independent, her grace and impetuosity acted on Sartre like a spell. He fell madly in love with *la petite Russe.*

When Olga was near, the roving crustaceans and their friends disappeared. Sartre, doing his utmost to please her, regained his customary lightheartedness. Olga became the antidote to his craziness, a living panacea. In one of the notebooks he kept from 1939 to 1940, he wrote, "I was at an all-time low at the time of my madness and of my passion for O.: two years. From March 1935 to March 1937."[42]

Olga failed the medical school entrance exam. Her parents, who wanted her to continue her study of medicine, decided she would take the year over as a boarder in Caen—a prospect that saddened Sartre and de Beauvoir. Sartre had no intention of losing Olga, de Beauvoir was afraid of seeing Sartre fall back into his neurosis, and Olga begged Simone to help her out of the unpalatable situation. To avoid the dreaded separation, they conceived the idea of convincing Olga's parents that their daughter, who had no particular taste for science, should undertake a *licence* in philosophy, for which de Beauvoir would be only too happy to serve as advisor and mentor.

De Beauvoir and Sartre had created their own little world, peopled with imaginary characters, and in a sense Olga would be their daughter. They had invented Little Noodle, an exquisitely handsome individual entirely devoid of inner life. They spoke of the tiny shoes made by the Lepricorne, who defeated doubt and unhappiness by cranking out footwear. They spoke of their own work in the same terms. There was Baladin, the eternal wanderer, whom they identified with Sartre. They eagerly renamed all their friends to put a little distance between them and daily life. De Beauvoir remained the Castor, Maheu and his wife the Lama and the Lamate. The Mops and the Bel-Eute denoted Madame Morel. Madame de Listomère was the Burma jewelry salesgirl, a friend of the Tapir. Olga was Iaròslaw, Merleau-Ponty was the Pont-aux-Merles, and so on.

A difficult or unpleasant situation was transformed into a psychodrama. Once removed from reality, even the most dreadful situation took on the qualities of farce. They entertained themselves with these little comedies in which they had the pleasure of watching themselves restructure reality according to their fantasy. Their quasi adoption of Olga was another story they told themselves.

De Beauvoir asked to meet Olga's parents, and they invited her to dinner. The strategy was laid, the actors were in place, and Simone had Olga's parents under her spell. Her manners, her air of distinction, the very way she spoke —everything about her carried the mark of rare quality. Olga's parents were in the presence of a fellow aristocrat. When she raised the idea of being entirely responsible for Olga's studies in Rouen, her hosts were enchanted. They thought their daughter spent entirely too much time with refugees and was probably spending more time in smoke-filled cafés than in the classroom. If her philosophy teacher wanted to take charge, that was an opportunity indeed. After all, if things had not taken their unfortunate course in Russia, Olga would have had governesses, tutors, and private instruction, so the proposed arrangement struck them as normal and fitting. It was settled.

Delighted, Sartre left with his parents on a Norwegian cruise, and de Beauvoir went backpacking alone through the Ardèche and the Cévennes for three weeks. Equipped with a thick sweater, a blanket, an alarm clock, a travel guide, and an assortment of Michelin maps, she left the beaten path and slept in haylofts. Each morning she bought a loaf of bread, filled her canteen with wine, and set off across the pastures. Sometimes, wrapped in her blanket in the dark, the solitude and immensity of the night would unsettle her, occasionally to the point of panic. At dawn, light-headed from insomnia, she would strike off again into the sun. She sensed in her blood, her lungs, and her muscles the aromas, the light, the breezes, the chirping of cicadas. She recognized the brewing of a storm in the rustling of leaves, and she liked to be lost in tempests. Nature was a privileged arena for exorcising her demons.

Sartre, who was a fine walker when he wanted to be, liked the countryside only in small doses and providing the hike promised a château, a museum, or some man-made monument as destination. De Beauvoir convinced him to join her that summer, and she dragged him from the Haute-Loire to Cévennes.[43] They lived in the open fields, eating hard-boiled eggs and sausage, singing and philosophizing along the way. The great outdoors succeeded in healing Sartre's frayed nerves. He had had enough of being mad, announced that he no longer was, and sent the lobsters packing.

THE PETIT-MOUTON HOTEL

Olga was in Rouen. Sartre and de Beauvoir had organized their protégée's course of study to the last detail. From the very first assignment —an essay that Olga was unable to begin, let alone complete—it became clear that the enterprise was destined to fail. Without official classes and classmates, the arrangement was too much like a vacation.

Sartre soon gave up on Olga's philosophy lessons, and de Beauvoir followed suit not long after. Olga had become "a most agreeable companion." She did not study a thing; she merely led a life of freedom, caprice, and fantasy, all with considerable enthusiasm. She read a great deal, engaged Sartre and de Beauvoir in discussion, went to cafés and brasseries. De Beauvoir taught her to play chess. While studying the moves, they drank inordinate amounts of cherry brandy, "a tipple to which we were vastly attracted."[44] Olga and Simone also played poker dice, a game made popular by American soldiers after World War I. They went to the theatre and the movies, listened to records, read, and pulled pranks. Such was life for this carefree charge under the supervision of her two mentors.

De Beauvoir had abandoned her room by the train station and taken another in the old quarter at the Petit-Mouton Hotel, a Norman-style building with exposed wooden beams and small leaded windows. Hidden away at the end of an alley, this modest hotel offered rooms by the hour or by the month, the two categories of accommodation symbolically separated by the central staircase. The Petit-Mouton Hotel became the gang's headquarters. Olga had a room there; Zuorro, assigned to the lycée in Rouen, moved into the bordello wing; Sartre, Poupette, Gégé, Simone Jollivet, Little Bost, Lionel de Roulet, and Pierre Guille all stayed there at one time or another. From her bed at night de Beauvoir could make out the rustling and scampering of mice as they dragged from the wastebasket the greasy paper in which cold-cuts had been wrapped. Occasionally she was awakened by tiny paws on her face. She loved "the somewhat coarsely cheerful patterns of my bedspread, wallpaper, and curtains." The room next door was occupied by a military officer who beat his wife nightly as a prelude to making love to her, bringing to mind the most pious of Simone's aunts, who had her husband whip her vigorously every evening. Come nightfall, the hotel corridors "echoed to amorous sighing."[45]

They all lived it up at the Petit-Mouton. Zuorro got a kick out of pretending to court the *patronne,* a madam with a pronounced fondness for pink
cotton stockings. Zuorro still intended to give up teaching for a career with
the Paris Opera. High-spirited and carefree, he attached no importance whatever to his reputation, and everything turned to adventure in his company.
Zuorro and Olga did the town together, dancing along the sidewalks, singing
at the top of their lungs. Zuorro specialized in thinking up shocking pranks
that were often as elaborate as they were improper. One night in a bar he
decided to fleece a client who could not keep his eyes off Olga. Zuorro
suggested to the man that he spend the night with Olga, and the three of them
proceeded to the Petit-Mouton, where they drank the better part of a bottle
of scotch. Rather, the visitor did; intending to remain clear-headed, Zuorro
and Olga discreetly poured their drinks out on the bed. But the victim was
not so easily put off, and he asked to get down to the real purpose of his visit.
Zuorro finally got rid of him by breaking down in tears and explaining that
he had given up the idea of selling his little sister.

Zuorro detested one of his colleagues, Paul Guth, who wanted to become
a writer.* The Petit-Mouton gang planned a nasty hoax. Zuorro told his
victim that he was well connected with Pierre Bost, who would soon be
coming to Rouen, and suggested that he arrange for the budding and the
established authors to meet, for which purpose he acquired a copy of the
novel Guth had just completed. On the day of the meeting, each of the
accomplices had a role to play. De Beauvoir was Bost's assistant, and she
waited in the café next door to the Petit-Mouton. Olga, seated at the bar, was
a prostitute. Zuorro arrived with the future author, introduced him to de
Beauvoir with utter seriousness, and let him outline his ideas for his next
book. Finally Sartre, who could be none other than Bost, showed up with the
manuscript under his arm. Sartre proceeded to rip the writing to shreds,
spouting odd and flamboyant criticisms, then took off, leaving the young
author shattered. A few days later Guth wrote Pierre Bost at Gallimard,
demanding further explanation of his criticism. Bost's reply, furious that
someone had used his name in such a way, made it obvious that it had all
been a gag. Ten years later, the man behind the episode remembered it clearly
and repaid Sartre and de Beauvoir's participation in a scathing article about
them for *Minerve,* published at the height of existentialist fever in Saint-
Germain-des-Prés.

When Simone Jollivet arrived at the Petit-Mouton, everyone went to

---

*Guth would become one of France's best-known authors (and "one of the worst," de
Beauvoir said).

great lengths to keep her entertained. At the seedy and decrepit Royal dance hall she ordered champagne and, sweeping Olga along, led her in performing a stylish paso doble, "her jewelry clanking, her tresses flying." Everyone stopped what they were doing to watch. Jollivet affirmed that Olga, like she, belonged to the race of dark angels and "declared her to be her goddaughter before Lucifer." At her suggestion, Olga would take drama courses with Dullin.

Hélène de Beauvoir and her friend Gégé checked into the notorious hotel, and Hélène painted Olga's portrait. In their rooms the gang frolicked and carried on, haunted by the strange feeling that youth was coming to an end and that tomorrow would require adult behavior. In the meantime, Gégé performed a belly dance, Bost lit matches with his toes, and Zuorro sang duets with Sartre, who wore women's clothing and a long blonde wig.

The life that de Beauvoir was leading with Olga in Rouen and her frequent trips to Le Havre were depleting her resources. When the end of the month came and she was short of cash, she took the gold trinkets her grandmother had given her to the pawnshop.[46] When that was not enough, Colette Audry generously lent her her phonograph, which promptly joined the jewels. At the beginning of the month Simone would redeem everything, and the routine would begin again.

DISTRACTIONS OF THE HEART AND MIND

*D*e Beauvoir and Sartre were no longer Olga's teachers; "we had become a trio," Simone wrote in *The Prime of Life*.[47]

This story, one that for two years would be at the center of their lives and their discussions, one that sparked in Sartre the temptation to abandon literature, one that caused de Beauvoir to doubt herself as well as Sartre's love for her, was a contest of two wills. As lovers, friends, and allies they confronted each other in order to measure their power over Olga. They idealized the stakes, imbuing Olga with the mythical purity of youth. In the heartfelt violence of Olga's likes and dislikes and her disdain for order and the bourgeoisie, they saw their own fantasies and anarchist tendencies made flesh.

They were caught in a trap, a trap that had long attracted them. When Sartre was serving in the military in 1929–1930, that is, shortly after the start of their liaison, one night in a bar in Montparnasse they had met "a very young girl, charming, half-drunk, and rather lost. We invited her to have a drink. . . . When we left her we amused ourselves by talking about how we'd adopt her."[48] De Beauvoir was only twenty-one and Sartre twenty-four when this singular temptation to incorporate a young girl into their lives first excited their imaginations. The idea of introducing a third party into a duo —so as to force each participant to discover himself in the scrutiny of the Other—was a theme that fascinated de Beauvoir and Sartre, one that would appear in *She Came to Stay* and *No Exit.* Sartre and de Beauvoir had devoted long hours to analyzing strange news items that intrigued them. One night a young couple, married for barely three months, took home with them another couple they had met in a nightclub. After a nightlong orgy, the strangers left and the young couple committed suicide. Sartre and de Beauvoir gave considerable thought to the implications of this act of despair, multiple couplings, the meaning of fidelity, sexual attraction, and the mysterious taboos that were powerful enough to push to suicide two human beings who were free to assume the consequences of their actions.

In Rouen, "enchanters and enchanted at once," their love went round in circles, turning first in one direction, then the other.[49] Olga called the shots, favoring de Beauvoir one day and Sartre the next. "We thought that human relationships remained perpetually to be made up as you go along." They organized their interaction on the basis of a perfect trio, without preferences, always maintaining an even distribution of feelings. They poured the full weight of their emotions, their pleasures, their imaginations into this elaborate construct of friendship and romance. They would keep this order of things until they died. They would alternate tête-à-têtes and plenary sessions with their successive friends. As their number grew, this arrangement came to be a true etiquette, a sort of court ceremonial with hours and days assigned to each member of the clan. Since some members of the Family adopted their organizational system, it made for very complex relationships and schedules.[50]

In the beginning this challenge to the conventions, this love reflected in three mirrors that should have gone on duplicating feelings, passions, and emotions down an infinite corridor, appeared to be a success that defied all psychology, every analysis of the workings of the human heart, and every warning issued by the mind and the spirit. In the beginning it was a somewhat diabolical arrangement that brought considerable joy to its participants. "Rouen began to glisten, shimmer, sparkle."[51] At a tea ceremony in Olga's little room at the Petit-Mouton they made up comedies, stories, and songs. Once again life became a merry escapade. In the spring they set out each afternoon for a deserted café buried deep in the forest. While Sartre and Olga chatted there, Simone, stimulated by a certain intellectual and emotional masochism, sat a little way off in a sunny corner, writing *When Things of the Spirit Come First.*

At vacation time the trio headed straight for Paris to take advantage of long walks through the city streets, long conversations on café terraces, and nights in the bars. Olga's parents, who had begun to worry, were campaigning for their daughter's return. She was supposed to be resolved to going home, and she thought she would never return to Rouen. "For two hours, seated on a banquette at the Dôme, we all three agonized in silence." Yet she did return; Sartre and de Beauvoir were both on the station platform to meet her when her train pulled into Rouen.

The trio began to worry their friends. Olga was a minor; they were playing with fire. The situation gradually became more and more trying. "Sartre never stopped halfway in any enterprise; and having sketched the beginnings of a friendship with Olga, he must needs bring it to a climax." On the other hand, de Beauvoir wrote, "Sartre, it was true, wanted to monopolize her, but in a purely sentimental fashion. . . . No one should mean as much to Olga as he did."[52]

De Beauvoir had not wanted all the complexities of this arrangement. "The edifice as such was Sartre's work. . . . For my own part, though I vainly tried to achieve satisfaction from the relationship, I never felt at ease with it."[53]

For Sartre the problem was simple: He was passionately in love with Olga. But this time it was not a Marie Girard, encountered far away in Berlin. This time it was a young friend of de Beauvoir whom Simone liked very much. For Sartre, the boredom of being a schoolteacher vanished as soon as he fell in love. "As for O., my passion for her burned my humdrum impurities like the flame of a Bunsen burner. I became scrawny like a cuckoo; farewell my creature comforts. And then we underwent, the Castor and I, the vertigo of this nude and instantaneous conscience which seemed only to feel with violence and purity."[54]

For de Beauvoir the situation was something else entirely. "It was too essential for me to agree with Sartre on everything to see Olga through any eyes but his." And yet, "when I tried to see her through Sartre's eyes, I felt I was playing my own emotions false." Sartre was no longer the same. Swept away by Olga, he would speculate unto infinity about the meaning of a gesture, a word, some frown or pout. He flew into fits of rage and bickered with de Beauvoir, who for the first time was seeing him in the grip of passion. He was experiencing worries, joys, and furies that he did not know with her, and she began to ask herself whether their love was founded on a lie. She had lost much in the trio, and when she considered the future she was afraid of losing even more. "Whenever I thought of the trio as a long-term project, stretching ahead for years, I was frankly terrified."[55]

The understanding with Sartre on which de Beauvoir had based her entire future took on unforeseen tones by virtue of the trio's darker moments. "I told myself it was wrong to bracket myself and another in that equivocal and all-too-handy word 'we.' There were some experiences that each individual lived through alone. . . . When I said 'We are one person,' I was dodging the issue."[56]

She had approached the trio as she had approached everything up to then, with the boldness of a woman who wanted to be the equal of the man she had chosen. She realized with clarity that *la petite Russe* had taken up such a large place in Sartre's life that he "began to doubt salvation through literature."[57] There was one more panel to this triptych to consider: Olga cared more for de Beauvoir than she did for Sartre. Worried about the possibility of losing Simone, Olga turned against Sartre, then turned against de Beauvoir, naïvely hoping that by paying increased attention to Sartre she would arouse de Beauvoir's jealousy and thereby capture even more of Simone's attention. Then she became terrified that her strategy might succeed. They were moving in circles and suffocating together. The psychology of an *amour à trois* had become a torment; they were living a strange love-hate relationship that offered no means of escape. "Both Sartre and Olga in turn would pour out their complaints to me and solicit my alliance." Although Simone often took Olga's side, this was, according to her, only for the sake of appearances; the most important thing was to preserve the integrity of her alliance with Sartre. She said flatly that Olga had lost at the outset. "Her role was . . . that of a child up against an adult couple."[58]

All things considered, the trio was an impossibility. Sartre did not find the pleasure he had anticipated in this complicated affair. Since Olga was being shared between Sartre and de Beauvoir, and had to divide her feelings between the two of them in turn, she constantly changed her mind, and this caused Sartre to "fly into a rage."[59] De Beauvoir grew impatient with being subjected to accounts and speculations she did not wish to hear.[60] She felt dispossessed yet refused to admit it.

La petite Russe, unbalanced by the disastrous train of events, resorted one day to a remarkable symbolic gesture. She slowly and deliberately touched a lighted cigarette to her own hand, "pressing it into the flesh with positively maniacal concentration," as though some magic purification rite was called for in her state of confusion.[61] She was the victim of a situation in which she had been cast in the role of a contingent being.

The arrangement was a violent and painful experience for de Beauvoir. Torn between her tender feelings for Olga and her immutable love for Sartre, she saw herself trapped in an infernal circle, bewitched to the extent that she was able to rid herself of the lingering spell only by transposing the story into *She Came to Stay* and killing off Olga in the last chapter. The novel's working title was *Self-Defense*.

In 1985 we asked Simone de Beauvoir if the trio had been an agonizing experience. She replied, "There were some very, very good times to the extent that each of us gave a great deal. It wouldn't have lasted as long as it did if Sartre and Olga or Olga and I hadn't spent some very happy times together. But it wasn't exactly agonizing, just a bit complicated. There were bad moments for everybody."

1936: PARIS

*I*n Rouen the gang was beginning to smell of heresy. Luckily for them, de Beauvoir and Zuorro had just been assigned to Paris. In order to stay within reach of the group, Sartre turned down a promotion in far-off Lyon and accepted a post in Laon.

For three years Simone de Beauvoir would teach at the Lycée Molière in Passy, a posting that amounted to a promotion. In five years she had passed through two of France's great lycées; her spell in purgatory had been brief. At the Lycée Molière, in one of the city's more bourgeois quarters, de Beauvoir behaved just as she had in Marseille and Rouen, ignoring those of her colleagues who did not share her anarchism. Her students, accustomed to the discreet garb of tradition-minded teachers, were surprised to see this twenty-eight-year-old woman standing before them, the very picture of elegance. One of her former students recalls the scene.

> That autumn day, Simone de Beauvoir strode rapidly through the door and stepped up on the rostrum. She was wearing a lilac silk blouse, a black skirt with sunray pleats, silk stockings, and high-heeled shoes. Her chestnut-colored hair, held in place by two combs, crowned her head in the very latest style. She had a fresh, clear complexion like a child's and her blue eyes sparkled. What's more, she was very made-up: a cherry mouth, the eyes outlined in blue, the lashes blackened, and the eyebrows penciled over.[62]

There was considerable talk about her at school. They whispered that she had a liaison with a teacher who displayed his nonconformity by giving classes without wearing a coat and tie (he wore a lumber jacket and a turtleneck sweater!). They said she wrote and categorically refused to do house-cleaning and cooking. She socialized with well-known people. It was common knowledge that she disliked teaching and did not plan to make it her career.

In class she lectured very rapidly without using notes. She reeled off the names of philosophers and philosophy terms so quickly that it was difficult to follow her. She jumped back and forth in the textbook or dispensed with it entirely, and her students had a rough time trying to understand when she spoke of Husserl and phenomenology. They tried their hardest to assimilate the most surprising ideas: Your conscience is conscious of something; you are all free; you are responsible for your choice and for your life. As she spoke her gaze was drawn constantly to the trees beyond the window. She ran her fingers over her face, toyed with the strap of her purse, and talked without stopping to take a breath. "We weren't prepared for the shock of her first class. Mademoiselle de Beauvoir dressed with audacity and imagination; however, for her duties at the Lycée Molière, she looked too silky and made-up." This inappropriate appearance served to counterbalance "the dazzling virtuosity of her mind, which intimidated us so."[63] At the end of several weeks, those students who were not completely out of their depth were fanatical admirers. De Beauvoir, as helpful as she was dazzling, gladly explained the more difficult concepts and suggested additional reading to those who asked. Her students discovered contemporary literature along with American and English authors. Every Thursday she brought to class a copy of *Marie-Claire* and placed the brand new magazine for women beside her purse.[64]

She rarely dallied in the teachers' lounge, for she had few friends there. She amazed, she disturbed. Her beige velvet jacket was too sporty, too modern. Her bursts of laughter were too spontaneous. She was constantly seen in cafés, correcting students' papers that she often returned splattered with coffee stains. Happy to be alive, avid, secretive, well informed about the latest trends, she disconcerted her colleagues. For her, happiness was absolutely everywhere, and she was determined to look for it, to find it, and to keep it. Others found her strength of character disturbing.

The long years of fanatical work to free herself of her family, to learn "what it meant to be me," had paid off. As a civil servant she would never be cold, never go hungry, never have to worry about tomorrow. She had succeeded in preserving her fierce independence without having to abdicate her intellectual autonomy, as she had feared. Sartre, impressed by the rapidity with which de Beauvoir grasped Hegel and Heidegger and the ease with which she synthesized the information, urged her to abandon literature in order to devote herself entirely to philosophy. After all, had she not advised Sartre to give up philosophy in favor of literature?

The years from 1936 to 1939 marked the end of their apprenticeship. The threat of war never stopped growing, but de Beauvoir would say, "It was still my individual relationships with people that counted for me, and I fiercely wanted happiness."

The principal component of this happiness was Paris itself. Simone took a room at the Royal-Bretagne Hotel in the rue de la Gaîté, near the Bobino music hall and the Montparnasse Theatre. De Beauvoir liked the music hall with its saucy songs and its audiences made up mostly of students, workers, craftsmen, and small shopkeepers from surrounding quarters, who screamed, whistled, and shouted, their emotions ranging from laughter to tears, quick to react with anger or jeers. In bygone days spectators had been served drinks during the show, and the seats were still equipped with little trays incorporated into the armrests. It was forbidden to toss anything onto the stage, yet all sorts of projectiles managed to land there anyway. All the big-name music-hall entertainers—Mayol, Chevalier, Mistinguett, Damia, Marie Dubas, Edith Piaf—got their start at the Bobino, where de Beauvoir, alone or with Sartre, went to laugh and have fun.

Since 1930 Gaston Baty had been putting on avant-garde plays at the Montparnasse Theatre, among them *Maya, Le Simoun,* an adaptation of *Madame Bovary,* and a Jansenist-inspired *Phèdre.* De Beauvoir attended all the shows produced by the Cartel.* Thanks to her friendship with Charles Dullin and Simone Jollivet, she attended all the final dress rehearsals and sometimes the working rehearsals as well. She was as sensitive to, and as liable to be carried away by, the magic of the stage as she had been as a child of six.

De Beauvoir resumed her old habits of Montparnasse days. She wrote seated in a booth at the Dôme. She renewed an active friendship with Poupette, and they saw one another almost daily. Hélène de Beauvoir's show at the Bonjean Gallery had been a success, enabling her to rent a large, run-down artist's studio near the wine market. With her sister, Simone socialized with avant-garde painters, particularly a student of Jacques-Emile Blanche, Francis Grüber, who influenced Bernard Buffet.

Marc Zuorro had moved into a hotel in the rue Delambre. He worked on his singing and taught at the Lycée Louis-le-Grand. Bost was taking courses and writing short stories. Olga, despite her parents' refusal to let her go, had hopped a train and joined de Beauvoir at the Royal-Bretagne. To earn

---

*The Cartel was a group of four avant-garde directors, Charles Dullin, Georges Pitoëff, Gaston Baty, and Louis Jouvet.

a little money, she worked as a waitress in "a sort of combined cafeteria, bookshop, and record store" on the boulevard Saint-Michel.[65] When Sartre came in from Laon, the trio fell back into its old patterns with the same complexities and the same attendant anguish. The vicious cycle of jealousies, rivalries, and quarrels began all over again.

Olga, idle and at loose ends, not at all certain what to do about a future in which she believed less and less, took to drinking Pernod to banish her anxiety. De Beauvoir could not bear to see Olga so easily defeated and took her to the theatre, movies, and concerts and encouraged her to read and to study acting with Dullin, whose pupils then included Célia Bertin, Madeleine Robinson, Jacques Dufilho, Sylvia Bataille, Lucienne Salacrou, Agnès Capri, Olga Barbezat, and Mouloudji. Jean-Louis Barrault taught them mime. De Beauvoir drilled Olga on the scenes she had to perform in class. In Mérimée's *L'Occasion* Olga was the very picture of innocence, blonde as one can be only in an English watercolor, pale as women are only in the poems of Musset. Supple and frail, she embodied weakness and abandonment, as though she had scarcely left childhood. "Do something! Act alive! React!" Dullin growled, terrifying her with a glance—at which Olga burst into tears and ran off.[66]

Zuorro was still wracked with passionate, stormy feelings for Little Bost, which the latter seemed to enjoy stirring up. Zuorro was secretly making plans for their future together, but his hopes were ended one day when, looking through the keyhole of his own hotel room, he saw Bost and Olga locked in an embrace. He had lent them his room so that they could listen to his record collection; arriving home early, he wondered what could account for the silence behind the door, and he saw what it was.

Lightning had struck the little clan. Olga had been Sartre's treasured image of the inaccessible young girl, and he bemoaned the end of his dream. Moreover, Gallimard had just turned down the manuscript of *Melancholia*. Zuorro, severely depressed, roamed Montparnasse with a revolver in his pocket. They were both so glum that de Beauvoir took them to Chamonix for a ski vacation. To prevent Sartre and Zuorro from moping away the nights quibbling and splitting hairs, she rented an attic loft with three beds. At bedtime Zuorro began sobbing, describing aloud his obsession with Bost, evoking his "white scarf, the purity of his smile, his youth and charm and unconscious cruelty."[67]

Back in Paris their lives became even more complicated. Zuorro made scene after scene over Bost, and Olga was morose because her love for Bost was not resolving her problems. Olga's younger sister, Wanda, had come for a visit and Sartre, the eternal seducer, disappointed at his failure with one member of the family, tried his luck with the new arrival and succeeded. A new passion had taken hold of him and would maintain its grip for some time.

De Beauvoir listened to everyone's complaints and confidences, spending long evenings first with one and then another, getting up early in order to be at work by eight-thirty, all the while relentlessly determined to keep on writing. She was so bone tired that she often fell asleep without warning on the métro or in a café near the Gare du Nord where she waited for Sartre on his regular visits from Laon. One night at the Select she developed a bad chill. Having never really been ill, she assumed it was the onset of a cold or flu; in fact it was a congestion of the lungs. Madame Morel arranged for an ambulance to take her to a clinic in Saint-Cloud, and she was carried from her room on a stretcher. "I learned afterward that when I was admitted one of my lungs resembled a chunk of liver, and the other was beginning to go the same way."[68]

When she was released from the hospital, Sartre got her a room in the more comfortable hotel where Zuorro lived in the rue Delambre. At noon he would bring her the plat du jour from the Coupole, taking small steps so as not to spill anything. Zuorro and Bost, more or less reconciled, accompanied Simone on her first outing to the Luxembourg Gardens, propping her up every step of the way. Madame de Beauvoir, Poupette, Gégé, Madame Morel, Olga, Bost, and Simone Jollivet had taken turns attending at her bedside. The Family had closed ranks to handle the emergency; no member would let another down in time of need.

As soon as she was strong enough, de Beauvoir shouldered her knapsack and set out on a hike through the south of France. For three weeks of silence and solitude, nature itself served once again as her refuge, walking as her therapy. She became one with stone, sunlight, and passing clouds, and in this cathartic communion she regained touch with her true self.

In the letters he sent to his "dear Castor," Sartre described the elaborate games he and Bost had gotten up to together. They had solemnly sworn, "with a pact and clasped hands," to spend eight days disguised as stinking tramps with no resources other than begging, singing in the streets, stealing, and forcing open the doors to railroad boxcars. Their companions would be vagabonds, they would live in fear of being found out by the police. " 'This will be unspeakably vile,' Bost said, in seventh heaven. 'There will be little old men who want to fondle us.' "[69] On the eighth day they would take Simone to dinner at Pierre's and tell her everything.

This imaginary theatre always amused them, and they willingly involved their friends. The games revealed their fantasies and would provided material for the two writers' work. One day they would play "bartender throwing out a drunk" with Bost as the bartender and Sartre as the drunk; another time Olga and Bost would play "who can insult the other the most." Bost, who wrote short stories, shared his most outlandish comic reveries with Sartre. "With loving care he has put the finishing touches to the following fiction: He has twenty-seven women. He's taken Tania* from me and even you, good Castor—incidentally he treats you quite honorably. He also has Poupette and l'Oranaise de Roulet, Gégé, etc. He buys the Theatre Hotel from the owners and sets up his women there, one to a room. You alone have the right to leave to exchange your books at Adrienne Monnier's."[70]

While de Beauvoir was scrambling up and down Provençal hillsides, recovering her health, Sartre kept her up to date on his relationship with Wanda, Olga's efforts to write a short story, and Poupette's affair with Jean Giraudoux, who, in love with her but fearing indiscretions, behaved cavalierly like a lover-in-a-hurry. Sartre scolded de Beauvoir for taking hikes longer than twelve miles. "That's not what you should be doing, you crazy Castor."[71] He prescribed three miles in the morning and three in the afternoon.

She returned to Paris cured. *Melancholia* was now retitled *Nausea* and was dedicated "To the Castor." Life picked up again, lively, lighthearted, and rich with hope and expectation.

---

*Wanda, Olga's sister.

6

Contingent Loves

"At once, as soon as we met, you told me that you were polygamous and that you had no intention of confining yourself to a single woman, a single affair: this was understood. . . ."

Conversations with Jean-Paul Sartre

ALL ABOUT LOVE

"The word *love* has by no means the same meaning for both sexes, and this is one cause of the serious misunderstandings that divide them. Byron well said, 'Man's love is of man's life a thing apart, 'tis woman's whole existence.' "[1]

De Beauvoir had accepted immediately the "contingent loves" clause in the pact Sartre proposed because she had every intention of experiencing love as a free individual. "The individual who is a subject, who is himself, . . . endeavors to extend his grasp on the world. . . . For woman, to love is to relinquish everything for the benefit of a master."[2] There was no question of relinquishing anything for Sartre's benefit.

The rule of transparency was also going to enable this man and this woman to understand, as accurately as possible, exactly what life and love entailed for the opposite sex. If, since time immemorial, male writers have drawn upon the confidences of their female companions for details of the feminine view of love, women writers, constrained by prevailing notions of what is and is not suitable for public discussion, compounded by prudishness and ignorance, were never able to describe love from the man's point of view.

For some time women's literature remained limited to the realm of sentiment. To speak without reticence of physical love, one had to be a man—or invent the clause not of frankness or sincerity but of transparency, a concept that extends so far and encompasses so many possibilities that it comes to a halt only where knowledge of the world and of oneself ends. The Greeks discovered the character of Tiresias, the seer who prophesied the misfortunes that would befall Oedipus and his family. The gods had given Tiresias a special privilege: In order to understand both halves of humanity, he had been in turn a man and a woman, and thus he was uniquely qualified to speak about what love is to each sex. For Sartre and de Beauvoir, the practice of transparency was as close as they could hope to come to the gift the gods had bestowed upon Tiresias.

Sartre had told a journalist: "Simone de Beauvoir and I never discussed her secondary loves. I considered them to be entirely secondary, without preoccupying myself with what might well have gone on in these affairs."[3]

De Beauvoir was equally straightforward in her remarks about Sartre's *amours.* "I accepted the fact without difficulty; I knew to what extent Sartre was obstinate about the project that governed his entire existence: to know the world and to express it. I was so certain of being intimately linked to this central concern of his, that no episode in his life could frustrate me."[4]

Nevertheless she recognized the dangers inherent in exercising transparency in the context of one's love life: "There is a form of loyalty which I've often observed and which is nothing more than flagrant hypocrisy; restricted to the domain of sexuality, its aim is not to create an intimate understanding between the man and woman but to furnish one of the two—most often the man—with a tranquil alibi: He deludes himself with the illusion that by confessing his infidelities he atones for them when in fact he inflicts a double violence upon his partner."[5]

Sartre and de Beauvoir both acknowledged the power of the transparency. "To have a radical understanding with someone is, in any case, a great privilege. In my eyes it is literally priceless," de Beauvoir wrote in *The Prime of Life.*[6] Sartre said much the same thing: "With Simone de Beauvoir it was 'life' in every sense of the word. Writing, obviously. I've often said that we thrashed it out with each other like nasty people. We each judge the other's writing harshly . . . so it was that, but it was also day to day life. It was perpetual reflections on what was going on in front of our eyes. . . . And then it was the things that crop up in life. What happened to each of us. . . . We put all that together."[7]

They lived their own truth, all justifications set aside. It had nothing to do with imposing this transparency on others. They were like gods at the center of their own world, seeing, commenting, deciding together without others being aware of the double light focused on them.

In 1937, as she approached thirty, Simone de Beauvoir saw herself as a woman who had had only one love in her life and had not rode the Colorado rapids in a raft or crossed the plateaus of Tibet on foot. In lieu of setting off to conquer the Himalayas, she went hiking in the Alps of Haute-Provence with Jacques-Laurent Bost, who alone could keep up with her. She left Sartre and Olga in Paris, each determined to win the other back, and walked from dawn to dusk, going wherever the trail led her, stopping in barns and village cafés along the way. Bost enjoyed de Beauvoir's company: "It was like being with a guy. With her you could walk around, get drunk, kid around. You didn't have to be on your best behavior like with other girls."[8] This was their second major expedition on foot.

They had set out at dawn, and as night began to fall the wind was blowing steadily and they had been climbing for two hours toward a hamlet where they hoped to find shelter in a barn. In *She Came to Stay* de Beauvoir would describe in pages full of tenderness and humor how Bost became her first contingent love.[9]

"I laughed," she told him, "thinking to myself what kind of face you'd make, you who dislike complications, if I suggested that you sleep with me." Sartre, informed by letter, approved of the new link uniting his "dear Castor" and the fellow he called Little Bost.

"Bost never loved anybody as much as he did Sartre. He was and would remain Sartre's only friend," de Beauvoir told us. For her he felt a love-friendship made up of admiration, attraction, and trust. Bost did fit without difficulty into Sartre and de Beauvoir's project to renew the basis of society. Sartre wrote the Castor that it was "for Bost"—for boys like him—that they had to "recreate man."[10] "We felt that for their sake we should have worked more for peace," de Beauvoir told us in 1985.

A new trio came into being, one quite different from that they had attempted to create with Olga, whom they thought to be a new Arthur Rimbaud.

Jacques-Laurent Bost represented youth itself. "He had its grace, casual nearly to the point of insolence, and its fragile narcissism as well."[11] He was without driving ambition, lighthearted, spontaneous; life's serious aspects made him laugh like a madman. A former boy scout, he knew his way around when it came to chores like cooking and cleaning. Over the years he would crisscross France and Italy on foot with de Beauvoir.

Once they had discovered their mutual attraction, they had to make up their minds about Olga. Should they tell her? She was not strong enough to practice transparency, which required fortitude and a difficult balance between philosophy and *le vécu*. They decided not to tell her.

At the end of this lively, wide-ranging journey—in the course of which de Beauvoir slipped and fell down a sheer incline without being injured seriously—the two intrepid walkers rejoined Sartre, who was waiting for them in Marseille. The trio set off for Greece. For three weeks they navigated from island to island, sleeping always under the stars, whether it was on the deck of a ship, on a hillside under the pines, or on a village terrace. They ate simple Greek fare and drank "a black syrupy substance that was in fact coffee" with large cool glasses of chlorinated water on the side.[12] Decked out in straw hats and carrying walking sticks and rucksacks, they climbed and clambered, sinking into soft cinder paths and baking in the unrelenting sunshine. One day, thoroughly exhausted, Sartre lost his temper. "I came out here to make the Grand Tour, and now you've got me playing at boy scout."[13] The heat had gotten the best of his stoicism. The traveling trio reached one destination in hopes of having lunch, but it was the height of the siesta time and the only soul they saw, a woman in black, scurried away at the sight of them. Sartre would use his memories of this, the village of Emborio, in describing Argos in his play *The Flies.*

Bost returned to France after three weeks, leaving Sartre and de Beauvoir to continue their exploration of Greece. Throughout their lives they would manage to set aside weeks to spend together in this way, most often abroad.

No sooner had she returned from Greece than de Beauvoir set out for an eight-day walking tour through Alsace with Olga. It was out of the question to abandon Olga; de Beauvoir had decided once and for all to take her on as a protégée. De Beauvoir would always look after their friendship with vigilance, so that it might never deteriorate. Her unpublished letters to Nelson Algren bear witness to a tenderness that would not waver over the years and demonstrate a constant concern for the well-being of this young friend: "I did not yet know how touching it can be to feel that one is useful, and how utterly devastating to believe oneself indispensable. The smiles that I provoked on her countenance from time to time gave me a deep joy that I could not have forgone without regret."[14]

While de Beauvoir was discovering the love of the young man "who had seemed so untouchable for so long," Sartre was making up for the trio's failure with Olga's younger sister, Wanda, who was dying to be an actress. He kept his word; five years after they met, he wrote *No Exit* for her, but the director Raymond Rouleau chose better-known performers. Sartre persevered. Wanda, using the stage name Marie Olivier, played Lucie in *Men Without Shadows*, Jessica in *Dirty Hands*, Catherine in *The Devil and the Good Lord*, Anna Damby in *Kean*, Véronique in *Nekrassov*, and Léni in *The Condemned of Altona*. Contingent though it may have been, this love was passionate and would endure. Sartre took care of Wanda all his life and left her a pension when he died.

Yet Sartre's romance with Wanda was a stormy one. In 1939, during the *drôle de guerre*, or phony war, when Wanda began spitting up blood, Sartre, already mobilized, resolved to marry her in order to obtain leave to see her, then abandoned the idea.

Wanda was not the only one; there were others, all duly recounted, each romantic interlude faithfully set down for the Castor in Sartre's letters. " 'Hold me tight, I want to feel tiny, tiny, tiny.' I felt like a dope. I held her conscientiously for a few minutes, then told her gently, 'You know, this is boring me stiff.' "[15] It was Lucile, one of Dullin's students. "There I was," he wrote, "an official groper." He specifies that "of all the girls who have honored me with their favors of late, not one is as pleasant a physical specimen as she and so pathetic when it comes to passion."[16]

Sartre went on to steal Martine,* a student with whom Maurice Merleau-Ponty was in love, right out from under his friend. "A very hot chick who sucked my tongue with the strength of an electric vacuum cleaner."[17] Although he deplored the fact that he had stolen Martine from Maurice ("I felt as criminal as possible"), he thoroughly enjoyed the fact that he had also taken her away from his former professor Jean Wahl, who hung around her. Then he tore himself away after "two beautiful tragic nights with her" and left with "a slightly bitter regret at having absolutely no room for her" in his life.[18] "Meanwhile, Martine was in love with a writer from the extreme right," de Beauvoir told us. "She was quite an exceptional girl."

In a café he described the entire affair to Olga, who was moved by the tale, and as a crowning touch, he swore to her that it was her sister whom he loved passionately, not Martine. Olga promised him she would keep an eye on her: "If Wanda acts like a fool, I'll try to straighten things out."[19]

In fact de Beauvoir was the one who looked after his little world. She mentioned to Sartre a short time later that Martine's face looked ravaged and

---

*Not her real name; she was a student at the Sorbonne and also took classes with Dullin.

that quite possibly she was on the way to losing her mind. Sartre denied that the passion he had inspired in her could have tragic consequences. De Beauvoir even worried about the financial situations of those people for whom she felt responsible. While Sartre was in the service she drew on his civilian salary and distributed it between Olga and Wanda. As a teacher she earned 3000 francs a month. Sartre wrote her, "If Paris becomes untenable, ship Wanda to Rouen or Marseille and do with the other [Olga] as you please."[20]

The only goal of an absurd existence, Sartre said, is to produce works of art. "As for life itself, it has to be lived as it comes, anyhow." For de Beauvoir he got down to basics: "I've never known how to properly conduct my sex life or my love life. I deeply and sincerely feel I'm a bastard, and a small-time operator on top of all that, a kind of scholarly sadist and civil servant Don Juan enough to make you vomit."[21] She serves as his "moral conscience" and his "little judge." She accepts Sartre's principle, "There is no excuse."[22] Each person is responsible for every one of his actions and all of his thoughts. And in assuming responsibility for everything she chose, she was accepting the consequences of her choice. She had chosen Sartre, totally and utterly as he was.

Nor did human relationships weigh all that heavily.[23] Olga was feeling ill and told him so. She was suffering from tuberculosis, although she did not know it yet. (She would undergo surgery and have a pneumothorax in 1941.) Olga began to worry. Sartre related his conversation with her: " 'Would you be on your last legs, Zazoulich?' Her reply is a big ironic laugh. For a good moment she discreetly pulls off the role of someone to whom everything seems extraordinarily absurd and insignificant because she's already full of death."[24]

In the end she told him she had spit up blood—a revelation that Sartre immediately corrected. "A tiny bit of pink had showed up in her saliva one day while she was brushing her teeth or rinsing her mouth. I breathed easily again: with her worries and reluctance, for a minute there I thought she was pregnant by Bost and determined, naturally, to kill herself. That would have cost us 1500 francs." "I've had enough of imaginary invalids," Sartre wrote.[25] Such was the offhanded cynicism and complicity of the couple, marked by their utter detachment from everything that was not them or their project.

Evidently de Beauvoir found these stories entertaining, for Sartre's letters continued to inform her of his affair with Martine, who vacillated "between two conceptions of her virginity." In the first variation, the man was to give his all in exchange for this munificent gift. "Consequence: She hangs on to her virginity indefinitely and can't enjoy herself as she pleases." The second variation is "reflexive." "What is virginity, after all? A nest of complexes and problems." He described their long sessions in bed without the slightest reticence.[26]

Zuorro (who became Daniel in *The Reprieve*) also supplied Sartre with an ample stock of amorous anecdotes. He had picked up a boy who had been sleeping on park benches and under bridges, and Zuorro's apartment was soon overrun with fleas. So Zuorro had the boy strip and sprayed him with Fly-Tox, Sartre explained, adding a description of the "pederastic dormitory with six or seven beds, in a miserable but immense apartment."[27]

Nothing went to waste, no detail was lost. Everything ended up on paper, to be sent to this other self whose echo he awaited. The stories go on and on, picturesque, full of life, executed with a never-failing sense of humor. It was a game in which two writers played ball with words, with people, with life. "My charming Castor, I send this morsel of letter without head or tail and especially without the least little *Erlebnis** so that you'll have it sooner since I think you are more partial to stories than to professions of love. All the same, know that there are constant stirrings for you in my heart."[28]

Sartre had his "fans" and de Beauvoir had hers, some of whom she encouraged.[29] The students were won over by the novelty and daring of their ideas. In her autobiography, *Nostalgia Isn't What It Used to Be,* the actress Simone Signoret describes how Sartre shook up tradition at the Lycée Pasteur, where he had been assigned in the autumn of 1937, by taking his students to cafés and treating them as equals. Some no longer left their teachers' sides. De Beauvoir strolled around with her favorite students, inviting them to cafés and sometimes restaurants. This liberal munificence, unheard of then in teaching circles, turned more than one adolescent's head. De Beauvoir constantly had a small crowd of admirers. In Rouen, in Paris, young girls grew attached to her, sometimes in pathetic fashion. In one of her unpublished letters to Nelson Algren she relates the story of Louise Védrine,† a student who was passionately taken with Simone and had a touching way of looking out for her. In 1939, when Sartre was mobilized and de Beauvoir was distressed and anxious over his departure, Louise invited her to her country home. She loaned de Beauvoir money to live on until the status of teachers was decided after the German invasion. This love would endure despite Louise's efforts to find a remedy. She began seeing a psychoanalyst, but years of analysis produced no change; she flung herself into marriage, hoping to find the solution there, and gave birth to a baby girl, but maternity was no

---

*In the phenomenological sense, "lived experience." Sartre used it to mean "emotion, rushes of affection, momentum of the heart" (Simone de Beauvoir).

†Not her real name.

help. She still loved de Beauvoir just as deeply, just as desperately. In 1948 de Beauvoir wrote to Algren that she found this love, which was fruitless for her, destructive for Louise. She believed then that one must live for oneself and not cling to the lives of others who do not reciprocate your feelings.

LIFE GOES ON

By the autumn of 1937, de Beauvoir had completed a collection of five short stories, *When Things of the Spirit Come First.* Here she had limited herself to creating written portraits of a few people she had known, trying to render tangibly events she had personally experienced. The fifth story is autobiographical, a satirical account of her childhood and youth. The manuscript was turned down by Gallimard and by Grasset, who reproached her for being content to describe a world in the process of disintegrating. At the same time, they encouraged her to continue—and continue she would.

Having been assigned to the Lycée Pasteur, Sartre took a room on the floor above de Beauvoir in a hotel between the avenue du Maine and the Montparnasse cemetery. They gave themselves over to writing and life's simple pleasures. They would have liked to buy a car and travel. (Sartre had a driver's license but had had two accidents.[30]) They did not buy a car, but they did travel. While de Beauvoir and her trusty knapsack roamed pathways and crested peaks with Bost, Sartre discovered the joys of writing perched in a sort of treehouse.

Returning to the city in the fall of 1938, they found Paris even more elegant than usual. The City of Light was outdoing itself with galas, receptions, and spectacular premieres. It proved to be one of the most brilliant seasons since World War I. Simone was happy in her multilevel loves.

Like all the women of Paris, de Beauvoir was seized with the urge to be part of the elegance around her. "I dressed with particular care that winter." She ordered a suit and blouses, sported a small boater hat with a veil, and hit upon the hairdo she would never abandon. Her hair, swept up off her face and sometimes held in place by a turban, flattered the regularity of her features and brought out the classic beauty of her face. Teaching did not bore her. She looked upon her sixteen hours of classes each week as "discussions between individuals rather than work."[31] She dressed up for work; feeling elegant pleased her. With seven years of teaching behind her now, she continued her established routine. In the evening she went to the Café de Flore

with Sartre, Bost, or Olga. For her the cafés were still the salons of Montparnasse. At the Flore, much activity revolved around Jacques Prévert. Everyone
who had anything at all to do with cinema gathered in the cafés facing the
church of Saint-Germain-des-Prés. Not everyone knew everyone else, but
everyone recognized everyone else and listened for snatches of conversation
in which illustrious names might be heard. Electricity was in the air, and there
was extraordinary activity around certain tables. Films were discussed; de
Beauvoir had seen them all. She went to the theatre, frequented cafés and
nightclubs. She plunged headlong into the whirlwind of *la vie parisienne intellec-
tuelle*—until Christmas vacation. The moment she was free, she took Sartre
off to Megève for skiing.

During Easter vacation in 1939 the two of them went to Provence. Sartre
read Heidegger in the sunshine while de Beauvoir scrambled up hillsides as
usual. Evenings at the hotel, she listened with rapt attention as Sartre explained to her for the first time what Heidegger's definition of man as "a
creature of distances" meant.[32] During the Pentecost vacation she walked all
over the Morvan with Bost and pushed on as far as Geneva to see an exhibit
of paintings that had been moved from the Prado in Madrid so as to be safe
from the bombardments.

Reading the daily newspapers was an exercise in anxiety. All the horrors
—the Nazi terror, the persecution of Jews, the imprisonment of those opposed
to the regime—could take place only in other countries, beyond French borders. France was strong, France was civilized, nothing could happen to France.
War could not happen.

DESCENT INTO HORROR

*I*n November 1938 at the German embassy in Paris there occurred
an event that would result in the deportation of 28,000 to 30,000 Jews from
the Third Reich.[33] A young Polish Jew whose parents had just been expelled
from Germany with 13,000 other Polish Jews asked to see the ambassador.
Received by Ernst vom Rath, the embassy secretary, he shot him in revenge
for the persecution of his compatriots. Vom Rath's death set off pogroms in
Germany and in Austria. During the night of November 9, synagogues were
torched, stores owned by Jews were ransacked, and Jews were tortured and
killed. Louise Védrine told de Beauvoir that a cousin who had managed to
flee Vienna had recently arrived at her house. The Gestapo had tortured him

for an entire night, and his face was covered with cigarette burns. He had told Louise that after vom Rath was assassinated his parents were awakened in the middle of the night and summoned to an assembly point where all the Jews were gathered. They were ordered to take off their clothes; fires were lit and the men were mutilated with red-hot pokers. Jews everywhere were being arrested and deported. Faced with her student's tears, de Beauvoir was ashamed. She was still staking everything on happiness; she still believed that Hitler would not attack France and that nothing would touch her personally. But it was no longer possible for her to ignore the persecutions, the tortures, the deportations. She mused, "Surely France at war would be worse than France under the Nazis?"[34] She remembered what she had seen and heard twenty years earlier. World War I had killed a million Frenchmen, and in the streets after the victory she had come across so many horribly mutilated men, so many women wearing widow's veils, so many orphans dressed in black!

Sartre explained to her that their lives as intellectuals would not be worth a cent under the Nazis, that peasants, workers, and bourgeoisie alike would all be treated as "a subhuman rabble to be sacrificed ruthlessly to the glory of the Reich."[35] De Beauvoir, convinced finally that war would break out, was gripped by guilt. She had never said a word, written a line, or lifted a finger to prevent this state of affairs. She had never taken a political position. She had been utterly uninterested in events, and now war was going to catch up with her and crush her. Her change in outlook was extreme and almost immediate; never again would her own personal happiness be her only concern. "I renounced my individualistic, antihumanist way of life. I learned the value of solidarity," she wrote. "In 1939 my existence was upset. . . . History took hold of me and never let go thereafter."[36]

THE LITTLE POLISH GIRL

*I*n 1939 de Beauvoir worked on *She Came to Stay,* while on every possible occasion Sartre described for her in detail what he called his "little stories of spring."

What is most extraordinary about their understanding is that it did not have the "heart's intermittences" that Proust denounced in the greatest loves. No less surprising is the fact that as soon as a very young girl attached herself to de Beauvoir, Sartre would not rest until he had succeeded in winning her over to him.

A series of letters that de Beauvoir must have considered important—she published them even though they are addressed to another person—gives us yet again a glimpse of a trio. These were letters written to Louise Védrine, whom de Beauvoir identifies here in a brief note as "a friend of mine with whom Sartre began an affair that the war quickly ended."[37] In his notebooks Sartre described the strength, the security, the happiness of the couple he formed with de Beauvoir: "Our relationship was so solid, so fascinating for others, that no one was able to love one of us without being prey to a fierce jealousy that finally turned into an irresistible attraction before having even met that person."[38] According to Sartre, this is how the trios came into existence. It was a recurring phenomenon. De Beauvoir told us that people often fell in love not with one of them but with the couple. It was to happen again in Brazil ten years after the trio with Louise.

A former student of de Beauvoir, Louise Védrine seems to have been poured from the same mold as *la petite Russe,* displaying the same vulnerability and the same fierce attachment to Simone. De Beauvoir sent Sartre Louise's letters, and Sartre assured his "dear little Polack, my love," that "our future is *your* future" and that "the Castor lives in a world where you are always present."[39]

In Sartre's first letter to Louise, dated July, he wrote that he had thought all day Sunday about how she was suffering, "and by Monday I already thought that things were a little bit better." The Castor had not left her side, which seemed altogether reassuring. He calls her "poor little martyr" and says that with every hour that passes she suffers less, which comforts him: "One whole corner of my horizon was truly blocked by pain." He announces that he will be visiting but "the good Castor" will see her every day, and he adds, "I'm very happy to think that you're completely flat."[40] Apparently Louise had just had an abortion.

Having taken care of Louise in the critical phase, de Beauvoir set out on a long trip across the Basses-Alpes. She and Sartre kept Louise roasting on the spit of their double affection while they vacationed. Louise did not understand why de Beauvoir had left her, and Sartre consoled her by explaining that as soon as good weather arrived the Castor was irresistibly drawn to the woods and plains. "Her need to see greenery becomes terrible and imperative . . . as urgent as the need to eat when she's hungry . . . don't mistake her behavior for a lack of tenderness. I know, more than you possibly can, how much the Castor loves you. . . . If your love for Simone makes you ache a little, think about how passionately I love you while you're waiting."[41]

All the time they were showering Louise with tenderness and promises, Sartre was living out his stormy romance with Wanda, and de Beauvoir, following her long hike across Provence, had joined Bost, who, on leave, awaited her in Marseille.

The new trio was superfluous—superfluous yet loving. "My love, my little passion, can you feel from far away how I love you? . . . What I want to affirm with all my might is that the Castor loves you as much as you could possibly desire. . . . I beg you not to torture yourself and to await our return both together."[42] Just when they planned to return remained vague. Sartre was with his parents in Saint-Sauveur, where he was going to visit the house in which Colette was born. He picked foxglove in the fields and wrote that his stepfather was dozing and his mother was concerned for Poulou's well-being.*

He plans his weeks of vacation with de Beauvoir and makes a list of expenses: He will get 4000 francs in July, and de Beauvoir will receive 3000 francs on August 1. He allocates 3000 francs to take Wanda to the Midi and 1800 francs to the Castor. But "Gégé wants 1200 francs," and Poupette has to have 700.[43] Therefore they will not have enough left to take the trip abroad that the Castor wants to take. Sartre pours on the charm and tries to make the disappointment more palatable by suggesting a trip on foot and by motor-coach across the limestone plateaus of south-central France and the Pyrénées. De Beauvoir hates being deprived of a project that she has carefully planned, and she does not give up her trip abroad willingly.

Sartre goes for a walk with Wanda and quarrels passionately with her before informing de Beauvoir in the sacrosanct name of transparency that Wanda had finally given herself to him in Avignon and that he had torn up de Beauvoir's letters so that Wanda would not see them. He had sacrificed de Beauvoir's letters, which, like his own, could serve as a writer's notes and which, like his own, might be published one day: "I received both of your little letters at the same time, the sad one and the serene one. Imagine: I quickly tore them up—I tore them all up, including the ones that you wanted me to keep—it's impossible to keep them; we're sharing the same room, and Wanda wanders around all morning while I'm asleep."[44]

This is what de Beauvoir would call the irresponsibility of youth, which Sartre, according to her, had so much difficulty overcoming. It was also a sentimental education that would serve as the basis for her reflections on woman's condition in *The Second Sex.*

---

*Poulou was Jean-Paul Sartre's nickname.

"LITERARY HONESTY IS NOT WHAT IT IS COMMONLY TAKEN TO BE"[45]

*I*f literature begins at the moment when "something in life goes slightly adrift," then the rounds of contingent loves, the attempts at making a trio work, the wealth of experiences and reflections on love, the endless analyzing and plentiful considerations of human conduct had to lead to this disturbing work. "The unfortunate episode of the trio did much more than supply me with a subject for a novel; it enabled me to deal with it."[46]

As she wrote, de Beauvoir rediscovered the joy of finding herself, for finally the very act of writing was changing her. The time for stylistic exercises and psychological analyses was past. Sartre was becoming a writer of note; after *Nausea,* which had not sold all that well before the war, *The Wall* met with success. De Beauvoir completed *She Came to Stay.*

She and Sartre used in their writing the same frankness that animated their conversation. But what the reader at Gallimard found acceptable in Sartre's work shocked him in de Beauvoir's, and he asked her to cut the first two chapters of *She Came to Stay,* in which she described her heroine's childhood and sexual awakening.

Olga Kosakiewicz had been their catalyst. De Beauvoir dedicated *She Came to Stay* to her, and Sartre did the same with *The Wall.* Sartre pushed de Beauvoir to abandon the purely stylistic and novelistic research she had been conducting until then. She was more interesting than her characters, he told her. "Put yourself boldly into your books," he urged.[47] As a result, few works of fiction would be as autobiographical as hers.

They wrote in collaboration a substantial portion of what they called *littérature alimentaire,* or writing that is done to earn a living. "If I had to come back to Paris in the middle of July it was because Sartre needed me for working at a movie script from his last play.* I told you that I always wanted to help him when he asked me and then that it is one of the ways of earning my life; my books would not be enough for me to live on and things like movie dialogues and so on help very much."[48]

---

*The play was *The Respectful Prostitute,* registered at the Society of Authors under the names Jean-Paul Sartre and Simone de Beauvoir. From an unpublished letter to Nelson Algren; in letters from Algeria in September 1948, de Beauvoir said she was working on the screenplay of *Dirty Hands* for the money. De Beauvoir's letters to Algren were written in English.

When separated, Sartre and de Beauvoir were linked by a correspondence in which they exchanged every detail concerning their work, their thoughts, their feelings, their friends, and others around them. There they found the source material for their novels. There is no character in their work who is not a composite of physical traits, linguistic habits, and biographical details borrowed from members of their entourage. Gerbert in *She Came to Stay,* basically a portrait of Bost, inherited Mouloudji's childhood. Roquentin in *Nausea* sports Politzer's flamboyant red hair. Xavière in *The Mandarins* is Olga, and Nadine speaks like Nathalie Sorokine.

In their Harlequin cloaks these creatures, half real, half fictional, are mysterious beings: characters in novels. And the lives led by Sartre and de Beauvoir are as fascinating as a made-up adventure because they lived and saw themselves like characters in a book. No wonder their entourage found their lifestyle surprising.

Their friend Madame Morel suggested they have a child just to see what it would be, and she offered to raise it for them so that the course of their daily lives would not be disturbed. They turned down this thoroughly Gide-like experiment but continued to rummage through their hearts and those of the other members of the Family, whose adventures became their joint treasure trove.

So it was that they spoke together of those around them, listening for the returning echoes of love addressed now to one, now to the other, provoking emotions and difficulties to be measured and recorded and examined until they reemerged in the form of a work such as *She Came to Stay.*

For de Beauvoir *She Came to Stay* was a catharsis as well as a realization. "In this novel I exposed myself so dangerously that at times the gap between my emotions and the words to express them seemed insurmountable."[49] She revealed herself more than she ever would in any other novel or even in *Memoirs of a Dutiful Daughter.* The characters are transposed nearly intact: Labrousse is Sartre, Françoise is de Beauvoir, Gerbert is Bost, and Xavière is Olga. Pierre Labrousse and Françoise Miquel live the same relationship as Sartre and de Beauvoir. "They stood together at the center of the world which it was their compelling mission in life to explore and reveal," she wrote, boldly setting in words the unabashed megalomania of the couple.[50]

Among the considerable good fortune on which her heroine, this avatar of herself, congratulates herself, "she put first that of being able to collaborate with him; the fatigue they shared, their efforts united them more surely than an embrace. There was not one minute of these exhausting rehearsals which wasn't an act of love." The novel is a psychodrama resembling those that she and Sartre played in difficult situations. The imaginary exorcising *le vécu,* the murder of Xavière, the motivating force and raison d'être for the entire novel were de Beauvoir's deliverance. She gave herself to the writing, and her throat constricted as though she were committing a real crime.

Writing *She Came to Stay* was no easy task; it took de Beauvoir four years to complete the book. In the meantime, new friendships had entered her life, new romances had appeared for Sartre, and the wheel of history had inexorably turned.

THE WAR

May that was cloudless and June stabbed to death
I shall never forget the lilacs, nor the roses
Nor those that the spring kept in its folds.
                                          Louis Aragon

THE FIRST DAYS OF THE END OF A WORLD

On March 15, 1939, in violation of the Munich accords, the German army entered Prague and Czechoslovakia lost its status as an independent nation.

On March 22 Hitler, who had stirred up secessionist agitation in Memel, a predominantly German city, forced Lithuania to surrender. France and England were rearming, and they signed a mutual assistance pact with Poland. Unwanted though it might be, the war was steadily approaching.

On April 6 Italy invaded Albania and the king of Italy and emperor of Ethiopia also became king of Albania.

On June 23 France, England, and Turkey signed a mutual assistance treaty.

At Sull Onda,* Madame Morel's summer home in Juan-les-Pins, on the still aristocratic and deserted beaches where only the terraces of a few magnificent villas encroached, it was easy to believe in peace and civilization. In the fragrant shadows of the tall pines, in the park facing the sea, Sartre wrote and de Beauvoir read and thought and let her projects ripen.

At two in the afternoon, when the heat was at its worst, everyone repaired to the large villa. The shutters were closed and the cool shadows were happiness itself. Lunch was followed by a siesta, laughter, games, a race along the beach, and a plunge in the sea. July slipped away and August brought alarming news. The guests began to exercise the daily routine with clenched teeth, taking no particular pleasure in their activities. Simone de Beauvoir grew impatient. She sensed the winds of war beginning to blow and found the lush calm of this rich estate unseemly. "The Castor doesn't like the good life," Sartre joked. To take her mind off things, he taught her how to swim and laughed at her "funny face," tense with concentration.

On August 23, 1939, Stalin and Hitler signed a nonagression pact that took everyone by surprise. Officially, Russia was engaged in negotiations with France and England, having been excluded from the Munich conference. People were stupefied to learn that all ideological questions had been swept aside and Nazi Germany had signed this pact with Soviet Russia. War was inevitable.

What no one knew was that on August 29 Albert Einstein sent President Franklin D. Roosevelt a confidential letter informing him that it was scientifically possible to envision the production of an atomic bomb.

At the Villa Sull Onda, as elsewhere throughout France, people began to open their daily newspapers with mounting apprehension. Time had vanished—it was zero hour. Sartre and de Beauvoir took leave of their friends with considerable emotion. When will we meet again? For that matter, *will* we meet again?

Sartre and de Beauvoir wanted some time to themselves; they intended to put matters into focus while walking along mountain paths in the Pyrénées. But they had gotten no further than the platform at Juan-les-Pins when absurdity smacked them in the face. The station was overrun, the train packed with young men helping themselves to the reserved compartments because they were already on their way to getting themselves killed on the Maginot Line.

Sartre and de Beauvoir braced themselves; unhappiness was certainly on

---

*Villa Puerta del Sol in *The Prime of Life*.

the way, but that they would face it together was a great consolation. In one final effort to keep themselves at arm's length from history, they visited the ramparts of the medieval city of Carcassonne, and sipped drinks on the tree-lined walks of still peaceful southern towns beneath a sky that already signaled the departure of summer. It was raining when they spotted the first mobilization posters. The dreaded moment had arrived: They must return to Paris.

Just a moment! Foix was such a lovely town, and this would be their last chance to celebrate in peacetime. They treated themselves to a magnificent luncheon in a restaurant noted for its cuisine, washing down "hors d'oeuvre, trout, cassoulet, foie gras, cheese, and fruit" with the local wine.[1] Carried away by the spirit of this reprieve, Sartre shared with de Beauvoir a revised plot outline for *Roads to Freedom*. Afterward their stroll beside the river reminded them of their walks along the Seine ten years earlier, when they were young *agrégés*. Paris might come to harm in the war, but the countryside and little towns like this would remain untouched, they told themselves. Later, when it was all over, they would return to find the tranquillity of small-town life, the unhurried pace, the mark of eternity etched into the very landscape. Without believing it for a minute they kept up a façade of confidence and calm.[2]

When they reached Toulouse the signs of war were unmistakable. The station was dimly lit by a few "feebly glowing violet lamps," their bulbs obscured by paint.[3] The express train for Paris shot through the station, too full to take on passengers. They waited for the next express and, by pushing harder than the surging, clawing crowd around them, managed to shove their way aboard and commandeer two corner seats.

It was all over, peace was finished, civility had peeled away. Already one lived at the expense of others; soon anything would be possible, and fear would come first.

The atmosphere was unnerving in a Paris devoid of its vacationing residents. The Communist newspapers had been banned. In the papers and in conversations overheard on café terraces de Beauvoir detected symptoms of "spy hysteria" and was uneasy.[4] There was talk of a fifth column that wanted to hand France over to the Nazis. France itself was divided: The right and part of the left were accusing the government of having led the nation to war when compromise was still possible. The right accused the Popular Front of having weakened and impoverished France with social reforms, particularly the forty-hour work week, instead of giving priority to rearmament. In *L'Action française* one could read:

S'ils s'obstinent ces cannibales	If these cannibals insist
A faire de nous des héros	On making heroes of us, well
Il faut que nos premières balles	Then our first bullets must be aimed
Soient pour Mandel, Blum et Reynaud.	At Blum, at Reynaud and Mandel.

Nothing was happening. No one knew anything, and everyone lived in apprehension of something. Sartre and de Beauvoir calmed their nerves by walking tirelessly through the streets of a Paris strangely stilled. Each new edition of the newspapers was scooped up quickly by people awaiting some new information, some easing of tension. Going to the movies was the only possible escape, and the theatres were packed. As soon as the show let out, the crowds descended on the newsstands for the late-night final edition of *Paris-Soir,* then scanned its pages anxiously for they knew not what.

De Beauvoir feared that a future barely begun would be yanked out from under her. She dreaded the idea of lost time because it meant the waste of talent, the waste of love, the waste of friendship. The general paralysis was gaining ground, people were moving in circles, playing an anxious game of waiting. The newspapers dispensed unsubstantiated and conflicting information. There were hopes that Mussolini would offer his services as a mediator. Some said that Hitler's threat to invade Poland was a bluff. And when, at dawn on September 1, the German army invaded Poland, the morning papers neglected to say so.

On September 2 de Beauvoir was having her morning coffee at the Dôme when a waiter announced what he had just heard from a customer who had read it in *Paris-Midi.* Others jumped up from the terrace and besieged the nearest newsstand. De Beauvoir ran back to her hotel to alert Sartre: The French Cabinet had announced a state of siege in France and Algeria and decreed a general mobilization.

At the hotel Sartre prepared to see his mother and stepfather before joining his regiment. Unwilling to leave his side, de Beauvoir accompanied him to Passy and waited in the métro while he said good-bye to his parents. The Mancys had never received Simone de Beauvoir as a guest in their home; *agrégation* or no, in their eyes she was nothing more than a hussy. Sartre's mother had invited her out for tea on several occasions, but Monsieur Mancy would never have consented to entertaining her under his own roof. The de Beauvoirs evidently preferred not to confront their daughters directly about their private lives. Simone's parents' financial situation was still chaotic, and she helped them out when necessary. Sartre loaned them money and reclaimed it without amenities: "Have your mother send me six hundred francs, and make it snappy. The bitch forgot to give me back the money."[5] Borrowing back and forth was a way of life for de Beauvoir and Sartre; "we borrowed from everybody."

On this particular day Simone was not thinking about the ostracism directed at her; she was waiting for Sartre. Night fell in Paris. Those who could, packed their bags and sent women and children to stay with friends and relatives in the countryside. Paris was sure to be the first target for bombs. A caravan of five cars left the rue Sébastien-Bottin carrying Gaston Gallimard and the manuscripts of the NRF authors. That night, in a Paris where curtains were drawn, street lamps extinguished, and windows blackened, unreality quietly settled in.

Like so many other couples, Sartre—in uniform—and de Beauvoir went out into the dark streets. They ordered coffee at the Dôme. While awaiting the hour of departure, Sartre wrote one last letter to Louise Védrine, dated September 2, 1939.

> My love,
>
> So it's idiocy that's triumphed. I leave tonight at five. The Castor is accompanying me to a square named Hébert, near porte de la Chapelle. . . . My love, I don't fear for my life; I'm not even afraid of being bored half to death, and I can't complain about the good Castor who is all courage and perfection, as always. What breaks my heart is your being all alone in your anguish, there in Annecy."[6]

He said he was taking photos of her with him and assured her that he was "a faithful one," that she would find him "exactly the same" as when they parted in Annecy. "Nothing can change us, my love, not you, not the Castor, not me! . . . I want you to know that I love you passionately and for always . . . and the Castor has told me to tell you that she'll be coming to see you before the end of September."

Dawn was breaking as a taxi left them at the Gare de l'Est. They sat on a café terrace and sampled one last ritual of ordinary life while waiting for the train, surrounded by people like themselves, all mouthing reassuring platitudes. The war will not last long, Germany is already rationing, it will crumble in no time, there is no great danger. Sartre is in the meteorological service; he will not be anywhere near the front lines.

As slowly as possible, people began moving toward the train that had just pulled into the station and would soon be full of soldiers. Faces appeared in every window as men jockeyed for a final glance, pushing their way forward for one last word and a parting gesture. Like all the other soldiers, Sartre passed beyond the barrier on the platform, de Beauvoir remaining on the civilian side. They found time for one more word. The last shred of life as they had known it was fraying away in an exchange that no longer seemed real. Sartre left. Freedom and initiative had come to an end. From now on, one pawn among others, he would go wherever the powers that be saw fit to send him.

De Beauvoir returned to Montparnasse on foot. People were still uncertain what was going on. The newspapers mentioned diplomatic maneuvers; it was not enough to muster hope, but it was sufficient to maintain the general torpor. The word SHELTER appeared on walls. Occasionally the windows of a shop whose proprietor's Alsatian name might lead to confusion offered clarification: FRENCH BUSINESS—FATHER MOBILIZED IN 1914—SON MOBILIZED. Jews were afraid. There was nothing to be done, nothing to do but go to the cinema, where you could cry discreetly, sensing the presence around you of others like you.

There was widespread fear that the Germans would use poison gas against civilian populations in the cities. Gas masks—a hood equipped with a snout, with two portholes for the eyes—were distributed. The contraption fit into a case that you had to take with you wherever you went. Night fell. Simone de Beauvoir did not return to her hotel room; she slept at Fernando's on a couch, then moved to Gégé's the next day and stayed with her until October 10.

TIME WITHOUT MEANING

*D*e Beauvoir was distraught; she found it impossible to endure the solitude of her own thoughts. Time, no longer hers to spend as she pleased, had been robbed of all meaning. Time slipped away, eluding her grasp. There were long, slow hours to fill, yet suddenly the day was gone. Sartre was gone. Bost was gone. People were certain that the Maginot Line was impregnable, that the army was ready. "We'll win because we're the strongest," it was said with assurance. There were 3,970,000 men mobilized. People counted on the blockade to starve out Germany, which had sacrificed butter for cannons. There was a general feeling that people had resigned themselves to the inevitable and wanted to get it over with as quickly as possible. Meanwhile, the reasons for fighting were not altogether clear. There was no obvious motivation, as there had been in 1914; this time there was no Alsace-Lorraine to recapture.

From *Paris-Soir* de Beauvoir learned that France had declared war at 5 P.M. and England had already been at war for several hours. Like everyone else, she drifted in a universe in which she was insignificant. With Hélène, Gégé, and other friends she went to the Flore to write other members of the Family, determined that the house of cards of contingent loves would not be blown down by the war. The manager announced that the Flore would close the following day. That left the Dôme. At 11 P.M. the cafés closed and their customers lingered on the dark sidewalks outside, reluctant to go home.

The sirens wailed for the first alert in the middle of the night on September 4. Simone peered out the window to see people hurrying to the shelters. She went downstairs, spotted the concierge wearing a gas mask, and headed back up to bed with the same calm disdain her father had displayed twenty years earlier, when Big Bertha was shelling Paris. The all clear would not sound until 7 A.M. In broad daylight people returned home in their nightclothes and slippers. Those who had no gas masks had wrapped pieces of linen around their heads. It was said that even underclothing would filter some gas in a pinch.

Sartre was with the 70th division in Essey-lès-Nancy. On the fifth Simone received his first letter, dated September 2.

> My love,
>
> I'm writing to you from Toul. . . . As for my feelings, not only have they not changed since I saw your poor ravaged little face for the last time, from the other side of the barrier at the Gare de l'Est, but they are even more "occupying" and almost painful. . . . If you were sleeping on the little bunk next to me, I would be completely at ease and my heart would be light. Oh, my love, how I love you and how I need you. Adieu. Now I'm going to write two little notes to my parents and to Wanda. I love you with all my might.[7]

De Beauvoir settled herself at the Deux-Magots to write her war journal. Sartre had asked her to take note of everything: It was up to her to describe for him the life he had left behind. Everything was literature, and nothing could stop these two irrepressible writers. "Books," Sartre wrote, "I still have the same unremitting determination to write them. Of that much I'm reassured, it's my nature—but who knows when they'll be published?

But there's one thing which will never change, which can never change: and that's that whatever happens and whatever I become, I'll become it with you. If there'd been a need to feel to what extent we're united, this phantom war would at least have had that much good about it that it would have made us feel that . . . it brings an answer to this question that tormented you: my love, you are not 'one thing in my life,' even the most important—because my life is no longer up to me, I don't even miss it, and that you, you are always me. You're much more—it's you who permit me to imagine any future.[8]

In a future in which death might play a part, Simone de Beauvoir had a mandate to carry on their common project. In the heart of the left bank, pen in hand, she watched as Paris sank into the war. This would be the most fertile period of her life. *She Came to Stay, Pyrrhus et Cinéas, The Blood of Others, Who Shall Die?,* "Moral Idealism and Political Realism," *Existentialism and the Wisdom of Nations,* and *All Men Are Mortal* would be written and published between 1940 and 1946. To this prolific output must be added her daily diary and her daily letters to Sartre.

THE DRÔLE DE GUERRE, *1939–1940*

*T*he blast of air raid sirens became a frequent and familiar sound. They wailed again during the night of September 5 and the following day de Beauvoir was at the Three Musketeers Café when the sirens went off. The owner lowered the steel shutters. In the streets people went on talking as though nothing was happening. De Beauvoir returned to her hotel, where the owner, utterly indifferent to the alert, was doing the dishes. De Beauvoir picked up a book and read until the all clear, then set off for the Dôme. "I have a close and affectionate regard for this little Montparnasse square. I love its half-empty sidewalk cafés and the expression of the switchboard girl at the Dôme; I feel part of the family, as it were, and that protects me against depression."[9]

On September 7 the French launched an offensive in the Saar, and the papers announced an improvement in the French positions. The cafés were full of talk about forts taken from the Germans along the Siegfried Line. Customers were requested to settle the bill when served, since an air raid alert might otherwise oblige the clientele to run for shelter without having paid.

At the Dôme, many spoke of plans to leave France for America. De Beauvoir dined with Fernando Gerassi at Dominique's in the rue Vavin. Gerassi had run into André Malraux, who was trying to do something for the foreigners who were being interned, in particular the Spanish Republicans, who were being forced to join the Foreign Legion. Gerassi had spent four days in prison, and Malraux, with whom he had fought in Spain, succeeded in getting him and some of their Spanish friends released. Gerassi intended to go to the United States with Stépha and his son. Malraux was trying to arrange to fight in Poland, the French air force having turned him down because of heart trouble.

Sartre's letters continued to arrive and were reassuring. Olga had moved into Gégé's empty apartment with de Beauvoir, but de Beauvoir felt trapped in the half-empty city with its blacked-out windows. Germans residing in France were relegated to internment camps, and signs clearly identifying businesses as 100% FRENCH proliferated in windows. Sandbags were piled high beside major monuments. The streets grew more and more deserted. Simone de Beauvoir took the train to Crécy to visit Charles Dullin, but despite her old friend's affection, she could not sit still and soon returned to Paris. On the Champs-Elysées she met Colette Audry, who in view of the already scarce fuel situation was the proud new owner of a bicycle. They asked themselves what would become of their numerous Communist friends, whom the authorities had lumped together with foreign agents. On September 26 the government had dissolved the Communist Party, confiscated its offices and resources, suspended the immunity of Communist deputies, repealed the legal guarantees accorded civil servants, and put all citizens suspected of Communist sympathies under house arrest at the discretion of local authorities.

Bianca begged de Beauvoir to join her in Brittany, and Madame Morel invited her to La Pouèze. She boarded the train, spent a few days in Brittany and a week at La Pouèze, taking long, solitary walks for the most part, but the general uneasiness spared no one. For a month she had been living like a sulfide on a sheet of water, outwardly calm yet ready to explode. Finally, as if awakening from a bad dream, she faced up to herself and reality: "Now I am about to adapt myself to a 'wartime existence,' and it seems ominous to me. Yet this morning I was seized by an almost panicky urge to get away from all this tranquillity, to come to grips with something again."[10]

A letter from Sartre, written in the code they had made up together, informed her that he was stationed at Brumath, near Strasbourg. Penniless, she borrowed money from Madame Morel and returned to Paris.

De Beauvoir immediately undertook the elaborate preparations necessary to obtain a safe-conduct pass to visit Sartre. She searched for a concierge who would agree to give her an official statement declaring that she had a permanent residence. On the same day she obtained a teaching post at the Lycée Camille-Sée and took a room at a hotel in the rue Vavin. It was time to get back to work.

Henceforth the necessity to continue work and to complete her novel justified everything—the patience, the waiting, accepting the unacceptable. She could be seen every day at the Dôme, writing away in a booth. Marie Ville, "the lunar woman" from Berlin, reappeared and took Simone to see Foujita's former model Youki Desnos and the colorful crowd she was entertaining. The atmosphere for which Montparnasse was known quietly reestablished itself. The Café de Flore reopened. People had learned to camouflage windows and glass doors with shades and thick drapes and were turning on the lights indoors in the evenings. If even a sliver of light escaped from curtains carelessly closed over windows splashed with blue paint, the local block captain would blow his shrill whistle until the offending party remedied the situation. Automobile headlights too were painted blue. People were certain that the least light would guide German bombers to their target. But the bombs were taking their time; the German air force was not yet darkening the skies above French cities. Poland had been crushed and Czechoslovakia lay conquered—perhaps that would suffice to fulfill Hitler's ambitions? The cost of living remained stable, and salaries were frozen. People had not taken to hoarding household staples, although everyone kept a little extra sugar, oil, and salt on hand. Real estate values, having fallen when war was declared, began rising again. There was no panic at bank windows, no sudden impetus to withdraw one's life savings in cash. While awaiting the victory that could not fail to come, people moped about, interjecting a spell of fretting now and then. Families grew bored in the country, and the men who had remained in the cities grew bored without their families. Should children be pulled out of school and sent off to the provinces? No clear danger had materialized. Administrators who had been shipped off to the provinces longed for Paris.

Factory employees worked forty-eight, then sixty hours a week, and workers staged the occasional slow-down strike. Soldiers posted on the Maginot Line were so bored that they occasionally resorted to playing soccer, and the soldiers manning the Siegfried Line across the border cheered them on. There was no fighting along the banks of the Rhine, just waiting. German propaganda had a field day in this climate of apathy. A radio station broadcasting in French from Stuttgart specialized in programs intended to shake up the French and turn them against their English allies. The daily appeals for reaching an agreement with Hitler emphasized that he wanted to be at war not with France but with England. Loudspeakers blared to the soldiers at the front: "You needn't die for Danzig or for England."[11] Jacques-Laurent Bost, in Paris on leave, told de Beauvoir that the Germans held up large signs to let the soldiers on the Maginot Line know that everything was England's fault and that the Germans had nothing against the French. Friendly little groups bearing messages from Hitler crossed the Rhine in small boats.

Auditoriums and theatres gradually reopened. Cinemas were authorized to operate until 10 P.M., cafés could do business until 11 P.M. With Olga in tow, de Beauvoir returned to familiar haunts, the Jockey and the other clubs around Montparnasse. She was determined to recapture the rhythm of a normal routine, to write her novel, teach her classes, see her friends, go out for dinner, go to cafés and bars and the movies. She intended to live her life as a citizen of Paris and a resident of Montparnasse, to have an identity and a clearly defined place in this society that was being pitched and tossed on uncontrollable waves.

When the first bout of collective anxiety had passed, a relative feeling of relief slowly gained ground. The German army was no longer expected to advance into French territory. People were bracing themselves for a long border war. Only one fear continued to haunt the populace: aerial bombardment and the use of poison gas. Local authorities had pails of water and sandbags on hand in every quarter. German radio propaganda aimed its message at the mothers of soldiers: "Don't sacrifice your sons!" And the leitmotif was always the same: "England—that's the enemy!" The government ordered the repression of defeatist attitudes and tactics. Any individual suspected of endangering national defense could be placed under house arrest. German propaganda seized upon this decree to attack Prime Minister Edouard Daladier for subjugating France "to the bankers of the City of London."[12]

Because those who were bored, particularly the idle and depressed troops stationed along the Rhine, were most susceptible to the propaganda, the number of leaves granted servicemen was increased. Theatrical performances for the army were encouraged, the sale of liquor was tolerated, the restrictions on sending packages were relaxed.

The civilian population was also treated considerately. The government advocated "the resumption of activity in ski resorts as well as the winter season along the Riviera." Safe-conduct passes were issued to wives of military men, enabling them to travel to see their husbands. De Beauvoir obtained a five-day pass at a police station and hoodwinked a doctor into writing her a medical excuse from work.

At 6 A.M. on October 31 she embarked for Brumath on a train that was overrun with soldiers returning from leave. De Beauvoir was lovely in her yellow turban, earrings, and high heels, and gentlemen told her so. She had an impression of everything's being fake—a phony war, phony soldiers. At police headquarters in Nancy there was general pandemonium as safe-conducts were being stamped. Just where was she headed? Not to see her boyfriend, by any chance? She denied this suggestion with a hearty conviction that utterly failed to convince the police officer whose stamp of approval she required. But he was a good sport and he gave her twenty-four hours, which amounted to a special favor because only married women were officially permitted to visit their men. Having hoped to spend five full days with Sartre, she felt her bile rise.

She had not been able to notify Sartre of her visit. Arriving in the middle of the night in a Brumath that was lit only by the full moon, she scouted around for a hotel in which to wait until dawn. The next morning she set off in search of Sartre, only to spot him, entirely by accident, walking toward her at the end of a street. They were able to talk for an hour, then he had to go. The police were strict; where had their freedom gone to? She had to have her safe-conduct stamped and extended, she was obliged to give up her hotel room to a couple, she was treated insolently at the Taverne du Cerf, and a drunken soldier threatened her, but if she made too much of a fuss, her safe-conduct might have been revoked. Sartre finally appeared and, having found her a room for the night, took her to dinner at the Lion d'Or. He gave her the first one hundred pages of *Roads to Freedom* and his notebooks to read; she showed him her journal, and they continued the dialogue they had been pursuing for ten years. She said she felt like a mature woman but had been asking herself, "In what ways am I typically 'feminine' and in what ways not?"[13] Sartre encouraged her to look into this idea more closely. And there, in the thick of the phony war, Simone de Beauvoir began laying the ground for *The Second Sex*.

After another twenty-four-hour reprieve it was back to a darkened station with sandbags everywhere, crowds of soldiers in uniform, evacuees, women in tears. Once more she felt hunted. "This station platform *is* the war," she thought.[14]

Paris had never before seen the stars stand out so clearly in the night skies. Owls could be heard hooting in the Luxembourg Gardens. Georges and Françoise de Beauvoir had recently returned from La Grillère; Hélène had remained in the Limousin to paint. Simone went to see her parents and listened in silence when her father offered his political analyses. She had

given up on having any sort of discussion with him. De Beauvoir described
the illusions of this father whom she loved and hated so, along with the
advertising world he frequented, in *Les Belles Images*. [15]

Teaching, writing, and holding up her end of an enormous correspondence still did not satisfy her or fill her time, and she plunged into the study
of music. She borrowed a phonograph and records and read the history of
music, music theory, and the lives of musicians and composers. She listened
avidly to the same piece ten times in a row. "I felt the same elation at the sight
of these silent yet sound-laden discs as I did when confronted by my new
books at the beginning of the term."[16] She spent hours at Chantecler's—a
record shop where one could sample the wares before making a purchase—
listening to records through crackly headphones. Saturdays and Sundays she
attended dress rehearsals and concerts at the Conservatoire, which were often
frequented by such celebrities as Cocteau and his friends or Colette, "wearing
sandals and no stockings." There was a patriotic ambience in the nightclubs
Simone visited with Olga; the striptease girls wore G-strings the colors of the
French flag and sang the Marseillaise. "Police raids were frequent, the flics in
shiny tin helmets examining customers' papers, using flashlights strapped to
their chests."[17]

Dullin was teaching again, and de Beauvoir accompanied Olga and
Wanda to class. She went to Férolles, where Dullin was preparing the set for
a production of *Richard III,* and she sat in on rehearsals at the Atelier. During
Christmas vacation she spent ten days skiing in Megève with Jean Kanapa,
a friend of Bianca and one of Sartre's former pupils. Only Simone de Beauvoir
could qualify this existence as "monotonous to the point of austerity."[18]

1940

*I*n February 1940 Sartre returned on leave, dividing his time equit-
ably among Simone, Wanda, and his parents. Sartre and de Beauvoir had
worked out a moral philosophy based on the idea of genuineness. "It required
every man to shoulder the responsibility of his situation in life; and the only
way in which he could do so was to transcend that situation by engaging
upon some source of action. Any other attitude was mere escapist pretense."
In her journal de Beauvoir admitted that not that long ago they had strived
to "keep our situation in life at arm's length by means of fantasy, deception,

and plain lies."[19] Together these few days they explored the paths that might lead them away from "bad faith" and toward the genuineness of a new attitude. On February 15, 1940, Sartre returned to the front. Simone observed the phenomenon of a platform divided into a mass of men who were leaving and a mass of women who would remain behind. The collective movement and the collective tension distressed her; individuals disappeared, melting into categories. De Beauvoir thought it was time to give back to each individual the right to exist.

A snowstorm hit Paris the following day, and because there was a labor shortage, no one cleared the streets. People were obliged to struggle over snowdrifts and wade through swamps of filthy slush that melted and froze in turn. Their feet soaked, shivering and worried, the people of Paris experienced winter as one cold, palpable oppression. The temperature fell to one degree Fahrenheit. Spring brought the first rationing. Specialty breads were a thing of the past, and pastry shops were closed three days a week. There were three "dry" days when the sale of alcohol was prohibited, and restaurants were allowed to serve only two courses.

Dissension burst out in the political ranks. The Communist leader Maurice Thorez was stripped of his French citizenship. General Maurice Gamelin relieved several other generals of their duties. Marshal Philippe Pétain appeared to be the only man with enough prestige to forge national unity. On January 26 Colonel Charles de Gaulle sent a memorandum to members of the French parliament and various ministers and military authorities, declaring that because they had tanks the enemy could easily break through the French lines and that it was essential to regroup all the dispersed French tanks into a single armored barrier and to make the rapid manufacture of additional tanks an urgent priority. He predicted that the conflict could be "the most violent of all those that have ravaged the earth."[20] His advice was disregarded.

On March 12 Finland signed a peace treaty that ceded important territory to Russia. Prime Minister Edouard Daladier left office on March 20, and Paul Reynaud replaced him, inspiring high hopes. In April, Germany invaded Denmark and Norway; this caused a general stupor in France and an even deeper depression and paralysis.

Sartre returned on leave in mid-April, having begun to work out a new philosophy at the front.

On May 10 de Beauvoir bought a newspaper at the intersection of the rue Vavin and the boulevard Raspail and there, below the balcony from which she had looked out on the world as a child, collapsed onto a bench and began to cry as she read the lead story: "This morning, in the early hours,

Germany invaded Holland and attacked Belgium and Luxembourg. French and British forces have crossed the Belgian frontier."[21]

On the same day Hélène de Beauvoir, who had been invited to Portugal by Lionel de Roulet's mother, arrived in Lisbon after an exhausting three-day journey and found herself exiled for the duration of the war.

On the morning of May 10 an airlifted contingent of 12,000 German soldiers and 4000 parachutists had been hurled at the cities of Holland. In Liège, 500 parachutists had landed at the fort responsible for the city's defense. In four days German armored tank divisions had crossed the Ardennes Forest, pierced the front at Sedan, and encircled the French divisions stationed in Belgium. Thus the German army was in a position to take the Maginot Line from the rear. Refugees were arriving in the Paris train stations en masse; on the roads, civilians were fleeing the advance of the army. In Paris the government prepared its evacuation. Fear started in official circles and filtered its way down to every level of the population. On the night of May 15 General Gamelin announced that the Germans were twelve miles from Laon. Thousands of terror-stricken people were already on the roads in a mass exodus. Government officials burned documents in the gardens of the Ministry of Foreign Affairs, and Parisians leaving the city could see the smoke from some distance. Paul Reynaud denied that the government was preparing to leave Paris and maintained on the radio that the city would be defended. In the afternoon the Chamber of Deputies affirmed its patriotism and unity.

But the Germans were not headed for Paris. They were marching toward the port cities along the English Channel, threatening to cut off the elite French and British forces that had come to Belgium's rescue.

Since May 10 de Beauvoir had been unable to shake the disproportionate, uncontrollable unhappiness that had overtaken her. She found it impossible to concentrate on writing, impossible to read. Nothing made sense; people were living from news report to news report, from radio bulletin to radio bulletin, and each announcement brought closer the inconceivable. To suppress her fear, she went to the cinema, the theatre, the opera. Despite the censorship, people kept well abreast of the tragic events that rapidly followed one another.

On May 29 the newspapers announced: KING LEOPOLD A TRAITOR. Belgium had collapsed. Hitler declared that he would enter Paris on June 15. De Beauvoir knew that the worst was yet—and certain—to come.

The war had just touched her directly: Jacques-Laurent Bost, wounded by shrapnel, had been evacuated to the rear lines. Olga left for Normandy to join her parents.

May 31 saw the Battle of Dunkirk. The entire British army and part of the French forces stood encircled on twenty-eight miles of beach, and German pilots had orders to destroy this pocket from the air. In an attempt to save the allies, warships, troop transports, trawlers, fishing boats, tugboats, yachts, motorboats, rafts, virtually anything that would float, crossed the Channel. For one day and one night the rescue craft ferried back and forth while German planes roared overhead. News of the debacle reached the capital.

Simone de Beauvoir considered going to Madame Morel's in La Pouèze; from there she figured she could cross the Loire. It was said that what was left of the army would regroup south of the Loire. She would set off in search of Sartre, but first she had to administer the baccalaureate exam on June 10. Then the Aisne and Somme fronts were attacked on June 5. The Battle of Paris had begun. "Life had finally ceased to adapt itself to my will."[22] She could not leave Paris. The examinations had not been canceled, and more than ever she needed her salary to live, for there was always someone she had to tide over or bail out.

Stépha and Fernando Gerassi traveled toward Spain with the hope of crossing the border clandestinely and somehow making their way to America. Bianca, who was Jewish, felt directly threatened; walking home from the opera one night, she told de Beauvoir that in the event of defeat she would kill herself. Antiaircraft guns were firing away in the distance.

Returning to her hotel on June 9, de Beauvoir found a note from Bianca begging Simone to join her in leaving Paris. De Beauvoir hurried to meet her at the Café de Flore, where Bianca told her that the exams had been canceled, all teachers were free to go, and she was leaving for Angers. De Beauvoir suddenly understood that the Maginot Line had not held. Where was Sartre? Taken prisoner? Dead? When would she know? Her life was unraveling. For the first time she had a true hysterical fit, her heart froze, her emotions went careening out of control. "This, as far as I was concerned, was the most awful moment in the whole course of the war."[23]

She packed a suitcase, taking all of Sartre's letters, and went with Bianca to meet some friends in the Latin quarter. They stayed up talking until 4 A.M. and drank champagne left behind by an Austrian woman who had been arrested and shipped off to a camp. At 7 A.M. de Beauvoir got up and went to the Lycée Camille-Sée to be certain that the exams were not being given after all. A few students were milling around, wanting to know the same thing. An evacuation order had arrived; the lycée was being moved to Nantes. De Beauvoir ran back to the Latin quarter to find Bianca. Students roamed the streets in a happy daze; what should have been a nerve-wracking examination day had turned into a sort of holiday. The streets were emptying, shops were closing. An endless stream of cars loaded with trunks and mattresses was inching its way down the boulevard Saint-Michel. De Beauvoir and Bianca took a seat on the Mahieu terrace to wait for Bianca's father to pick them up in the vehicle they would share. Unreal details jumped out at them as they watched the people of Paris abandoning their city, joined by refugees from the north who were fleeing the advancing German troops.

Six million French people had taken to the roads. The main route was congested with cars, carts, bicycles, and people on foot carrying their possessions on their backs. The stream of humanity moved forward at less than a mile an hour, spilling from the roadsides into the farms and fields, crawling ahead like one great unified mass. Cars with engine trouble and untethered horses were scattered everywhere.

With Bianca's father at the wheel, one of his women employees surrounded by packages and suitcases in the back seat, Bianca and Simone in the front, and a bicycle lashed to the hood, their automobile resembled all the others. Cafés and restaurants along the way had run out of food. Alarming rumors spread from group to group: Planes were gunning down people who were fleeing by road, Italy had entered the war, the trains had stopped running, Evreux was in flames. There were stories whose absurdity made one uncomfortable: On some roads workmen continued to lay tar, and the hapless refugees walked and rode over the fresh tar, which splattered them, burning and staining their skin.

By evening they had reached the tiny village of Illiers, and de Beauvoir spent the first night of the exodus in the town that had served as the model for Proust's Combray. At daylight de Beauvoir hurried down to the café to write Sartre. There, hearing on the radio that Paris had been declared an open city, she was unable to choke back her tears.

She planned to stay with Madame Morel at La Pouèze, where she would not be far from Nantes when classes resumed at the Lycée Camille-Sée. She left Bianca and began to make her way south. In Laval the telephones were working, but there was pandemonium surrounding their use. Simone left her suitcase with Sartre's precious letters at the baggage check and fought her way through the crowds to phone Madame Morel.[24] When she returned to claim her bag, it had disappeared; all the letters Sartre had written to her since 1929 were gone, lost forever. A bus was leaving for Angers, and de Beauvoir fought her way aboard and stood the entire trip. The bus let her off in Angers at 8 P.M., and she managed to secure herself a chair at the sidewalk café near the station. Thousands of people, stranded, were seated on their possessions or wandering in circles. Children had been lost in the crush, bombs had exploded, people had been sprayed with machine-gun fire. Finally a car arrived to take her to the Morel home.

The flood of refugees brought the latest news as it streamed through La Pouèze. The Germans were on the way. When it was reported that the enemy had reached Le Mans, the streets emptied and the shutters clacked shut. Truckfuls of French troops passed through town, followed by officers in cars, a column of tanks, straggling foot soldiers, then nothing. The town was empty, the road clear. "Then something exploded under our windows, the plate glass in the restaurant across the way flew into slivers, a guttural voice barked out some words in an incomprehensible language, and they were upon us."[25]

De Beauvoir peered out between the slats of the closed venetian blinds, observing and remembering. Later she would reconstruct this pain and anxiety in the pages of *The Blood of Others* and *The Prime of Life*.

On June 21 the terms of the armistice were published, the fighting stopped. The status of prisoners of war was not at all clear, and de Beauvoir was worried. Would all prisoners be taken to Germany and kept there until the end of the war? It seemed unlikely that Germany would be willing to house and feed three million men. Refugees who had begun to return home told themselves that thousands of soldiers had probably managed to hide from the Germans and were heading for home dressed as civilians.

Perhaps Sartre had managed to slip through the net somehow and was already in Paris. There was no way of finding out short of returning to Paris immediately. De Beauvoir found a Dutch couple who were about to return to their cleaning and dyeing establishment in Paris and were willing to take her along. She said good-bye to Madame Morel and at 5 A.M. squeezed in among the packages and suitcases. The car, with a mattress lashed to its roof, retraced in reverse the path of the exodus from Paris.

The Occupation had already begun in Le Mans. Military vehicles were noisily circling the central square, their loudspeakers blaring military marches and announcements in French and German. In the sunshine it all resembled a country fair. The Germans entered cafés, saluted, clicked their heels, and laughed, "well-groomed, cheerful, and courteous."[26] The newspapers and the radio encouraged people to return to their homes.

All well and good, but no one could return anywhere until there were new supplies of gasoline. Powerless, the French crowds milled around, buying whatever was offered for sale, eating what they could find, sleeping where there was room.

De Beauvoir refused to resign herself to anything. It was 105 miles to

Paris, and she set out to cover the distance on foot, walking along the tarred highway beneath a scorching sun. When a German truck pulled up, two women rushed to board it and de Beauvoir followed them. It was suffocatingly hot and uncomfortable under the tarpaulin roof, and de Beauvoir was jostled and tossed until she was sick to her stomach, yet she was happy to be making progress, passing the many people stranded along the way. She would not be victimized by a situation, no matter what it might be.[27]

The truck took her as far as Mantes, where she spotted a Red Cross vehicle about to depart and hitched a ride, finding herself squeezed in between two nurses whose vehement anglophobia surprised her. The desert surrounding Paris surprised her even more: Bridges had been destroyed, there were bomb craters in abundance, and the area was as still as the lunar landscape it resembled. She was left at the Red Cross bureau in the rue François-I, where people had lined up for news of the prisoners of war. She crossed Paris on foot, passing through mostly empty streets, spotting an occasional line outside the rare shops that remained open. At her hotel in the rue Vavin the owner confessed to having thrown away all her belongings, convinced that she was gone for good. Nothing remained; she would have to start all over again.

De Beauvoir then learned of the existence of enormous camps where it appeared that prisoners of war would be kept for years. "I don't think I have ever felt so utterly depressed as I did during that walk back through the deserted streets . . . the one thought in my mind was of Sartre, literally and physically starving to death."[28]

She realized that her stubborn love for him made her a woman like any other, riveted to a single overriding hope: the return of the one prisoner who mattered. She heard the women around her wherever she went, in the cafés, on the street, in the métro; they all talked about "him." He had returned, he was going to return, would he return? You had to be patient, you had to wait, he would write.

De Beauvoir found her way to her "native land," the carrefour Vavin, after three weeks of flight in a sort of collective nothingness that had been humiliating and terrifying. What she saw was a strange Montparnasse in which an unfamiliar fauna—German soldiers in gray or green uniforms— seemed to have become acclimatized. They did not look very different from tourists. "I observe them but register nothing," she noted with surprise in her journal. She moved into her grandmother's empty apartment and the room where she had proudly discovered her independence ten years earlier. "Quite suddenly, and with my whole heart and soul, I find myself believing the war will end, that there will be an 'afterward.' The proof of this is my purchase of a bottle of ink and the notebook in which I'm writing an account of the past few days."[29] In the meantime she did as she had always done to conquer her anxiety, walking for miles and miles through the suburbs just outside Paris.

Olga came into town for a visit and spent several days in the nearly vacant, neighborless apartment. Bianca made an appearance, only to leave soon after. Signs announcing OUT OF BOUNDS TO JEWS appeared in more and more shop windows. Factories fired employees who were either Jewish or foreign-born. Bianca's father had arranged for an Aryan friend to handle his affairs and was preparing to go into hiding. Bianca's life was in danger. In the face of her friend's genuine and warranted distress, de Beauvoir experienced "an uncomfortable feeling very much akin to remorse." She remembered how some years earlier, in a display of humanism and idealism, she had told Olga that there was "no such thing as 'a Jew,' there were only human beings," and added in retrospect, "How head-in-the-clouds I had been!"[30]

The Third Republic was abolished on July 10 and Vichy declared the seat of government. On July 14, French Independence Day, several soldiers paraded before the War Memorial, Marshal Pétain presiding. At the same hour in London, a number of French soldiers who were resolved to continue the struggle against the Nazis marched to the cheers of the English. France was now divided into two zones, and nothing was simple any longer for anyone. The France that had welcomed exiles, the France that had stood for liberty, had become unrecognizable overnight. All civil servants were required to sign an affidavit affirming that they were neither Freemasons nor Jews. De Beauvoir underwent a moment of powerless rage, then signed. Finally a letter from Sartre arrived, postmarked once by the postal authorities and once by the government of Paris.

My love,

I'm a prisoner and not at all unhappy. I hope to be back before the end of the month.[31]

He was in a camp at Baccarat. For de Beauvoir there had been only one month of silence and anxiety. Sartre was alive, he had managed to write her. She was among the privileged; she had not lost anyone.

Other letters, brave and reassuring, reached her. "All in all, my captivity boils down to camping out." He looked forward to being released soon. "My sweet little one, as soon as we're together we'll be able to live." He told her, "I've begun writing a metaphysical treatise: *Being and Nothingness.*"[32]

De Beauvoir wrote him every day, and Sartre sent her a long, wide-ranging letter the day he received seven of her envelopes all at once. "I'm so happy thinking that you're safe." He tells her he had experienced events "with the liveliest interest." The debacle had lasted ten days, and he had written down everything he saw and heard. He was still keeping his note-books, he was writing *Roads to Freedom.* He knew she probably thought he was behaving admirably and hastened to qualify: "I'm neither stoic nor genuine but locked up, padlocked like one of Freud's patients, without the least effort." He asked her to send two packages, one containing "mounds of food" and the other books. He concluded by telling de Beauvoir, "You're my whole life," and recommending that she not mention to Wanda or Olga that he was writing to her every day.[33]

Sartre was betting on the future, and he would be ready when it arrived. The course of events had not robbed him of a single page or one observation. In direct contact with the world, buoyed up instead of being crushed by contingencies, Sartre set de Beauvoir an example of freedom in action. To write, de Beauvoir would say, had become an act of faith. Every morning and every evening she took her place at the Dôme and set to work.

De Beauvoir made plans to visit Sartre, but he discouraged her: "It's possible that we'll be leaving this place." To give her hope, he added, "Surely one day you'll see me show up behind the statue of Balzac."*[34]

On October 26 he wrote, "My love, it's our eleventh anniversary and I feel so close to you." He scolded her a bit: "My love, you must never again dream that I don't love you anymore. . . . Never have I loved you so much. . . . My sweet little one, have faith and patience." He described life in the stalag—from which, he told her, he had a superb view. "We sleep on the floor in groups of fifteen and live primarily in a reclining position." He performed calisthenics every morning and had managed to become an interpreter at the infirmary because he spoke fluent German. He had taken it upon himself to create a popular university in the camp and gave classes for an audience "almost exclusively made up of priests—I won't give up disciples," he wrote to make the Castor smile. Sartre had applied himself to writing plays in order to distract the prisoners. Fifteen hundred spectators approved his work, so he threw himself into it. *Bariona* featured sixty characters wearing masks. "Know that I'm writing my first serious play and that I'm giving it my all. . . . I certainly have talent as a dramatist, I made a scene where an angel announces the birth of Christ to some shepherds which took everyone's breath away. Tell Dullin about it."[35]

He went on to say that he had discovered "an entirely new theatrical

---

*A statue of Balzac by Rodin is in the carrefour Vavin.

form." He was making great progress, but, he reassured de Beauvoir, "Don't get it into your head that I'm living through something that separates me from you and leaves you with catching up to do."[36]

He appeared to be faithful to his companion; they had traveled this far together, and they would go on navigating the road to come. "You'll see how exciting it will be for *us* when I return . . . and this whole interesting life that I'm leading here—it's with you that I lead it. We are not separated." And, buried in the body of the letter, a little sentence revealed a great deal about his intentions: "I am waiting . . . resolved, that if the heavens don't help me, I will help myself."[37]

In Paris, where shortages were beginning to be felt, de Beauvoir ate in little restaurants where she was known and the proprietors managed to lay their hands on reasonable supplies. Jerusalem artichokes and rutabagas, vegetables largely forgotten since World War I, had reappeared. In the autumn of 1940 rationing began to weigh in earnest on the population, with specified allotments of staple foods per person: bread, 8.8 ounces per day; meat, 6.3 ounces per week; fats (oil and butter), .5 ounce per day; cheese, 1.4 ounces per week; sugar, 17.6 ounces per month.

Recourse to the black market and fraud became essential in order to survive. A meal served without ration coupons cost 100 francs for a meat dish and some cheese, and the average salary was 1000 francs a month. Fabric, clothing, linens—everything was in short supply. The black market took shape and expanded. The winter of 1940–1941 was one of the coldest of the century, and fuel was scarce. Women took to wearing pants as a defensive measure; they wore ski pants, took in their husbands' old trousers, pieced together makeshift slacks from other garments. The Paris Prefecture of Police chose that miserable winter to prohibit the wearing of "masculine clothing" by women—an edict Simone de Beauvoir would not soon forget.

She rejected the entire Vichy regime out of hand. At the lycée, "thinking right" was the order of the day. "Henceforth the family would be the sovereign unit, the reign of virtue was at hand, and God would be spoken of respectfully in the schools . . . the same violent prejudice and stupidity that had darkened my childhood . . . now extended over the entire country, an official and repressive blanket."[38] Nevertheless she went right on teaching Hegel to her students.

De Beauvoir's future as a writer suddenly looked far less promising, and Brice Parrain at the NRF could say nothing to reassure her. The entire "left bank" had moved to the south of France. She would not be able to publish her novel without the censor's approval.

She took refuge at the National Library and immersed herself in Hegel,

whose "amplitude of detail amazed me."[39] Her thirst to know would come
to the rescue once again, but even the strength of Hegel's speculations could
not allay completely the fury and anguish brought on by the realities of daily
life in Occupied France, and de Beauvoir turned back to Kierkegaard with
passionate interest. She recalled how she had felt as a student when she
vacillated between philosophy and literature, asking herself endless questions about Spinoza and Dostoevsky. "When I read Spinoza and Dostoevsky
alternately, at one moment I was convinced that literature was mere meaning-
less fury, at the next that metaphysics was nothing but idle speculation and
logic-chopping. . . . From an intellectual viewpoint this confrontation of the
individual and the universal was the merest cliché; but for me it was as
original and actual an experience as my revelation concerning the existence
of rational awareness in others." Her reading and thinking brought her to the
conclusion that she was inseparably bound up with and responsible to her
contemporaries; she could no longer consider herself detached from her fellow human beings and her nation. "Heidegger," she wrote, "had convinced
me that 'human reality' is accomplished and expressed in each separate living
entity."[40]

She had traveled through the dark night to arrive, as had Sartre, at the
same crossroads of freedom. She discovered responsibility and solidarity and
saw that "in Occupied France the mere fact of being alive implied acquies-
cence in oppression. Not even suicide would have freed me from this dilemma; on the contrary, it would have set the final seal on my defeat. My
salvation was bound up with that of my country as a whole."[41] Now she was
ready to take a stand and play an active part.

THE BLOOD OF OTHERS

"When you get this note, be sure to stay in touch with the
Hotel Denmark, as I'll be phoning there as soon as I arrive to let you know
where to meet me."[42] Sartre was going to be released. One evening in late
March de Beauvoir returned to her hotel to find a note from him: "I'm at the
Three Musketeers Café." The hardest part was over.

She ran the length of the rue Delambre and the rue de la Gaîté and burst
into the café only to find no sign of Sartre. One of the waiters handed her
a sheet of paper with the scribbled message that Sartre had waited two hours,
gone for a walk to calm his nerves, and would soon return—which he did.
His captivity had lasted from June 1940 to March 1941.

Paris surprised Sartre. In the camp he had sworn not to give an inch, not to bend. He believed that the people of Paris had made too many concessions, too many compromises. Why had de Beauvoir agreed to sign the declaration that she was neither a Freemason nor a Jew? How could she stoop to buying anything, whatever it might be, on the black market? He was impatient to do something, to *act*. He got in touch with old friends who belonged to the Resistance movements. De Beauvoir had moved into the Hotel Mistral, having pushed her few belongings through the streets on a handcart, and there the new Socialism and Liberty group held its first meeting. Socialism and Liberty was more than a name; it was a working outline for the goals of its members, who included Jacques-Laurent Bost, Jean Pouillon, Cuzin, Jean-Toussaint Desanti, and Maurice Merleau-Ponty. Their activities were to recruit further support, gather information, distribute tracts, and establish contact with other Resistance workers. They met Jean Cavaillès at the Closerie des Lilas and held meetings, without taking any particular precautions, "in hotel rooms or someone's study at the Ecole Normale." The first issue of their news bulletin proclaimed that "if Germany won the war, our task would be to see that she lost the peace."[43]

The news was so discouraging that a German victory seemed possible in 1941. In North Africa and in Greece, the Germans and the Italians were advancing on all fronts. England no longer had a base on the Continent. In June, Hitler attacked Russia and won victory after victory; Kiev was taken, Leningrad besieged. The Nazis were masters of Europe from Norway to the Mediterranean, the Italians were in Somaliland and Libya, the Japanese had invaded China. In France many people saw no way of escaping Germany's power and looked upon collaboration as the wise course of action. It was then that the V, the symbol of an English victory, and the Cross of Lorraine, the Gaullist emblem, began to appear on the walls of Paris and in the corridors of the métro.

At the beginning of summer Sartre and de Beauvoir set out to contact all the writers who had relocated in the Free Zone and to secure their backing for Socialism and Liberty. One of de Beauvoir's students at the Lycée Molière, Nathalie Sorokine, a stateless Russian, got them bicycles by dubious means. Friends had given them the address of a café where a guide would meet them and take them across the demarcation line. The man in question was arrested a few days before their arrival, but a middle-aged woman took his place, leading the small group through fields and woods under cover of night.

The next morning they were in the Free Zone. They had sent their bicycles ahead, and while waiting for the arrival of the train that carried them, Sartre and de Beauvoir eagerly read the newspapers and were disappointed to find that they were no different from the newspapers in Paris. As soon as they had their bicycles they pedaled to Bourg, where Sartre had himself officially demobilized. The American films being shown in Lyon or Marseille gave them an additional illusion of freedom and they "went to literally anything for the sheer pleasure of seeing an American picture again."[44] Only German propaganda films were being shown in Paris.

De Beauvoir was delighted to be pedaling alongside Sartre: "I had been so afraid of losing everything—not only Sartre himself, but all the happiness I had known."[45] She no longer had the harsh tendency to consider pleasure and happiness as her due, like any other quality or result that could be achieved through sheer application and willpower. She had seen her relative powerlessness in the face of the power wielded by others. She realized there had been a fundamental change in her attitude when the front tire on Sartre's bicycle blew out and she took the troublesome interruption in stride. "Previously the idea that this trip could be brought to an abrupt halt, against my express wishes, would have filled me with rage."[46]

They covered mile after mile, stopping to stay with people whom their friends in the Resistance had told them to look up, sleeping in their tent in open fields or woods by night. They pedaled all the way to Grasse to see André Gide, who had taken up residence there in a hotel. Gide welcomed Sartre and listened to what he had to say, changing café tables three times so that no third party could follow their conversation, but he failed to display an interest in Sartre's project. They took to their bicycles again to see André Malraux at Cap-Martin. Sartre was received at La Souco, the sumptuous villa where Malraux lived with Josette Clotis. They lunched on chicken served by a maître d'hôtel. Malraux told Sartre that he did not see the practical effectiveness of purely intellectual action. In his opinion, you either fought or were silent; only tanks and planes were likely to win the war.

They set off for Grenoble, where Colette Audry was staying, in hopes of interesting her in Socialism and Liberty. The road was narrow and winding, and while coasting downhill with poor brakes, de Beauvoir swerved to avoid hitting two other cyclists, skidded, fell, and lost consciousness on impact. Sartre revived her. Since she "felt as though all the cells in my body were jarring and grinding against each other," she traveled the remaining ten miles in some discomfort. Her face and lips were badly swollen, her skin was scraped raw, and she had lost a tooth. Nevertheless she mounted her bicycle again the following day. Having ridden ahead of Sartre and stopped to wait for him, de Beauvoir had a sterling opportunity to meditate on the male psyche when a man, roaring with laughter, called out to her, "Still waiting for him after all he's done to you?"[47]

Near Chalon a ferryman took a group of twenty cyclists, including Sartre and de Beauvoir, across the border, through woods and under barbed wire, in broad daylight. Their next stop was Angers for a few days of vacation with Madame Morel before returning to Paris for the start of classes. They had covered more than 1250 miles.

In Paris the political climate had darkened. Red or yellow posters proliferated, announcing the executions of Frenchmen. The Germans had decreed that any person convicted of disseminating Communist propaganda would be shot "and had set up a special tribunal to judge those charged with anti-German activities."[48] Sabotage and Resistance attacks on the Germans were increasing, and for each German killed, a disproportionate number of hostages would be shot. Socialism and Liberty was too weak and isolated to organize efficient action, and the group gradually disbanded. Sartre attempted to contact the Communists to form a united front but was rejected. The Communists wanted no part of him; some even said that his liberation only served to prove that he was an agent provocateur.* As Simone de Beauvoir had felt all along, literature was the only form of resistance work that was effectively open to them. She began work on her second novel, *The Blood of Others,* in which she described the Occupation and the Resistance, but she did not expect to see it published before the victory in which she forced herself to believe.

She was convinced that the writer owed it to himself to take action through his works. She had not given up telling herself, "I am a writer, a woman whose entire life is dominated by literature." "To write remains the major concern of my life."[49] The Occupation depressed everyone, but de Beauvoir kept her faith in words, in literature.

Georges de Beauvoir died on July 8, 1941. Weakened by months of undernourishment, overwhelmed by the defeat and disgusted by the Occupation, he had lost the will to live in a world that was no longer his, and he let himself slip into death without a struggle. He asked that he be spared a priest's visit, and he died, detached and disdainful, with his daughter at his bedside. De Beauvoir admired "this departure to no destination . . . amazed at the peaceful way he returned to nothingness."[50] He had this to say to Simone, who kept watch over him until the last: "You earned your own living early on. Your sister cost me a fortune." Poupette had tried to succeed as a painter. "She lived at home and my father was barely feeding her. Really, the bare minimum." He did not leave a cent, and Françoise de Beauvoir had to

---

*To make up for his support of collaboration policy at the NRF, Pierre Drieu La Rochelle called for the release of a number of writers being held prisoner in Germany. Jean-Paul Sartre was among them, according to Herbert L. Lottman in *The Left Bank.*

go to work for a living. She found a job with the Red Cross, someone got her a bicycle, and with Simone's help she was able to get by.

Obtaining the material goods one needed to survive was a particularly daunting task, and de Beauvoir applied herself to meeting the challenge with such diligence that she was effectively distracted from her darkest thoughts and worries.

She was not fond of domestic chores, but she met them with her familiar formula: Turn a disagreeable situation into a virtual obsession, and emerge victorious. At the Hotel Mistral she had a room with a kitchen, and she became a makeshift chef. Foodstuffs had to be tracked down; rutabagas or cabbages were a real find. "I resurrected one of my favorite childhood games —organizing a strict economy for a very poor household." She would write Nelson Algren that for three years she cooked for Sartre and Nathalie. The poverty she had experienced at 71 rue de Rennes surfaced from her memory along with an extra measure of courage with which to meet the present situation. Because most people were subsisting in poverty, it was no longer a humiliating condition to find oneself in. She covered miles in searching for provisions. Paradoxically, it was during the war that she discovered the pleasure of writing while a savory-smelling soup simmered away on the stove. "Though I was not in the true sense of the word a housewife, I had a glimpse of a housewife's joys. Yet I was not really more up against the hard facts of life than I had ever been."[51]

Her father's death entitled her to ration coupons for fabric, and this enabled her to have an overcoat and a dress made. Because of the cold, de Beauvoir resorted to wearing ski pants except at the lycée. Wooden clogs had begun to take the place of leather shoes, for which materials and repairs were rationed. As heating fuel was increasingly difficult to come by, de Beauvoir got into the habit of going to the Flore to work. Often she arrived just as the place opened in order to claim a seat next to the stovepipe. Thierry Maulnier, Dominique Aury, Jacques Audiberti, Arthur Adamov, and Mouloudji also went to the Flore in search of a bit of warmth. The vast majority of the customers were hostile to collaboration and fascism; some were actively involved in the Resistance, others not. Collaborationist journalists were also known to frequent the Flore. Alfred Fabre-Luce described the scene: "On the little marble tables you saw, in lieu of beverages, inkwells. They worked there, between the telephones and the toilet stalls, amid drafts and questionable odors."[52]

When de Beauvoir set up shop permanently on the second floor, others imitated her and it soon resembled a study hall. The news reports circulated, and those who had heard Radio London added what they knew. It was a privileged locale for taking the pulse of events as they unfolded—and for gathering material for *The Blood of Others.*

Collaboration with the Occupation forces made de Beauvoir indignant. She had an unpleasant surprise when, with Dullin listening in silence, Simone Jollivet held forth on how one must move with the times if one hoped to leave one's mark and how Nazism had obviously triumphed. This was the first argument for collaboration that she had heard among her friends. She was overwhelmed to find articles in the recently reestablished pro-Nazi newspaper *Je suis partout* indicting all the political figures of the Third Republic, all Jews, all Communists, and all writers who were attempting to maintain their dignity by living in the Free Zone in the south of France.

Her circle of intimate friends was reduced to Olga, Gégé, Dullin, and Jollivet. Bost returned to Paris as soon as his wounds were sufficiently healed. Olga, seriously ill with tuberculosis, went into a sanitorium, and Bost married her so as to be allowed to visit her, but he spent most of his time with Simone. ("I saw a lot of Bost in those days."[53]) There was also the irrepressible Nathalie.

Nathalie Sorokine, whose parents had fled the Russian Revolution and taken refuge in France, was de Beauvoir's finest pupil at the Lycée Molière in Passy. Nathalie's aggressive nature had amused de Beauvoir from the start: She asked endless questions that were tempered by a demanding intellectual stance. She would have liked to continue studying philosophy, but insofar as she was not French, the world of teaching was closed to her. Her father wanted her to become a chemical engineer, a fate to which she refused to submit.

To an even greater extent than Olga, Nathalie felt exiled in the land where she had been raised. The only country she knew was not her own. Stateless, she had neither the security nor the privileges that go with being French. To compensate, "she reacted by believing that she possessed absolute rights over everything, in the teeth of the entire world."[54]

She interrupted in class, took issue with the material, and talked back to the teacher. Faced with the casual cruelty of those who would humiliate her by reminding her that she had no nationality, she learned to defend herself with irony. Even her appearance betrayed a need to affirm her difference. Clad in skirts that were too long and shoes that were too large, Nathalie impressed de Beauvoir, who admired her intellectual rigor and her baroque vision of the world. Accepted and understood, Nathalie clung to this teacher who was as different from the rest of the faculty as Nathalie was from her peers. De Beauvoir's young admirer waited faithfully at the entrance to the lycée or at the door of de Beauvoir's hotel, then tagged along, describing her adventures. Whether she was telling the truth or making things up as she went, Nathalie's vivid imagination and sharp pictorial sense kept de Beauvoir entertained and half incredulous.

Nathalie prided herself on having shoplifted with a girl friend when she was fourteen; she described her parents' cruelty and brutality and spoke of the chemistry studies her father had forced her to undertake and which she had conducted with rage and considerable breakage. De Beauvoir's own uneasy adolescence remained vivid enough in her memory to generate empathy, and she could not help sympathizing with Nathalie's predicament. Nathalie seemed utterly lost from time to time, and de Beauvoir was disarmed by her tears; she devoted more and more time to Nathalie, who demanded still more in return—and got it.

Uncertain about what she should do with Nathalie, Simone had taken up the question with Sartre. In January 1940 he had written, "So you have lost your heart to your little Sorokine, my love? But you will not let her down, by no means. What is it? You are all stories and all loves and all charm."[55] He wrote again from the stalag:

> I find your harem of girls very amusing. I encourage you very much to love your little Sorokine, who is quite charming. But I can hear you say, "I would have to give her up at the end of the war." You are naïve, my love, for either you won't care for her then . . . and you will spit her out of your life, you nasty little one, or you will become fond of her and then I know that you will be fierce enough to keep her in spite of everyone. It would be a real pity to give up this pure and charming little heart.[56]

In another letter, "You are mean with Sorokine, my little one, don't grumble, I am not minding your business, but I believe that it broke her heart not to spend her night with you."[57]

Sartre commented often on Nathalie's invasive love, as in this letter from Brumath:

> As for Sorokine, like you I find her instability fairly annoying, but you should keep in mind that there's a vast array of tender gestures that a man, even one wellborn, can permit himself in a dance hall with a woman and that a woman with another woman must forbid herself. That must make things a bit aggravating for her. Despite the fact that she loves you roughly, this whole story makes me laugh, my dear little one. My, but you're kind and pleasant in the middle of all this, little

too-loved one. Not too much for your merits, of course, but for what you want out of all this.[58]

When Sartre saw the debacle coming, he implored de Beauvoir not to await the German invasion in Paris. It was the stateless young girl's welfare in particular that concerned him, for she was in greater danger than the others. He wrote the Castor:

> You know, my dear little one, if you can possibly swing it you must absolutely take Sorokine with you in case of evacuation. Never mind about the mother's curse. I'm not considering in the least the affection she has for you, but you can do so much in bringing her along; you'll save her from the chaos of a forced evacuation and a total lack of money and then she'll be with you, and if not, maybe she'll go for months without being able to send or receive news. Take her with you, and if it costs us a few pennies, never mind, what else can you do? And then, above all, we are privileged, and this will be the only concrete help that I understand and accept: the full support of an individual.[59]

The jealous and possessive Nathalie did not like this omnipresent Sartre to whom Simone wrote every single day. He was far away, and she would see about him when he returned, but she did not hide the fact that she wished him dead.

Nathalie was responsible for introducing de Beauvoir to the Swiss sculptor Alberto Giacometti, and that was the beginning of a lasting friendship. At the Dôme, Giacometti had noticed the tall, blonde magnificence that was Nathalie, struck up a conversation with her, and been won over by her vivacity and nonconformity. He invited her to dinner at the Dôme, sometimes with Picasso, sometimes with other fascinating personalities. Nathalie found them all superficial and badly informed on philosophical theories; she would get up and leave the instant she had finished eating. Since she was a strapping young girl with a healthy appetite that the student cafeterias rarely satisfied, Giacometti found the way to keep her at the table a little longer: No sooner had she finished her meal than he would order her a second, which she devoured eagerly. For him she was so amusing that he allowed her to use the courtyard adjoining his studio to repaint the bicycles that she seemed to unearth as if by magic. Since gasoline had been requisitioned for the war effort, the bicycle remained the sole means of transportation for most Parisians. Having given de Beauvoir an ill-gotten bicycle, Nathalie made a present of one to Sartre when he returned to Paris. She gave illicitly acquired, artfully camouflaged bicycles to all her friends.[60]

Nathalie became part of the Family and wrote a parody of life in their little group, *The Peashooter Family* (*La Famille Sarbacane,* unpublished).

Nathalie's mother, unhappy with the life her daughter was leading, accused de Beauvoir of abducting a minor—a criminal offense punishable by law. Friends intervened and the criminal charge was dropped, but after twelve years of teaching, de Beauvoir was barred from the University, and she was lucky that the matter went no further, for the offense carried a jail sentence. She could no longer teach anywhere in France; she would have to find a new way of earning a living.

In 1943 de Beauvoir knew many influential people in theatre and publishing circles. Sartre's screenplay for *Les Jeux sont faits* had just been accepted by the director Jean Delannoy, and a journalist named Delange, who had contacts in the film industry, told de Beauvoir that he could arrange a contract for her with the national radio network. A single one-hour radio script per month would give her an income of 2000 francs. Sartre told the Castor, "The script has finally been accepted. Don't worry; you won't need to work next year, we'll live quietly."[61] Sartre signed a contract with Pathé for a series of screenplays, and the money began to roll in. He wrote de Beauvoir, "We can really tell the Alma Mater to go to hell." Gallimard brought out *The Flies* in April, and Sartre wrote articles for *Les Lettres françaises,* which was being published clandestinely. An excerpt from his novel *The Age of Reason* was published, and in June Gallimard released *Being and Nothingness,* dedicated to the Castor. The paper advertising band wrapped around the book bore Sartre's words "What is important in a vase is the emptiness within." This monumental work went almost entirely unnoticed. The media were not particularly taken with the field of philosophy; only such marginal publications as *Confluences* and *Fontaine* printed favorable reviews.

In June Charles Dullin mounted a production of *The Flies* at the Sarah Bernhardt Theatre, renamed the Theatre de la Cité in view of the fact that Bernhardt was Jewish. Dullin himself played Jupiter, Olga (now known as Olga Dominique) played Electra, and the play ran for twenty-five performances. De Beauvoir attended all the rehearsals. Sartre gave an interview to *Comœdia,* and Dullin consented to be interviewed by the collaborationist paper *La Gerbe* to help launch the play. In general the critical response to Sartre's play was harsh, and no one spoke of its political implications. The crowd at the Flore made no mistake about the deeper meaning of *The Flies,* but it was a partial failure all the same. Sartre had established some solid friendships in joining the National Writers' Committee (CNE), a clandestine academy that assembled the most prestigious names in literature, be they Communist, as was the case with Aragon, or not, as with Mauriac, Father R.-L. Bruckberger, and Jean Paulhan. De Beauvoir had the committee's support for the publication of her first novel, *She Came to Stay,* which appeared in August. The book was an immediate success; both the underground and the collaborationist press gave it glowing reviews, and de Beauvoir became famous overnight. In a time of paper shortages and limited press runs, 23,000 copies were printed of *She Came to Stay.* Her name was mentioned for the Prix Goncourt, and the CNE informed her that they had no objection to her accepting it if she refrained from giving press interviews and publishing articles in connection with the prize.[62]

"Gallimard's new woman novelist," "the hope of French literature," mounted her bicycle and with Sartre in tow left for La Pouèze to spend a few days with Madame Morel. When they returned to Paris, she moved from the rundown Aubusson Hotel to the Louisiane Hotel, which she would help to make famous. Several years later, Juliette Gréco and Anne-Marie Cazalis would ask for de Beauvoir's old room, number 50. From this beloved furnished room with kitchen, de Beauvoir had a view of the sky and "a great sea of rooftops. None of my previous retreats had come so close to being the apartment of my dreams, and I felt like staying there for the rest of my life."[63] Sartre lived in a room at the end of the hall when he was not with Wanda, who was performing at the Lancry Theatre.

Nathalie too moved into the hotel, taking a room on the floor below with a former student of Sartre, a young Spanish Jew named Bourla. Bourla had fallen in love with her, and she lived with him until he was arrested. A previous lover, a wealthy student who had an apartment, had asked her to move in with him, and she had jumped at the offer because above all else she wanted to get away from her family. But she had soon become bored, for "he wanted to make love all the time," and she asked Simone to give her a small allowance, which Simone could not do. She accused de Beauvoir of forcing her onto the streets. Life with Bourla was fun; he stole from his father to add to his allowance, and he offered Nathalie sumptuous dinners bought on the black market. Every night she asked de Beauvoir to come and give her a kiss and tuck them in. De Beauvoir had ambiguous feelings toward Nathalie, to whom she dedicated *The Blood of Others.*

The publication of *She Came to Stay* marked a turning point in de Beauvoir's life. When the first review of the book came out, she marveled, "Here was a review, written by a real critic, printed in a real paper, to assure me in black and white that I had written a real book . . . I could not contain my joy."[64] Michel and Zette Leiris had her over, and she met Raymond Queneau and Albert Camus. She wrote Sartre that the time had come for her to resign herself to fitting in with important folk.

Albert Camus was recruiting members for *Combat,* an underground newspaper that had evolved from a Resistance movement founded early in 1942.
Combat's goal was to gather information about the Occupation forces, to
sabotage their installations, and to bring down the enemy with weapons.
Jacqueline Bernard, an assistant editor of *Combat* and the person responsible
for communications between the publication's production teams, told Camus'
biographer Herbert Lottman that, toward the end of the summer in 1943,
Camus brought a couple of volunteers to a staff meeting. Since everyone used
a code name, it was not until she went to see *No Exit* that she discovered that
"Castor" and "Miro" were de Beauvoir and Sartre. At the time they were
participating in these clandestine meetings, an anonymous tract was circulat-
ing in Paris that called the existentialist writers "pseudo-resistants."[65]

THE FIESTAS

*T*he year 1944 would bring further reasons for believing in a
happy future. "We awaited Hitler's downfall with feverish exultation."[66] In
January de Beauvoir went skiing in Morzine with Bost. As soon as she came
back the Leirises invited her to be part of a special evening to be held in their
home on March 19, which would feature a reading of Picasso's play *Desire
Caught by the Tail.* In January 1941 Picasso found it too cold to paint and took
to writing in a schoolboy's notebook. On the first page he sketched himself
in the process of writing, all bundled up. He listed the cast of characters on
the second page: Big Foot, the Onion, the Tart, the Cousin, Round End, the
two Doggies, Silence, Fat Anguish, Thin Anguish, and the Curtains. It was
a surrealist farce in six acts that took place in the Sordid's Hotel. The stage
directions indicate just how difficult it would be to produce the play faithfully. Act Two: "A corridor in the Sordid's Hotel. The two feet of each guest
are outside the door to their room, doubled up with pain." Act Six: "In the
combination sewer-bedroom-kitchen-and-bathroom of the Villa of Anguish" there was a bathtub full of suds in which Onion, Big Foot, and Round
End were courting the Tart and the Cousin. The play was published by Marc
Barbezat in his luxurious review *L'Arbalète,* which he printed himself on a
handpress in Lyon. His wife, Olga-the-brunette, was one of Dullin's students
and was friendly with de Beauvoir and Olga.

The performance of *Desire Caught by the Tail* was held in the Leirises'
apartment on the quai des Grands-Augustins. Their windows looked out on

the Seine, and the walls were hung with modern masterpieces by Juan Gris and Picasso. The art dealer Kahnweiller, who had Picasso under contract and handled the work of most of the great contemporary painters, was Zette Leiris' brother-in-law. Camus directed the play and was a sort of master of ceremonies; he signaled each change of scene by rapping a large cane on the floor. Sartre played Round End, Leiris was Big Foot, Picasso's mistress Dora Marr was Fat Anguish, Zanie Campan, the only real actress in the cast, was cast as the Tart, and de Beauvoir appeared as the Cousin. The spectators assembled in the Leirises' large drawing room included the painter Georges Braque, the actor and stage director Jean-Louis Barrault, the actress Madeleine Renaud, the playwright Armand Salacrou, the poet Georges Bataille, the philosopher Jacques Lacan and his wife, the film actress Sylvia Bataille, and the poet Georges Limbour—in short, the elite of the avant-garde.

Everyone was enchanted. Each night the blackout plunged deserted streets into darkness and silence, but here was a night-long celebration in the middle of Occupied Paris. From now on, it was decided, they would hold nocturnal fiestas, unqualifiedly joyous occasions that would offer a fleeting alternative to the worry and uncertainty of daily life. They proved to be magical interludes, an anticipation of the victory to come. The fiestas were held either in Simone's room at the Louisiane, which had become a mecca for the intelligentsia, at Bost's place in Taverny, or at the Batailles' apartment in the cour de Rohan. Each guest used his ingenuity to supply food and drink. Records were played, dances were danced. Everyone made an effort to keep the company entertained. "We had pantomimes, diatribes, parodies, monologues, and confessions: the flow of improvisations never dried up."[67] Sartre outdid himself on these occasions and was always in demand for songs and comic sketches. Bost recalled a dinner in de Beauvoir's hotel room with Camus, Zette and Michel Leiris, and Picasso in attendance. De Beauvoir had combed the city for something to serve and was unable to buy anything but beans. All morning long de Beauvoir, Bost—who served as chef for the Family when there were guests—and Nathalie sorted beans full of weevils. Camus collapsed with laughter at the sight of the enormous bowlful of beans: "You'd think we were back in the barracks."[68]

Finding food was a major problem. Madame Morel sent packages from the country, but delivery was so slow that more often than not the meat they contained was half spoiled or crawling with maggots on arrival. De Beauvoir soaked the suspect meat in vinegar, boiled it, and seasoned it liberally. One day, while Bost and de Beauvoir looked helplessly on, Sartre grabbed a spoiled rabbit and tossed it out of the window.[69]

On June 5, in the vast apartment in the rue de la Tour-d'Auvergne that

Dullin and Simone Jollivet shared, Sartre and de Beauvoir organized one of the more memorable fiestas. The place lent itself to festivity; it was there that Victor Hugo had once housed his mistress Juliette Drouet. A spacious circular drawing room opened onto a garden full of flowers. Jollivet had given full sway to her imagination, and the house was decked out with ribbons and garlands and bouquets, the buffet was miraculously well stocked, and the liquor flowed in quantities reminiscent of peacetime.

De Beauvoir and Sartre had invited all their friends and brought the Family. The NRF was represented, the young Gallimards were there, and Camus had come with Maria Casarès, who was starring in his play *The Misunderstanding,* then in rehearsal at the Mathurins Theatre. De Beauvoir was impressed by Casarès' strange beauty and the violet and mauve striped Rochas dress she wore. Her talent as a tragedienne had taken Paris by surprise; she was a Spanish Republican in exile, her father having been a government minister before Franco's victory.

The evening was an exceptionally lively one, the men and women present bursting with talent and ambition. This was the group that would give the postwar era its zest and ideology, and fate seemed to have chosen this date. Late that night, at precisely 1:30 A.M., American paratroopers began to land on the Normandy beaches. D-Day was under way; the Allies would soon be landing in force. When the party broke up at dawn, de Beauvoir, Bost, and Olga set off toward Montparnasse. At the railway station they saw posters announcing that all train departures were canceled until further notice. With her heart beating wildly, de Beauvoir ran back to her hotel. People were abuzz in the entryway and on the stairs. A cyclist had ridden past with the news: The Allies had landed in Normandy and the battle was raging.

De Beauvoir, along with all the others who had participated in the night's festivities, had the impression that somehow, by premonition, they had celebrated the decisive turning point in the war. Now Germany's defeat was certain. The end was near for the Occupation army, and the consequences were immediately apparent. Surveillance of underground movements intensified.

Jacqueline Bernard was picked up by the Gestapo while on her way to a meeting of the group that wrote and distributed *Combat* (she would be deported to Ravensbruck). All members of the group were now in danger. Bernard managed to warn Camus, who immediately notified Janine Gallimard. The very next day, Camus and Michel and Pierre Gallimard left Paris on three bicycles, with Janine Gallimard doubling up with each man in turn. Before leaving, Camus had gotten word to Sartre and de Beauvoir that they too should go into hiding. They stayed with the Leirises temporarily, then put

"I promised myself that when I grew up, I would never forget that a five-year-old is already a complete individual."

"Every year my parents spent three weeks at Divonne-les-Bains with a troupe of amateur actors who put on plays at the Casino."

The Carrefour Vavin in 1914. Simone de Beauvoir was born in the apartment above the Café de la Rotonde.

Simone de Beauvoir and Elisabeth L., "Zaza Mabille" in her memoirs.

"My sister always came first in my affections." Hélène de Beauvoir.

Simone de Beauvoir as a Lycée professor.

From left to right, top: Jacques Lacan, Cécile Eluard, Pierre Reverdy, Louise Leiris, Zanie Campan, Pablo Picasso, Valentine Hugo, Simone de Beauvoir, Yves Brassai. Bottom: Jean-Paul Sartre, Albert Camus, Michel Leiris et Jean Aubier, in Picasso's studio, June 1944.

De Beauvoir was only 21 and Sartre 24 when this singular temptation to incorporate a young girl into their lives first excited their imaginations.

Wanda Kosakievicz performing as Marie Ollivier in Sartre's play **Les Mains Sales.**

Olga Kosakievicz performing as Olga Dominique in Sartre's **Les Mouches.**

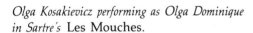

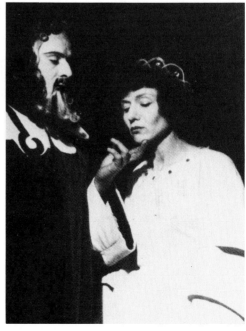

Nelson Algren, "My husband of the Mississippi." (Stephen Deutch)

At the Café de Flore. "Writing has remained the great love of my life."

Sartre and de Beauvoir with Fidel Castro in 1960.

De Beauvoir and Claude Lanzmann received by Nasser in 1967.

Receiving the Sonning Prize in 1983.

De Beauvoir as the guest of François Mitterrand. With Yvette Roudy, minister of the Department of Women's Rights.

"I have been faithful to thee, Cynara, in my fashion." De Beauvoir and Sartre in Crete, 1978.

Sweden, 1981. "I have never met anyone in the whole of my life who was so well equipped for happiness as I was, or who labored so stubbornly to achieve it."

"He corresponded exactly to the dream companion I had longed for since I was fifteen: He was the double in whom I found all my burning aspirations raised to the pitch of incandescence. I should always be able to share everything with him."

themselves and their bicycles aboard a train for Neuilly-sous-Clermont, where they hid in a tiny apartment above a combination inn and grocery. There they remained for three weeks while events took their course. Absolutely incapable of going even a few days without writing, however, they ended up installing themselves in the lobby with paper and pen, among the local inhabitants, who played cards or billiards. Leiris and Bost brought them the news that was not reported in the papers: the German attack on the Vercors maquis, the peasant massacres, the destruction of villages, the execution of Resistance fighters.

On August 11 the radio and the newspapers announced that the Americans were on the outskirts of Chartres. Sartre and de Beauvoir packed their bags and began pedaling furiously toward Paris. At night flickering red flames seared across the sky, indicating the launch of another V-1 rocket, and de Beauvoir imagined it striking London and killing civilians. The main road was congested with German troops retreating under the machine-gun fire of RAF planes. Sartre and de Beauvoir took to the side roads, pedaling as fast as they could, with one goal in mind: They must not miss the actual liberation of Paris, they dared not be cut off from Paris, they had to be there, to be a part of it! In Chantilly they caught a train that was peppered with machine-gun fire just a few miles down the track, but they made it to Paris in time. As a precaution, they switched hotels, moving into the Welcome Hotel just down the street.

They found themselves on the Flore terrace, having a drink with Camus, who, with the Gallimards, had also returned by bicycle. He told them that the Resistance leaders were all agreed on one point: Paris should liberate itself just as soon as the Allies seemed to be sufficiently close to the capital.

The Germans were beginning to retreat, and military convoys were a frequent sight. Daily life had become difficult in view of the severe food shortage; people were waiting, preparing themselves for the uprising to come. The first issue of *Combat* intended for the general public was ready. Camus and his colleagues were going to offer their readers something new; they would tell all those who had suffered under the Occupation what they wanted to hear. Resistance fighters and freedom fighters, together they would try to transform the nation. Camus and his staff offered a new morality, a new political stance, and hope for the future.

Camus asked Sartre and de Beauvoir to cover the liberation of the city and to write a series of articles. They agreed that only Sartre's by-line would appear but that de Beauvoir would work alongside him.

The Allies' plan was to force the Germans to evacuate the city or to surrender without fighting in Paris itself. The American Third Army had Paris surrounded. It was understood that the French soldiers who had fought beside the Allies would be the first to enter the capital to accept the German surrender. Resistance leaders had decided to recapture the public monuments and official buildings, one after the other, replacing the swastika banners with the French tricolor. Yet the Germans still possessed considerable strength in Paris, and the mobilization of the Resistance obliged General Dwight Eisenhower to speed up the movement of General Philippe Leclerc's forces. On August 21 the Parisian Liberation Committee called on all citizens to intensify the struggle: "Cut down trees, dig antitank ditches, barricade the roads. A people victorious shall greet the Allies."

The insurrection would claim nearly 1500 lives, including those of 582 civilians. Public buildings were assaulted, and snipers posted on rooftops and behind windows made crossing the streets nearly impossible. "Bullets were flying everywhere. FFI* patrols were handling passersby like traffic policemen: 'Stop!' they would yell, and then 'Go'—at which one scurried across the street."[70]

De Beauvoir gathered the raw material for her reports by roaming the streets. Shots occasionally rang out, much too close to her, and bullets embedded themselves in nearby walls. The latest news was delivered by cyclists who crisscrossed the capital. Sartre was more or less permanently posted with the committee of theatre people at its headquarters at the Comédie-Française.

He and de Beauvoir went to see Camus at *Combat* headquarters in the rue Réaumur, where the entrance was guarded by young men carrying machine guns. The first issue of the newspaper was dated August 21 but carried the legend "number 59, fourth year" to mark its long clandestine existence. "From Resistance to Revolution" was the paper's slogan. Like all Camus' friends and comrades, de Beauvoir believed that together they would bring about a new France. In *Force of Circumstance* she described her own attitude: "We were writers, and that was our job, to address ourselves to others . . . it was our turn to carry the torch."[71]

In their joint reports in *Combat* (on August 28, 29, 30, 31; September 1, 2, 4) one finds the exultant joy of the liberation by following step by step a writer who is putting the most vibrant days of his life into words, his joy heightened by the joy of others.

The final sentence of *The Prime of Life,* the second volume of de Beauvoir's memoirs, which recounts these years, reads: "Thus each book thenceforth impelled me toward its successor, for the more I saw of the world, the more I realized that it was brimming over with all I could ever hope to experience,

---

*Forces Françaises de l'Interieur—the Gaullists.

understand, and put into words."[72] At the time of the liberation, it was the immense collective happiness that filled her with radiant satisfaction. In the times to follow, her life, already rich in work and ideas, would overflow to the point of enriching other lives. The word for this is glory.

VIOLETTE LEDUC

*B*efore the entrance to a cinema on the Champs-Elysées, one of Simone de Beauvoir's women friends introduced her to Violette Leduc, a tall, slim, ugly yet elegant woman who wanted to publish a book. Leduc asked de Beauvoir to read the manuscript of *L'Asphyxie,* which she delivered to her at the Flore. De Beauvoir made suggestions, had Leduc rewrite the ending, and then recommended the revised manuscript to Albert Camus, who had recently been put in charge of a new division at Gallimard. Camus accepted it. Violette Leduc, taken by a strong passion for Simone de Beauvoir, invited her to dinner in the very best restaurants twice a month, where de Beauvoir feasted on lobster and champagne. Although Paris had been liberated, obtaining food remained a major problem, restrictions were severe, and ration coupons were required for everything. Leduc had survived the war by making trips to the farms outside Paris and returning with contraband comestibles that she resold to restaurants at black market prices.

As dish followed dish during their dinners, de Beauvoir's hunger, her greediness, her epicureanism stirred and sharpened Leduc's desire, rendering her pathetic. She tried to soften de Beauvoir's resistance by describing her loneliness, then crying and begging. Yet no sooner had de Beauvoir chewed and swallowed the last morsel and drained her glass of champagne than she rose from the table and escaped into the night, leaving Leduc in tears. She to whom de Beauvoir referred as "the ugly woman" threatened to kill herself. "What can I do?" de Beauvoir wrote. "She gave me her diary to read, it is written with a real talent, she speaks in it of her love for me, it's very embarrassing."[73]

Nevertheless de Beauvoir had discerned her talent and would never refuse to help her and listen to her. Leduc was a tormented, passionate woman. It was de Beauvoir who comforted her when, wracked with sobs, she came to tell her how Jean Genet had hurt her. Genet had called her a pedant and maintained that she had no talent whatsoever. Genet did not like women, least of all those who wrote. Seated beside de Beauvoir during the premiere of her play *Who Shall Die?* *(Les Bouches inutiles),* he kept up a steady stream of merciless criticism throughout the performance. When *All Men Are Mortal* was published, Genet invited de Beauvoir to lunch, complimented her on her book, and concluded the meal by asking her for money. "He had a new lover."

De Beauvoir defended Leduc against Genet's attacks. She was willing to listen to her troubles, but she rejected "the ugly woman's" advances. Their relationship was a strange one. The twice-monthly dinners continued for years. In *L'Affamée* and *Ravages* Leduc described her pathetic longings in a very intense, baroque prose. When she was away from Paris she wrote de Beauvoir every day, and on one occasion she drew up a will that named de Beauvoir as her heir. Twice she tried to commit suicide, once by attempting to run under a truck, once by turning on the gas in her kitchen. When Nelson Algren became de Beauvoir's lover, he asked her not to see Violette again; de Beauvoir refused, arguing that Leduc needed her too much. At the same time she told Leduc that she no longer loved Nathalie Sorokine. Leduc was "exhilarated." A few days later de Beauvoir had a dream in which Nathalie and Violette were the same person and were killed in a motorcycle accident. In her psychological dilemma, de Beauvoir killed off—in a sort of ritual act— the protagonist, as she had done with Xavière/Olga in *She Came to Stay.*

Twenty years later, famous the world over, de Beauvoir would write the preface to Violette Leduc's *La Bâtarde* and thereby help Leduc to reach her own audience at a time when de Beauvoir's books were translated into thirty languages. This introduction, which has the dimensions of an essay, is the existential analysis of a woman adrift, rendered guilty by a mother who reproached her for being born a girl instead of a boy, "for being a woman and therefore condemned to the miseries of the feminine condition." For Leduc, literature had meant salvation and "the reworking of a destiny by a freedom." De Beauvoir described this salvation through literature that she too shared. "To manufacture reality with imaginary materials: that is the prerogative of artists and writers. . . . The failure to relate to others has resulted in that privileged form of communication—a work of art."[74]

8

Existentialism

Man is sole and sovereign master of his destiny if only he wants to be; there you have the affirmation of existentialism; that is truly an optimistic view.
Existentialism and the Wisdom of Nations

"It Was Our Turn to Carry the Torch"

*T*he people who now held important positions in the media were friends and acquaintances. The Resistance fighters were in power, and Sartre and de Beauvoir were part of the group for whom victory would open up the future; politics had become a family affair. De Beauvoir was well aware that her happiness depended on the course of events.

After the liberation there was a time when it looked as though all paths were opening up. But the euphoria did not hold up under the burden of terrible news, and each new revelation brought back the horror of the days of the Occupation. Georges Politzer had been executed by the Germans; many friends were missing. The newspapers gave accounts of massacres and deportations. A shattered and incredulous public discovered the mass graves, torture rooms, and gas chambers of the concentration camps. People learned that the Germans were still firing V-2 rockets at London, that retreating German troops had devastated Holland and slaughtered Belgian villagers. Fear that the situation might somehow reverse itself tempered the jubilation of liberation, and restrictions, rather than being lifted, were tightened.

Simone de Beauvoir entered a new period, one characterized by thought and reflection, which she called her "moral period." In 1943, in the philosophical essay *Pyrrhus et Cinéas,* she brought to bear against inert reason the inescapable evidence of a living affirmation. This 123-page essay was very well received when it appeared in 1944. For four years the public had been starved for literature and philosophy; now the novelty of existentialism and the euphoria of the liberation came together, and new ideas aroused enormous curiosity. De Beauvoir dealt also with the relationship between individual and universal experience and demonstrated the importance of the concept of "situation"* that Sartre had introduced in *Being and Nothingness.* In 1982 de Beauvoir would say, "We argued quite a bit about *Being and Nothingness.* I was opposed to some of his ideas. . . . In the first version of *Being and Nothingness* he spoke about freedom as though it were equally complete for everybody. Or at least that it was always possible to exercise one's freedom. I, on the other hand, insisted that there exist situations in which freedom cannot be exercised or is nothing more than a hoax. He agreed with that. As a result, he gave a lot of weight to the situation in which the human being finds himself."

In *Pyrrhus et Cinéas* she presented two opposing attitudes. Cinéas argues, "What's the good of leaving if you just end up coming home again? What's the point of starting if you'll only have to stop?" Pyrrhus maintains that he will not stop until he has conquered the world; "it's today that I exist, today I throw myself into a future defined by my project at hand." Cinéas' attitude appears to be wise, but it leads to immobility and inertia. In contrast to Cinéas, Pyrrhus wants to choose and to take action; he resists the temptation of indifference. Because man lives, he must give a meaning to his life. De Beauvoir maintained that the concrete possibilities open to people are unequal and that an activity was good when it aimed to conquer, for the individual and for others, the means of freeing oneself, of "freeing freedom." De Beauvoir said that she wanted to reconcile her own inclination with Sartre's ideas. Sartre maintained that the concrete possibilities that present

---

*Those concrete human relationships taken together which, at a given moment, join a subject or a group to the environment and circumstances in which it must live and act. "My position in the midst of the world . . . that is what we call the situation. It doesn't have to do with choosing your time but with choosing yourself within it" (Sartre).

themselves to individuals have no meaning or value other than through the judgment those individuals bring to bear on them. For example, even a slave in chains is free because he can choose to want to break his chains or to want to remain a slave. If he wishes himself free, he "chooses for himself the past of a man who is free by nature, unjustly enslaved; if he chooses to remain a slave, he chooses for himself the past of a man who is a slave by nature, by the will of God, by virtue of the immutable social order, etc."[2]

De Beauvoir argued that neither the prisoner in a cell nor the woman in a harem could escape his or her situation through the choice of an entirely mental freedom: "I reestablished a hierarchy among situations."[3]

The notion of freedom in the context of situation as de Beauvoir presented it in *Pyrrhus et Cinéas* seduced a great number of readers and contributed significantly to the success of existentialism. Never had France known a comparable conjunction between literature, philosophy, and politics in the intellectual milieus. The era immediately following the war saw the flowering of political periodicals, nearly all of which claimed to be on the left while at the same time declaring themselves independent of the French Socialist Party and the French Communist Party.

The rejection of the Third Republic and the Vichy government impelled intellectuals in their search for new formulas. The period following the war, which posed enormous problems for a Europe where everything had been thrown into question, proved favorable for the tumult of ideas. Japan having surrendered, the autumn of 1945 was the first autumn of peacetime. Along with Leiris, Merleau-Ponty, and Camus, Sartre and de Beauvoir contemplated giving the world a new ideology. Sartre wanted to found a review with this small team; the result was *Les Temps modernes.* The editorial staff seemed to assemble the liveliest forces the new France had to offer. Maurice Merleau-Ponty served as editor-in-chief and political director. Raymond Aron, returned from Free French headquarters in London and advising André Malraux, then minister of information, was part of the staff, as was Jean Paulhan, moral heir to the departed *Nouvelle Revue française,* where he had served as editor-in-chief. Albert Ollivier, who along with Camus and Pascal Pia was one of three directors of *Combat,* also joined the staff. Wanting to devote himself to literature, Camus refused to be a part of the new publication but opened the columns of *Combat,* which had a press run in excess of 200,000 copies, to his colleagues at *Les Temps modernes.* The first editorial committee took shape at the end of 1944, with the war continuing and resources in pitiful supply. In order to publish the review they had to obtain an allocation of paper. Simone de Beauvoir took on this challenge. Still aglow from the recent success of *Pyrrhus et Cinéas,* she went in search of Jacques Soustelle, who had followed Malraux at the Ministry of Information, and succeeded in winning him over.

The first issue of *Les Temps modernes* appeared on October 15, 1945. In its pages Sartre presented his concept of committed literature and the revolutionary role of the writer, which filled certain intellectuals with dismay. André Gide attacked the notion of commitment in the short-lived weekly *Terre des hommes.* Nevertheless the first issue met with enormous success. In *Situations II* Sartre wrote that "it is not pleasing to be treated as a public monument in one's lifetime."[4] De Beauvoir declared, "I was pushed out into the limelight."[5]

The history of *Les Temps modernes* is that of the polemics of Sartre and de Beauvoir with other intellectuals, for ideological differences quickly appeared among members of the staff. Between 1945 and 1950, Aron, Merleau-Ponty, and Camus moved away from *Les Temps modernes.*[6]

Meetings were held in an office at Gallimard until the day the Sartrians attacked André Malraux. Evicted, they set up shop in the attic of a rival publishing house, Julliard, in the rue de l'Université. At the outset it had seemed possible for them to share certain objectives with the Communists and to join with them in certain campaigns while maintaining their independence. But from the moment *Les Temps modernes* appeared, Communist Party ideologists reproached them for attracting young people. Sartre was described as a "disciple of that Nazi Heidegger" and became a target of *Pravda,* which defined existentialism as "nauseating and putrid concoctions." For the Communists, Sartre was "a hyena with a fountain pen."[7] Garaudy, writing in *Les Lettres françaises,* which was edited by Aragon, attacked "a false prophet, Jean-Paul Sartre."[8] Jean Kanapa, an old friend of de Beauvoir, published (under the auspices of the Communist Party) *Existentialism Is Not a Humanism,* wherein he held the Sartrians up to ridicule: "Is the Sartrian simply a little animal already out of style, bad-tempered but harmless?" His doctrine is "a little ideological deliquescence aggressively playing at the game of reaction." Kanapa ranked the existentialists among the ideological enemies of Communist intellectuals along with "surrealism, the Trotskyism of literary cafés, aestheticism à la Paulhan and Malraux."[9]

Sartre countered by taking up the defense of Paul Nizan, who had left the Communist Party in August 1939 when the party approved the pact between Hitler and Stalin. At that time Maurice Thorez had called Nizan a police informer and a government spy, and Nizan's death at the front in 1939 did not put an end to the attacks.

In 1947 Sartre, Raymond Aron, André Breton, Julien Benda, Albert Camus, Jean Guéhenno, and François Mauriac drafted a declaration, "The

Nizan Case," in which they defended Nizan and demanded that the Communist Party prove its allegations. No such proof was ever offered. *Les Temps modernes* published "The Nizan Case" and the rupture with the Communist Party was confirmed.

The earliest issues of *Les Temps modernes* carried a series of important articles by Simone de Beauvoir. In "Moral Idealism and Political Realism," which appeared in the second number, she maintained that to reconcile morality and politics is to reconcile man with himself, provided he takes upon himself the full burden of responsibility. But this demands that he give up the idea of taking refuge in the subjectivity of traditional morality or the objectivity of realistic morality.

For the third issue she reviewed Maurice Merleau-Ponty's doctoral dissertation and wrote "Existentialism and Popular Wisdom."

DANIEL SECRÉTAN

*I*n February 1945 de Beauvoir's brother-in-law, attached to the French Institute in Lisbon, invited her to Portugal to deliver a series of lectures on the Occupation. Camus assigned her to do a series of articles on Spain and Portugal for *Combat*. She had not crossed a border for six years, and it had been fourteen years since she last saw Spain.

At the border she was kept waiting for an hour, then the barrier was raised and, suitcase in hand, she walked the mile and a half of no man's land between the border and Irún, where she would board the train. "By the side of the road a woman was selling oranges, bananas, and chocolate; my throat gagged with desire and revulsion: all this plenty only a few yards away from us, why was it forbidden?"[10]

The food shortage was not inevitable, and de Beauvoir became aware of the lack of organization that prevailed on a global scale. There was no rational universal economy, there was no humanity; the one system that existed prevented neither wars nor those scourges of medieval times, famine and mass death. She had seen the photos that Bost brought back from Holland, the photos that Camus had spread out across his desk, saying, "We can't publish these!" They were "pictures of children without bodies and without faces: nothing but eyes, huge, mad eyes." The Dutch had gnawed at the bark of trees and tried to scratch up their roots. This was Europe, this was civilization in 1945. And now she was in Irún, which had been nothing more than a heap of ruins since the civil war. The Spaniards who saw de Beauvoir did not fail to notice the clothing of one of the first Frenchwomen to come their way: "She must be poor; she has no stockings!" No, she had no stockings, and she did not color her legs with tincture of iodine to give the illusion of stockings. Nor did she have leather shoes; she was wearing wooden clogs. Her clothes were old—the color, the texture, everything about them betrayed years of wear. "A furious solidarity with the poverty of France raged inside me."[11]

When the train stopped, vendors offered fruit, candy, ham, fresh bread, and drinks for sale. Stalls overflowed onto the sidewalk. What an awakening after the long sleep of the Occupation! On the other side of the border people had been eating their fill and living in peace. Yes, but in 1936, when Spain was convulsed by civil war and refugees were corralled in camps north of the Pyrénées, it was de Beauvoir who had eaten her fill. "I knew then that my destiny was bound to that of all other people; freedom, oppression, the happiness and misery of men was a matter of intimate concern to me."[12]

In Madrid the café terraces packed with people, the shops overflowing with silk clothing, leather handbags, and wool coats left her breathless. It dawned on her that she could eat and drink whatever she liked: brioches, pastries, crayfish, fried eggs, wine, real coffee, chocolate. She went on a binge of bulimia. Food and freedom suddenly seemed much the same thing, as they had when she was a child in the park at Meyrignac. She ate while walking, she went into cafés and ate some more. And while she was eating she watched the passersby, who knew nothing of her story, just as she had known nothing of the refugee camps. She stopped short before a window display of magnificent photographs. "It was a German propaganda center. I stood there, I saw with my own eyes these pictures of heroic crusaders, members of the S.S." She was overcome with anguish; a conscience other than her own was at the center of things; the thread of time, her time, was broken. "Until that moment, the subject of history had been France."[13] She walked as far as a hill where the University of Madrid campus had once been and from there saw houses reduced to rubble, construction sites, and vacant lots. She visited a sordid shantytown just north of the city; it was unquestionably 1945 here, as elsewhere. She wrote about what she had seen, and as soon as her article appeared, the Spanish media reacted.[14] Radio Madrid accused de Beauvoir of "inventing slanders without leaving Paris" and of having done so for a great deal of money.

Combat propounded no specific political view, intending to remain free to criticize all parties and all governments. Since Francoism and the Salazar government both came under attack regularly in its pages, *Combat* began publishing de Beauvoir's articles on Portugal. So as not to compromise her brother-in-law, she wrote under the pseudonym Daniel Secrétan. As an official guest of the French Cultural Services in Lisbon, she had experienced a minimum of red tape and had been able to speak with the Portuguese without difficulty. The misery of the population had moved her. What she wrote in "Portugal Under Salazar's Regime" is an indictment.

> People told me: "Of course Salazar's regime is an authoritarian regime, but it's a tempered authoritarianism . . . he's done a tremendous amount for Portugal." I visited Portugal. I went looking for what Mr. Salazar has done for his people. And I saw.
>
> In this country of seven million inhabitants there are 70,000 who eat. I can still hear the voices of the children of Braga at the door of a candy shop where I was buying some marzipan: "We have nothing to eat."
>
> They are deprived of vitamins to the point where they are afflicted with a kind of scurvy that makes their teeth fall out, and pieces of their gums, their ears, their noses.
>
> I shall not soon forget those two children wearing bits of burlap rummaging through garbage cans one rainy morning in Porto. . . . The little girl I saw going through the garbage of Porto someday will be looking for some way, any way, to earn a few escudos. . . . Out of 194 prostitutes given medical care in a certain community clinic, 43 percent were minors: women are eligible to register as professional prostitutes starting at age 14. They do not need their parents' authorization to obtain this registration because the tax collected on these cards is an important source of revenue for the State.[15]

This was the first in a long series of articles, prefaces, and interviews that, paralleling de Beauvoir's novels and essays, mark her commitments and indicate the stands she took.

Daniel Secrétan's articles troubled and disturbed readers. In an era when French journalism was above all a journalism of opinion, a journalism more emotional than factual, de Beauvoir had written a documented report that was supported with figures. By setting the scene with people and facts, she inaugurated the kind of journalism that is practiced today by all major French newspapers.

Hers was a pitiless report. The Portuguese embassy intervened, pressures were brought to bear on *Combat,* and the journal, seeing its quota of newsprint diminish and not wanting to attract reprisals, halted publication of the articles. Albert Camus, on a lecture tour of the United States, could not intercede, and the remainder of the series appeared in *Volontés,* edited by Michel Colli-net. Simone de Beauvoir had the makings of a great reporter. She was inter-ested in everything and afraid of nothing, and she knew how to prompt people to confide in her—traits that she would bestow on Henri Perron in *The Mandarins.*

LITERATURE AND METAPHYSICS

The Blood of Others appeared in September 1945, and this second novel had an even better reception than the first. De Beauvoir wrote that she "received floods of compliments."[16] Camus told her enthusiastically, "It's a *fraternal* book."[17] *The Blood of Others,* in which she spoke of the Resistance, freedom, responsibility, and "the original curse that constitutes each individ-ual's coexistence with everybody else," would go through thirty-two print-ings in two years.

Two years earlier de Beauvoir had begun a new novel, *All Men Are Mortal,* for which she read Léonard Sismondi's chronicles of Italy. The Swiss historian described what took place in many besieged villages during the fourteenth century. When a long siege resulted in famine, the authorities, in hopes of holding out longer, declared that all provisions were reserved for the comba-tants, and *les bouches inutiles,* or useless mouths—women, children, the elderly, invalids—were expelled from the town and forced into ditches at the foot of the city walls. De Beauvoir thought about the men who delivered up their loved ones to the enemy and was seized by the horror of this action. "I remained quite still for a moment or two, staring at nothing, while a wave of intense excitement surged through me."[18] The practice of abandoning the weak to face certain death outside the city gates was not only mass murder sanctioned by custom but was seen as a heroic act exercised in a spirit of sublime prudence and high virtue. The subject seemed terribly topical after a war in which millions of people had been killed. De Beauvoir strove to understand the feelings of men who condemned their wives and children to die in the ditches before their eyes. She tried hard to imagine the thoughts of the condemned, sent to their fate by their spouses, their fathers, their sons.

In three months she wrote the play *Who Shall Die? (Les Bouches inutiles),* situating the action in fourteenth-century Flanders, where an entire town grapples with its conscience. The town is besieged and the governing council is faced with a dilemma: Either everyone receives a food ration and supplies run out quickly or only the soldiers are fed and the rest of the population, the useless mouths, are left to starve. The council decides to sacrifice the ill, the aged, children, and women in order to save the town. Then the hero, Jean-Pierre, convinces the council to give true freedom to the town by allowing everyone the right to choose his own destiny. The people resolve to set their town afire and to storm the enemy in a final effort that will give them either victory or death.[19]

De Beauvoir was eager to see performed this play she had written for Olga, and at the Café de Flore she met the writer's dream, a man named Néron who told her he was ready to invest money in the production of *Who Shall Die?* A few days later he gave her 100,000 francs, and Sartre delivered the money to the stage director Michel Vitold. The following day Simone was summoned to police headquarters at the quai des Orfèvres; Néron had embezzled the money. Sartre went to his publisher to borrow the money to make up for the theft, the judge requested autographed copies of their books, and the charges were dropped. Néron, a megalomaniac, later committed suicide.

The play was staged at the Carrefours Theatre by Michel Vitold, with whom de Beauvoir took bicycle trips. She had envisaged an uninterrupted portrayal of an entire community acting and reacting, but the actual production was divided into scenes with pauses between them to accommodate set changes. The weather turned cold and the theatre was poorly heated. Elevated métro trains had a tendency to drown out the actors in passing, and the performers themselves were not quite up to the demands of the text. De Beauvoir had insisted that Olga play the role of Clarice. The play ran for fifty performances.

The critic Jacques Lemarchand saw in *Who Shall Die?* "an important event." He admired the strength of the dialogue and the violent and tragic quality of the subject; in de Beauvoir he saw a dramatic author who would establish herself, and he attributed the production's weaknesses to the inexperienced cast and director.[20] But overall the reviews were poor. A disappointed de Beauvoir would not let the critics defeat her and, having concluded that the play had not really been given a fair chance, moved on to other things.

The war had thrown everything into question and revealed a horrifying aspect of mankind. For de Beauvoir, people were defined by their bodies, their needs, and their work, and only the novel permitted one to evoke "the original outpouring of existence in its complete, remarkable, and worldly truth."

In *All Men Are Mortal,* the novel de Beauvoir began in 1943, the hero, Fosca, who is immortal, tries to identify with the world and to have an impact on it. She imagined the strange existence of this man who remained alive while everything around him died out, his friends and loves, institutions, religions, societies, nations. He discovers "that the world resolves itself into individual liberties, each of which he is unable to attain."[21] He learns that the search for a universal good leads to persecutions, massacres, and destruction, causes unhappiness, and brings forth evil. Finally he sees that good does not exist as a universal value; there are only men—forever divided, hostile, exploiting and exploited, conquering or conquered—and he can do nothing for them. His grand dreams of progress and freedom collapse as he realizes that men do not want happiness, they want to live. Despite the experience of a life hundreds of years long, despite the power he has wielded on countless occasions, Fosca does not succeed in improving men's lives, establishing justice or the greatest good for the many. History unfolds and there is no progress, for humanity always returns to violence, oppression, and injustice in all its forms.

Fosca sinks into despair. His memory is burdened with horrors, and his impotence to remedy the situation tortures him. It was Sartre's belief that "man is a useless passion," and the novel is dedicated to him.

De Beauvoir believed this metaphysical novel to be "the best by far," superior to *She Came to Stay* and *The Blood of Others.* Raymond Queneau at Gallimard suggested a first printing of 75,000 copies, but the book did not sell well.

This tale that spans six centuries and takes its hero around the globe to demonstrate that "the dimension of human enterprise is neither the finite nor the infinite but the indefinite" was translated almost immediately in Germany.[22] Existentialist philosophy had its metaphysical novel; Fosca was a new Faust, a Faust eager not for knowledge but for action, a Faust who sought to make men happy.

THE EXISTENTIALIST OFFENSIVE

A critic noted that in one week *Who Shall Die?* was playing, the first issue of *Les Temps modernes* appeared, and Sartre delivered his famous lecture "Existentialism Is a Humanism," which proved to be a dramatic event complete with fainting women, spectators coming to blows, explosions of enthusiasm or hatred in the press, and frenzied excitement in that intellectual circle which proclaimed itself the avant-garde. All this was referred to as "the existentialist offensive."

The misunderstood word "existentialism" was also the latest, most fashionable word. Sartre and de Beauvoir were on their way to becoming the leading authorities on a philosophy that was rising like a tide on all sides and seeping into the least expected corners of Parisian life. Neither Sartre nor de Beauvoir wanted a label, and this one irritated them as much as any other. "I don't even know what existentialism is," Sartre declared during a symposium organized by the Dominicans. But their protests were in vain. "In the end, we took the epithet that everyone used for us and used it for our own purposes," de Beauvoir wrote.[23]

The existentialist philosophy may be defined, according to Sartre's famous phrase, as "Existence precedes essence."[24] Existence does not demonstrate itself; it is there, it imposes itself on consciousness. In order to justify his existence and give meaning to his life, man, "born for nothing," can rely only on himself. Of course he is plunged into a set of historical and material conditions that define his situation, but each individual must experience his own life and create himself with recourse to his strengths alone. For Sartre, as for de Beauvoir, each man is responsible for himself and cannot hope for aid from heaven or some ready-made doctrine. The result is "the anxiety" which is the consciousness of "our total and profound responsibility." Each individual must assume or shoulder this responsibility in exercising his freedom. As soon as a human being hides behind tradition, doctrines, systems, or ideologies, he becomes "a bastard"; if he refuses to *s'assumer*, or come to terms with himself, he falls into the realm of bad faith.* The opposite of bad faith is authenticity, or genuineness. The authentic act is that through which man assumes his situation and surpasses it in taking action. His acts, once accomplished, define the man and do so without recourse: "Man is what he makes himself." "Man is nothing other than that which he makes of himself." And he is constantly confronted with new choices, for life is a perpetual state of becoming.

Sartre's atheistic existentialism was even less well understood than a religiously inspired existentialism such as that of Gabriel Marcel, who rec-

---

* *"Assumer* does not in any way mean 'to accept' even though in certain cases the two go hand in hand. When I *assume,* I assume *in order to* make a given use of that which I assume . . . moreover, to assume means to shoulder or to claim responsibility for oneself . . . the first act of assuming which can and does create human reality returning back on itself is the assuming of one's freedom; an act which can be expressed by this formula: *On n'a jamais d'excuse* (there is no excuse)" (Jean-Paul Sartre, *Carnets de la drôle de guerre,* pp. 143–144).

onciled the existence of God, the source of values, with human freedom.

Trendiness entered into it. Everything became existentialist; there was the existentialist crime, the existentialist black sweater, the long hair of the existentialists, the existentialist cellars where people danced, or drank, or sang existentialist songs. Juliette Gréco was an existentialist singer. Mouloudji, accomplished as an actor, singer, and novelist, was the existentialist heir apparent, Sartre was the king, and de Beauvoir the queen in this trumped-up kingdom that existed only in the imagination of journalists with a cocky sense of humor, a kingdom that delighted those who came to gape in admiration before the Flore terrace when their noses were not buried in the latest twaddle about their new idols. Photographers harassed Sartre and de Beauvoir in the street, and people asked for their autographs.

De Beauvoir gave two lectures on the novel and metaphysics. No one fainted this time, but the tumult of the simultaneous glory and scandal surrounding her and Sartre was growing by the minute.

She had never written in the cocoonlike silence of a study. She lived in cafés and hotels and was one of those people who like to be in the thick of the crowd. Her natural, easygoing style pleased some and shocked others. Scandalous rumors circulated. She practiced an emotional and sexual independence which prompted indignation. Commentary spilled forth from the newspapers. The uproar made its way abroad, and existentialism soon became the mirror in which the rest of the world admired the recalcitrant and exciting reflection of the new France. De Beauvoir called it "an idiotic glory."

"However," de Beauvoir pointed out, "if circumstances happened to be so favorable to Sartre, it was no accident; there existed, at least at first glance, a remarkable agreement between what he was offering the public and what the public wanted."[25] In fact the public had just experienced a world war, and Sartre and de Beauvoir offered an ideology that allowed the public to "assume" its condition and to surmount the countless traumas inflicted on the world between 1939 and 1945. There had been the horror of combat, the discovery of the abominable death camps, the humiliation of the Occupation, and the return of a gamut of scourges that had been presumed to be gone for good: famine, enslavement, torture, tyranny, informing, and murder. Monstrosities were lodged in everyone's memory and remorse remained in the collective conscience on such a scale that existentialism arrived like a sweeping wind that dispels the fog, chases away the miasma, disinfects, and restores life to the welcoming earth. It dispersed the evil spell that had made the world rotten for five long years.

It was no small thing to face up to and accept the horror; it was extraordinary to reconcile recent history, the current situation, and the possibility of freedom. To confront the absurdity of the human condition, to say that it was neither imposed nor fatal nor permanent, and to proclaim that man was free and responsible and able to transcend his past actions and make goodness triumph was something new for many people of good will. "Sartre seduced them by maintaining, on the level of the individual, the rights of morality."[26] But this morality was disconcerting, and the notion of freedom combined with that of individual responsibility was difficult for a public accustomed to thinking in terms of social classes and strict categories in accord with religious teachings. The notion of authenticity—to flee all lies, all equivocation, all carefully maintained illusions, all instances of bad faith, all excuses good or bad—was frightening.

"In Sartre the bourgeoisie recognized themselves without consenting to the self-transcendence he exemplified."[27] For de Beauvoir the situation was particularly unpleasant. As a woman, she was subjected to blame. And what furor, what noise! Twenty years later François Mauriac would apologize for having spoken unkind words and would make amends: "Of course, if one set aside religious values, anyone would agree it's a beautiful life that Simone de Beauvoir recounts for us, despite its disorderliness and its excesses . . . these pleasurable lives led by Simone de Beauvoir and Sartre are only a brilliant fringe. The reality is frenzied, uninterrupted work and the thirst for justice, which dictated a political choice."[28]

Existentialism aroused the animosity of both Catholics and Marxists. The attacks came from all sides; thinkers attacked the principle, litterateurs attacked the aesthetics. Existentialism was accused of demoralizing youth, it was accused of quietism.[29] It was accused of "miserabilism" as well as decadence. What is an existentialist? It is a man who is disgusted, who is bored, who is completely detached from the pleasures and obligations of existence. And the woman existentialist, how to define her? On the one hand, de Beauvoir was made out to be a madwoman, an excentric lacking in moral restraint who indulged in every conceivable vice and led a life befitting a sideshow; on the other hand, people maintained that she spent all her time at her writing table, that she was pure brainpower, that she had all the allure of a den mother in her low-heeled shoes and tight chignon. One way or another, the lady in question was abnormal. She resisted all attempts at classification: leftist but not looked upon kindly by the Communists, living in a hotel but not in the least bohemian, famous but unwilling to play the part and mix with high society. Thanks to her books she was wealthy, yet her lifestyle was not on a par with that usually associated with success. She had come through the war working, writing. She had gotten through a poor and difficult childhood, one filled with humiliating comparisons with her cousins and girl friends, without losing the tremendous momentum and spirit that allowed her to become what she wanted to be: a writer.

"PEOPLE WILL SPEAK OF THE EXISTENTIALIST ERA"[30]

*D*uring the Occupation the area bounded by the rue de Seine, the rue des Saints-Pères, the Senate, and the rue Dauphine had remained almost provincial. The concentration of publishing houses—Gallimard, Grasset, Plon, Stock, Mercure de France—attracted numerous well-known and would-be writers, artists, filmmakers, and actors to the cafés of the neighborhood. The Lipp, the Deux-Magots, the Flore, the Rhumerie, the bar of the Pont-Royal, the Bar Vert in the rue Jacob, all frequented by intellectuals and a few politicians from the neighborhood, kept their old-fashioned look and shared a native clientele.

This sleepy quarter woke abruptly at the liberation and became general headquarters for the city's youth. The young people had a style all their own, one that succeeded the Zazous without resembling them.* The boys had discovered tons of clothing sent by Jewish charities in New York to their needy coreligionists, the surplus having ended up in the used clothing stalls at the Saint-Ouen flea market.

Soon thousands of checked shirts, narrow trousers, horizontally striped socks, and—the biggest novelty of all—sneakers invaded the streets of Paris. They could be had for a song, and all you needed to complete the look was a GI-style crewcut. The girls adopted black wraparound skirts, clingy black sweaters, and long, straight hair in the style launched by Juliette Gréco.

At the Bar Vert in the rue Jacob, one group bemoaned the fact that they had no place of their own to drink and dance. Among them were Anne-Marie Cazalis, who had just won the Prix Valéry for poetry, her inseparable friend Juliette Gréco, the future filmmaker Alexandre Astruc, the young comic actor Marc Doelnitz, and other young actors and painters. One of the crowd, Yves

---

*The Zazous, or "hepcats," wore their own version of the zoot suit: baggy jackets down to their knees, long stovepipe trousers, and platform shoes. Winter and summer, rain or shine, umbrellas swung from their arms. Their extravagant attire was seen as a protest of the Occupation, and collaborators often hunted them down to shave off their slicked-back hair or to force them to swallow castor oil. Their nickname came from a song sung by Charles Trenet with a chorus of *"Je suis swing, zazou, zazou,"* accompanied by a dance during which the index finger remained extended and pointed skyward.

Corbassière, habitually arrived in a 1922 red-and-black-checkerboard open touring car covered with autographs. For years a photo of this car and its not yet celebrated occupants adorned the tile walls of the Saint-Germain-des-Prés metro station, alongside other posters commemorating the quarter's heyday. The Bar Vert's owner found the nook his customers were looking for —the *cave,* or cellar, of a tavern. When Gréco, Cazalis, and Astruc first ventured down to the basement area that served as a catchall storage and junk room, they spotted the words *le Tabou* painted on one of the beams.

A young embassy attaché, Frédéric Chauvelot, financed the enterprise, and Robert Auboyneau, the nephew of an admiral, was the doorman. Alain Quercy, son of the Socialist minister Christian Pineau, played popular jazz tunes on a piano that had been lowered into place with considerable difficulty. The bar sported subdued lighting, not because shadows were consciously sought but because costs had to be kept down. The stools were wobbly, but the booths looked quite acceptable in the prevailing dimness. Cazalis, Gréco, and Doelnitz took charge of the refreshments; you could order anything you liked as long as it was rum and Coke. The Tabou acted like a magnet. It was a private club, and at 10 P.M. a crowd of friends swooped down on the premises and made a dash for the minuscule dance floor (the entire cellar measured only 50 by 26 feet), where they bebopped the night away. Boris Vian, who with his two brothers had formed an orchestra, played trumpet.* The Tabou yielded just about enough for its backers to buy themselves one meal a day. Soon all of intellectual Paris would venture into the *cave* at 33 rue Dauphine. Claude Mauriac was a faithful visitor, and his father, François Mauriac, took the plunge. Queneau, Merleau-Ponty, Camus, Lemarchand; writers, painters, and musicians were in attendance. Those who already counted and those who soon would—Marcel Duhamel, Jacques Prévert, Christian Bérard, Jean Cau, Roger Vadim, Robert Hossein—found themselves surrounded by hordes of photographers drawn by the novelty and the celebrities. The trio of Gréco, Cazalis, and Doelnitz alone could create pandemonium.

The Tabou became famous when the editor-in-chief of the sensationalist weekly *Samedi-Soir* sent a reporter to cover the club. With the help of two or three habitués, the reporter filed a stirring account, and on May 3, 1947, the Tabou became a legend and its members became "the existentialists."

The famous article was accompanied by a photo of a young girl who leans against a rough-hewn cellar wall as a young man shows her the way

---

*A writer, poet, and musician, Vian earned notoriety with his novel *J'irai cracher sur vos tombes* (*I'll Spit on Your Graves*), which he pretended was a translation of an American novel.

by the light of a candle. The guide was Vadim, the girl was Gréco. The caption
explained: "A whole generation of youth loves, sleeps, and dreams Bikini [the
Bikini atoll was the site of atomic bomb tests the previous summer] in the
caves of Saint-Germain-des-Prés." On that fateful day the journalist Jacques
Robert created a myth and a style.

> There's no point in looking for existentialists at the Café de Flore.
> They've all taken refuge in the *caves.* After the Vatican cellars, those of
> Saint-Germain-des-Prés. . . .
>
>   In the beginning, all the existentialists were poor; but since then,
> Sartre, Simone de Beauvoir, and Camus have made money in literature;
> Jacques-Laurent Bost in the cinema; Mouloudji in proletarian realism;
> others in journalism. Headquarters for these rich existentialists is the
> Pont-Royal, and their drinking habits extend to cocktails. Oddly
> enough, wealthy existentialists are few in number, while poor existen-
> tialists are legion. The poor existentialists are extremely poor. They're
> between 16 and 22 years old. They generally come from good families.
> Nearly all have been cursed by their fathers. Nearly all of them claim
> to be actors. Michel Radiguet, nephew of the author of *Le Diable au corps,*
> figures among them. One of the oldest in their ranks, Michel de Ré, age
> 22, is really named Michel Gallieni; he's the grandson of the general
> . . . he's six foot six and hasn't combed his hair for a year."[31]

The reporter noted that the young existentialist actresses walked around
with white mice in their pockets and let them scurry across their shoulders.
The actresses never wore makeup. The writer offered examples of existentialist graffiti:

"When you hear Hello! Hello!, don't you think of the Seine?"*

"Man, this animal who sings the Marseillaise."

"Order an arsenic soda to quench your thirst for eternity."

"An existentialist is a man with Sartre on his teeth."†

Having defined the Tabou as the sanctuary of the new generation, where
"the existentialists, whom you can't make out anymore except through a fog,
launch shrieking into frenzied jitterbugging and boogie-woogieing" or "completely exhausted, remain seated while staring down their glass of lukewarm
water," the journalist explained how they spent their time: "Between eleven
in the morning and the end of the night they make their way from the Flore

---

Allo! sounds like *à l'eau* ("to the water").

†*Sartre* rhymes with *tartre,* the French word for tartar.

to the Bar Vert, from the Tabou to the Deux-Magots, from the Bal Nègre to their favorite restaurant, Aux Assassins."[32] The article was destined to make the rounds of the foreign press. When *Life* magazine got hold of it, armies of camera-clutching American tourists headed straight for the existentialist lairs. And when Ali Khan, Maurice Chevalier, Marlene Dietrich, Orson Welles, and even Greta Garbo dropped in, the *cave* received consecration on an international scale. Thus the Tabou was a casualty of its own success. Born as something of a joke, it died from overexposure in the press, the aggression of tourists, and the protests of weary neighbors, who succeeded in imposing a midnight curfew.

In his *Guide to Saint-Germain-des-Prés,* Boris Vian maintained that the quarter's sudden popularity was in large part due to the literary renown of Simone de Beauvoir and Jean-Paul Sartre. One no longer separated this couple whose legend grew along with the popularity of Saint-Germain-des-Prés. "If the local barkeeps had one shred of honesty, Simone de Beauvoir and Sartre should drink for free in all the bistros they put on the map. That's a good idea, Castor, isn't it?" He went on to describe the muse-in-spite-of-herself of *cave*-centered existentialism: "Young, lively, a pleasantly hoarse voice, hair dark and eyes like delft china, clear of gaze and flat of shoe, she enjoys traveling and talking in equal measure, forty kilometers on foot per day and forty hours of discussion when the discussion interests her." And Vian stood up for her against a journalist who had written of "prodigious intelligence whose only fault is to be too organized." "No intelligence," Vian wrote, "would know how to go about being too organized, and this undeniable organization in no way detracts from its owner's charm."[33]

The existentialist *caves* began to multiply, and the young people who flocked there to dance were dubbed cellar rats. Jean-Paul Sartre was crowned the pope of existentialism, and de Beauvoir received the title Notre-Dame-de-Sartre. People confused completely a philosophy that few understood with the manner in which a considerable number of young people chose to live. French and foreign newspapers only fed the misunderstanding. "The existentialist *caves* shelter strange and bellicose bacchanals," *La Presse* declared on January 3, 1949. *La Gazette de Lausanne* for November 24, 1948, stigmatized the Tabou habitués: "The Tabou . . . in the back, an orchestra, twenty couples dance, a limp, shapeless mass beset with spasms in a space three yards square. Nothingness, nausea. Somebody says 'existentialism.' The Tabou's young regulars have found a name for their disgust." Even the *Literaturnaia Gazeta* had its say: "This is the youth of Paris' depths, a curious mildew of hate, jealousy, stupidity, and the most vulgar sexuality. Such is the face of existentialism."[34]

Completely contradictory captions appeared one after another: "Saint-Germain-des-Prés makes too much love"; "Isidor Isou* wants to teach love at Saint-Germain-des-Prés, the most chaste quarter in Paris"; "In Existentialist intimacy, nothing, absolutely nothing happens. And that's revolting."[35] It was a competition for the most amusing anecdotes. One journalist assured his readers that before his cleaning lady began work on his office, she asked to borrow his copy of *The Roads to Freedom.* "Beat it, existentialist!" became the latest insult.

People spoke of existentialist painting, existentialist political economy, even existentialist hats. Sartre and de Beauvoir's robust appetites were notorious, and their favorite dishes, pork, sauerkraut, steak and french fries, and cheese, became existentialist specialities. People repeated what other authors had to say. The poet Léon-Paul Fargue maintained, "It's the philosophy of shit!" Yves Gandon quipped, "Existentialism is excrementalism." On the right as on the left, existentialism was looked upon as an unhealthy philosophy that rejected pleasure in living and turned the conventional order of values on its head. André Gide, aggravated to see his role as "leader of youth" swept out from under him, joined in: "In 1920, after the Great War, there was the dada movement; in 1944, after the other Great War, there's the caca movement."[36] Gabriel Marcel, a Christian existentialist philosopher, gave a lecture on "Techniques of Degradation from Buchenwald to Jean-Paul Sartre."[37] Some maintained that "the firm of Sartre and Company" dominated the literary marketplace through publicity: "Each day trucks of the absurd pull out in orderly lines from existentialist factories. Their anthracite inundates even foreign markets. Everywhere, in bookstore window displays, in the columns of the press, in the wings of public meeting rooms, the foul merchandise piles up. It's one of today's most thriving businesses."[38]

"It's a policy of silence toward all those who aren't part of the brotherhood," wrote a journalist who attributed the success of existentialism to a lack of education, cowardice, and a sabotaged syntax.[39] People reassured themselves by writing that the whole thing was nothing more than a game among aesthetes, thought up in café booths where budding Roquentins experienced their first bouts of nausea over their cups of coffee. Paul Guth affirmed in *Le Figaro* that "existentialism was a word secreted by Saint-Germain-des-Prés between the terrace of the Flore, the rue Saint-Benoît, and the rue Jacob." In a strangely chaotic account, he cited "the ancestors of existen-

---

*Isou devised *lettrisme,* a literary theory in which poetry consists exclusively of the sonority of letters.

tialism: Kant, Pascal, Heidegger, Jaspers, Kierkegaard, Schelling, Gabriel Marcel."[40]

"A philosophical abstraction that bears the barbarous name of existentialism," proclaimed the text of a three-column article devoted to Simon de Beauvoir and Sartre in *Samedi-Soir* for November 17, 1945. The piece was titled, "Hotel Louisiane, rooms 17 and 50, the decor of *No Exit* yet more hellish." Existentialism is a philosophy, but who are the existentialists? "Above all, there is Madame Simone de Beauvoir. She is endowed with this historical circumstance: She lives at the Hotel Louisiane in room 50. She is also a teacher. She wears a University-style braid and has very bright, pretty dark eyes." Simone de Beauvoir's blue eyes must have glared darkly indeed at this reporter.

"She writes novels, philosophical essays, plays. *Who Shall Die?* is currently being performed in Paris. An unknown gentleman named Néron offered her 100,000 francs to produce the play. She accepted; he was a con man. A few days later the police came knocking at the door of room 50 at the Louisiane. They had come to arrest the author of *Who Shall Die?* At that very moment they saw a sheet move, and strangely enough, beneath it they found Mr. Sartre."

Sartre and de Beauvoir, "writing shoulder to shoulder on café tables, compose hefty novels or fashion themselves a mythology of nausea and abortion midway between shady hotels and nightclubs. They imitate Heidegger and American novels pell-mell." The journalist described Sartre seated before his *café crème* at the Flore, bandying about incomprehensible philosophical terminology and saying, "I'm living my selfness. And the entire Café de Flore is prepared to sell its soul for the splendors of selfness."[41]

One year later, *Samedi-Soir* had this to say: "Existentialism, we're informed, has colonized the Gallimard publishing house. It has its own monthly magazine, *Les Temps modernes,* and its boss, Mr. J.-P. Sartre, before occupying the cinema with a film cheerfully entitled *Typhus,* got his hooks into two theatres. At the Verlaine Theatre they're performing *No Exit,* while the Antoine Theatre is spreading terror with *The Respectful Prostitute* and *Men Without Shadows.* Every evening some spectators find themselves ill, others scream, others walk out, letting the door slam in their wake. Onstage rise the shrieks of pain of Resistance fighters being tortured by militiamen. Mr. Sartre wishes to retain only the world's most horrible aspects and its suffering." A caricature three columns wide illustrates the article: Sartre is shown leaning against the Pont-Royal bar while Simone de Beauvoir scribbles away at a table, with endless sheets of paper piled up and strewn about her feet.[42]

Yet a few voices were heard to ask: And what if Jean-Paul turned out to be as great as Jean-Jacques Rousseau? And what if Simone were as great as Germaine de Staël or Colette? If the caricatured aspect of certain articles did not entirely mask the reality, it painted a revealing portrait of the tumultuous era that followed the war.

De Beauvoir, Sartre, and their friends rarely went to nightclubs, but they were frequently in bars where, depending on the evening, they might run into Camus, Vian, Merleau-Ponty, Arthur Koestler, Manès Sperber, Romain Gary, Jean Cau, Jacques-Laurent Bost. According to what Simone wrote Nelson Algren, some of their crowd became aggressive when fortified by too much liquor. Bost attacked his so-called rivals, Sartre became bellicose and refused to let himself be put into a car to go home. One night Koestler slammed a taxi door in Camus' face, leaving him with a black eye. Camus became irritable when he had been drinking. Koestler undertook to seduce de Beauvoir. Sartre was interested in Koestler's wife and had an *amour passionnel* for Michèle Vian, with whom he strolled, holding hands, followed by Boris Vian. De Beauvoir had a brief crush on Koestler, whom she would portray as Scriassine in *The Mandarins.*

The members of the group helped one another out. Camus edited the Espoir editions at Gallimard and published the work of de Beauvoir's friends. The first novel in the series, Violette Leduc's *L'Asphyxie,* was followed by Bost's novel *The Last Professional* and *Gamble to Lose* by Colette Audry. De Beauvoir, Sartre, and Camus, as the leading thinkers and trendsetters for youth, were the most read, most admired, most commented upon, and most disparaged. They were loved, they were hated, but people talked only of them.

On December 11, 1945, de Beauvoir spoke before the Maintenant Club in a small lecture room at the Learned Societies in the rue Danton. She praised the metaphysical novel, whose aim is "to place the whole human being opposite the whole world," in contrast to the thesis novel, which subordinates events and characters to a preconceived system. She developed this proposition in her essay "Literature and Metaphysics," which would be reprinted in 1948, along with three other essays that had appeared in *Les Temps modernes,* under the title *L'Existentialisme et la sagesse des nations (Existentialism and Popular Wisdom).* This volume was brought out by Nagel because Gallimard could not manage to print copies of *Les Temps modernes* quickly enough to meet the demand—each issue was literally snatched from the newsstands. De Beauvoir defended existentialism against those who had labeled it the philosophy of despair. With pointed humor, she scoffed at popular wisdom as expressed in proverbs and clichés. She demonstrated the weakness of a civilization based on man's self-interest and contempt. As proof she offered numerous proverbs that are variations on the theme "you don't go out of your way for nothing" and "charity begins at home." All weaknesses are excused by the catchall phrase "that's human nature." "Since above all men dread responsibility . . . they're so afraid to put their freedom on the line that they prefer to renounce it." According to de Beauvoir, this explains the violent reactions against existentialism, based as it is on freedom and responsibility.[43]

In an interview with the Italian newspaper *Il Politecnico* de Beauvoir underlined the fact that she believed in a universal basis for morality. Freedom, she said, is the respect of freedoms. She emphasized the importance of continuously creating new rules that permit open agreement among all the members of a group and avoid anarchy.[44]

At the age of thirty-seven, Simone de Beauvoir, now a public figure, was pleased with her position. Throughout her youth she had devoted herself to a fundamental undertaking: to know and to convey knowledge. As a committed author, she put into practice a moral code, one that she had taken from Sartre's brand of existentialism and that followed precisely those paths she wished to follow. She defined man in terms of action and the weight of responsibilities. In *Les Lettres françaises* of December 1, 1945, de Beauvoir replied to Dominique Aury that man is not explained solely by his behavior but also through his relationships with others and with the world. She pointed out that no moral doctrine is implicated in existentialism and added, "For my part, I've tried to extract one." According to existentialism, God does not exist, but contrary to what Dostoevsky has Ivan Karamazov say—"If God does not exist, everything is permitted"—the existentialist conclusion is, "God does not exist; nothing is permitted." Since God is not on hand to permit or punish, each individual is completely responsible for his actions. Each person is what he makes of himself. "At the heart of the world as given, it is man's task to make the reign of freedom triumph."[45]

In order to extract a moral from existentialism and to respond to its detractors, de Beauvoir wrote a 223-page philosophical essay that aroused the same lively interest as had *Pyrrhus et Cinéas* and was immediately translated for readers in the United States. In *The Ethics of Ambiguity,* dedicated to Bianca, she defended existentialism against those who called it a "nihilist philosophy, wilfully pessimistic, licentious, despairing, and ignoble."[46] She criticized the notion of a monolithic humanity, countering with the collective reality each person carries within himself. And she raised one of the era's burning questions, that of the end and the means, and maintained that the end never justifies the means.

Albert Camus, who according to de Beauvoir "sometimes failed to pursue his thought as far as he might" in the name of clarity, in turn expressed his reservations after having read the essay and reproached de Beauvoir for a lack of clarity. While he remained deeply attached to the classic values of French literature, de Beauvoir was wresting herself away from them. She considered writers who believed in art for art's sake to be irresponsible because for her the writer, who has only one life to live, must work toward changes in the society that surrounds him. She wanted to transform man's social condition and his self-image. More revolutionary than Camus, she thought he was "keeping himself covered" from eventual criticism while she actively elicited it.[47]

In the lectures she delivered that year in the United States she returned to the ideas she had expounded in her essay. At Vassar she noted the abandonment of the tradition of art for art's sake, declared that the writer must recognize his responsibility vis-à-vis his readers, and emphasized literature's power as an active political and moral force. For her the essential thing was to communicate with the social group to whom the future belonged: the masses who had already accepted Marxist ideology. The existentialists' goal was to incite the public to think about freedom, hope, and brotherly love. "The writer can lay new foundations for a justified hope and for an ethical course of action."[48]

She underlined the writer's responsibility in recalling that the intellectuals who had betrayed and collaborated during the German Occupation had been judged mercilessly by the French courts, while those who collaborated along economic lines were sometimes acquitted. She declared that the writer is morally obliged "to take part and be committed in world struggles, even if the war was over."[49] In 1947 literature was judged far more by its political and social content than by its aesthetic value. De Beauvoir's writings were an affirmation of optimism.

9

THE AMERICAN LOVER

America is one big box full of surprises.
America Day by Day

AMERICA! AMERICA!

*T*he myth of America had set de Beauvoir dreaming ever since her adolescence. She had seen every Hollywood film that made its way across the Atlantic, devoured the novels of Faulkner and Hemingway, given in to the melancholy of the blues, and felt her eyes mist over when the saxophonist at the Jockey sobbed out American tunes. America was the skyscrapers of Manhattan, the Arizona desert, the California beaches, and immense open country. It was freedom and adventure and violence, gangsters gunning down their rivals in the streets of Chicago, millionaires throwing parties at which drunken guests in black tie and evening gown tumbled into the giant swimming pool.

From America had come the tall young men, carefree and laughing, the GIs who had rescued Europe from the Nazis and who now ambled about Paris as tourists.

Since returning from a reporting tour for *Combat,* an exultant Jacques-Laurent Bost had not stopped talking about what he had seen in America. In 1946 Nathalie Sorokine had married an American GI, Ivan Moffat, a photographer in director George Stevens' Army Signal Corps unit, and she was living in Los Angeles, where her husband worked as a director and screenwriter. She begged Simone to come to the United States. And no sooner had Sartre, sent on special assignment for *Combat* and *Le Figaro,* returned to France than he turned around and headed straight back to do a lecture tour of American universities.

De Beauvoir wanted her part of America too, and she set the wheels in motion for a future visit. She was the existentialist novelist everyone was talking about; she was much in demand for lectures on the metaphysical novel and existentialism, that brand new philosophy that sparked people's imaginations and stirred debate wherever it was mentioned. She traveled to North Africa on a lecture tour on behalf of the Alliance Française. When she returned to Paris she found herself alone: Sartre was in New York, Nathalie was in California, Bost was in Italy, and Camus was packing for a trip to America. De Beauvoir managed *Les Temps modernes* with Merleau-Ponty and spent long, animated evenings in Saint-Germain-des-Prés with Boris Vian. Finally, in May 1946, Philippe Soupault asked her whether she would like to go to America. "Of course I want to go, and I insisted, and I'm bursting to go."[1]

It would be a speaking tour of American universities, which were clamoring for the new writers whose existence had been revealed only after the war. Contact was being reestablished, and cultural exchanges were starting up again.

While Soupault worked out her American itinerary, de Beauvoir was invited to Switzerland with Sartre, who had just returned from New York. For three weeks she delivered lectures, autographed copies of her books, and attended official dinners. She noted with amusement that they were interviewed as a unit, never separately: Their success was equal. After Switzerland, Holland extended an invitation to de Beauvoir, and lecture followed lecture. Her workload was prolific beyond the ordinary; she produced articles, gave interviews, and went on speaking tours without letting up on her writing. She was taking wake-up pills, amphetamines, and she drank a lot.

Finally her American cross-country tour was set and her travel arrangements complete. De Beauvoir boarded a plane for the United States on January 25, 1947. She would speak on the moral problems of the postwar writer, a subject that concerned all intellectuals, for responsibility and commitment are central preoccupations with those who want to see that wholesale slaughter, concentration camps, and torture can never happen again.

The New Yorker devoted an enthusiastic item to "the prettiest existentialist." The "Talk of the Town" writer had expected "a grim half hour" of arduous conversation and was pleasantly surprised to find "the female intellectual counterpart of Jean-Paul Sartre" brimming with kindness and modesty and just as fascinated by New York as a farmer from the sticks. She had already been all over Manhattan, discovered Brooklyn, and had a glass of orange juice at a drugstore lunch counter, a Coke at a soda fountain, and a whiskey in a bar. Having asked her to talk about her life, the reporter scrupulously noted that de Beauvoir rose at 8 A.M. and worked for four hours at a table at the Flore, devoting the rest of her time to lunching, dining, and talking with friends.[2]

De Beauvoir told us that the *New Yorker* piece had been written by Janet Flanner before Simone left Paris. "Flanner liked women, and one day she summoned me to the Scribe, where we had a drink. Thanks to her article, I was introduced to New York intellectual circles." And soon she *was* the talk of the town. She was invited to cocktail party upon cocktail party and met Harold Rosenberg, Mary McCarthy, Richard Wright, and Bernie Wolfe, Leon Trotsky's secretary, who told her the story of Trotsky's assassination in 1940 (which would be the subject of Sartre's play *Dirty Hands*).

At Princeton, de Beauvoir addressed her audience in French and kept them enthralled for an hour. "The writer must commit himself, make a choice, and feel responsible because he is free." This was her message, repeated from university to university. Everywhere she went mention was made of her elegance, vivacity, and beauty.[3] Journalists emphasized that she saw existentialism as an optimistic approach and that she practiced it in such a way as to dispel lies and myths. The left-leaning *Partisan Review* journalists told her that French intellectuals were playing into Moscow's hands, and she denied it.

The New York Times Magazine commissioned an article from her, which appeared on May 25, 1947. "For an Existentialist," de Beauvoir wrote, "it is in the nature of human existence to assert itself against the inertia of the given by dominating things, by invading them, by incorporating their structures into the world of man." This is why she was quite taken by drugstores and dime stores, where "the abundance and variety of the industrial products displayed all pointed to a magnificent and immediate taste for the transformation of mere things into instruments adapted to human purposes." Her praise for pragmatism pleased her audience. "American dynamism" won her over. In less than two hundred years a continent had been equipped with a history and a civilization. "A humanist," she wrote, "cannot but marvel at this magnificent triumph of man."[4]

She stated her case with such clarity and simplicity that existentialism sounded like the world's most normal and moral doctrine.

> Man is not a stone or a plant and cannot calmly rest his case on the fact that he is present in the midst of the world; man is man only by his refusal to be passive, by the urge which thrusts him from the present toward the future, which thrusts him toward things with the aim of dominating them and shaping them; for him, to exist is to remake existence, to live is to will to live.
>
> We hold that man is free: but his freedom is real and concrete only to the degree that it is committed to something, only if it pursues some end and strives to effect some changes in the world. That is why we approve, to some extent, the American way of judging a man by what he has done.[5]

She taught the people of America that they were existentialists without knowing it, and she congratulated them.

On April 15 she arrived at Smith College, where a colloquium on "Woman's Role in Contemporary Society" was held. Well-known women in science, the arts, and the business world participated. De Beauvoir, already at work on *The Second Sex*, took advantage of the occasion to question these American women. She did not waste a minute. The Gerassis, who had been in New York since the beginning of the war, took her everywhere.

Sartre had put her in touch with the writer Richard Wright and his wife, Ellen. The author of *Native Son*, then a Communist, took her on a tour of Harlem and spoke to her of racial problems. They became friends. She also looked up Claude Lévi-Strauss, who was then the director of French cultural services in New York ("He was not very nice, and I saw him only once").

In speaking with college students at the schools she visited, de Beauvoir was surprised to hear that they thought Faulkner old-fashioned and no longer read Hemingway.[6] She noted that not only the past but also the present was condemned in favor of the future. Young Americans lacked a tragic sensibility toward life and seemed to do without the feelings of sin and remorse and anxiety that were so basic to the French. She thought of herself at nineteen and her own restlessness and worry, and this made her increasingly curious about the reality of America. But how to get at it? The answer was to write a book that looked closely at daily life in the United States. She wanted to seize America "with her hands, her eyes, her mouth." She walked around and looked around, went into stores and movie theatres, bars and restaurants. Her friends, completely done in by her energy, were not up to the task of guiding this indefatigable explorer who wanted to get to the bottom of city life, to decipher the secrets of its days and the mysteries of its nights. "I walk slowly. I want to wrap these lights around my neck, caress and eat them . . . I desire nothing except a myth: New York which is everywhere and nowhere . . . I didn't think I could love another city as much as Paris."[7]

NELSON ALGREN

*H*er lecture tour took Simone de Beauvoir to Chicago, where she faced a thirty-six-hour layover. Chicago was a myth whose very name fascinated her. In New York, de Beauvoir had met a young intellectual, Mary Guggenheim,* whose lover was a writer who lived in Chicago.[8] Guggenheim had shown her his picture ("He is my love") and given her the address of Nelson Algren, whose novels *(The Man with the Golden Arm, A Walk on the Wild Side)* described the seedy side of Chicago with its shady characters, social outcasts, and drug addicts. This was just what de Beauvoir wanted to see; she called him.

Thirty-five years later, Nelson Algren remembered the phone call— rather, the calls—that interrupted his dinner that February night in 1947. The first time the telephone rang he made out a hoarse, incomprehensible screech, assumed it was a wrong number, and hung up and returned to the stove. This happened three times, and then the operator interceded: "Would you mind holding the phone for a minute, don't hang up for just a minute, there's a party here would like to speak to you."[9] Algren heard a woman's voice, a very thick French accent, a name he could not quite catch. She would await him at the Palmer House, a copy of *Partisan Review* under her arm.

Algren watched her for a few minutes, saw her get up four times, walk as far as the door, then sit down again. He invited her to the bar for a drink, and since she was French and he did not know what else to tell her, he began talking about his experiences in the war. Later she admitted to him that she had not understood a word. Yet they found each other pleasant company, and she promised to return to the city when her speaking tour was finished. He promised to show her "the real Chicago."

---

*Nelly Benson in the memoirs.

She returned, and they fell madly in love with each other. This was a fierce and passionate love, a true understanding on every level. Nelson Algren was a handsome man with regular features and a broad forehead under a mass of blond hair. He stood over six feet tall and was robust and slender, a Scandinavian. He was an adventurer, a free spirit, a rebel; he gave the impression of having stepped out of a movie or a novel. De Beauvoir told him in parting that she would return but added that "my life was permanently fixed in Paris; he believed me without at all understanding what I meant."[10] Algren could not possibly have known just what sort of relationship was in store for him. He loved Simone de Beauvoir deeply and in all simplicity. Simone, who had a short liaison in New York with a married man, did not plan to become involved with Nelson. Returned to Paris, she had to admit that she was in love with him and that "forever" she would be "his loving wife." She wrote him that she would never forget the two days she had spent in Chicago. Often in her letters she recalled their first encounter and the time they had spent in each other's arms.

In 1981 Nelson Algren answered questions put to him by W. J. Weatherby, a writer who had come to interview him about his last book, *The Devil's Stocking*. He recounted some of his memories.

> But the topic that seemed to excite him more than anything was a love affair of twenty-five years ago. His encounter with Simone de Beauvoir, the French author and long-time companion of Jean-Paul Sartre, became a romantic episode in her novel *The Mandarins*. Algren still hadn't forgiven her.
>
> He told me indignantly, "She gave me a disguise, another name, in *The Mandarins*, but in a later book, I think it was called *The Prime of Life*, she tried to make our relationship into a great international literary affair, naming me and quoting from some of my letters. She must have been awfully hard up for something to write about or maybe she thought of herself as another Colette. The publisher asked my permission to quote the letters. I thought about it for a few days and then I reluctantly said okay. Hell, love letters should be private. I've been in whorehouses all over the world and the women there always close the door, whether it's in Korea or India. But this woman flung the door open and called in the public and the press.[11]

Algren got more and more worked up, and his interviewer, knowing that Algren at seventy-two had heart trouble, tried to calm the writer and change the subject, but it was a lost cause.

He was too steamed up about de Beauvoir. He confided that in his bare, half-furnished cottage at Sag Harbor, Long Island, New York, was a tin box containing about three hundred love letters from the French writer. As she had published some of his letters, he intended to auction hers. "If one half of a correspondence is made public," he said, "then the other half should be. They're no longer of any sentimental value to me. You can't commercialize half and keep the other half sacrosanct. Let's make it all public!"*

His wrath showed no sign of abating, and the flustered journalist excused himself. The following day a reception was scheduled at Algren's house to celebrate the release of his new book. The first guest to arrive pushed the door open to find Algren stretched out on the floor, dead of a heart attack. Love had killed him. His final rage had been directed at Simone de Beauvoir, whom he had been unable to forget despite two marriages and two divorces. It was an unceremonious adieu; the American lover died alone after sharing his final confidences with a journalist who was frightened by so much emotion, so much passion.

When de Beauvoir first met Algren he was considered an important writer, a hard-hitting journalist, and a poet when the spirit moved him. Algren was the eternal rebel. His parents were born in Chicago, but his paternal grandfather, Nels Ahlgren, had come from Sweden. This Swedish nonconformist found the truth he had been seeking in the Bible, converted to Judaism, and decided to call himself Isaac Ben Abraham. Ahlgren emigrated to the United States and sold furs; then, finding that line of work monotonous, he embarked with his wife and children for Jerusalem, where he posed as a rabbi. Unable to tolerate the phony rabbi's pipe dreams and interminable discussions, his wife gathered their remaining dollars, took the children, and set off to return to the United States. At the last minute her husband came running up the gangplank as it was being lifted. On board ship, Nels Ahlgren had a new inspiration. Lending his unique interpretation to the biblical ban on making false idols, he decreed that since man was made in God's image, all images of man were sacrilegious. He wrested away his wife's cache of dollars, showed her Washington's likeness, shouted "Sacrilege!" and threw the offending bills overboard. After this display of lunacy his wife would have nothing to do with him. He roamed the world, changing his religion in accordance with local preference and posing as a missionary wher-

---

*Only a few lines from Algren's letters actually appeared in the memoirs.

ever he went. In his absence his family fended for itself, the children quitting school and going to work. Nelson Algren felt certain affinities with this grandfather, who returned to his family, then left again for Florida, where he died.

The youngest child, Nelson Algren Abraham was named after his paternal grandfather.[12] His maternal grandfather was a German Jew who repudiated Judaism. Nelson attended a Protestant Sunday school in an Irish neighborhood. In this environment he became a nonconformist. His older sister, a teacher, paid his tuition at the University of Illinois, where he took courses in journalism. Impatient to tackle life and armed with a virtually worthless diploma, Algren took to the open road, doing odd jobs where and when the opportunity arose. His wandering led him to Texas, where, penniless and without fixed occupation, he was jailed on a vagrancy charge. A lawyer offered to get him out for two hundred dollars—a fortune—but Nelson decided to wait for the judge, who came through the locality every two months. The judge tried the case and let him off with a five-dollar fine.

Algren went in search of further adventures and settled on an abandoned ranch in Alpine, Texas. This small town housed a sparsely attended teachers' college, and in one of the campus buildings Algren discovered an abandoned classroom equipped with thirty typewriters. He got into the habit of going there regularly to write, and no one took notice of him.

Because he could not make ends meet on the money he occasionally earned at odd jobs, Algren decided to return to Chicago. Having grown attached to the typewriter he had been using, he decided to take it with him. He got a cardboard box, packed the machine carefully, took it to the post office, and sent it to Chicago. Then he boarded a train. At a stop near San Antonio, Algren left the stuffy compartment to stretch his legs, rolled a cigarette, and waited for the "All aboard!" A sheriff happened along, and in conversation Algren mentioned that he had just left Alpine. The sheriff asked his name, then told Algren he would have to turn back immediately, giving him no explanation. Algren obediently returned to Alpine. The post office clerk had not shipped the typewriter—he had notified the sheriff, and Algren landed in jail. The judge passed through this town only twice a year, so the twenty-two-year-old Algren waited under lock and key from November to March, when the judge gave him a two-year suspended sentence. He had to leave Texas and return in two years to swear he had committed no further crime. Algren never returned to Alpine and remained officially sentenced to the two-year suspended sentence.

This happened in 1929; on the other side of the Atlantic, one dutiful daughter had just passed the *agrégation* competition with distinction.

For the next three years Algren continued to roam the country, travel-ing by freight train. It was okay to ride in a boxcar provided you did not get caught; if you were caught, you went to jail. Sometimes Algren lived on his own, sometimes he joined other hoboes. He earned a few dollars as an ac-complice to a carnival huckster with a game-of-chance scam. Nelson was the one who hit the jackpot and made it look easy to unsuspecting custom-ers. Algren played and won as agreed, and with an appreciable sum in his possession, he took advantage of a sheriff's presence to pocket his "win-nings" and stroll away, leaving his partner high and dry and none too pleased.

After the freight trains, Algren took to the highways. He ate at the Salvation Army and other charitable institutions. And he talked with men who were down on their luck, thieves and bandits, drifters and the disadvan-taged who complained they could not get an even break. He had a soft spot for unbalanced people and was taken with their originality; drawing on the people he met and the tales they told, he wrote poetry.

His ill-fated romance with the Texas typewriter stemmed from a deep-seated need to write. Algren was a born writer. On America's endless high-ways he had discovered what he wanted to describe, what he wanted to say, and the people he wanted to write about. He had witnessed accidents and seen people die. He had seen the absolute misery that was the lot of thou-sands of Americans who were trying to hang on, struggling to survive during the Great Depression, a time of woeful mass migrations as the disenfran-chised sought work in the southern and western states. Misery reigned in the big cities as well. Everything they had taught him was untrue. They had told him, "Kid, you go to college, you get a diploma, you become a reporter, you work for a good paper, you marry a nice girl, you have nice kids, and that's America." That was not it at all. Society was badly put together, his head had been filled with nothing but lies at school, and what he had learned about journalism was useless. That was not what writing was.

Algren was twenty-four when he returned to Chicago. He found a type-writer and a place to work in a club founded by young writers. A newspaper published his account of one of his adventures, and as a result Algren received a letter from a publisher asking if he would write a novel. Algren hitchhiked to New York, where the director of the Vanguard Press asked him three questions: "What do you need? What would you do if you had some money? How would you write a novel?" Algren replied in three sentences of his own: "I'd need thirty dollars a month. I'd go back to the Southwest. I'd give you a manuscript in three months."[13] He got ten dollars for travel expenses and ninety dollars to cover three months. The novel did not meet with success. Algren married. Four years later he divorced and wrote another novel, which attracted some attention.

Like many other left-leaning American intellectuals, Algren enlisted in the army in 1942 and remained in the service until 1945. His regiment was sent to Europe, but Algren served in the medical corps and never saw combat.

In 1945 a vast camp was set up north of Marseille to accommodate the American troops waiting to be repatriated. Tens of thousands of soldiers lived in a gigantic tent city until ships arrived to take them home. Algren made gambling money by supplying the black market with cigarettes, clothing, and any other American goods he could get his hands on. He got a kick out of the ruses people tried on him. One of the classic stunts consisted of telling a GI:

"Sell me your jacket."

"How much?"

"Twenty bucks."

The "buyer" dropped the money, the seller bent over to pick it up, and while he was looking at the ground he got conked on the head—and the "buyer" ran off with the jacket. Algren did not bend over; he had seen the outcome too often.

He drank sensibly in the bars, for a drunken GI was quickly shoved into a corner and relieved of jacket, boots, and money. One always had to give the appearance of sobriety. Algren looked on with amusement as soldiers entered a brothel that the military police raided every half hour, dragging out any hapless GI caught on the premises in a state of undress. The citizens of Marseille sat on the curbs and applauded.

Algren returned to Chicago in 1945 and began work on a novel. His new home was at 1523 West Wabansia, in one of the poorer neighborhoods. The rent on his unheated one-room apartment with a spacious kitchen but no electricity was ten dollars a month. Algren helped himself to some electrical wiring and bought a stove. At the YMCA he swam for an hour, lifted weights, and took his daily shower as well, since his apartment lacked a bathroom.

Algren was happy in the modest room he shared with a legitimately gotten typewriter. After years of bumming around and a stint in the army, he had a home of his own. And it was there that Simone de Beauvoir appeared one February day in 1947. He had just had his first success with *The Neon Wilderness*, in which he described a part of American society that was unfamiliar to his readers: the social outcasts who live in the lower depths of the big cities—thieves, drug addicts, prostitutes.

"*MA PETITE GAULOISE*"

*T*his was the Chicago Algren showed de Beauvoir. He took her to lowlife bars and to a police station at night, when the paddy wagons delivered all sorts of characters, and he showed her the electric chair. They went to burlesque shows, the zoo, the racetrack. Algren told her about the American left and what was going on in intellectual circles. The Communist cell in Chicago was shaken up over the case of a black member accused of having repudiated the party's teachings. The party organized a "confessional trial" that was closely followed by the entire intellectual left; rather than be expelled from the party, Comrade Ross chose to be in full agreement with his accusers without saying a word in his own defense. In *The God That Failed* Richard Wright described the surprise of American Communist writers who saw in "the Chicago trial" another form of totalitarianism. It was a whole new world for de Beauvoir. Thanks to Nelson Algren, she could grasp what interested her most: real life as it was lived.

She left Algren, in tears, and arrived in Paris "in a dreadful state."[14] She loved the tall, fair-haired American writer and adventurer. Her relationship with Jacques-Laurent Bost having lost its meaning, she arranged for them to be "just friends." Bost was writing for *Combat* and had published a novel with the NRF. His blossoming success and the liberation had thrown multitudes of women into his arms, and Simone's companion had become a public figure. Bost was not angered when she broke things off. "He knew I did not *love* him, but there remains some uneasiness between us."[15]

Then there was Sartre. He too had become entangled in a romance on American soil. In 1945 he and eight other French journalists were invited by the State Department to report for the French press for two months about the American war effort. In New York, he met Dolorès Vanetti,* an actress who had performed under Gaston Baty's direction at the Montparnasse Theatre before the war. De Beauvoir had often admired her at the Dôme, where her stunning entrances never went unmarked. At the beginning of the war she left for the United States, where she hosted a radio program in French, became André Breton's mistress, then married a wealthy American doctor. Sartre had made his conquest in New York, and they had talked of marriage. Vanetti

---

*M. in *Force of Circumstance*.

resolved on divorce. Sartre thought a great deal of her and wanted to spend
three or four months a year with her, but he did not want to disturb the
careful equilibrium that allowed him to carry on simultaneously his career
and his various love relationships. Vanetti, like Nelson Algren, found it
difficult to understand the subtle nuances of Sartrian love. In 1945 and again
in 1946, Sartre spent several months with Dolorès in New York. When he
came back he told his friends that she would come to France. He spoke of
her so passionately that his mother thought that he was going to marry her.
Simone de Beauvoir saw in this brilliant and beautiful woman a real threat
to her relationship with Sartre. Dolorès arrived and Sartre managed to strike
a delicate balance between Simone and Dolorès. Sartre preserved his hours
of work, and he preferred to keep de Beauvoir out of reach of Vanetti.

Sartre and de Beauvoir moved into "a little hotel near Port-Royal on the
outskirts of Paris," where they could work. Sartre took a leave of absence to
spend days in Paris with Dolorès, but that was not enough. She telephoned
in tears. In the end Sartre gave in to her and they went on a trip. "His excuse
was that, while refusing to alter his relationship with me, he cared for her
intensely and wanted to believe that some compromise solution could be
found," de Beauvoir explained in *Force of Circumstance.* It proved to be an
awkward, spoiled spring. De Beauvoir, steeped in nostalgia, wrote her essay
on America. She was thinking about Algren, she wanted to see him, and she
had the money to do it. Why not go back to Chicago? "I asked myself that
question with an anxiety that bordered on mental aberration." Since she
always experienced her feelings fiercely and her senses remained as imperious
as ever, she summed up her state of mind and heart with, "That is hell."[16]

After those months of turmoil Sartre accompanied Dolorès to Le Havre,
where she reembarked for America. But the sweet, simple joy of living was
slow to return. "Sartre was very quiet, and so was I. I wondered in terror if
we had become strangers to one another."[17]

A trip to Sweden with Sartre eased the tension between them, but as
soon as they were back in France, de Beauvoir cabled Algren to ask whether
he wanted her to return. Indeed he did. She left to rejoin him.

Finding Algren in his hovel, de Beauvoir felt immediately she had been
"right to come back."[18] They shared two weeks of radiant happiness. She read
the first draft of his new novel, and they discussed it together. She met his
friends, who were writers, actors, radio and television reporters; they tended
to be liberal nonconformists, and de Beauvoir enjoyed their company. She
researched and completed her book on America. She and Nelson worked side
by side and were happy. Algren discovered the fullness and satisfaction of

a life shared with a woman who, like himself, was a writer, a woman whose intelligence and talent created between them a relationship that reached heights he had never before known. This equal, this marvelous intellectual companion was also a passionate, happy woman; he asked her to stay on forever. Having no understanding of the power of the pact she had made with Sartre, he was upset by her refusal.

De Beauvoir and Sartre did not want to destroy their understanding. Their work mattered above all else, yet by a strange twist of fate they had both fallen in love with partners who demanded marriage. For several years de Beauvoir would try to make good a transatlantic liaison and to reconcile her love for Sartre's genius with her love for Nelson Algren.

LOVE LETTERS

*I*n the metal box Nelson Algren described to the interviewer on the eve of his death were two sprigs of dried bellflower that had been picked in some corner of France. They were pressed in the folds of a letter, preserved for thirty years, and they are there still, among the 1442 pages de Beauvoir wrote to Algren. These love letters show us an unexpected Simone, tender, mischievous, subtle, and passionately in love.

The letters have something de Beauvoir's memoirs lack. They are the spontaneous witnesses to a passion, the thoughts of a writer who allowed her pen to wander where her heart led it. Through their transparency we see the life of a likable, touching, sensitive woman. One of the letters had been torn up by a furious lover, then lovingly pieced together again by the same man. Algren had once sold the entire collection in a fit of anger and immediately bought it back. The letters, nestled in their metal box, remained by his side to the very end.

"Nelson my love," "My own Nelson," "My dear love, I am closer to you every day." She speaks of her "obstinately faithful" heart, and from letter to letter the same words return: "my beloved spouse," "my friend, my lover, my husband," "my husband of spring," "my husband of the Mississippi," and, mixing French with English, "Nelson, dearest you, *mon cher amour,*" "I will be your wife of Wabansia."[19] She returned to France with a silver ring on her finger that astonished her friends.

In the letter accompanying the mauve bellflowers she wrote, "I am impatient to melt into your arms again . . . my far-away love." A crumpled sheet of paper cries out, "Don't go, stay with me, talk to me!" and each letter is signed "your own Simone."

She kept Nelson posted on her life, but there was a language problem: "I am jealous at your writing such nice letters—it is not fair. I cannot say what I wish, writing in a foreign language. You seem so witty, and describe so well and tell a story in the best way, I can just write a broken childish English, yet I am not so stupid, you know. I am afraid that you are going to feel so much better than I and have a haughty contempt for me." She wrote him about Sartre, the Family, and friends; about Bost, Olga, Wanda, Bianca, Michèle Vian, Juliette Gréco, Violette Leduc, Jean Genet, Mouloudji; about rehearsals for *The Flies,* which Dullin was staging again, and the goings-on at *Les Temps modernes,* what she was writing, what she saw, her travels. She tells him that she dreams of him and the burn of his kisses. She tells him, "I look for you from street to street all over Paris." She is terror-stricken by the idea of death: "I don't want to die . . . I cannot bear the idea that you could die before me." She recalls Nelson's having said to her, "Let's die together at seventy-six." That would be best, she agrees, but seventy-six is a bit too soon. She calls him "Nelson, my only love" and confirms for him that their meeting was the luckiest thing that ever happened to her. Their love did not fluctuate in its intensity, but it came with lengthy separations and the freedom to devote themselves deeply to their writing.

She wrote him from the Riviera that she saw him seated beside her and that she loved him in this French garden and in Chicago at the same time, "for I am in our house in Chicago just as you are in France with me. We are not separated and we will never be separated. I am your own wife forever." Was the writer's all-powerful imagination peopling her daily life with well-loved presences as realistically as it peopled her novels with characters? Did the imaginary hold a privileged place here? If fictional beings can be made to rise out of the pages of literature, why then should the same minds that create these characters not have exceptional powers for making illusion reality? "Every day, after lunch, I rest a little on my bed, without reading, just half dreaming, and every day you come silently and lovingly and you lie in my arms as long as I can keep you. Once it was true, do you remember, Nelson? Every day I remember and I want you."

It is impossible to doubt the sincerity of the urgent appeal repeated from letter to letter. "We must not feel separated. On the contrary, when we will meet again in nine or ten months, we will be more close, even more intimate than when we separated. These three months we have to try to live them together."

She gave an account of her daily routine. She wrote from 9 A.M. to 1 P.M., then had lunch with Sartre, then wrote from 5 P.M. to 8 P.M. She was translating one of Algren's short stories, "Too Much Salt on the Pretzels," which would appear in *Les Temps modernes*. [20] She was hard at work and wanted Nelson to go on working too. Knowing all the while that he needed Chicago in the same way she needed Paris, she admitted that she could not live apart from him. He called her "my true wife," and she said, "So I am."

She describes herself seated on the second floor of the Café de Flore, before the open windows through which she can see the trees lining the boulevard Saint-Germain. She had given Sartre the first chapters of *America Day by Day* to read, and she tells Algren she is sorry that this narrative that concerns the two of them should be written in a language he does not understand. And what if he learned French? She sends him a little translation exercise to do, as simple as a child's composition, as sweet as a lullaby and naïvely sentimental.

> *Mon bien aimé est très loin. . . . Je penserai à lui jusqu'à ce que je le retrouve et alors je n'aurai plus à penser. . . . Il est très loin mais personne n'est plus près de moi parce qu'il habite mon coeur. Son nom est Nelson Algren.* [21]

(My beloved is far away. . . . I'll think of him until I'm with him once again and then I won't have to think anymore. . . . He is very far away but no one is closer to me because he lives in my heart. His name is Nelson Algren.)

He too was sentimental. He sent her a bouquet of white flowers, and she cried on receiving this message from her distant love. She learned his letters by heart, and if they were long, so much the better. At first she had loved him for the way he loved her, and in time she came to love him for himself. "I will never grow old and I will never die as long as you give me your love." She wrote that she thought of his arms holding her tight and trembled and ached all over. Night and day she dreamed of this love that enveloped and protected her. In the beginning she had been afraid to admit that she had fallen in love with him, "for to love with such intensity makes you vulnerable." She noted that her happiness was now in his hands. "I would have preferred to keep it under control."

She promises lightheartedly that she will let him work in peace, that he can be by himself while she washes the dishes, sweeps the floor, and goes out for eggs and bread, and that she will not caress him or run her fingers through his hair or stroke his shoulder without his permission. She promises not to be morose when he is in a bad mood and not to hamper his freedom. Then, jesting aside, in one great surge, she asks if he could not arrange the thing she desires most with all her soul, with all her body, with all her heart: for him to live long months at her side.

This letter ends with a graceful pirouette. "May be you smile to see me so serious, may be you think I am a talkative little frog. May be you are right. This is why love frightens me; it makes me rather silly." She says she is unhappy with this epistle—"it is difficult to make love by correspondence" —and concludes in French, *"Vous êtes mon amour."*[22]

When she moved to the rue de la Bûcherie she wrote him that the apartment would be theirs. Only one man would sleep there—him—and she added with emphasis, *"You'll* do the *cooking."* On one of the sheets of blue stationery imprinted "Simone de Beauvoir, 11 rue de la Bûcherie," she added "and 1523 W. Wabansia."[23]

It was difficult to admit to this dearly beloved that he belonged to the category of contingent loves and that this terminology described an arrangement which was normal and beneficial for literary work. Sartre, she explained, had helped her. He needed her, and she could not "let him down" because the links between them were indestructible.

Shocked, the American lover had only one choice: to take what he was offered, this "sharing," or lose her altogether. He was subjugated by a love-admiration for the writer who led her life as freely as a man might. He felt outdone by this amazing woman's nonconformity.

When she left, he waited for her; she returned in May 1948. Excerpts from *America Day by Day* appeared in installments in *Les Temps modernes.* Just before her departure she had published an extract from *The Second Sex.*

Still more famous and controversial, she arrived in the United States to see Algren and lure him away from Chicago. She wanted to see the Mississippi River—Chateaubriand's Meschacebé, the Father of the Waters of Indian legend—and middle America too. Nelson had planned to show her the lower depths of Chicago and had arranged for her to meet thieves and morphine addicts, but she had done all that on her last visit. A disappointed Nelson, realizing that she was bored, bought train tickets for Cincinnati. The following day they boarded a paddle-wheel steamer complete with smokestack, a bell to summon the passengers, luxury cabins, and a restaurant. It was a genuine nineteenth-century riverboat, one of the Green Line stern-wheelers, restored to take tourists up and down the Mississippi in good weather.

De Beauvoir marveled at the beauty of Old Man River, this "wide watery landscape," and "the enchantment of its evenings, its moons."[24] Splendid garnet-colored sunsets turned to romantic moonlight, and the mighty Mississippi carried her slowly along to the rhythm of Chateaubriand's prose. All the pages about the forests of the new world came alive.

On deck, Nelson took photos and Simone translated one of Algren's stories that she wanted to publish in *Les Temps modernes*. They chatted, drank scotch ("one of the keys to America"), and loved each other.[25]

Their itinerary included New Orleans, the Yucatan, Guatemala, and Mexico. They kept a joint travel diary; she recorded her impressions on one page, and he wrote on the facing page.* Disconcerted by such a methodical approach and the constant concern for work, Algren sulked a bit but was resigned.

He was unhappy. He had his caprices; he refused to accompany de Beauvoir when she set out to explore monuments and ruins and insisted on examining every stone. De Beauvoir did not want to understand the reason for his sulking; or rather, she understood it all too well and asked herself how to behave without driving Algren to despair. Worse, she had put off telling him that she would be leaving him on July 14 to return to Paris because Sartre had asked her to help him with a screenplay. It was a complete reversal of the conventional roles: The woman was the stronger, more celebrated, in control of her destiny, and she had to tell her lover, My career, my work, and someone supremely important oblige me to leave. Wait for me.

De Beauvoir would have liked to be able to return whenever the spirit moved her. Nelson rebelled. In New York de Beauvoir flared up at this intractable lover who was making himself increasingly disagreeable. She announced abruptly that she could leave that very day. Nelson, cornered and facing the worst, laid bare his heart. "I'm ready to marry you this very moment," he mumbled. She did not want to change her style of life; why would Algren not just come to live in Paris?

Algren sensed that he would not be able to write far away from Chicago, and he refused to adjust his life to accommodate de Beauvoir. Their parting was painful. No sooner had Simone returned to Paris to rejoin Sartre than Dolorès Vanetti came back into the picture. She telephoned Sartre from New York to say she wanted to see him again. Sartre took her to the south of France for a month. There was no further mention of the screenplay, and de Beauvoir, finding herself alone, cabled Algren to say she was ready to return. The vexed lover replied, "No, I have too much work to do." When Sartre returned he and Simone left together for North Africa, where they recovered from their American romances and worked on the movie script.

Algren, however, did not appear to be recovering. He wrote de Beauvoir twice a week, admitting he would have liked to have a wife, perhaps even a child. He found himself alone and lonely.

---

*This little notebook is included among de Beauvoir's unpublished letters to Algren.

De Beauvoir too was having a difficult time coping with their separation. She wrote him burning, unhappy letters and confessed that she sometimes cried all night. Passionate and apologetic, their letters crossed the ocean until, at the beginning of June 1949, Algren dispatched himself to Paris. De Beauvoir put on the white coat she had worn two years earlier in Chicago and went to meet him at the station. She put him up in her apartment at 11 rue de la Bûcherie. There was a Picasso on the wall, but Algren took more notice of the fact that rainwater was leaking through the ceiling and buckets had been positioned to collect it. There was a view of Notre-Dame from the sixth-floor window, and if you leaned out, you could see a café full of North Africans whose music and shouting drifted up day and night.

Nelson was thrilled to be taken around like a tourist, and Simone made sure that he saw everything from Montparnasse to Saint-Germain-des-Prés, from Notre-Dame to Montmartre, and all the way to the top of the Eiffel Tower. It was the heyday of existentialism, and she introduced him to Sartre, the Family, and their friends: Gréco, Vian, Cazalis, Mouloudji, Giacometti, Genet. She taught him to appreciate Paris as he had taught her about Chicago. Then they set off for Italy, Tunisia, and Algeria. They spent September in Paris.

After the months of celebration it was time to part. De Beauvoir accompanied Algren to Orly, certain that she would be seeing him the following year. When he got back to the United States he discovered that he had won the National Book Award for *The Man with the Golden Arm.* A round of cocktail parties, interviews, radio and television appearances followed. He wrote tenderly that he was waiting for her. It finally seemed as though contingent love could not be working better.

In October 1950 de Beauvoir returned to visit Algren at his Forrest Avenue home in Chicago. It was her fifth trip. She went swimming in the lake, rested, and wrote *Must We Burn Sade?* They shared several happy weeks, but at the end of the month Algren announced that he was going to remarry his former wife. "I didn't know which I would miss most: a man, a landscape, or myself." He drove her to the station. They avoided talking to each other. Finally she told him that she was happy that they still had a friendship. Nelson brutally corrected her: "It's not friendship. I can never offer you less than love." She took it as a defeat. The ambiguity of the situation was intolerable to her. Was everything over or not? Was he going to remarry? Did he love her? She cried for hours, in the taxi, on the train, on the plane, and at her hotel in New York.[26]

In Paris, a letter from Algren told her what she already knew too well. He could not love a woman who did not belong to him, who would always put Sartre before him without leaving him the slightest hope of being in first place, the only place. He did not want to give his entire life to someone he could see only for a few months from time to time.

The correspondence continued. For years de Beauvoir wrote to her "blond husband," her "dear Crocodile," her "Brute from nowhere," to "Nelson my love," to her "Old Owl," "my man with a golden brain." She understood his need to share his bed with a woman, but she asked him to keep their friendship intact even though he left their love behind.

In a long letter, she tried to make Algren understand the place Sartre held in her life. She was most eager to work on her own book but had not been able to touch it for a month because Sartre had asked her to go over the manuscript of his *Saint Genet: Actor and Martyr.* She described how the concentrated critical reading she had given this 850-page epic had absorbed her and completely worn her out. In discussing Genet, Sartre touched on morality, taboos, and oppression, took issue with the laws of society, and expounded upon his ideas and his philosophy. She wanted Algren to understand that Sartre's manuscript came first—ahead of her own writing, ahead of everything.[27]

Algren refused to admit that this intellectual pairing, maintained in spite of all difficulties, really counted that much in de Beauvoir's life. She attempted to hang on to Algren by describing Sartre's romances simply and without jealousy. With humor and detachment she explained that Sartre was persuaded that it was not enough to have a brunette Arlette, a blonde Wanda, and two bleached blondes, Michèle and Evelyne; he was missing a redhead, and he found one in Brazil. Since in Brazil it was not permissible for young girls to "sleep with a man," if "that nutty Sartre" went too far he would be obliged to marry the young lady in question—unless he wanted his skin punctured by a dozen rounds of ammunition.

Neither de Beauvoir's detachment vis-à-vis the philosopher Don Juan's conquests nor her explanations of the intellectual links that bound her to him satisfied Algren. He reproached himself for having given so much of himself to her.

"Let's tell each other everything trustingly," she went on repeating, as if transparency practiced between them could create some form of subcontract within the paramount pact with Sartre. But it was useless; Algren wanted nothing more than for his wounded pride to heal.

One day Algren wrote, "Not one to risk her own freedom, Mme. de Beauvoir sensed she could trust Jean-Paul Sartre to be faithless." He added, "Anybody who can experience love contingently has a mind that has recently snapped. How can love be *contingent*? Contingent upon *what*?"[28] In *Force of*

Circumstance he discovered and reacted to the two-year contract, the liberties granted, the fidelity that Sartre and de Beauvoir called "a certain fidelity" and that had little in common with the conventional definition of the word.

But this love refused to die, and would reunite the lovers several times despite the passing of time and other love affairs.

10

Paths of Glory

A writer is hoisted up onto à pedestal only to scrutinize him more closely and conclude that it was a mistake to put him up there in the first place. All the same, as long as he hangs on up there, the distance between himself and the public will blunt the edge of their malice.

Force of Circumstance

"ONE IS NOT BORN, BUT RATHER BECOMES, A WOMAN"

*V*olume I of *The Second Sex* rolled off the Gallimard presses in June 1949, and nothing would ever be quite the same again. *Les Temps modernes* had carried the chapter "The Myth of Woman in Five Authors" in February, followed by "Woman's Sexual Initiation" in May and "The Lesbian" in June. Cries of indignation rose in the press. Twenty-two thousand copies of Volume I were sold in one week. Volume II appeared in November and sold as many. Similarly, each issue of *Les Temps modernes* had been snatched from the newsstands. The scandal was at its height.

Few books have provoked such an avalanche of bad faith, hypocrisy, rudeness, and indecency. In *Le Figaro littéraire* François Mauriac wrote indignantly, "We have literally reached the limits of the abject. This is the ipecac

they made us swallow as children to induce vomiting. Here perhaps is the
moment of the final nausea: that which delivers."[1] He appealed to the general
public and began an investigation in the name of the readers. He railed against
Emmanuel Mounier's collaborator, Domenach, who wrote in the left-wing
Christian review *Esprit* that Madame de Beauvoir had given, with her "courageous articles in *Les Temps modernes,* a course in normal sexuality." Domenach
had also suggested that such novelists as François Mauriac were furious
because de Beauvoir demystified the subterranean reaches of sexuality from
which those novelists drew their material.

De Beauvoir chose the provocative slogan "Woman, this unknown" for
the eye-catching paper band wrapped around her book. Ever since the advent
of men and writing implements there had hardly been a subject more famous,
more cursed, more described, more sung, more analyzed, more glorified than
woman. De Beauvoir was challenging every novelist, every playwright, every
psychologist. Left and right attacked her with the same vehement indignation. Readers felt compelled in the name of truth, goodness, and beauty to
send her lewd letters.

François Mauriac continued his crusade, going so far as to write to one
of the staff of *Les Temps modernes,* "I've learned all there is to know about your
boss's vagina."[2] The reactions appear all the more astounding when one takes
into account the fact that *The Second Sex* is not in the least erotic, let alone
pornographic. Armand Hoog wrote that de Beauvoir was "agonizingly conscious of being imprisoned in her condition by the eyes of men" and unexpectedly called her a "suffragette."[3] André Rousseau admitted that *The Second
Sex* pleased him for its lively polemical tone, "Not that I approve of this
bacchante ripping apart certain of my friends." He demonstrated deliberate
or feigned myopia: "In raising my eyes from Mme. de Beauvoir's book I look
around me in search of the dens of females and the harems, the herds of
female slaves whose lives, because of masculine imperialism, might be divided up between servile tasks and male pleasure." He declared that the goal
of "our Amazon, in stirring up one half of humanity in revolt against the
other, is comparable only to the world's great revolutions. One sees nothing
further but the problem of the black race on which to focus our attention.
. . . It's not the one thousand pages of these two volumes that make me feel
crushed, but my responsibility in an inequality on the order of half the human
race." He added, with a knowing wink, " 'The eternal feminine' is homolo-
gous to the 'black soul,' Mme. de Beauvoir writes. . . . I have very little faith
in the future of this revolution based on pedantry and bedroom. This attempt
to destroy woman by a woman of letters left me afflicted more by lassitude
than disgust."[4]

Paris Match devoted seven full pages to *The Second Sex* with a marked change in tone. The article reflects the common sense and curiosity of the public that will follow de Beauvoir down the path she opened. "A woman summons women to freedom. Simone de Beauvoir, lieutenant to Jean-Paul Sartre and expert on existentialism, is without a doubt the first woman philosopher to appear in the history of man. It has fallen upon her to extract from the grand human adventure a philosophy of her sex."[5]

According to *Paris Match*, de Beauvoir confronts her readers, male as well as female, with

> all the problems that characterize the modern woman's restlessness and worry: the freedom to live, abortion, prostitution, sexual equality, marriage and divorce, giving birth painlessly, etc. The accession to political equality, acquired by women four years ago,* justifies that the eternal "feminine question" be treated, in modern terms, by a young woman philosopher who is levelheaded and lucid. She explodes clichés.
>
> Coming from a man's mouth, the epithet "female" sounds like an insult. . . . On the other hand, he is proud if it is said of him, "That's a male!" . . . Biology alone won't yield an answer. It's a matter of knowing what humanity has made of the human female.[6]

The article was accompanied by a photo of "the first woman philosopher" seated on the terrace of a café in Saint-Germain-des-Prés: "Her simplicity is restful to the eye. She is unaware of the luxury furriers and the couturiers of the rue Royale. Her only coat is one she brought back from America; the black writer Richard Wright picked it out for her. Paris loves Simone de Beauvoir's diadem-shaped tresses and her hoarse, steady, slightly tragic voice. She is part of Parisian mythology, but her true face is in her books." With *The Second Sex* she took on the face of all the women who had ever wanted what she wanted: to change woman's lot. In 1789 Olympe de Gouges proposed that there be a Declaration of the Rights of Woman to parallel the Declaration of the Rights of Man. She died at the guillotine.

Although it *was* placed on the Index, *The Second Sex* was not burned at the executioner's hand, nor was its author condemned to burn for sorcery. Yet an incredible fanaticism was unleashed against de Beauvoir, and it has not entirely subsided to this day.

To reduce *The Second Sex*, as numerous critics have done, to a dictionary of feminine demands is to miss completely the point of a work based on a philosophical system that poses each individual as its subject.

---

*Women were granted the right to vote in France in 1945.

Every subject plays his part as such specifically through exploits or projects that serve as a mode of transcendence; he achieves liberty only through a continual reaching out toward other liberties. There is no justification for the present existence other than its expansion into an indefinitely open future. Every time transcendence falls back into immanence, stagnation, there is a degradation of existence into the *en-soi* —the brutish life of subjection to given conditions—and of liberty into constraint and contingence. This downfall represents a moral fault if the subject consents to it; if it is inflicted upon him, it spells frustration and oppression. In both cases it is an absolute evil.[7]

The originality of *The Second Sex,* like that of Descartes' *Discours de la méthode,* lies in its having proposed that received ideas be systematically questioned. The book's true impact would not be perceived in France until later, when the American feminist movement had attracted attention and brought forth a sudden awareness of feminist consciousness in France. The majority of feminist writers throughout the rest of the world took their inspiration from Simone de Beauvoir. *The Second Sex* was translated into English in 1953, and two million copies were sold in English-speaking countries. It remained on Japan's best-seller list for a full year. It was translated into German, Arabic, Danish, Spanish, Hebrew, Hungarian, Italian, Dutch, Norwegian, Polish, Portuguese, Serbo-Croatian, Slovak, Swedish, Tamil, and Czech. Simone de Beauvoir was the most widely read feminist author in the world. The work remains topical, and it has inspired an impressive number of scholarly papers and university theses. This book launched women's studies as a serious academic discipline. Whether a feminist movement is "Beauvoirian" or utterly different—that is, hostile—it can be related beyond any question to this ground-breaking essay.

De Beauvoir did not open the doors to freedom for women alone with her slogan, "One is not born a woman, one becomes one."[8] In demonstrating the effect that culture can have on the human condition, she posed not only the problem of liberation for women but all the problems that are related to cultural oppression. She called into questions laws, religions, customs, and traditions, and in her own way she demanded that society and all its structures be reevaluated.

THE MANDARINS

*D*e Beauvoir was not interested in the political action that attracted Sartre more and more; she intended to act by means of the written word. She had begun *The Mandarins* in 1949. "I wanted it to contain all of me . . . and above all to tell the feverish and disappointing story of what happened after the war." What was referred to as "the failure of the Resistance" Simone de Beauvoir had experienced as "a personal defeat: the triumphant return of bourgeois domination" and the end of an illusion.[9]

In 1948 a great many pacifist movements saw the light of day. De Beauvoir approved of Sartre's joining the Rassemblement Démocratique Révolutionnaire (RDR), founded by David Rousset, Jean Rous, and Georges Altmann, which quickly became known as "Sartre's party." The RDR refused to situate itself in the political spectrum. Its goal was to disintoxicate the public and to establish contact with all European democratic movements in order to "place Europe in the forefront of peace."[10]

Sartre thought the RDR could attract the reformist lower middle class and the revolutionary proletariat. Since the Communists recruited their members from the very same environments, Sartre became their direct competition. *Liberté de l'esprit,* the Gaullist-inspired review created in February 1949 under the direction of Claude Mauriac, attacked Sartre. Disagreement intensified between the staff of *Les Temps modernes* and the Communist Party. After the publication of the the United Nations report on forced labor in Soviet work camps, Sartre and Merleau-Ponty in a joint editorial reproached the Communists for their bad faith: "There is no socialism where one citizen out of twenty is in a camp." A series of events had spoiled their relationship with the Communist Party. First was the condemnation of *The Second Sex,* which held the rare distinction of displeasing the Communists and the Vatican at the same time. Next, Aragon continued to stalk Paul Nizan with a hatred so implacable it would continue beyond the grave; he depicted him as the traitor Orfilat in his novel *The Communists.* Then Elsa Triolet launched the book war, and the Communist writers slung mud at the "bourgeois literature" of Breton, Camus, and Sartre.

The Kravchenko case ignited the powder keg. The USSR itself was on trial in this affair that lasted for weeks. Hordes of witnesses testified, and one undeniable truth emerged from their evidence: the existence of work camps.

"We began to wonder whether the USSR and the People's Democracies deserved to be called socialist countries." Sartre resigned from the RDR in October 1949, stating in his unpublished notes that the movement "did answer to an abstract need . . . but not to any real need among the people."[11]

That spring, at the suggestion of Michel Leiris, who specialized in the ethnology of black Africa, Sartre and de Beauvoir left on a trip that would take them through Algeria (Algiers and the Ahaggar Mountains), Mali (Gao, Timbuktu, Bamako), and Upper Volta (Bobo-Dioulasso) and finish in the Ivory Coast, where terror had reigned for two months since "the Europeans had tried in vain to repeal the Houphouët law voted by the Constituent Assembly in 1947, which suppressed forced labor."[12]

This was Sartre and de Beauvoir's first "political" trip. They were to contact the Rassemblement Démocratique Africain (RDA), find out what was really going on, and publish their findings in *Les Temps modernes*. Since *The Second Sex* had appeared, de Beauvoir had been exposed to aggressiveness and belligerence from a substantial segment of the press, and even the far reaches of the Sahara were no exception. At Tamanrasset, where they spent eight days, they learned that the region's European settlers spied on one another across hundreds of miles. De Beauvoir found the gossip and tittle-tattle that thrived at the ends of the earth spicy and entertaining. As always, everything amused and interested her; she liked diving to the heart of people's daily lives. One night she stood at the bar, drinking and joking with the picturesque innkeeper and two young truck drivers, "one of whom was as blond and handsome as Jean Marais at twenty."[13] They filled her in on their expeditions across the desert in less than genteel language, which did not bother de Beauvoir as she was capable of employing the same sort of vocabulary when necessary, and they talked until 3 A.M. Several days later she read a full account of her "alcoholic and verbal debauch" in the pages of *Samedi-Soir*. The article was so vile, and went so much further than previous excessive attacks in the press, that de Beauvoir grew worried. She rebelled at the thought of having to live on the defensive, watching her every word, and she found anything that threatened to limit her autonomy intolerable. Sartre reassured her by pointing out that they could do whatever they pleased because no matter what they did, it could not possibly be worse than what had already been said about them.

On each leg of their African journey they hoped to find a message from the RDA, but none was forthcoming. The trip, undertaken to see "the blacks who were fighting the administration," was a disappointment. Everywhere they went they were received by the local authorities; at Bamako the head doctor at the hospital for lepers spoke warmly of *The Second Sex*. But from a political standpoint the trip was a fiasco. They stopped in Morocco for two weeks to recover from their exhaustion. De Beauvoir was put up in the Djalnaï Palace in the sultana's room, which opened onto a patio. Tourists came in the open door and walked around her as though she were "an exhibit in a museum," uncertain whether they should examine the famous author or the bedroom of the sultan's wife.

De Beauvoir was preparing to rejoin Algren in the United States. After receiving the National Book Award he had gone to Hollywood, then, with money in hand, he had bought a house in Miller, near the shores of Lake Michigan. It was there that de Beauvoir intended to spend two months in his company.

As she was about to catch her plane she was seized by a wave of panic. The Korean War had just begun, she believed that China would attack Formosa, and in that case World War III seemed to her inevitable. People were lining up at grocery stores in Paris to stock up on staple goods, and the Red Army was expected to arrive at any minute. Sartre thought that war would not break out for several years, and he encouraged de Beauvoir to leave. He was depressed; after endless quarrels, he and Dolorès Vanetti had broken up.

In Chicago, de Beauvoir found Algren morose, doing what he could to wean himself away from Simone. But he extended his hospitality to Sartre and de Beauvoir in the event World War III were to break out, and he offered them from $200 to $300 to settle in South America.

Returned to Paris, de Beauvoir set about writing seven to eight hours a day. Friendships were falling apart around her. Maurice Merleau-Ponty left *Les Temps modernes* in 1951; he had believed that the RDR was the start of a great revolutionary movement comparable to that of the Bolsheviks, but the RDR was the target of attacks from every party from the Communists to the Gaullists. Unable to constitute a viable party, Sartre drew closer to the Communists. Francis Jeanson became the managing editor of *Les Temps modernes*.

Next came the break with Albert Camus in May 1952. Camus' *The Rebel* had appeared in August 1951, throwing the editorial staff of *Les Temps modernes* into a quandary. In *The Rebel* Camus had taken moral, philosophical, and political positions that ran counter to the beliefs of Sartre and his followers. Camus' declarations against Stalinism had won him the support of the anti-Communists and the right. According to *Le Figaro littéraire,* Camus had just written one of the greatest books of the era. For *Le Monde,* no book of comparable merit had appeared since the war. *Aspects de la France,* the mouthpiece of Action Française, saw in the book a return to nationalism and even to God. Among Camus' adversaries, Claude Mauriac pointed out "an obscure and extremely odd nostalgia for murder."[14]

Each time the editorial committee of *Les Temps modernes* met, de Beauvoir valiantly attempted to hold to the agenda with the reminder, "Remember, we have to review Camus' book." Twenty editors were present, and every one of them shied away from the matter. They said that Camus had not read Marx and Engels thoroughly and that he was dealing with things he did not understand in the first place. Finally Francis Jeanson was assigned to do the article. On a day before the review appeared, Camus went into a café in the place Saint-Sulpice where Sartre and de Beauvoir were sitting and spoke to them of *The Rebel,* convinced that they had liked the book. They were too embarrassed to admit to what they really thought; he was an old friend, and they had admired him for such a long time.

Jeanson's twenty-six-page article concluded with the words, "*The Rebel* is above all a great book manqué."[15] Camus was so disturbed by the Sartrians' rejection that he confided to Maria Casarès that he was no longer able to work and that he had even lost his taste for life. Finally he responded to *Les Temps modernes.* "Camus, affecting to ignore Jeanson's existence, sent Sartre an open letter seventeen pages long in which he addressed him as '*Monsieur le directeur.*'"[16] He wrote that he had grown tired of receiving lessons in efficiency from censors "who have never placed anything but their armchairs in the direction of history."

Camus' letter was published, and Sartre responded to it in the following issue: "A violent and ceremonious dictatorship that relies on an abstract bureaucracy and claims to maintain moral law has taken a firm hold on you." Sartre regretted the broken friendship because for him Camus had been "the admirable conjunction of a person, a course of action, and a body of work."

De Beauvoir also regretted the loss of this friendship that had lasted more than seven years, but they had drifted too far apart in their views. She thought Camus was wrong to attribute man's unhappiness to Nature, when in her opinion the unhappiness of man was a result of culture. She believed in the possibility of changing society through socialism.

Plenty of ink flowed as Sartre and Camus fought it out, and the press reprinted substantial portions of the two writers' open letters. *Samedi-Soir* declared, "Sartre and Camus Break for Good" in an article three columns wide.[17] All of intellectual Paris was abuzz with this public split, and the two men's most biting replies were circulated. If Camus had written that only Sartre's armchair was facing in the direction of history, Sartre had replied that Camus "brought along a portable pedestal" wherever he went.

The RDR's neutrality proved to be an impossibility. In 1952 the Sartrians sided with the USSR.[18] The terror there had reached its height during the final months of Stalin's life. Camus detested the Soviet Union and criticized the Sartrians for tolerating authoritarian socialism. De Beauvoir wanted to return to the United States but was refused a visa because of the political stance of *Les Temps modernes.* She wrote Nelson Algren, "Why don't you come over with the money I set aside for the trip?"[19]

Les Temps modernes, with the addition of two new writers, Marcel Péju and Claude Lanzmann, was repoliticizing. Sartre was closer to the Communists than he would ever be. This was the period when he published a series of articles on *The Communists and Peace.* Sartre and David Rousset's *Conversations on Policy* had publicly put an end to the friendship that had joined Raymond Aron and Sartre since their days at the ENS. Maurice Merleau-Ponty became increasingly distanced from Sartre's positions; he began expressing a "new liberalism" and looked upon parliamentary government as the only known institution "that guarantees a minimum of opposition and truth."

De Beauvoir had lived at the heart of events, at the core of all the ideological movements. This group of intellectuals was her own, and she sensed that she could describe it so that an entire generation would recognize itself. Like Hugo, she felt herself to be at the center of everything, like "a resounding echo." "If the desire to write a novel became imperative for me, it was because I felt situated at a point in space and time at which each of the sounds that I could draw from myself had a chance to awaken echoes in a great many other hearts."[20]

She had been at work on *The Mandarins* for three years, and in its pages she described her love for Nelson Algren, the surprise of their encounter and the terrible wrenching of their partings. She freed herself by transforming into literature a love that would not die.

She gave the manuscript to Sartre to read, and for the first time his criticisms worried her. She was convinced that the book would be a failure. At night she dreamed of her characters so intensely that upon awakening she jotted down the phrases that had been spoken in her dreams. At forty-four she thought her life was over. " 'I'll never sleep again warmed by another's body.' Never: what a knell! When the realization of these facts penetrated me, I felt myself sinking into death."[21]

Death, which had haunted her since childhood, suddenly became more tangibly menacing when she discovered a breast tumor. She asked herself, "What if it's cancer?" She remembered vividly her secretary's long, agonizing death. She saw a doctor, who concluded that in view of her age it would be wise to remove the growth. And if the tumor were not benign, would she agree to have the breast removed? She agreed. The beauty of her body no longer concerned her; she assumed her sex life was over. Since her breakup with Algren she was not about "to quibble over a mutilation." Sartre analyzed her chances: After the operation she could count on another dozen years or so, and sometime between now and then "the atomic bomb will have wiped us all out anyway." The next morning, on her way into the operating room, she resigned herself to the worst. When she came to, she heard a voice in the fog saying, "You don't have cancer." Full of wonder, she took an intensely renewed joy in living.

Several days later she set off on an automobile trip with Bost, Sartre, and Michèle Vian, who, separated from Boris Vian, had become Sartre's companion.

De Beauvoir overflowed with vitality and fought fiercely with Bost over who would get to do the driving. They stopped in Saint-Tropez, where Sartre wrote on a café terrace and de Beauvoir took long, meandering excursions in her car with as much pleasure as she had formerly taken at covering ground on foot. Merleau-Ponty and his wife arrived in Saint-Tropez, now a gathering spot for literary and artistic Paris, and de Beauvoir took them for a spin around Les Maures. Sartre and Michèle Vian left for three weeks in Italy. De Beauvoir went too, taking along Bost and Olga, who had joined them. They all returned to Paris, whereupon de Beauvoir, infatuated with her car, decided to go back to Italy. Sartre would join her there, and they would travel together by car for two months.

Bost, about to write a tourist guide to Brazil, asked his friends to a farewell party, and de Beauvoir suggested he invite one of the new contributors to Les Temps modernes, whom she found attractive, Claude Lanzmann. "The way his mind worked reminded me of Sartre."[22]

Lanzmann's father had been one of the first Resistance fighters, and Claude himself had fought in the maquis from October 1943. He proudly insisted on being recognized as a Jew and "beamed whenever he discovered that some famous man was a Jew."[23] He was a Marxist but not a member of the Communist Party. He had a solid grounding in philosophy. Politics came first for Lanzmann. He was seductive and exuberant.

When Lanzmann called the day after the party to invite her to see a film, de Beauvoir accepted, hung up the phone, and much to her surprise burst into tears. What she had blindly hoped for had come to pass. "We went out for a drink, and we spent the next afternoon and night together." Claude Lanzmann was seventeen years her junior, and his youth would rescue Simone de Beauvoir from the anxiety of aging. In Force of Circumstance she wrote that "after two years in which the general apathy had coincided for me with the breakup of a love affair and the first warnings of physical decline, I leapt back enthralled into happiness."[24]

She had to meet Sartre in Italy. When she got behind the wheel, the emotion brought on by the separation from Lanzmann was so powerful and distracting that she became hopelessly lost in the suburbs until she managed to find the highway. She picked up two English girls who were hitchhiking and almost killed them when she slid off the road and into a wall. She plowed into a stone road marker along the shores of Lake Maggiore, wrenching it from its mooring, and arrived in Milan with one of the car doors flapping. Reaching over to close it, she realized that her purse, containing her money and her papers, was no longer on the seat beside her. Horrified, she got out of the car to search the roadside, when she spotted a cyclist riding toward her with her bag.

Sartre was waiting for her at the Caffè di la Scala, and they climbed into the car for their first motoring trip together. Michèle Vian was spending the vacation with her children, and Lanzmann was in Israel. As they drove they continued the conversation they had begun twenty-five years before, interrupted by exclamations from Sartre, who could not bear being passed by other motorists. "Pass him, go on, pass him," he would urge, and de Beauvoir, glued to the wheel, did her best to overtake the vehicles that zigzagged to prevent her doing so. Women drivers exasperated the machismo of Italian men.

"AM I PAST THE TIME OF LOVING?"[25]

*A*t the age of forty-four Simone de Beauvoir exercised a privilege generally reserved for men of that age: She began her life over with a man seventeen years younger than she. Everything was new for Lanzmann, and for de Beauvoir everything basked in the light of a fresh day's dawning. Sartre and de Beauvoir were famous as a couple, and there was no question of destroying that image so carefully built and maintained.

De Beauvoir had always lived apart from Sartre and had refused to live with Algren, but she decided to share her life with Claude Lanzmann, and he moved into her studio in the rue de la Bûcherie. "I had loved my solitude, but I did not miss it."[26] They arranged their housekeeping. Books, newspapers, and other paper doubled in volume and overflowed onto furniture and floor. Mornings she wrote at home, afternoons she worked with Sartre in the rue Bonaparte, where he had gone to live with his mother. The only problem was that of the two months each year that Sartre and de Beauvoir always spent abroad on vacation together. Since such a long separation between de Beauvoir and Lanzmann would have been painful, it was decided that Lanzmann would join them for ten days of that time. De Beauvoir made La Palette on the boulevard Montparnasse her headquarters and ate her meals with Lanzmann or Olga at La Bûcherie, a restaurant across the square from her house. She refused to enlarge her circle of relationships and did not even want to meet Faulkner, whom she had admired since her youth. The day Sartre dined at Michèle Vian's house with Charlie Chaplin, de Beauvoir chose to go to the movies with Lanzmann, whom she had not seen for a few days. They saw *Limelight,* Chaplin's latest film. De Beauvoir, who had been seized by "the horrors of declining age" since thirty, had discovered in this young love her own youth, complete with its passions, ecstasies, and trances. She dragged Lanzmann all over France and Europe and walked with him for seven or eight hours a day.[27]

Lanzmann urged *Les Temps modernes* to throw in its lot with the Communists. He attacked de Beauvoir's resistance daily, but she could not accept Stalinism.[28]

Politics absorbed and burdened Sartre, who had never written so many articles or participated in so many meetings. He was a member of the National Writers' Committee and vice-president of the France–USSR Association. The life that de Beauvoir and Sartre led together was no longer quite the same. Their respective affairs of the heart had not separated them, but their political beliefs threatened to do so. Would their destinies, hitherto intertwined, diverge in the end? Claude Lanzmann occupied such an important place in her life that she feared her understanding with Sartre would suffer. And yet, she wrote, "the equilibrium I had achieved, thanks to Lanzmann, to Sartre, to my own vigilance, was durable and endured."[29]

In this atmosphere of political polemic, de Beauvoir reworked her novel yet again. Sartre criticized it ardently, and she was on the brink of shelving it altogether, but Lanzmann and Bost persuaded her to continue. She wanted to call the novel *Les Suspects;* Sartre suggested *Les Griots* ("we rather liked comparing ourselves to those blacksmiths-cum-witchdoctors-cum-poets whom certain African societies honor, fear, and despise all at the same time; but it was too esoteric"[30]), and Lanzmann came up with *The Mandarins.* * The book is dedicated to Nelson Algren.

---

*In France a mandarin is a writer and an intellectual of some influence.

THE PRIX GONCOURT

The Mandarins was published after the failure of the European Commission of Defense in October 1954, the year in which the French army was defeated at Diên Biên Phu, Indochina won its independence, and the Algerian war began. De Beauvoir traveled throughout the year. In January she spent two weeks in Algeria with Lanzmann, who was making a study of the problem of independence. She accompanied Sartre to Holland, where Elsa Triolet had invited him to participate in a conference of writers from East and West, at the end of which he was invited to Moscow. In May she visited the Morvan with Lanzmann. On the day she returned to Paris, Bost informed her that Sartre was in a hospital in Moscow. One of the terrible nervous crises to which she had been prone since childhood overcame her; no one filled the world and made it complete as Sartre did—and suddenly she realized that he was mortal.

Recovered from his attack of high blood pressure and fatigue, Sartre returned and left for Italy with Michèle Vian. De Beauvoir and Lanzmann went to Spain. Sartre still did not feel quite well; he complained about not being able to put two ideas together. De Beauvoir persuaded him to take a trip to Alsace, Germany, Austria, and Czechoslovakia. She became worried their first night in Strasbourg when Sartre, seated and staring, declared solemnly, "Literature is a lot of horseshit." She worked at getting him back on his feet by taking him for healthy promenades and preventing him from drinking too much; soon he felt better and began writing again. Sartre took the train to Paris, and Lanzmann, who had joined them in Vienna, continued on to Italy with de Beauvoir.

On the way back, arriving at a hotel in Grenoble, de Beauvoir read a praise-filled article on *The Mandarins* in *Paris-Presse*. This came as a surprise because she had been expecting the same nasty reception *The Second Sex* had received. Sartre told her that *Les Lettres françaises* had given the book an excellent review. *The Mandarins* was treated as kindly by the right-wing press, which thought the novel "had a pleasing odor of anti-Communism," as it was by the Communists, who saw it as an expression of sympathy for them.[31] The book sold 40,000 copies in less than a month, and Gallimard began talking about the Prix Goncourt.

She had put so much of herself into the book that "there were moments when my cheeks burned at the idea of indifferent or hostile eyes moving across its pages."[32] She had endowed Anne, the psychiatrist, with many of her own memories and reactions. Henri, the writer, to whom she attributed "the joy of existence, the gaiety of activity, the pleasure of writing," incarnated de Beauvoir's free and creative side.[33] She was surprised when the critics assumed that Henri was Camus. In *The Mandarins* she described the Family, the *Temps modernes* crowd and the magazine's misadventures, and her failed affair with Arthur Koestler, who appears in the novel as Scriassine. The character of Dubreuil evokes Sartre by virtue of his immoderation and his fame; like Sartre, Dubreuil is fanatically devoted to politics and literature. The character of Nadine has the traits of Nathalie Sorokine, and Lewis is Nelson Algren, to whom de Beauvoir had written:

> This book of yours is a novel about French people from 1945 to 1948; I try to tell the happy revival we felt when the war was over and so many things began again, and the slow disappointment, after. It will be a very big book with lot of people and lot of stories. I try to tell something of *our* story—1) because it seems to be quite a nowaday kind of story, this love from Paris to Chicago, with airplanes making the towns so near yet so far, all that—2) and chiefly because I enjoy remembering those things on paper. Now I am just writing that part and I want it to be very good. I work hard at it. And it's not a wise thing to do because I have too good a memory and when I remember things they seem so real and so near, and I get very blue. So it was not easy to write to you. I felt too much useless love. You look so nice the way I remember you. Your own Simone.[34]

Gallimard assured her that she stood a very good chance of winning the Goncourt. The night before the award was announced, de Beauvoir moved to a friend's house with Lanzmann in order to avoid the possibility of reporters' invading her studio. When she wanted something she always wanted it fiercely, and she had already founded so many projects on the Goncourt money that she was itching with impatience.* De Beauvoir spent the entire morning of December 6 glued to the radio, her heart pounding, waiting for the award to be announced. At noon the prize was hers. The jury had chosen *The Mandarins* by a vote of seven to two over *L'Heure exquise* by Raymond Las

---

*The Prix Goncourt carries a cash award of only 100 francs (about $15), but it virtually guarantees a boost in sales and an accompanying increase in revenue. The Goncourt brothers, Edmond Louis Antoine de Goncourt (1822–1896) and Jules Alfred Huot de Goncourt (1830–1870), established the prize to honor a particularly meritorious French novel.

Vergnas. The defeated candidate was an old classmate of Sartre and Nizan at the Lycée Henri-IV. In 1945, in *L'Affaire Sartre,* he had attacked existentialism: "We've had enough of these excremental paths where it is better not to venture except on stilts."[35]

Michèle Vian threw a luncheon party, and Sartre gave the Castor the pompously appropriate gift of André Billy's recently published book on the Goncourts. De Beauvoir took the occasion to remind Sartre that fifteen years earlier he had received the Prix Populiste for *Nausea.* That evening Michèle Vian, Sartre, Olga and Bost, Lanzmann and his friends the writer Scipion and the journalist J.-F. Rolland assembled for a celebration dinner.

Her memory of the scandal surrounding *The Second Sex* still stung so vividly that de Beauvoir refused to give interviews, except to J.-F. Rolland for *L'Humanité-Dimanche,* for she wanted to make it clear that she was not hostile toward the Communists. *La Nouvelle Critique,* a Communist political review that rarely took note of novels, published a sixteen-page article about this one. The only photo shows de Beauvoir with her mother in her mother's studio. A great number of articles soon appeared, having more to say about what people imagined of her life with Sartre than of her life as a writer. De Beauvoir was forcefully taken to task in a fifty-page diatribe, *Madame de Beauvoir and Her Mandarins,* signed with the pseudonym La Vouldie and published by the Librairie Française.

Several critics reproached the Goncourt jury for having crowned an already famous author, which went against the criteria laid down by the Goncourt brothers. Numerous critics saw every scene in the book as a reproduction of reality and matched the names of public figures with those of the novel's characters. De Beauvoir was wasting her breath in declaring that *The Mandarins* was not a roman à clef and that she had "refracted, diluted, hammered thin, blown up, mixed, transposed, twisted, sometimes completely reversed, and in every case recreated" all the material she drew from memory.[36] Did Wanda see herself in one of the characters? De Beauvoir wrote Algren that in a fit of anger Wanda began stabbing a copy of *The Mandarins* with a kitchen knife, pierced her hand, cut the veins in her wrist, and lost so much blood she nearly died.[37]

The money the Goncourt brought her way—130,000 copies of *The Mandarins* were sold in one month—enabled Simone de Beauvoir to buy the artist's studio in the rue Schoelcher where she lived until her death in April 1986.

In July 1956 the Holy Office placed *The Mandarins* as well as *The Second Sex* on the Index of prohibited books. *L 'Osservatore romano* explained the Church's decision:

The works of Simone de Beauvoir exude the deleterious atmosphere of a certain Existentialist philosophy. . . . The more a society feeds on such literature, it reveals itself to be truly corrupt and subject to all forms of decay as well as all forms of slavery. The author considers the institution of marriage to be a farce and takes up the defense of free love. All methods are good, she maintains, as long as they permit the woman to escape from the slavery of motherhood. She defends the emancipation of woman from everything, especially moral laws, and she accuses the Church of being opposed to this emancipation. The Church must energetically condemn these immoral doctrines that trample underfoot accepted standards of good behavior and the sanctity of the family.[38]

De Beauvoir was inundated with letters. Some were "angry, hurt, indignant, moralizing, insulting," and many were admiring.[39] The press would make mention of The Mandarins for a long time to come. In February 1962 Pierre Aubry, writing in Actualités, responded to a reader who did not understand why the book had been put on the Index: "It's a thoroughly rotten world which Mme. de Beauvoir describes for us in this unwholesome and corrupt novel that takes place in French intellectual milieus immediately following World War II."[40]

The works of Simone de Beauvoir continued to provoke strong reaction and incessant controversy.

11

THE TIME of ACTION

If the contest is neither lost nor won beforehand, one must strive and take risks from minute to minute.
Existentialism and the Wisdom of Nations

THE TRIP TO CHINA

On February 20, 1955, Sartre gave a short speech during a France–USSR Association meeting commemorating the victory at Stalingrad. His play *Nekrassov* premiered in June and was praised by the Communists. Sartre was invited to the World Assembly for Peace in Helsinki, and de Beauvoir, as in her youth, wanted to "be useful and take part" and accompanied him to Finland. There she met the Cuban poet Nicolás Guillén, the Brazilian writer Jorge Amado, Georg Lukács, and Ilya Ehrenburg, who told her that in Moscow the intellectuals who knew French read *The Mandarins.* For de Beauvoir as for Sartre, "the Iron Curtain had dissolved . . . the realms of socialism were now part of our world."[1] Charles de Gaulle had initiated a reconciliation with the Soviet Union.

The Chinese government invited de Beauvoir and Sartre to spend two

267

months in China. They would stop in Moscow for a week on the way back. She plunged into preparations for the trip with a passionate interest, reading and dreaming endlessly of this Orient about which she knew next to nothing.

Sartre and de Beauvoir landed in Peking on September 6, 1955. De Beauvoir, who had no familiarity at all with contemporary Chinese writing, found herself completely disoriented. She met writers whose work she read on the spot in English when translations existed. Only a handful of specialists in French literature had heard of her and Sartre; it was the first time in her travels that she had encountered reciprocal ignorance.

She and Sartre had been invited there to witness the new China's progress, and she gave this project her all. Guided imperiously by the Chinese, she began her customary ambitious expeditions on foot and found that she learned more about a city and its inhabitants by walking the streets of Peking, Shanghai, and Mukden than through her reading. Much about the Far East baffled her, but "for the first time I understood fully the meaning of the words 'underdeveloped country,' " and she saw what poverty on a scale of six hundred million people represents.[2] Yesterday the Chinese had suffered from chronic malnutrition, epidemic illnesses, and an extremely high rate of infant mortality; today people had clean clothes, food, and shelter.

De Beauvoir tried to compare the history of China and the socialist experiment. The practicality of some reforms struck her; for example, domestic service had not been eliminated, and servants were decently paid. Austerity was universal, shared alike by the new political elite and the workers.

Returned to France, she wrote her essay *The Long March.* Having studied China from an historical standpoint, she concluded that it is only when one sees the most populous nation on earth in terms of its evolution that the true country comes to light, "neither paradise nor an infernal hive of activity but a region of this earth where men who have just broken the hopeless cycle of an animal existence struggle hard to build a human world."

In December 1955 she wrote Nelson Algren that the book she was writing was "full of lies" for she talked about things she did not see, so she did "a lot of research."

After her trip to China, de Beauvoir understood that the Western world's prosperity, which had been her only norm, was in fact a privilege when compared to the standard of living in the Third World. The sheer enormity of the Chinese population obliged her to revise her view of the world. Henceforth the Far East, India, Africa, and South America would bring their full weight to bear on her conception of mankind. The journey to China had swept away those points of reference she had formerly used for judging a great many realities. Such words as city, village, family, work, and culture took on new meanings in light of a civilization where these words did not have the meanings they had in French civilization. Her view of her own environment changed completely.

Sartre planned a lengthy study of his travels through China; he did not complete the project, but *Les Temps modernes* published a special issue on "China Yesterday and Today."

Sartre and de Beauvoir spent a week in Moscow on their way back from China. After two months of Chinese poverty, Moscow amazed de Beauvoir with its richness much as New York had amazed her in 1947, after Europe's wartime shortages. In 1955 Moscow was undergoing extensive construction and expansion. Trucks, bulldozers, and cranes cluttered the streets; here nobody moved dirt around in baskets. "What joy to come back to the kind of food and drink one can get high on!" The "terrifyingly good health" enjoyed by the Russian writers who invited them to lunch fascinated de Beauvoir. These robust writers had celebrated all the previous night, and that day's luncheon featured four bottles of vodka and ten bottles of wine for a total of six people! The quantity of food was in line with the quantity of drink: an enormous side of roast lamb accompanied by other hearty dishes. The Russians emptied all the bottles without apparent effect. Sartre "managed to get up and talk quite sanely about the role of the critic"; de Beauvoir's head was on fire. She had to write two articles, give interviews, and talk on the radio, all of which led to her spending her final day in Moscow in bed, exhausted.[3]

The invitation from the Chinese government sought their testimony vis-à-vis the Western world, which politicized them even more.

A ROOM OF ONE'S OWN

Once back in Paris, de Beauvoir and Claude Lanzmann moved into the apartment she had bought in the rue Schoelcher, a ground-floor artist's studio with large bay windows, divided by a mezzanine leading to the bedroom. She moved the two Venetian glass swords that Sartre had given her, the lamp that had been a gift from Giacometti, the painting by Picasso, and the souvenirs of her many travels, from the rue de la Bûcherie to her new home in the 14th arrondissement. Chinese shadow puppets ornamented the mezzanine. Under the wooden staircase stood a small desk—practically a grammar school model—at which de Beauvoir wrote. A ladder whose steps overflowed with books and papers doubled as a coatrack. For the first time in her life, the walls that surrounded her belonged to her. An impression of permanence led her to think, when going to bed at night, "This is the bed I shall die in."[4]

Things were not going well in the Family. Olga had been forced to give up the theatre after a pneumothorax. Depressed, she quarreled with her husband, Bost, who walked out slamming the door and swearing he would not come back. Olga threatened to kill herself after killing Bost, and de Beauvoir was afraid she might commit suicide. Despite her liaison with Sartre, Michèle Vian had never gotten over a former lover who was killed in a car accident from which she emerged without a scratch. Michèle had thought about marrying Sartre, but Sartre continued to devote himself to Wanda and her acting career. That year he fell in love with Claude Lanzmann's sister, Evelyne Rey, an extremely gifted actress. She was a member of the Centre-Ouest company and made her Paris debut in Chekhov's *Three Sisters*. Sartre offered her the role of Estelle in *No Exit*, which she followed with Arthur Adamov's *Ping-Pong* before embarking on a television career. Like her brothers Claude and Jacques Lanzmann, she was politically committed to the far left. Of all Sartre's romances, this one ran deepest. In the United States, Nathalie Sorokine had divorced Ivan Moffat and married a professor from the University of California at Berkeley; she had two children, had adopted a third, and led a life so disorganized it horrified de Beauvoir. Her health broke down rapidly, and one day her husband found her dead on her bed.

The year 1956 began with a two-week ski vacation in Switzerland with Lanzmann. De Beauvoir had not been on skis for six years, and she attacked the slopes, coaxing Lanzmann along on lengthy downhill expeditions that were rewarded by a wood fire, fondue, and *fendant*—a Swiss white wine—in the chalets that clung to the peaks. That spring she drove with Lanzmann to London, then to Milan to attend the opening of an exhibition of her sister's paintings, and then they roamed the coast of Brittany. Success assured her freedom. *The Mandarins*, recently translated into English, was selling briskly in the United States, where it fostered discussions about political commitment and a crisis of conscience for left-wing intellectuals, just as it had in France. As for de Beauvoir, she devoured kilometers.

In the first days of summer a mini-caravan—de Beauvoir and Lanzmann in one car, Sartre and Michèle Vian in the other—set out for Italy, Yugoslavia, and Greece. A group of Yugoslavian intellectuals welcomed them, and they were treated a little like idols and a little like magi. They were asked all sorts of questions on subjects ranging from surrealist poetry to politics, and they were clearly expected to pronounce liberating words of such wisdom and power that, appearing as headlines in the following day's newspapers, they would help people to live and to think. Sometimes the questions took them completely by surprise. "How can we integrate surrealism into popular culture?" they were asked in Belgrade. The same question surfaced in Macedonia. For de Beauvoir and Sartre, as for many French intellectuals, surrealism was an adventure that had ended; they were surprised that these writers were so isolated, so far behind the times—and they had no idea of the influence the surrealist movement would have on the art and literature of Latin America, or that it would flourish again on the walls of Paris in 1968.

De Beauvoir and Sartre were together again in Rome, which became their summer headquarters. Until Sartre's death they spent two or three months every summer at the Albergo Nazionale. De Beauvoir loved their lengthy conversations and the relaxed, easygoing atmosphere in the Roman capital.

The Italians had succeeded in doing what Sartre had attempted to do in France: unify the left. "Almost all the intellectuals were in sympathy with the Communists and the Communists had remained faithful to their humanist traditions." De Beauvoir enjoyed the Italian leftist newspapers, which were well written and aimed at a large audience. She read them from first page to last and was particularly taken with the minor news items, for she found "the whole of Italy reflected in them."[5] Politically, however, the year left de Beauvoir with few opportunities to maintain her serenity and joie de vivre. De-Stalinization was in full swing in the Eastern-bloc countries, and in Poland the people demanded the reinstatement of Wladislaw Gomulka, who had been imprisoned in 1948 by the Stalinists.

REVOLUTION IN HUNGARY was the headline of the newspaper de Beauvoir read on October 24. That evening she and Sartre had dinner with the Communist painter Guttoso. They were appalled, shattered, uncertain what to make of it. The newspapers spoke of Soviet tanks invading Budapest and described insurgents battling the Russians in the streets. Sartre, bound by the efforts he had made to get along with the Communists, struggled with his feelings of helplessness and confusion by gulping whiskey. For de Beauvoir the choice was clear: It was necessary to disassociate oneself from a regime that used the army to impose its politics and support the rebellion of a people who called out for independence from the USSR.

De Beauvoir was incapable of cloistering herself within the happiness of her private life when the daily papers brought her images of death. Returning to Paris, she found her friends just as distressed as she was. Nasser had nationalized the Suez Canal. During the summer France and England had begun military preparations, and people were expecting a joint French and British landing in Egypt at any moment.

The international atmosphere had become stifling. On November 8 de Beauvoir signed the Manifesto Against Soviet Intervention. The staff of *Les Temps modernes* was hard at work on a special issue on Poland, to be followed by another special issue devoted to Hungary in January. De Beauvoir still took an active part in preparing the magazine, and she read through stacks of deeply distressing reports.

THE COURSE OF WORLD EVENTS

Of all the tragedies taking place around the world, de Beauvoir was torn most by the Algerian situation. In the 1950s the movement in a predominantly Moslem Algeria toward separation and independence from France led to war and created deep political divisions within French society, much as the war in Vietnam would bitterly rend American society in the 1960s. De Beauvoir believed that one had to join the struggle of the Algerian people "to deliver both the Algerians and the French from the tyranny of colonialism."

De Beauvoir was convinced that Algeria would win its independence— but, she asked herself anxiously, at what price? Since the time of the Occupation she had experienced persecution, torture, or humiliation inflicted on others as a personal attack. She made no distinction based on race or sex; the rights of each human individual were and are a requirement rooted in his sensibility, in his mind and spirit. *Les Temps modernes* called for independence for the Algerian people and considered it to be embodied in the National Liberation Front (FLN). The Sartrians found it necessary to make a distinction between their real allies and their adversaries in the left. De Beauvoir defined the problem in "The Thinking of the Right Today." As in all those essays that reflect her intellectual certainties, here she carried on the discussion with rigor and a certain righteousness. "If one wishes to explode empty theories, one must not flatter them but attack them tooth and nail."

The new non-Communist left was split over Pierre Mendès-France, who had become prime minister. Jean-Jacques Servan-Schreiber and the magazine *L'Express* supported him. *Les Temps modernes* did not see Mendès-France as a representative of the left, and that was what Simone de Beauvoir told *L'Humanité*. In her opinion, the left that supported him was in opposition to the authentic left. *Les Temps modernes* denounced Mendès-France's partisans in a series of articles in 1955. As she wrote in "The Thinking of the Right Today" (which would be republished in *Privilèges,* a collection of essays), de Beauvoir saw in Mendès-France's supporters a gradual movement toward the thinking of the right along with all its political, economic, and social consequences. The thinking of the right was outdated, de Beauvoir wrote, and it had no ideal to offer humanity. "Truth is one, error is diverse"; today Marxism is truth and pluralistic and diffuse bourgeois thinking is error, she said.

Raymond Aron attacked her essay in *Le Figaro littéraire.* "The foolish affirmations of intelligent people are always entertaining and sometimes instructive. Taken overall, Mme. de Beauvoir's study of the right's thinking is one of the most surprising that one has read in a long time. In breaking it down in detail one comes across a number of apt or shrewd remarks."[6] Time served only to deepen the gulf between the two philosophers.

When Ahmed Ben Bella, one of the FLN leaders, was captured—the French authorities hijacked and rerouted his plane—de Beauvoir understood that the government "was going to persist with this war." Detailed reports made their way to *Les Temps modernes,* and friends brought testimony of massacres, rape, torture, and other atrocities on both sides—information that was not to be found in the press. She saw that matters were sinking deeper and deeper into violence.[7]

"The course of world events is the very texture of my own life"—de Beauvoir had lived this thought before recording it in her memoirs.

And the world was not evolving peaceably. Nelson Algren wrote from America to say that his passport had been revoked simply because he had belonged to a committee to save the Rosenbergs (who were executed in June 1953). Algren was a Communist sympathizer, and the witch-hunts were in full course. De Beauvoir was revolted by the intolerance and excesses of McCarthyism. She had loved America, its liberty, its efficiency, its respect for the individual; she could not remain indifferent to a nation that had included "the pursuit of happiness" among the inalienable rights set down in its Constitution. She had seen the general good in many individual quests. In 1956, so far as she could tell, the nation that had delivered Europe from the Nazis was nothing more than a society of consumers avidly consuming. She accused it of measuring worth solely in terms of success, leaving open "no road to freedom except that of anarchic revolt; this explains the corruption of its youth, their refuge in drug-taking and their imbecile outbreaks of violence."[8] She no longer got along with the writer Richard Wright, who had become openly anti-Communist.

Disenchanted with America, where she saw only racism, capitalism, and conformity, and with Europe, which was entering a period of oppression, violence, and agression, no matter which way she turned, de Beauvoir had the impression of breathing poisoned air. The Algerian situation made her ill to the depth of her being. Suddenly she saw herself rejected by a large sector of public opinion, accused of being against her own country. She accepted the challenge with defiance: "I had been labeled anti-French. . . . I became so."[9]

Much as the publication of *The Second Sex* had led people to insult her in the street, de Beauvoir's stand in favor of Algerian independence made her a target for outrageous remarks in public places, and merely leaving the house became an unbearable ordeal. She chose to remain at home, where she felt cut off completely from her fellow citizens. The horror of the ongoing tortures obsessed her, and she deemed herself an accomplice to the executioners because she was powerless to halt their atrocities. Even at her own sister's house she felt excluded when her brother-in-law asserted that instances of torture were exceptional and a stop had been put to terrorism. Her reaction was so severe that she became ill; she was under mounting tension and stress, and she suffered violent headaches. Her disgust pursued her into her dreams. De Beauvoir wanted the war to end because she had "a Christian, democratic, humanist conscience."[10] De Beauvoir and Sartre believed that there were legal ways to help Algeria obtain its independence. Both were available and willing to write, to publish, to sign appeals and manifestos, but clandestine action did not suit them. They were not ready to follow Francis Jeanson, their friend and colleague on *Les Temps modernes*. Jeanson, who had written perceptively about Sartre and his writings, had worked in Algeria, was friendly with many Moslems, and was active with the FLN, for which activities he would later be tried.

Writing had always helped her in taking the more decisive steps in her life, and she immersed herself in it again. The writer took leave of the world that was causing her pain and stepped through the looking glass of time via the pathways of memory. For eighteen months de Beauvoir worked on *Memoirs of a Dutiful Daughter*. She resuscitated the curly-locked little girl who observed the world from her balcony overlooking the carrefour Vavin, the model pupil, the dutiful child with her secret daring, the ambitious, unrelentingly hard worker, the writer making her first attempts at a novel, the lovestruck twenty-year-old meeting the person who fulfills her every wish. Like Montaigne isolated from the civil wars in his library, she escaped by making herself the raw material of her book.

January returned, bringing the temptation of the snow, and de Beauvoir went skiing with Lanzmann at Davos, the ski resort in Switzerland. Then came summer and the temptation of the sea and sun-drenched villages, and she and Lanzmann left for Sicily. She did her best to practice Camus' maxim,

"Hang on to your own happiness, no matter what." When in Paris with Sartre, with Lanzmann, she spent evenings in the large white studio with its violet, green, and yellow cushions that Sonia Delaunay would not have disowned, surrounded by two stories of precariously shelved books. They chatted beneath the Chinese masks, and more often they listened to records. This was their haven following the passage of the turbulent hours of their overburdened days. The walls were covered with countless photographs that recorded the stages of their lives and the procession of their friends. On a tabletop a casting of Sartre's hands reached toward the light of the picture windows, serving as a perch to tiny birds fashioned from colored feathers, welcoming gifts of flowers and rings, seeming to juggle these lightweight objects, these imponderable colors, like the assured hands of a wandering minstrel. Yet even their evenings of relaxation were somber and gloomy; de Beauvoir saw that Sartre tolerated badly an amphetamine that he crunched incessantly to keep himself going at the frantic pace he maintained. Alcohol had a strong effect on him from the first glass: He slurred his words and lost control of his gestures, yet he insisted on having a second and then a third, in the name of relaxation. De Beauvoir refused to stand by and watch him destroy himself. She told him he had had enough and sometimes flew into a violent temper and smashed a glass or two on the tiled kitchen floor. She cried rivers of tears, all in vain; Sartre was working furiously on his *Critique of Dialectical Reason,* and nothing could make him slow down.

In January 1958 the tragedy of the Algerian war touched de Beauvoir personally. Jacqueline Guerroudj, one of her former students in Rouen, had gone to Algeria to teach and had married a Moslem. Guerroudj had become involved in the struggle for independence, and in the previous month she had been sentenced to death along with two others for her part in a bombing. De Beauvoir applied all her energy to the campaign the left was leading to save the three. Jacqueline Guerroudj and Yveton were pardoned; the third prisoner, Taleb, was executed.

There was no escaping the horrors of history, for it was built upon human suffering. De Beauvoir, a writer above all, completed her manuscript, submitted *Memoirs of a Dutiful Daughter* to Gallimard, and in the spring took off for London with Lanzmann.

Returning, she felt isolated and detached once again, no longer in solidarity with a France she judged to be "politically apathetic and inert."[11] In May Lanzmann left for North Korea with a delegation of journalists representing the far left. Without her young companion at her side to talk of the course of events—it was virtually impossible for them to correspond—de Beauvoir resumed her diary, her conversation with herself, her oldest recourse against anxiety.

Memoirs of a Dutiful Daughter became an international best-seller upon its appearance. Here was a new genre of autobiography, one in which the author followed her own existence as it unfolded. Her view of the world, her family, and herself expands with the passing years; her conscience and self-aware-ness develop before the reader's eyes, much as the thought processes of a character in a novel appear in consecutive layers without explanation. The actions, thoughts, and reactions we read of are *le vécu* of the child turned adolescent and student. The author never anticipates the action to come and never backtracks; life appears to be seized from within from day to day. This autobiography seems to have been written with the same sincerity with which Jean-Jacques Rousseau penned his *Confessions.*

THE DEMONSTRATIONS

On May 13, 1958, when the formation of the Pierre Pflimlin government was announced, there had been an uprising in Algiers and the formation of a committee of public safety. On May 28 Pflimlin stepped down, and on May 29 President René Coty called upon "the most illustrious of Frenchmen," General Charles de Gaulle.

For de Beauvoir the time for taking action had come. She decided to go into the streets on May 30 to take part in an anti-Gaullist demonstration.

De Beauvoir and Sartre took a taxi to the Reuilly-Diderot métro station, from which Hélène de Beauvoir and her friend Gégé, accompanied by her family and all the employees of her fabric design studio, soon emerged. Then came Pontalis, Chapsal, Adamov, Pozner, Tzaral, and the contributors to *Les Temps modernes.* De Beauvoir and Sartre marched behind the Rights of Man banner, Sartre singing loudly the Marseillaise and "Le Chant du départ." The crowd marched from the place de la Nation to the place de la République chanting slogans. Anxious to know more, de Beauvoir led Olga and Bost in the direction of the Elysée Palace. A traffic jam of elegant cars prevented them from making much headway, and de Beauvoir reflected that "our bourgeois democrats would much rather put themselves in the hands of a dictator than revive the Popular Front."[12]

Riddled with anxiety, de Beauvoir did not want to be alone. She had lunch with Lévi-Strauss and Jean Pouillon, one of the earliest contributors to

Les Temps modernes, who was a secretary to the National Assembly. She spent the afternoon with Sartre and the evening with Olga Bost.

She tried to tame her rage and put a stop to her gloomy predictions by listening to others talk. Lanzmann had been living with her for six years, and his absence seemed to create a ready-made void to accommodate her anxiety. She dragged her friends from café to café across town; from Montparnasse to Saint-Germain to the Champs-Elysées, she took the pulse of Paris in the hours that she believed were the Republic's last.

The following day she decided to demonstrate with the antifascist committee of her own 14th arrondissement, and she went to Sartre's house to see what he was planning to do. Lanzmann's sister, Evelyne Rey, showed up, having just left Serge Reggiani, with whom she had been trying to free a friend who had been arrested for distributing tracts.* Olga and Bost arrived, and the group headed for the carrefour Sèvres-Babylone, where the Communists had instructed everyone to create a traffic jam. They were then to proceed to the place de la République to adorn the large statue there with flowers. De Beauvoir went into a florist shop and emerged with a tricolor spray of red gladioli and blue and white irises.

The carrefour Sèvres-Babylone had become the meeting place of the Paris intellectual left, where everyone greeted one another and fraternized. The Desantis—Jean Toussaint a philosopher and Dominique a novelist— joined Sartre and de Beauvoir; they had known one another since the distant days of Sartre's Resistance group, Socialism and Liberty.

De Beauvoir's colorful bouquet drew attention. A procession of Communists appeared, and de Beauvoir and company blended in with them. Once more Sartre sang the Marseillaise.

On June 1 the National Assembly granted de Gaulle's investiture as *président du conseil.* † The Fifth Republic was about to begin.

De Beauvoir's frustration was so great that she had an attack of high blood pressure. That evening she and Sartre analyzed the intellectual's role in politics, a question they had been debating since they first started exchanging views. André Malraux had just been named minister of information and culture. Sartre, disenchanted by the RDR's failure, supported the notion that the intellectual, "even if he supports the government, should remain a latent

---

*Reggiani appeared in several of Sartre's plays; in *The Condemned of Altona* in 1959 he was Frantz, Evelyne Rey was Johanna, and Wanda was Leni.

†*Président du conseil* designates the office now referred to as prime minister. René Coty, the president of France, named de Gaulle as his *président du conseil*. De Gaulle then dissolved the National Assembly and called for a referendum to rework the Constitution. Under the Fourth Republic, the president was elected by the deputies and senators; De Gaulle's reform, which became the Fifth Republic, called for direct election of the president by popular vote.

278   SIMONE DE BEAUVOIR

source of opposition and criticism; in other words, he should judge policies, not execute them." De Beauvoir, who did not think otherwise, saw only one case in which the intellectual should agree to be part of the government, "in underdeveloped countries that are short of trained people."[13] André Malraux troubled and upset them. He believed that literature and art were the triumphant answer to the absurdity of destiny. Yet from 1936 Malraux had committed himself to action. He had fought during the Spanish civil war, writing his great novel *Man's Hope* at the same time. In 1940 he had attempted to make contact with de Gaulle, but the letter Malraux sent never reached its destination because the messenger, captured in a roundup, had swallowed it.* Malraux believed he had been rejected by the Free French forces. In the spring of 1944 Malraux, working under the name Colonel Berger, played a principal role in Zone R5. On July 14, in liaison with London, he organized the largest operation since the airdrops into Norway in 1940: For six hours American and British aircraft, flying in relays, dropped arms and ammunition into a drop zone twelve miles square designated by a gigantic Z made by tacking down the bedsheets of all the families in the region. One thousand five hundred Resistance fighters, men and women, encircled the Z, standing by to carry off and hide the supplies as they floated to earth. And now André Malraux was part of the government.

De Beauvoir blamed herself for not trying to do more, but she justified her behavior by reasoning that Sartre was working for them both. Yet this rationalization did nothing to assuage her conscience. The severity of her reactions surprised her; "I really don't understand why I'm as upset as I am."[14] The anxiety that she could neither pin down nor abolish disappeared temporarily when she received from her readers testimony of the importance of her writings and their liberating effect. A young American woman, a student whom she saw from time to time, told de Beauvoir that in the United States people wrote dissertations based on her work and that the flow of studies, articles, research, courses, and seminars was proof of the influence she and her writing had had on young intellectuals. Far from appeasing de Beauvoir, this American acquaintance's open admiration served only to add remorse to her feelings of helplessness and confusion. "I ought to be writing new books, better ones, I ought to be proving my worth afresh, proving that I really deserve to exist like that for other people."[15]

Claude Lanzmann's brother, Jacques, just returned from a trip to Mexico, Cuba, and Haiti, told de Beauvoir of the tortures inflicted on the revolutionaries there. De Beauvoir was too distraught, too distressed to start writing

---

*This fact is contested by Clara Malraux.

again, and Sartre managed to convince her to leave for Italy. She got behind the wheel of her car and tried to escape this gloom that was so unlike her.

The Alpine scenery she passed made her more than a little nostalgic. Never again would she embark on the long and strenuous walking tours, forging ahead for ten and twelve hours at a stretch for the sheer challenge and joy of pushing herself to the limits of exhaustion, covering majestic ground at six or nine thousand feet and sometimes higher, sleeping in tents and barns—that time was past.

When Sartre joined her in Milan, the sight of him working diligently had a rejuvenating effect on her. She decided that the best approach would be to force herself to write ten pages, even in rough draft, each day. The only way to recover from her indefinable unease would be to knuckle down to work on a new book. Her anxiety returned by night, however, and she would awaken thinking, "We're going to be seventy years old, and then we'll die, it's a fact, it's certain, it's not just a nightmare!" She was fifty at the time. She repeated to herself Georges Bataille's words, "I have my schedule for suffering." With difficulty she worked on the rough draft of what would become *The Prime of Life* and worried about her mood. "If only I could write when I'm drunk!" she told herself.[16]

Back from vacation and alone in her apartment—Sartre had remained in Pisa with Michèle Vian, and Lanzmann was in the provinces—de Beauvoir was lonely. She decided to join an anti-Gaullist campaign against the referendum of September 28, in which de Gaulle was putting to a popular vote the project for a new Constitution. On September 4 she took part in an extremely violent demonstration during de Gaulle's speech at the place de le République. The previous night she had taken part in a meeting of the anti-Gaullist committee of the 14th arrondissement, of which she was copresident. "It was pitiful and touching." On September 13 she went to Bièvre to lecture before a group of Protestant teachers, "hoping to drag a few no's out of them."[17] She put together posters, wrote articles for the neighborhood paper, and accepted an invitation to talk to some students at the Cité Universitaire. On September 26 she spoke at a meeting of the liaison committee for the 14th arrondissement, before a crowd of 2400 people. She was throwing all her weight against the Gaullist referendum.

Sartre had returned from Italy feverish and exhausted by the furious pace at which he forced himself to work. Having to write an article for *L'Express,* he proceeded to work on it for twenty-eight hours straight, had a little sleep, then returned to it for another twelve hours of concentrated effort, after which he went to deliver a speech. De Beauvoir revised and cut "The Frogs Who Want a King" and got it to *L'Express* on time. A paragraph of

Sartre's article addresses those women who are fascinated by the myth of the great man: "How many solitary and betrayed women have extended their resentment to the entire species: Everything human horrifies them, they love dogs and supermen."

The article was a call to participation in the life of the city: "If millions of men today are indifferent to the referendum, if they don't care about the respective powers of the president and the legislative bodies, it's our fault, it's that we've never known how to make them understand that they are taking action that affects other men through the simple ballot they deposit in the urn, and that the citizen's political activity is the fullest affirmation of his freedom."[18]

De Beauvoir expected a slight majority of yes votes. She broke down in tears upon learning that 80 percent of her countrymen had voted for changing the Constitution.

Buying the newspapers that morning, she recalled the beginning of the war: "I felt almost the same distress." She was "against a whole country"— her own.[19] The majority of her fellow citizens did not want what she and Sartre wanted for France at all. In the article in *L'Express*—whose ideas she upheld—one read that "a nation's greatness is not measured by the quantity of blood it spills but by the number of human problems it solves."[20]

De Beauvoir wanted to see an end to the hostilities in Algeria, to work toward greater cooperation between the Eastern and Western blocs and thus toward peace, to reconcile all the left-leaning factions under one well-defined program, which would give France an economy comparable to those of other European nations, would raise productivity in such a way that the major beneficiaries would be the workers themselves, would help develop the scientific, literary, artistic, and political interests of the most disadvantaged branches of society, and would create a program of agricultural education. According to Sartre and de Beauvoir, these reforms would transform France within ten years. De Beauvoir saw in the outcome of the referendum a repudiation "of all that we had believed in and wanted for France, an enormous collective suicide."[21]

On top of all her other anxieties, Sartre became seriously ill. He had violent headaches, and she feared the possible consequences of a stroke. He pumped himself full of amphetamines. His handwriting and spelling became appalling. He suffered abrupt changes of mood and sudden fits of rage. When de Beauvoir suggested that he take a rest, he answered her "with a violence that was uncharacteristic of him." He was finishing his play *The Condemned of Altona*; de Beauvoir had told him that the text upheld none of the promise of the subject, and he had started over. She had the play's premiere put off until the autumn, and the doctor succeeded in convincing Sartre to work more slowly. "The most painful part for me during this crisis," she wrote, "was the solitude his illness condemned me to." She listened with consternation as Sartre and Michel Leiris discussed their sleeping pills and sedatives and stimulants as they dined together at La Palette on the boulevard Montparnasse, the waves of passersby rolling along just as they had in the days when de Beauvoir first discovered bars and cocktails. She asked Leiris about the effects of the antidepressants he had been taking since his suicide attempt. Leiris explained that "you know everything's just as awful as it was before, only you're not depressed." She saw Leiris and Sartre as two survivors, and hearing them talk about their various medications in a spirit of solidarity made her think, "Well, that's it, we're on the other side now, we're old."[22]

A melancholy conversation with René Maheu served to convince her of her decline. There was nothing to look forward to but their own deaths or the deaths of those close to them, de Beauvoir insisted despite protests from Maheu, who thought they were not quite that far gone yet.

"BRIGITTE BARDOT AND THE LOLITA SYNDROME"

*T*wo years earlier Sartre had met a seventeen-year-old high school student who would come to hold a privileged place in his life. In 1965 he would legally adopt her and designate her as his executor. Arlette El-Kaïm was originally from Constantine, Algeria; cut off from her country and far from her family, she had become attached to Sartre. This serious relationship with a young girl brought gloom to de Beauvoir. "At first we got along very well," de Beauvoir said. "She told me about her childhood." Later the Sartre–de Beauvoir relationship became strained as Sartre explored new intellectual directions with Arlette. To make matters worse, Claude Lanzmann at thirty-three had his eyes on the future. When he took the initiative in their separation, de Beauvoir was unprepared and experienced the end of their affair as a clear sign of her entry into old age. This trial, coming on top of Sartre's illness, his new liaison, and the failure of her political hopes and ideas, was particularly painful.

The year 1959 commenced in solitude. No sooner had she gotten over a bout of moroseness than a fit of melancholy overtook her. When she chatted with Françoise Sagan, Jacques Chazot, or younger friends, she felt out of step. She saw herself as an exile from current events, from youth, and henceforth from love—love that she had experienced without restraint.

Esquire magazine asked her for an article. Having just read Vladimir Nabokov's *Lolita,* she wrote "Brigitte Bardot and the Lolita Syndrome." Bardot had recently attained international fame as a film star, and the Nabokov novel was creating a sensation in the press. De Beauvoir detected the birth of a new eroticism in this joint success. The accusations of immorality leveled against Bardot's films were reminiscent of the attacks on existentialism. In the city of Angers, three young people from good families had murdered an elderly man who had fallen asleep on a train, and the local PTA denounced Brigitte Bardot to the town's deputy mayor: "It is she," they claimed, "who is really responsible for this crime. Her films are perverting our youth." De Beauvoir wrote that "it is no new thing for high-minded folk to identify the flesh with sin and to dream of making a bonfire of works of art, books, and films that depict it complacently or frankly." De Beauvoir had shocked people with the descriptions of sexual relations in her novels; Brigitte Bardot, she said, is not perverse, not rebellious, not immoral, and that is why morality has no hold on her. Good and evil are conventions it does not even occur to her to think about. She eats when she is hungry and makes love with the same simplicity. Moral flaws can be corrected, but how is one to cure this new woman of the amazing virtue of genuineness? For this is most certainly a new woman, in de Beauvoir's view, and a new eroticism as well. The consummate vamp is no longer a Marlene Dietrich, her thighs clad in silk, carefully made up, and cloaked in mystery; she is an ambiguous nymph who goes barefoot, wears pants, is slim, muscular, and nearly androgynous. "In the game of love, she is as much a hunter as she is a prey. The male is an object to her, just as she is to him. . . . A free woman is the very contrary of a light woman."*

Love can do without mystery but not without eroticism, for in an era when woman speculates on the stock exchange, drives her own car, and exposes herself unceremoniously at the beach, it is not possible to revive the vamp and her air of mystery. "The adult woman now inhabits the same world as the man, but the child-woman moves in a universe which he cannot enter. The age difference reestablishes between them the distance that seems necessary to desire. At least that is what those who have created a new Eve by merging the 'green fruit' and 'femme fatale' types have pinned their hopes on. . . . She is without memory, without a past, and, thanks to this ignorance, she retains the perfect innocence that is attributed to a mythical childhood."[23]

---

*A light woman: "a woman of easy virtue." De Beauvoir wrote the article in English.

It was this same indefinable charm that had attracted Sartre to Olga, Wanda, Martine, Lucile, Louise—and, at the age of fifty, to the seventeen-year-old Arlette.

"WHAT HAS BECOME OF MY FRIENDS?" [24]

*O*ne night Lanzmann took her to a rehearsal by Josephine Baker, whom she had admired twenty years earlier. This was no longer the black dancer of old, pulsating with passion, ardent and fiery, and de Beauvoir thought it indecent to watch the woman making a heroic attempt to outlast herself. She became brutally aware of the years that had sped by; Baker was wearing a mask, that of old age.

Old age, which she had so detested even before its handiwork began to stare back at her from the mirror, surprised her every time she saw the traces it left on the faces of her contemporaries. Suddenly, as if to remind her that old age is not always the threshold to death, Boris Vian died at thirty-nine. She had held a great deal of affection for him, and with his passing disappeared the era of Saint-Germain-des-Prés and the frenzied delirium of existentialism.

The year 1960 also began badly as a new death shook and distressed her. She was alone in Sartre's apartment in the rue Bonaparte when Lanzmann called to tell her that Camus had just died in an automobile accident. It was January 4; Camus was returning from the south of France with Michel and Janine Gallimard and Anne, Janine's daughter. They had set out after breakfast; Michel was at the wheel, with Camus seated beside him and the two women in the back seat. Janine had the impression of a bend in the road when in reality it continued on straight. She found herself in a field. Anna lay on the ground about twenty yards from the car, and Michel Gallimard lay in the field, bleeding profusely. Camus had been flung against the rear windshield, his skull fractured and his neck broken; death had been instantaneous. The car had swerved on the wet and slippery road, struck a plane tree, then another about fourteen yards down the road. The asphalt was torn up for fifty yards, and debris was spread over a radius of one hundred fifty yards. The Gallimards were taken to the hospital. Camus' body was laid in the auditorium of the Villeblevin town hall. Someone placed a spray of flowers beside the body and stopped the clock. His briefcase was found in the field; it contained his passport, the manuscript of *The First Man,* his journal, a French translation of Nietzsche's *Die fröliche Wissenschaft,* and a French translation of *Othello.* Michel Gallimard died ten days later.[25]

Simone's throat was tight and her lips trembled as she hung up the telephone. She choked back her tears, telling herself that Camus no longer meant anything to her. When Sartre and Bost arrived, they spoke of nothing but Camus. Late that night, unable to sleep, de Beauvoir went out to calm her nerves. She walked until dawn. She had forgotten everything that separated them, all their quarrels had vanished, he was dead as she had loved him. She had lost the friend and companion of 1945, the young writer of the hopeful years who adored life, friendship, and glory.

She recalled the couscous luncheon in honor of the Prix de la Pléiade for *The Misunderstanding* and the evening they had been so close: They had had dinner at the Brasserie Lipp and continued their conversation at the Pont-Royal. They had so much left to say when closing time came that they bought a bottle of champagne and took it to the Louisiane, where they went on talking until 3 A.M. Camus had read aloud from his journal and spoken about the gap between his life and his work. Camus, dead, suddenly became a heartbreaking presence. Watching the sunrise, de Beauvoir said to herself, "He can't see this morning," and, led by his powerful presence, she passed over to the side of the dead: "All day I teetered on the edge of that impossible experience: touching the other side of my own non-being."[26]

Camus' face staring out from the front pages of the newspapers blinded her with tears. By ceasing to exist, Camus had taken up permanent residence in the no-man's-land of great men, forever to endure. In an official *hommage,* Malraux said of him: "For more than twenty years the work of Albert Camus was inseparable from the obsession with justice. We salute one of those through whom France remains present in the hearts of men."[27]

On January 7 *France-Observateur* carried Sartre's eulogy for Camus. "He was, in this century and against history, the current heir to that long line of moralists whose works perhaps constitute that which is most original in French letters. His stubborn humanism, narrow and pure, austere and sensual, battled uncertainly against the massive and misshapen events of this, our time. But, inversely, through his obstinate refusal, he reaffirmed, in the heart of our era, against the Machiavellians, against the golden calf of realism, the existence of morality."[28]

Finally something came along to tear de Beauvoir away from a France where death claimed her friends and the political situation revolted her. Franqui, the director of the Cuban newspaper *Revolución,* invited her to Havana to observe a young revolution at work. This breath of hope that blew in from Cuba renewed her desire to throw herself into the future.

CUBA

*H*avana gave Sartre and de Beauvoir an enthusiastic welcome, complete with crowds, bouquets, cheers, and a horde of journalists. Their first luncheon took place amid a hubbub of flashbulbs. De Beauvoir was asked a battery of questions concerning "abstract painting, Algeria, the commitment of French writers, of American writers, and existentialism."[29] It was February, Carnival month; in a delirium of song, dance, and masquerade, a jubilant crowd blended ancient rites with a celebration of its recent victory. De Beauvoir delighted in celebrating the honeymoon of the Cuban revolution, for this was a revolution to her liking. She and Sartre were photographed with Fidel Castro and Che Guevara and appeared on television. Everyone recognized them; even taxi drivers called out their names as they drove by.

The interviews, with their rapid assaults of questions, kept coming. De Beauvoir responded: She had been influenced by Dostoevsky and certain American novelists, Faulkner, Hemingway, and Dos Passos in particular. Her work as a writer did not prevent her being interested in economic and political problems. She received letters from all over the world and always replied to them. People occasionally sent her manuscripts; she recommended them to publishers when she thought they had merit. No, she did not attend literary cocktail parties; they were a waste of time and she preferred to see a small circle of friends, Sartre, Giacometti, contributors to *Les Temps modernes.* Yes, she loved the theatre but did not possess the lyricism necessary to write plays. As for the cinema, André Cayatte, the director of *Justice Is Done* and *We Are All Murderers,* had asked her to write a screenplay about a couple whose love is broken. She had counted on finishing it while in Havana, but she was so passionately absorbed by her discovery of the Cuban revolution that she had not even touched the script since her arrival.

What did she think of the *nouveau roman*? That it had reached a dead end. The practitioners of the *nouveau roman* were too devoted to disengagement and entertained an excessive taste for form that was a clever way of evading real problems. Nathalie Sarraute, Alain Robbe-Grillet, and Michel Butor were the most interesting but, lost in their formal research, the *nouveau roman* writers "neglect to show us the existential dimension of man."

They interrogated de Beauvoir like an oracle, they took her everywhere, they wanted her to tell the world about the revolution. She and Sartre were accompanied by young ministers. There was not yet a bureaucracy in the new Cuban regime; the people were in direct contact with their leaders, and the militiamen radiated youth and gaiety.

De Beauvoir reflected upon violence. For the first time in her life she was "a witness to happiness that had been achieved by violence." She had come from a France where she had discovered violence in "its negative aspect: the rejection of the oppressor."[30] Here violence took on a new meaning. She and Sartre spent three days in a spirit of familiarity and friendship with Castro, who like all cultivated Cubans spoke French. He personally led them across Cuba on an extraordinary tour from the impressive modern quarters of Havana to the fields of sugarcane. People broke into cheers spontaneously whenever Castro passed. De Beauvoir had the impression that a society was being born before her very eyes, a society authentic, free, responsible, and— in a word—existentialist. She heard Castro speak for two hours before a crowd of five hundred thousand people.

All this fanfare swept her off her feet. Any negative aspects of the revolution escaped her attention. Dazzled by the happenings, she enjoyed herself to the point of acclaiming everything with a naïve enthusiasm. Years later she would denounce the Cuban revolution for failing to live up to its promises. She compared the Cuban rebels celebrating their victory and the Algerian rebels still engaged in their struggle. She had just learned that their friend Francis Jeanson had narrowly escaped arrest when the police rounded up several members of his underground network.

On their return trip to France, de Beauvoir and Sartre had an eight-hour layover in New York. Simone would have loved to spend the entire afternoon sightseeing with Sartre; it was the first time they had been in the United States together. But a young Cuban attaché had organized a cocktail party for the press at the Waldorf Astoria, so they toured Manhattan only until 6 P.M. and then went dutifully to the party. De Beauvoir was pleased with all the attention she received, and she felt "still far from the resigned wisdom of old age."[31] She had recaptured her taste for happiness because she was in a position to influence public opinion toward a cause she held dear. The feeling of hopelessness that had paralyzed her in France was gone.

The reception at the Waldorf did not disappoint her. The French and American pro-Castro journalists in attendance admired Sartre and de Beauvoir, who returned the compliment.

"GIVE ME BACK THE AGE OF LOVE"[32]

*R*eturning to her Paris apartment, de Beauvoir did not even have time to turn the key in the lock when Nelson Algren flung open the door and said, "It's you!" Reunited, they "felt as close as during the best days of 1949" despite "the stormy summers" of 1950 and 1951, despite the nine years apart, despite all the misunderstandings.

She had left him in 1951, taking with her all his hopes for a shared life, after telling him one last time that she could live and write only in Paris.

Algren had remarried his first wife, Amanda, in 1953 and redivorced her not long after. He continued to lead his life with the greatest possible extravagance. He turned down fabulous Hollywood contracts, lost fortunes at poker. He nearly froze to death one day, having fallen into a trench filled with icy water that came up to his chin. On another occasion he barely escaped from a burning brothel. His literary agent shot herself, and he signed disastrous agreements with his publisher. As soon as *The Mandarins* came out in America, journalists hounded him, asking whether he was Lewis. He was. It was all there, barely modified, the tale of his romance with the same Simone de Beauvoir whose relationship with Sartre was known the world over.[33] Then he sent word to de Beauvoir that he would be telephoning. She awaited his call with some anxiety, but the phone did not ring. She sent him a note, he wrote back, and gradually they renewed the correspondence they had broken off. The witch-hunts were finished in America and Algren had a new passport. He wrote to ask if it would be all right for him to come and spend a few months in Paris. De Beauvoir replied that she would very much like to see him again before she died. He soon announced that he was arriving on March 10. She would be in Cuba until March 20, but Olga and Bost could pick him up at Orly and let him into her apartment.

Ten years fell away. Wabansia Avenue flowed straight into the rue Schoelcher, bringing with it waves of memories, books, the daily *New York Herald,* sheafs of the yellow paper Algren favored, his electric typewriter, the latest jazz and blues records, every conceivable sort of American gadget. Long nights devoted to bar and club hopping were revived. They went to the music halls and the fashionable night spots. Friends of Algren often rang the bell, and de Beauvoir met Americans who lived in her own building, unknown to her until Algren came along. They made a pilgrimage to her old apartment in the rue de la Bûcherie, visited the flea market, and returned to all the restaurants and bistros they had enjoyed together. They sipped onion soup at Les Halles in the hours before dawn. There were dinners aboard a *bateau mouche,* at the Lapin Agile, at the Abbaye. Nighttime Paris had gone crazy again, and all their friends joined in: Gréco, Mouloudji, Cazalis, Giacometti, Jean Genet, Violette Leduc, Olga, Bost, Wanda, Michèle Vian, Sartre. They left together for Spain at the beginning of May, and their relationship was clear sailing.

Algren seemed to have staked everything on one last attempt to forge stronger, more permanent links between them. He could not understand Sartre and de Beauvoir's arrangement. They lived separately, he in the rue Bonaparte, she in the rue Schoelcher. They saw each other nearly every day, and there was always a manuscript to read or discuss, important decisions to make together, appointments with writers and journalists. For Algren they were a sort of business enterprise, a single entity, Sartre de Beauvoir & Co. He would attempt to explain this situation to a journalist in the wake of the sensational publication of the second volume of de Beauvoir's memoirs, *The Prime of Life,* and after having himself written *Who Lost an American?* This intellectual rapport, this business relationship no longer overwhelmed him. In an interview he affirmed that Sartre and de Beauvoir had not had a sexual relationship "since the 1930s" and had always carried on separate love lives. Algren described de Beauvoir in *Who Lost an American?*

> Simone de Beauvoir's eyes were lit by a light-blue intelligence: she was possessed by something like total apprehension. Her judgments seemed a fraction sooner than immediate and her decisiveness shook the arrondissement.
>
> "Now, tell *me* about Existentialism," a male interviewer once settled himself down to amuse himself, and get a story too, at a café table where she sat; with pencil and notebook ready and self-contentment coming out of his ears.
>
> "You do not care about Existentialism, you do not care about anything"—and, taking her own notebook and pencil from her handbag, she bent to her own work. The interview was over.
>
> She did not even bother to glance up when he left.
>
> Yet to the fool trying not to be a fool, to the perplexed or the half-maddened, to the man or woman in trouble, to all those making an effort to understand themselves, she put down her own work with the same immediacy and struggled with others' problems as though they were her own.[34]

Her absolute fidelity to the relationship with Sartre could be explained. But that this understanding, however perfect it might be on the intellectual plane, could exclude love and a life shared with Algren—whom she had called her "only husband" so many times in her letters—was beyond his comprehension. He loved de Beauvoir, his love for her was simple and straightforward, he would love her until his final day. He knew that Sartre had always had affairs with other women, and the concept of contingent loves left him incredulous. "Being able to love only contingently means being able to live only contingently."[35] For Algren, Simone was another Alice in Wonderland; she had stepped through the mirror and was living in a topsy-turvy world. In his review of *Force of Circumstance* for *Harper's* magazine in May 1965, Algren mused on the domino theory and the possibility of a nuclear war's bringing an eventual end to civilized life on the planet: "Then a low dread pall of greenish-gray will enwrap and enwind earth, forest, skyscraper, and sky in an endless orbit through endless space through endless time, in a silence without end. Except for one small hoarse human voice burbling up from the ancestral ocean's depths—'In this matter man's sexuality may be modified. Sartre needs peace and quiet. The dead are better adapted to the earth than the living. Bost is on the Cinema Vigilance Committee. I want to go skiing. Merleau-Ponty' "—and Algren caps his assessment with, *"Will she ever quit talking?"*[36]

Despite his sense of humor, he did not succeed in understanding her. He had decided to devote six months of his life to this recaptured romance in the hope that their relationship would endure. But de Beauvoir had even less time to give him now than she had in 1947, when she was still on the brink of fame. She had been invited to the reception given by Khrushchev at the Soviet embassy during his official visit to France, she had just given Gallimard the completed manuscript for *The Prime of Life,* she had finished an article about the Cuban revolution for *France-Observateur,* she was actively involved in the production of *Les Temps modernes,* she had written a preface to *The Fear of Loving* by Dr. Weill-Hallé, whose *Family Planning* she had prefaced the year before.

Dr. Weill-Hallé, a gynecologist, had resolved to shake the medical establishment out of its inertia in the face of the abortion issue. In 1955 she had presented a report on "voluntary maternity" to the Academy of Ethical and Political Sciences. The vast majority of her male colleagues had attacked her, and their violence reminded her of the scandal *The Second Sex* had provoked. Armed with her convictions, Dr. Weill-Hallé had founded the French Family Planning Movement in 1958 and called on de Beauvoir for support. The author of *The Second Sex* shared Weill-Hallé's ideas. She considered it only proper that women have the right to choose maternity freely, and she approved of the French Family Planning Movement's efforts to spread the use of contraceptives. She saw the law prohibiting abortion as a surefire means of oppressing women and was surprised by the reaction of the Communists, who denounced the campaign for contraception as a conspiracy to weaken the proletariat by depriving it of children. De Beauvoir also lent her support to a campaign in favor of contraception launched by Colette Audry.

Algren began to apprehend the growing importance of de Beauvoir's role. It was impossible for a left-wing writer like himself not to take an interest in what she was doing. The Algerian war became a reality for him on the morning de Beauvoir received a telephone call from Gisèle Halimi. The young lawyer had just returned from Algiers, where she had taken on the defense of a young Algerian woman, Djamila Boupacha, who was accused of participating in a bombing. Djamila had been tortured and sexually abused in prison, and Gisèle Halimi wanted to file an official complaint, start a new trial, and sue the torturers. She asked de Beauvoir to write an article about the case, which de Beauvoir did immediately and submitted it to Le Monde. The next morning, because of this article, Le Monde was impounded in Algiers. And the American press picked up the story. In 1960 the American women's movement adopted The Second Sex as the theoretical basis for its activities, and everything Simone de Beauvoir said and did was immediately the object of analysis. Thus the Djamila Boupacha affair was soon a matter of international concern. Gisèle Halimi wanted the case removed from the jurisdiction of the Algiers courts and transferred to France, a maneuver that only the minister of justice could request. Halimi asked de Beauvoir to accompany her and two former deportees, Germaine Tillon and Anise Postel-Vinay, to see Michelet, the minister of justice, who referred them to Patin, the president of la Commission de sauve garde. Djamila Boupacha was transferred to the prison at Fresnes, in the north of France, and a judge from Caen was put in charge of investigating the tortures she claimed to have undergone. De Beauvoir and Halimi formed a defense committee for Boupacha.

Nelson Algren wanted to see Marseille again, and he and de Beauvoir spent several days there. Then they visited Greece and Turkey. For two weeks happiness and nostalgia blended. They returned to Paris; "not a single shadow of disagreement had troubled our five months together," she noted.[37] Nevertheless they were going to part. Both were free, yet both were tied to their obligations as writers. Talent, success, a demanding audience tugged at them, pulling them to their respective roots.

She did not "tear herself to pieces" as she had at their previous separations. She accepted the fact that their love had no future and consoled herself with the tragic observation that, come to think of it, they did not have that much time left either. In 1961 and again in 1962 she planned to go to Chicago, but it was wishful thinking on her part. She kept telling him that he was "her last houseguest." When he told her he was involved with one of her friends, the journalist Madeleine Gobeil, she wrote no more about going to the United States. As for Algren, serenity was never to be his lot in life. In his writing he would evoke his lost love and the woman who had been so different from the rest.

> Friends sometimes had to remind her that it might be just as well to hang up last winter's dress, midsummer having come to France. Most Parisian of Parisians, she was least the *Parisienne.* As a court had to prevent Sartre from blocking the French economy, Castor's friends provided her with needle and thread and buttons. Nothing more was then needed except a volunteer to sew them on.
>
> "If one gives time to trivial things, the important matters will never be settled," she disposed of all sewing of buttons, all washing of dishes, all sweeping of all floors, all shopping, all cooking, all childbearing—she not only did not know one end of a broom from the other, but was actively opposed to other women differentiating between either end. It was understandable that she should resent husbands honoring themselves with the freedom to drink and chase the girls while wives lived between bed and stove. But I worried a bit about how the human race was going to perpetuate itself once Castor took over. She struck me as a bit preposterous.

Then he renders homage to her initiative and actions.

> And, indeed, in 1949 her one-woman opposition to the single standard *was* preposterous. It was preposterized in every newspaper and magazine edited by the French bourgeoisie. She was cartooned, ridiculed, sometimes made gentle fun of and, at other times, reviled with no restraint.
>
> When I came again to Paris, in 1960, there was no more laughter: she was feared. She had broken through the defenses of the bourgeoisie, of the church, the businessmen, the right-wing defenders of Napoleonic glory, and the hired press. She was, at once, the most hated and the most loved woman in France. It had become plain: she *meant* it.[38]

There is a great deal of admiration in his final remark about her.

In taking his leave of her, Algren mentioned that while out for a walk, his steps had once more automatically led him back to her former apartment in the rue de la Bûcherie. She recognized the regret and the spirit of love in his voice. She let him go. He would never forgive her: "Let all clocks of Paris strike hard on the heart."*

In 1965 he wrote an article full of anger in which his spurned and ridiculed love came through in insults: Under the "philosophical jargon . . . she and Sartre erected a façade of *petit-bourgeois* respectability behind which she could continue the search for her own femininity. . . . Procurers are more honest than philosophers."[39]

On the eve of his death he was still raging against the woman he had loved so dearly and who had delivered up their love to the world. It was her letters he was thinking of during the final hours of his life.

THE TRIP TO BRAZIL

*T*he strange obsession with old age that served alternately as a source of horror and a source of consolation was not rooted in a visible reality.

In March 1960 Maria Craipeau, interviewing de Beauvoir for *France-Observateur*, described her as being "fresh like a rose, her countenance smooth and clear." The reporter noted with surprise that de Beauvoir's rebellion against her family and her upbringing could certainly not be ascertained from her appearance: a carefully ironed blouse, a discreet perfume, neatly manicured nails, all in all, elegant and reserved. "No middle-class mother would find fault . . . she is not aggressive on the surface."[40]

All those who came near remarked on the delicacy of her complexion and the slender, muscular body that had kept its élan and elasticity as a result of her many walks, climbs, and hikes. At fifty-two she was attractive, she had a beauty all her own. The article in *France-Observateur* explained her clear-headed renunciation of Algren, and de Beauvoir explained why she reproached women: "They think of themselves too much. To become a Marie Curie, it is necessary to think of something other than oneself." She admired those women who surpass themselves with a political or social passion, an active passion. Those who can manage their housekeeping, their family, and their career "are complete beings, marvelous and rare."

From the outset she had chosen to attain excellence, and it was "exultant to make it to the point where a man is already blasé. When I was twenty-two

---

*Algren remarried in 1966 and was divorced three years later.

I remember what a conquest the *agrégation* was for me, while Sartre, on the other hand, complained, 'Now that I'm *agrégé,* it can only be monotonous from here on in.' "

She was a pioneer.

Now the women who follow in our footsteps become "little lawyers," "little" this or that. They say that's good enough for a woman. They don't try to go farther, to become truly outstanding in their professions . . . they're hybrids, hybrids who feel guilty. A career isn't always obvious or self-evident, there's always this dilemma: Should I have a career? Should I stay home and take care of a family? For men the question doesn't come up—they don't have a choice. They have to have a career, they have to prepare for it, they have to apply themselves wholeheartedly. Women are divided against themselves and intimidated by society, which harasses them in a thousand different ways. If they choose freedom and a career they're labeled "adventuress." If *Le Rouge et le noir* were written today, Julien Sorel would be a woman.[41]

A few days after Algren's departure, de Beauvoir involved herself more deeply in the tragedy of the Algerian war. Some draftees were refusing to serve, crossing borders and choosing exile rather than the war.

A group of intellectuals took the initiative with a manifesto declaring the right to insubordination. Sartre, de Beauvoir, and the entire staff of *Les Temps modernes* signed this document, known as the Manifesto of the 121, and it was published in the August issue of *Les Temps modernes,* which was confiscated. Like Sartre, de Beauvoir hoped that by committing themselves they would succeed in radicalizing the left.

After her trips to China and Cuba, her support of Djamila Boupacha, and the Manifesto of the 121, de Beauvoir gave the appearance of being a militant writer. The influence of Castro was becoming apparent in Brazil, and the writer Jorge Amado and other Brazilian intellectuals asked Sartre and de Beauvoir to come to their country to speak about the Cuban revolution and to see what it meant to be an underdeveloped country. They would lecture and give interviews; their fame gave them an authority "that they had the responsibility to make use of." They decided to go, and they were impressed from the moment they landed in Recife. Amado was there to welcome them under a brilliant sky, and a crowd of photographers and journalists proffered outstretched hands and flowers.

Amado took them directly to a friend's immense *fazenda* with its chapel, mill, palm trees, banana plants, and the undulating landscape of sugarcane. Sipping her first *batido da cajou,* de Beauvoir let herself drift off for a moment into the most heretical of dreams, slipping "under the skin of a great land-owner."[42]

Perhaps it was a sudden burst of nostalgia—transposed into tropical lavishness—for the estate at Meyrignac in the days when her grandfather took her walking in the park where peacocks fanned their tails, where the "English stream" with its artificial waterfall ran beneath the water lilies, near an aviary full of exotic birds, under trees with fairy-tale names like *auraucaria,* magnolia, and *wellingtonia.*

De Beauvoir and Sartre crisscrossed Brazil, covering 7500 miles with Amado, who proved to be an excellent guide. His influence was such that, because he called for a modern port for the city of Ilhéus in his novel *Gabriela,* the government immediately set to work to provide one. They were welcomed listened to, and cheered everywhere. At the University of Rio, de Beauvoir lectured on the condition of women—the first time she had been asked to discuss that particular subject. She was more interested in the influence of Castro and the projects of the Brazilian left, which wanted to establish economic ties with the African nations. The Algerian war stirred considerable interest; Sartre spoke about Algeria and Cuba to packed auditoriums. In everyone's eyes he and de Beauvoir formed an indivisible intellectual and ideological unit. When Sartre agreed to autograph copies of his book *The Sugar Hurricane* to demonstrate his solidarity with Fidel Castro, de Beauvoir too was invited to sit down and sign copies of Sartre's volume. After a moment's hesitation, she accepted.

President Juscelino Kubitschek received them in Brasilia. The city of Rio made them honorary citizens. They held a press conference and were interviewed on television in São Paulo. Students were invited to discussion groups with them. A group of elegant women whose ideas were far removed from those of de Beauvoir gave her a warm welcome in a vast auditorium which they had filled with flowers. *The Second Sex* was still making its way around the globe. De Beauvoir did not like to see herself confined to issues related to the feminine condition while Sartre was asked to hold forth on the colonial system, Algerian independence, the Cuban revolution, agrarian reform, and the possibility of a revolution in Brazil. She felt left out of the real world.

Sartre had awakened a fierce passion in a young Brazilian redhead and thus he found himself in an unforeseen predicament. In Brazil a young lady from a good family must be married promptly by her seducer; social custom did not tolerate the sexual liberty to which Sartre was accustomed. "That nutty Sartre," de Beauvoir wrote Algren, "might just get shot if he refuses to marry her."[43]

De Beauvoir told her biographers a more Beauvoirian tale.

It was a very complicated story. Christina T. was in love with our couple. She was a leftist Catholic, and she had been told before we came that we were the incarnation of the devil. She lived in Recife and came along with us to know what it was to be atheists and to know what the devil looked like. Sartre wanted to go to bed with her, but she did not want to because virginity was sacred. She was with us for six weeks. When I caught some type of fever and spent a week in the hospital, Sartre after the third *batido* would tell her, "I have to marry you." I liked her very much. If I had to rewrite *She Came to Stay,* I would use Christina. She is a much more interesting character than Olga. She was extremely committed politically.

During their stay in Brazil, they lived a trio revisited. Yet Sartre was wavering; he really wanted to marry Christina and did not know what to do about Arlette. Christina tried to kill herself. Sartre hesitated, then finally made his escape.

> If love has wings
> Are they not for taking flight?

Beaumarchais always supplied Sartre with an exit line.

THE UNINDICTED INDICTABLES

The trial of their colleague Francis Jeanson was about to begin, and his lawyers wanted Sartre, director of *Les Temps modernes,* to return to testify. Sartre dictated his statement over the telephone, and it was read before the military tribunal.[44] He defended Jeanson and clandestine action, affirmed that independence was an acknowledged fact, and quoted President de Gaulle, who "now finds himself constrained to admit, 'Algerians, Algeria is yours.' "[45] The strong language of the statement is easily explained: Sartre had resolved to have himself formally charged for having signed the Manifesto of the 121 as soon as he returned. The headline in *Paris-Presse* on September 8 declared, JEAN-PAUL SARTRE, SIMONE SIGNORET AND 100 OTHERS RISK FIVE YEARS IN JAIL. The French embassy in Rio was letting the world know that Sartre would be arrested when he got off the plane in Paris. Claude Lanzmann informed de Beauvoir by telephone that the Jeanson trial had concluded in a "despicable verdict" and that all signatories of the Manifesto of the 121 were no longer allowed to appear on radio or television.[46] There had been searches and arrests on the premises of *Les Temps modernes, Esprit,* and *Vérité et Liberté.* The October issue of *Les Temps modernes* had been seized. Five thousand veterans had paraded on the Champs-Elysées shouting, "Shoot Sartre!" and *Paris Match* carried the headline, SARTRE: A CIVIL WAR MACHINE. Lanzmann gave de Beauvoir precise instructions: They were to land in Madrid and proceed to Barcelona, where Jacques-Laurent Bost and Jean Pouillon would meet them.

The trip to Brazil had lasted from August 24 to October 23, 1960. During that time, trade unionists and academics in Paris had launched a call for "a negotiated peace." Television actors had gone on strike in solidarity with Evelyne Rey, who had been thrown off a program. Laurent Schwartz had been relieved of his chair at the Ecole Polytechnique, and Jean Pouillon and Bernard Pingaud, undersecretaries at the National Assembly, had been suspended. Marshal Alphonse Juin had initiated a manifesto against "the teachers of treason." The list of the 121 names had been posted in officers' mess halls and in the headquarters of the National Union of Fighting Men and the National Union of Reserve Officers with the demand that sanctions be taken against "the madmen and traitors."

En route to France, Sartre and de Beauvoir stopped in Havana, where they were welcomed as warmly as they had been on their first visit. They held a press conference for radio and television. Two hours before their plane was due to depart, President Fidel Castro came roaring up in his jeep unannounced and insisted on giving them a quick tour to see the progress that had been made since their last visit. He showed them around the town and the university campus at breakneck speed, returning them to the airport just in time to make their flight.

Bost and Pouillon were on hand to meet Sartre and de Beauvoir when they reached Barcelona. They drove to the French border, where customs officials warned them that Paris had to be informed of their arrival and instructed them to notify the police as soon as they reached the capital.

They returned to Paris on November 4. On the same day, in a televised speech, President de Gaulle spoke the words "Algerian Republic." De Beauvoir and Sartre were absolutely determined to get themselves indicted. On November 8 the police arrived at de Beauvoir's studio to take her statement and Sartre's. The judge who was to hear their case reported himself sick the night before their court date, and the hearing was rescheduled, then postponed indefinitely at the last minute. Then it was announced that no further indictments would be made. It is difficult to get yourself indicted when you are a national asset! They decided to call a press conference at their headquarters, de Beauvoir's apartment. About thirty French and foreign journalists attended. Sartre expressed their joint views and declared that he would campaign for a "no" response to the referendum on self-determination. "If the question the government were asking was, Are you for self-determination through a peace *unconditionally negotiated* with the FLN? I would vote yes. But the left must reply no to any question that leads to a *bestowed upon* or *granted* solution to the Algerian problem."[47] The press softened what he had to say, and the incident was closed. They remained "the unindicted indictables."

In November 1960, *The Prime of Life* appeared with great success, forty thousand copies sold in advance of publication. This second volume of memoirs, dedicated to Jean-Paul Sartre, covers the period 1929–1944. Reviewers had high praise for the book in France and abroad, and de Beauvoir's audience continued to expand. She made a major commitment to the campaign for a "no" vote on the referendum on Algeria's self-determination. At the Antony Cité Universitaire, the students punctuated everything she said with outbursts of applause. Students representing the extreme left wing of the Belgian Socialist Party invited her to Brussels to lecture on "The Intellectual and the Government." The auditorium was packed not with politicized students but with curious members of the upper middle class, elegant women, a smattering of government ministers and businessmen—people with whom she had nothing in common and who had come out of curiosity to hear a famous writer speak. Socialist members of Parliament asked her to speak at City Hall and before a union group.

Soon after she returned to Paris, de Beauvoir took part in the National Writers' Committee sale at the Palais des Sports, where she signed copies of *The Prime of Life.* The Communists had criticized the Manifesto of the 121, and de Beauvoir felt that by participating in the sale "we would be demonstrating the solidarity that still existed between us."[48]

She was too famous not to pay a price. Much as during the glory days of the existentialist period in Saint-Germain-des-Prés, she was unable to go into a restaurant or a café without being assaulted by expressions of sympathy or hostility. The public figure had stolen a lead on the private individual. Her refuge was the intimate group of friends to which two new additions, André Gorz and Bernard Pingaud of *Les Temps modernes,* had recently been made. This little group was the mainspring of an important machine that brewed words and ideas full time and was sought out by all opposition movements. De Beauvoir's studio in the rue Schoelcher, where everything seemed to end up, was one of the most important centers of the international left.

Claude Lanzmann handed Simone de Beauvoir a report on the tortures inflicted on the Moslem residents of the Goutte d'Or quarter of Paris by the *harkis,* Moslems who had served in the French army in North Africa. Having learned that people were being tortured in the cellars of Paris, she had the report published in *Les Temps modernes.*

Sartre received the Italian Omonia Prize for his struggle against the Algerian war and donated the prize money—one million francs—to Algerian prisoners. *Les Temps modernes* sent Claude Lanzmann and Marcel Péju as delegates to the Conference on Anticolonialism held in Tunis in order to show that their solidarity with the Algerian independence fighters extended to the whole of the Third World.

The Secret Army Organization (OAS) had just come into being, and four generals had engineered a putsch, seizing power in Algiers on April 22.* On the following day President de Gaulle, in uniform, spoke to the nation on television: "An insurrectional government has been established in Algeria by a military pronunciamento. . . . In the name of France, I order that all means, I say all means, be employed to thwart these men everywhere until they are brought down." Prime Minister Michel Debré "was begging the people of Paris to stop . . . with their bare hands" the paratroopers who were expected at any hour.[49] The putsch collapsed on April 25. Not long after that, some leftists began to receive threatening letters, and the threats were followed by bombings. The offices of *L'Observateur* were devastated by a bomb. All the signatories of the Manifesto of the 121 were likely targets. Sartre, who lived in his mother's apartment, moved her into a hotel and went to live with de Beauvoir. The Algerian minister Aït Ahmed, held in Fresnes prison, made it known that he wanted to talk to them, and they went to see him in his cell. He asked them to testify on behalf of the Algerians, and once more de Beauvoir measured the efficiency of writing in "the struggle for world truth."

She was in Antibes on May 4 when a telephone call informed her of Maurice Merleau-Ponty's death. Time had just taken away the companion of her youth, Zaza's great love. Their ideological disagreements had reverberated in the press. Merleau-Ponty had accused Sartre and de Beauvoir of having "ultra-Bolshevik" opinions; de Beauvoir had replied by writing "Merleau-Ponty and the Pseudo-Sartrism," but they were again on friendly terms the following year.

In 1961 a powerless de Beauvoir watched the play of outside forces: history, time, death. "I had exhausted all my capacities for revolt, for regret, I was vanquished, I let go. Hostile to the society to which I belonged, banished

---

*Patrick O'Brian, translator of *Adieux,* defines the OAS as "an armed and violent body opposed to the independence of Algeria."

by my age from the future, stripped fiber by fiber of my past, I was reduced to facing each moment with nothing but my naked existence." To Sartre she said, "If we've got another twenty years to live, let's try to enjoy them."[50]

The bombings accelerated. On July 19 a plastic bomb exploded in Sartre's building. On September 9 President de Gaulle barely escaped an OAS attempt. The studio in the rue Schoelcher was an easy target. Sartre's secretary, Claude Faux, rented a furnished apartment in his own name in a building still under construction on the boulevard Saint-Germain. The windows faced a wall in the rue Saint-Guillaume, there was no daylight to speak of, and the electric lights had to be left on even during the day. The staircase was filled with construction rubble, and the workers hammered all day long. The combination apartment-refuge was gloomy and sinister. It was here that de Beauvoir wrote the preface to Gisèle Halimi's book about Djamila Boupacha, in which she qualified Algerian repression as genocide and declared that repression followed by pacification had resulted in more than a million victims. The relocation camps, in her words, "are in fact death camps, serving on the side as brothels for elite troops."

There exists among the public, she said, an often unconscious refusal to acknowledge evidence—a collective case of bad faith. Torture is "publicly advocated, openly taught, sanctioned by a great number of ecclesiastics, systematically practiced. The exceptional thing about the Boupacha affair is not the facts themselves but their revelation." She had first encountered the incredulity of readers in 1945, when she described the Occupation and the Nazi concentration camps. "After all, if it was that dreadful, we would have known about it," people in Portugal had told her.[51]

Sartre, de Beauvoir, Schwartz, Vigier, Lanzmann, Péju, and Pouillon participated in the creation of a League for Antifascist Movements that, on November 18, organized a march for Peace in Algeria. De Beauvoir linked arms with Sartre on one side and a stranger on the other and marched down the street chanting, "Peace in Algeria—solidarity with the Algerians—OAS murderers."

The following month she attended another demonstration on Sartre's arm. Soon after they arrived in front of the Saint-Paul métro station, de Beauvoir realized that they were boxed in by the ranks in front of them, which were backing up, while the ranks behind them continued to move forward. She felt smothered, about to faint. She lost a shoe and clung to Sartre to keep from being swept away by the crowd. Lanzmann, who was much taller than Sartre and could see what was happening, managed to maneuver them into the protection of a crowded cross street. They made it to the place des Vosges and took refuge in a café. Bianca had been demonstrating with them, and she lent a wool stocking to de Beauvoir, who had been hobbling around in one shoe.

On January 7, 1962, the building where Sartre and de Beauvoir had believed themselves safe was bombed. The shirt shop on the corner was demolished. Three days later a plastic bomb aimed at Sartre's apartment exploded in the building at 42 rue Bonaparte; the apartments on the two floors above his were blown up, the staircase was left dangling in midair, the apartment door was ripped off its hinges, and papers were scattered all over the floor. Simone de Beauvoir's letters had vanished in the blast.

Two policemen were posted outside the front door of the building on the boulevard Saint-Germain. When the owners discovered that Sartre and de Beauvoir were such a hazard, they asked them to move. And they did, to a vast modern apartment on the quai Louis-Blériot, with large picture windows overlooking the Seine. That very day a second explosion occurred near the building they had just left on the boulevard Saint-Germain. When de Beauvoir went to collect her mail at her apartment in the rue Schoelcher, the concierges told her they had received a telephone call announcing, "Watch out! Simone de Beauvoir is getting blown up tonight!" Student volunteers moved into her studio, and nothing happened after that. When she wanted to move back in, however, there were quite a few young people in residence who did not want to leave; it would have been necessary to use force to eject them. She wrote Algren, who was tall and athletic, that she would have needed a strong American to scare them off and liberate her studio. She resigned herself to staying on for a while on the quai Louis-Blériot.

On February 8, 1962, the left organized an anti-OAS demonstration that ended tragically: Eight people died in the Charonne métro station. The unions organized an enormous demonstration on February 13, the day of the victims' funerals. The League for Antifascist Movements took part. All the workers of Paris went on strike, an enormous crowd marched through the streets, and the sidewalks were packed with onlookers. There were more than half a million demonstrators.

De Beauvoir and the staff of *Les Temps modernes* took part in all the demonstrations. Under pressure from the Communists, the League for Antifascist Movements became the Front for Action and Coordination Among University Teachers and Intellectuals for an Antifascist Movement (FAC). On March 15 the FAC held a meeting at the Mutualité auditorium. A telephone call warned the organizers that the hall would be bombed, but this turned out to be a false alarm. The Communists did not look favorably upon the FAC. De Beauvoir pointed out that nothing had been accomplished either with them or without them; nothing had changed since the days of the Democratic Revolutionary Movement, "Sartre's party."

On March 18 a cease-fire agreement was signed in Evian-les-Bains, effective in Algeria the following day. The April 8 referendum showed that the majority of the French people wanted peace.[52]

For de Beauvoir the seven long years of the Algerian war had been a turning point. Sartre and, in his wake, de Beauvoir were perceived by European youth of the extreme left and by the revolutionaries of the Third World as symbols of defiance to world order.

BACK TO THE USSR

Simone de Beauvoir and Sartre traveled extensively in 1962. On June 1 they left Paris for Moscow as guests of the Soviet Writers' Union. This was the time of the "thaw" in Soviet relations, and there was talk of coexistence. They were received less officially than they had been in 1955: no banquets, no toasts.

Sartre and de Beauvoir had accumulated substantial royalties in Russia, sums that had to be spent within the country. Until 1966 they were to go to Moscow every summer. They struck up friendships there. Ilya Ehrenburg received them at his dacha, where he owned an imposing collection of paintings: works by Picasso, Léger, Chagall, and Matisse. He had lived in Montparnasse for some time and often went to Paris. They stopped in Poland on their way back, spent the summer in Rome, returned to Moscow to celebrate the Russian Christmas, and brought in the New Year with the Russian writer Konstantin Simonov in the lobby of a theatre where elegant young people danced the latest Western dances to jazz melodies.

The following summer they returned to the Soviet Union for the Congress of the Community of European Writers (COMES), created in Italy in 1958. The French delegation included Frénaud, Robbe-Grillet, Nathalie Sarraute, and Pingaud. Caillois represented UNESCO. The thaw had already slowed, and the cultural situation was no longer the same. Khrushchev had attacked abstractionism and formalism and accused Ehrenburg of inciting Sartre to leave the Communist Party, neglecting to acknowledge that Sartre had never been a member of it. The Soviet writers present at the Congress defended socialist realism, while the French contingent, especially Robbe-

Grillet, defended the *nouveau roman.* The Soviets denounced degeneracy, cynicism, and all other vices of the West, including the striptease. Sartre was
asked to draw up a concluding statement to the debates; he did so and was
applauded, but there had been no real exchange of ideas.

Nevertheless Khrushchev invited a COMES delegation to his dacha in
Georgia. A special plane transported Sartre and de Beauvoir along with English, Italian, Polish, Rumanian, and Soviet representatives. De Beauvoir
discovered the Mediterranean climate of the south: Khrushchev's property
was luxuriant with vegetation, a vast wood "planted with the rarest and most
beautiful trees in the entire Union," and it featured an enormous glass-walled
swimming pool. All this luxury came as a surprise to de Beauvoir. Khrushchev's welcome had been friendly, but the speech he gave his guests was far
less so. De Beauvoir attentively heard him heap invective on his visitors,
calling them "henchmen of capitalism." He extolled the merits of socialism
and justified the Soviet intervention in Budapest. The violence of his outburst
surprised her. The next stop was the pool, where bathing suits had been laid
out for those who wished to swim before lunch. The visitors dutifully soaked
up some sun. Then a splendid meal was served, followed by a poem read
aloud, in Russian, that lasted nearly an hour. De Beauvoir did not know the
language of Pushkin.[53]

The delegates took leave of their host, who remained cold and reserved.
Not until their return to Moscow did de Beauvoir understand why Khrushchev had given them such a chilly reception. That same morning, Maurice
Thorez, the president of the French Communist Party, who was vacationing
nearby, had visited Khrushchev and put him on his guard against these
staunchly anti-Communist writers who were merely posing as members of
the left.

Sartre and de Beauvoir departed for Rome, their summer headquarters.
October saw the appearance of the third volume of her memoirs, *Force of
Circumstance,* which covers the period 1944–1962. These years were a time of
literary triumph, travel, political commitment, and disenchantment, and de
Beauvoir tells of her "anxiety before the horror of the world." *Force of Circumstance* is also a celebration of her extraordinary and singular understanding
with Sartre. De Beauvoir shares her life "in its surging vigor, its moments of
distress, its jolts and starts" with her readers. She reveals herself in full
maturity, from age thirty-six to age fifty-four, in constant struggle with her
emotions and her natural ferocity, mastering a fiery nature and doing what
is necessary in order to devote herself entirely to literature. In giving precedence to her relationship with Sartre, even to the point of sacrificing her love
for Nelson Algren, in letting herself go in numerous adventures, affairs with

men and ambiguous relationships with women, she tells a unique story, that of a woman who is first of all a writer, capable of sacrificing everything for glory, in the classic sense of the word, that is to say, for her calling. This volume is a summing up and assessment of her illusions. The world did not bend to her expectations; the "force of circumstance" carried her along, and she concludes with the now famous words, "I was gypped."

A VERY EASY DEATH

*I*n November Simone de Beauvoir was invited to Czechoslovakia by the Writers' Union. There she gave interviews and wrote articles as she had in Cuba, Brazil, the USSR, and Poland. In her memoirs she describes in detail her discovery of other societies, other cultures. From trip to trip she never ceased to learn and, wherever she went, to measure "the human reign that is the truth of the world."

In Rome a telephone call informed her that her mother had had an accident. It was October 24, 1963. She returned to Paris, then left for Prague but came back immediately. For the month to come she followed along, powerless and outraged, as death approached. She wrote to Nelson Algren:

> November was a long sad month, for indeed my mother was dying and at last she did it. How these old women cling to life. My mother fell down and broke a bone in the hip. . . . She had two very happy weeks, everybody taking care of her, my sister and myself spending our days and nights in her room. Not from love in any case, but from a deep and bitter compassion. She wanted so much to live! She began to feel very tired and pains began too, and we ordered the doctors to give her a lot of morphine and in fact to kill her slowly. They were obedient.

Twenty years earlier, her father had accepted death with a sort of fatalism. Embittered, weak from the deprivations caused by the war, he had passed away. Françoise de Beauvoir put a great deal of stock in life and held tight to its gifts. As a widow she had discovered the joy of working and of being independent. She enjoyed traveling, she had plans and projects ahead. To a certain extent Simone de Beauvoir recognized herself in this woman who refused to accept death. She felt compelled to bear witness to the scandal of the end of an existence, and in a few short months she wrote *A Very Easy Death*. She touched upon what hurt the most: the unhappiness of being over and

done with, of being stripped of the world, of losing one's self. Three lines of
verse by Dylan Thomas serve as the epigraph.

> *Do not go gentle into that good night,*
> *Old age should burn and rave at close of day;*
> *Rage, rage against the dying of the light.*

The words reflect de Beauvoir's attitude in the face of death, this "un-
warranted violence," this "brutal adventure" that haunted her: "Awakened,
I feel its shadow between me and the world." Death is a leitmotif, the
counterpoint to the hymn to joy that runs through all her work. In *The
Mandarins* Anne is tempted by suicide. Françoise kills in *She Came to Stay. The
Blood of Others* unfolds beside the deathbed of a dying woman. *Who Shall Die?*
depicts the deaths of half a city's population. *All Men Are Mortal* is a meditation on death. The theme reappears in *Les Belles Images,* in *The Woman Destroyed,*
in the memoirs—death is present everywhere. Of all French writers, she alone
—along with Chateaubriand—noted the passing years with such insistence,
ever conscious of the ticking clock, of life's running out and slipping away.
Mémoires d'outre-tombe resounds with the same knell, the same recollection of
escaping time, of death's approach. Sartre never felt the imminence of death;
in a certain way he felt himself eternal.[54]

On May 30 de Beauvoir returned to the Soviet Union. She and Sartre had
been invited to the celebrations being held in Kiev in honor of the 150th
anniversary of the birth of the Ukrainian poet Taras Shevchenko. This time
they had hesitated to accept the invitation. Anti-Semitism was resurfacing.
A "virulently anti-Semitic pamphlet" had been published by a Professor
Kichko at the University of Kiev. The Soviet government had officially disa-
vowed him, but his pamphlet was republished five years later.[55]

They began to ask themselves whether the USSR really wanted cultural
coexistence between East and West. At a banquet they posed the question
directly: Did they or did they not want to work together with Western writers
to achieve cultural coexistence? The reply was that cooperation was more
necessary than ever in the face of the growing danger China represented. De
Beauvoir saw that the situation was deteriorating. Fights had broken out
between Russian students and the black students sent to Moscow from various African nations. The young Jewish poet Joseph Brodsky had just been
sentenced to imprisonment in Arkhangelsk.

De Beauvoir had been observing the changing face of the Soviet Union
since 1962: modernization, the thaw in relations, the return to a state of

tension. Despite the restrictions imposed on all foreign visitors, de Beauvoir made the most of their opportunities to explore the country. She led Sartre to Estonia, where they managed to wander around by themselves for two full days, unaccompanied by any official presence other than the welcome company of their interpreter, Lena Zonina, who became a close friend in the course of their many visits. Sartre, who had grown particularly attached to her, would leave her a pension in his will. Once back in Moscow they were "free from all constraint at last" and could wander as they pleased without being officially shown official sights by official guides.[56]

Upon her return to Paris, de Beauvoir undertook a novel on a theme that obsessed her, old age. She worked on it six or seven hours a day for an entire year but, unhappy with the results, abandoned it.

A major American publisher, Macmillan, asked de Beauvoir to write an introduction to an English-language edition of Perrault's fairy tales. It was surprising that they should approach this famous existentialist novelist, whose philosophy was considered subversive in some quarters, whose *The Mandarins* and *The Second Sex* were on the Index, this left-wing intellectual who had no children of her own and had declared that the family was an institution in need of dismantling. She accepted the offer and put within the reach of children a message of which Perrault had never dreamed. According to her, all the suspense of his tales resides in the reestablishment of social justice by means of the imaginary. Well before Perrault gathered these tales and wrote them down, they had made their way around the world by word of mouth; they were part of a universal folklore. Puss in Boots leads a poor miller's son to a noble fortune, Cinderella marries the handsome prince, Bluebeard is punished for his evil doings, the weak win out over the strong, and the poor make out nicely against the rich. "Hope, act; heaven will help you if you help yourself," de Beauvoir concluded after throwing a revolutionary light on *Tales from Mother Goose*![57]

The editor of *Clarté*, a magazine published by young Communists, asked de Beauvoir to defend the concept of commitment against those who supported the *nouveau roman*. At the Mutualité auditorium, before six thousand people, she reaffirmed the relationship between literature and *le vécu*, underlining the growing connection between literature and information and the difference between the two. Information keeps the reader at a distance, while literature is communication: The reader must enter into the author's world, and this world must become his own. In de Beauvoir's opinion the new novelists were suppressing the story, the historical dimension, the praxis, that is, the commitment, and they were suppressing man in the bargain. "Then there's no more misery or unhappiness, there's nothing but systems." Her speech was published in *Que peut la littérature?*[58]

De Beauvoir and Sartre had decided to accept no further literary prizes in order to maintain a complete ideological independence. They were having lunch together at the Oriental, a peaceable restaurant in the 14th arrondissement, when, fork in hand before a plate of pork and lentils, Sartre discovered that he had been awarded the Nobel Prize for Literature. He immediately gave a statement to *Le Monde:* "A writer who takes social or literary positions must act only with his own means, that is to say, the written word . . . the writer must refuse to let himself be transformed into an institution." He informed the Swedish Academy that he was turning down the prize. The press reacted by trying to account for his refusal: He was unhappy because Camus had gotten it before he had; he was turning it down because Simone de Beauvoir was jealous. As always, an attack aimed at Sartre reached de Beauvoir. The philosopher Gabriel Marcel called Sartre an "inveterate denigrator," a "systematic blasphemer spreading the most pernicious teachings, the most toxic advice which has ever been lavished upon youth by an established corrupter," and concluded, "It's a gravedigger of the West that the jury has hoisted onto its shoulders."[59]

In 1964 de Beauvoir and Sartre were as indivisible in the eyes of the public as they were in real life. "In more than thirty years, we have only once gone to sleep disunited," de Beauvoir wrote in the epilogue to *Force of Circumstance.* Sartre used to say that they never quarreled except over futile things. In Naples in 1939 they came to verbal blows over the subsidized public housing that Mussolini had just had built. Should the Neapolitans be obliged to move into these impersonal bunkers, or should they be left to dwell in unhealthy alleyways? De Beauvoir was in favor of their moving. Sartre called her a fascist, and she shot back, "And you, you'll never amount to anything!"

The unconditional help they gave one another as writers surprised their close friends by its despotic nature. Their disagreement on an idea, on a text, could be total at first and express itself in biting and startlingly excessive terms. Bost, who often lunched with the couple, sometimes heard "savage brawling" that carried through the door and clear to the other end of the hall, and he much preferred to return when the "discussion" was over and silence was restored.

"WHAT LOVE IS—AND ISN'T"

McCall's magazine asked de Beauvoir to write an article about love. Her love life intrigued like that of any other celebrity, and she was in no way sheltered from the indiscreet curiosity of her readers. Her liaison with Sartre was one of notoriety, and their lifestyle seemed to be a successful example of free love. Had de Beauvoir discovered the secret of happiness? "A celebrated Frenchwoman explains what love is," the August 1965 *McCall's* announced to its readers.

The article, "What Love Is—and Isn't," takes the form of elegant banter, a shortened version of *On Love,* de Beauvoir style: "Why do you fall in love? Nothing is more simple. You fall in love because you are young, because you are growing old, because you *are* old; because spring is fading, because autumn is beginning; from excess energy, from fatigue; from gaiety, from boredom; because someone loves you, because he does not love you. . . . I find too many answers: perhaps the question is not so simple, after all." Love is a mystery. Why this one or that one, rather than another man, another woman? All lovers have said, "You are different. You are an exception. You are not like anybody else." These words explain the attraction between two human beings to the exclusion of all others; they signify that the loved one has been chosen in comparison with and against all others. The love relationship involves not two people but the whole of society. "A person who is too harmoniously adjusted to society may never know love."

For de Beauvoir, love arises "in defiance of a husband or a wife, in defiance of your parents, in opposition to friends and surroundings, in defiance of all those who in some way have thwarted you." "The first great romance in the West, Tristan and Isolde, is the story of a revolt." In effect, Tristan betrays the mission with which his uncle has entrusted him. Tristan is to take to the king Isolde, his fiancée, and instead he steals her out from under him. Isolde gives herself to Tristan when she is destined for King Mark. The lives of the two lovers will be nothing more than a revolt against the laws that others impose upon them, a revolt against laws both religious and moral, against the laws of chivalry. Their indestructible love, at the dawn of Western literature, is the model for rebel lovers who make of their love a defiant challenge to all of society.

In choosing Sartre and freedom, de Beauvoir did so against her family, against her class, in opposition to moral and religious laws. And when she wrote that lovers forget the existence of all those who hold the laws against them, that they forget societal customs, she was speaking from experience.

It is by defiance, she wrote, that lovers choose to be "alone in the world." Love at first sight, the love that unites two people, is a revolutionary experience that abolishes the rights of others and suddenly liberates the lovers.

De Beauvoir went still further in this analysis of love: Love represents not only defiance and liberation but also vengeance. "Love would not have its somber violence if it were not always, at first, a kind of revenge: revenge against a closed society to which you can suddenly belong." The entire story of Cinderella is based on the device of love's vengeance, for love will lift Cinderella out of her servanthood to make of her a princess who shall rule over her former oppressors. But love is also a happy conquest. The loved one introduces you to a new world and immediately gives you all its keys because everything is shared between those who love. De Beauvoir remembers having discovered America through the love of Nelson Algren. "To explore an unfamiliar country is work, but to possess it through the love of an appealing foreigner is a miracle. In this case, as in many others, love is a marvelous shortcut."

De Beauvoir notes that women are particularly predisposed toward love since they rarely possess the means that would allow them to enlarge or change their universe otherwise. Love is their only chance when they have no profession or talent. "Even the most privileged often prefer the unexpected and wonderful joy of receiving everything without so much effort."

Things are not the same for men. The man of action can change his relationship to the world; he can even change the world. If he devotes himself entirely to his project, then love has no hold on him, he knows only flings that have no future.

According to de Beauvoir, love is defiance, liberation, vengeance, a conquest which fills a need that may be "ambiguous, indefinite, or even infinite." It is a force, a strength, a blossoming forth, a self-revelation.

Her conclusion to this essay in praise of love ends where it began, with the lighthearted banter that veils the unconventional thinking that peeks out from between the lines: "Why do you fall in love? Nothing could be more complex: because it is winter, because it is summer; from overwork, from too much leisure; from weakness, from strength; a need for security, a taste for danger; from despair, from hope; because someone does not love you, because he does love you. . . ."[60]

HUMAN RIGHTS

*I*n the sixties Simone de Beauvoir was seen as the theoretician par excellence on the condition of women. In the United States *The Second Sex,* published in paperback by Bantam Books, became the bible of feminism. Gloria Steinem, Kate Millett, and Betty Friedan drew inspiration from it. When American universities created women's studies departments, *The Second Sex* served as the basic text. Echoes of these developments reached France, where several parapolitical organizations, such as the Union of French Women, or apolitical organizations, such as the National Council of Women, the League for Women's Rights, and the French Family Planning Movement, already existed. Around 1965 the French women's movement, following the American lead, took on new life. De Beauvoir developed the themes of *The Second Sex* in interviews, discussions, and introductions. So it is that the themes of mutilation, manipulation, and the oppression of women emerge from the analysis of Violette Leduc's childhood in de Beauvoir's preface to Leduc's autobiographical novel *La Bâtarde.* The crushing of this writer's personality is explained by the interiorization of her humiliating situation and by the negative image she created of herself. In her preface de Beauvoir pointed out an oppressed woman who shouldered her situation, surpassed it, and freed herself.

Francis Jeanson wrote a biographical study of de Beauvoir, who gave him two interviews during which she spoke at length about the feminine condition. She attributed the fact that she was never conscious of the inferiority of her status as a woman to her religious education: "God loved me just as much as he would have if I'd been a man." It was to this notion of moral equality that she attributed her conviction that the difference between the condition of men and that of women is a purely cultural development. God guarantees the equality of souls, or human beings, here on earth and in the realm of eternity. Laws are made by humanity, and what one civilization may establish, another may undo. The second-class status of women is not a "natural" or "God-given" fact, and civilizations are mortal.

She rejected the idea of a specifically feminine nature, which would make of all women an inferior caste. In her introduction to Phyllis and Eberhard

Kronhausen's *The Sexually Responsive Woman,* de Beauvoir questioned the physiological aspect of woman's destiny that dooms her to a secondary place in society.

For de Beauvoir, women's rights were inseparable from human rights. She took a stand against the oppression of the individual whenever the opportunity arose. De Beauvoir agreed to preface Jean-François Steiner's *Treblinka,* which describes a death camp in which 800,000 Jews were gassed in ten months.

De Beauvoir had been struck by "the fact that the course of events was a perfect illustration of Sartre's theories on serialization* . . . in the camps the Nazis serialized their victims with Machiavellian ingenuity, so that they turned against one another and were reduced to impotence." When, at immense sacrifice, the deportees of Treblinka managed at last to form a group, "they became a powerful force and rebellion broke out."[61]

Steiner had tried to make people understand from a technical standpoint how the Nazis had succeeded in obliterating an enormous number of people one by one; he was reproached for having presented the Jews as cowards. De Beauvoir immediately took up his defense, pointing out that no category of deportees had been able to resist the Germans. Along with Claude Lanzmann and Richard Marienstrass, de Beauvoir spoke on behalf of Steiner, and their discussion was published in *Le Nouvel Observateur* under the unmistakably clear heading "They Were Not Cowards."[62] Her comments were immediately attacked by David Rousset. Steiner was accused of anti-Semitism. De Beauvoir declared that she was "personally involved in these attacks" and refused to have her introduction removed from translations of the book, an action that drew many indications of hostility but also numerous marks of respect. Jean-François Steiner received the Prix de la Résistance.

According to de Beauvoir, the extermination of six million Jews can be explained by Sartre's theory of serialization, which also explains the oppression of hundreds of millions of women. De Beauvoir supported the idea that only group solidarity permits action, struggle, resistance, and victory. The isolation of individuals leads them to disaster. "Unlike men, women rarely belong to a group: a sporting club, a union, a political party . . . they live a shared condition in dispersal."[63]

---

*"Serialization takes place when individuals, each separately experiencing a condition common to them all, become hostile to one another, as in the case of a panic or a traffic jam" (*All Said and Done,* p. 145).

"I SHALL NEVER SEE MOSCOW AGAIN"

In July 1965 de Beauvoir returned to the Soviet Union. Khrush-chev had fallen from power, Solzhenitsyn's works were being published, Pasternak was in print again, and Akhmatova's poems and a portion of Ehrenburg's memoirs were available. Ehrenburg invited Sartre to attend the Peace Congress in Helsinki and suggested that he write Anastas Mikoyan, president of the Presidium of the Supreme Soviet, to ask that Joseph Brodsky be pardoned. Not long after, Brodsky was released from exile in Siberia.

De Beauvoir and Sartre decided to visit Lithuania with their friend and interpreter Lena Zonina.[64] A delegation of writers accompanied them every step of the way. They had planned to sightsee like simple tourists, but their modest trip turned into an official tour complete with the laying of wreaths at monuments to the dead. In Moscow and Leningrad, however, they led the life they chose with their many friends, a privilege only granted to "fellow travelers."*

In May 1966 the situation changed. Two Soviet writers, Sinyavsky and Daniel, had been sent to a labor camp for "reeducation," the former for seven years, the latter for five. Only sixty-two of the six thousand members of the Writers' Union had signed a petition in their favor, and they did this at considerable risk. Ehrenburg asked Sartre and de Beauvoir, "What are you doing here in the midst of all this?" They did not cut short their trip, however, and they proceeded to visit Yalta, Odessa, Kishinev, and Lvov.

The following year, de Beauvoir refused to attend the Congress of the Writers' Union as a sign of disapproval that the two writers had been con-victed and sent to Siberia.

The entry of Soviet tanks into Czechoslovakia marked her final break with the USSR. A grand illusion had come to an end.

---

*"Fellow travelers" means Communist sympathizers.

JAPAN

*H*er Japanese publisher, Kazuho Watanabe, and the University of Kyoto invited de Beauvoir to Japan. *The Second Sex* had remained on the best seller list for a full year; all her books, and those of Sartre, had been translated into Japanese. The invitation particularly enchanted de Beauvoir, who knew nothing about Japanese culture. She threw herself into the classical and modern literature of a country she approached without taking a political position.

Tomiko Asabuki, who had translated her books, served as guide and interpreter. De Beauvoir had a great deal of esteem and friendship for this woman, who was a friend of her sister, Hélène de Beauvoir. An aristocrat ruined by the war, Asabuki had gone to Paris to make a start in the world of fashion. She published an account of her departure from bomb-ravaged Japan and her journey across an Asia devastated by war, and it was such a success that she gave up haute couture and continued to write. On September 17, 1966, de Beauvoir and Sartre took off for the Land of the Rising Sun, where Tomiko Asabuki awaited them.

At the Tokyo airport, in the middle of the night, a crowd of young people lined up in the rain, chanting Sartre's and de Beauvoir's names and stepping all over each other to shake the French couple's hands. A hundred journalists and photographers surrounded the new arrivals with a media barrage. The lively welcome took everyone by surprise.

The director of education for the University of Tokyo received them in the city's finest restaurant, where he had assembled a number of literary and film personalities. The geishas in attendance asked them to sign a stack of books for their husbands. Students brandished signs of welcome when, the following day, Sartre and de Beauvoir, one after the other, each delivered a speech to a packed house.

De Beauvoir embarked upon an exhaustive study of the country's daily life, institutions, means of production, and current ideas as circumstances permitted. Her hosts, well informed as to her tastes and personality, had organized a visit that, in one month, was designed to satisfy the most ardent curiosity. She had enjoyed the bars and the entertainment quarters, so her guides led her through Tokyo by night. She loved the festive nocturnal atmosphere with its aggressive neon lights and omnipresent paper lanterns, and they visited popular music halls and cabarets. Everywhere they went, hordes of young people asked for autographs. A young man silently handed de Beauvoir a flower, a young woman kissed Sartre's hand and presented him with a box of crackers.

De Beauvoir wanted to see a Noh play. Thirty-five years earlier, Simone Jollivet had thrilled her with a description of this ancient art form, and now Watanabe organized a private performance just for de Beauvoir, with one hundred guests invited in her honor. The play had been adapted from the *Tale of Genji,* the masterwork of Japanese literature, written by a woman. De Beauvoir also discovered Bunraku, "the only puppet theatre for which literary masterpieces have been written." She found an ancient taste for abstract art, "another universe" in which the actors' masks and the puppets' sculpted faces "have nothing human about them," where chants, songs, and cries take the place of language. Noh and Bunraku did not entail an imitation of reality: "It is in a total shattering of reality that the meaning of the drama is isolated in brilliant purity." She loved the balance between stylization and realism in Japanese art, a balance to be found in *Les Belles Images,* which she wrote while preparing for her trip to Japan.[65]

After Tokyo the next stop was Kyoto. When a traffic jam slowed them on the way to the train station, the train was delayed three minutes to accommodate them. In a country where the high-speed trains are electronically controlled and run very much on time, this modification in the timetable was an extraordinary honor.

While visiting a lamasery in Kyoto, a city of 1700 temples, they were surprised to find that the lamas were interested in existentialism and further surprised to hear them speak warmly of *The Second Sex.* All the same, one lama informed de Beauvoir that according to their religion she would have to be reincarnated as a man in order to enter paradise, since she could not be admitted in her present form.

After the temples they visited the industrial zone of a port where the dockers, whom de Beauvoir interviewed for Japanese television, were women. She climbed down into a ship's hold, where eight hours a day, seven days a week, the women shoveled chemical fertilizer into sacks, working in clouds of acrid dust. They were paid less than men, and they were expected to take care of the housework at home as well. De Beauvoir did not conceal the fact that this was not what she had had in mind for women.

At the hospital in Hiroshima, surrounded by journalists, de Beauvoir was given a bouquet and, under the glare of photographers' flashes, was guided toward the bed of a patient suffering the effects of the bombing. At the Hiroshima Foundation she and Sartre found themselves installed behind a podium with a television crew and yet more journalists and photographers in attendance. She did her best to converse with survivors and learned that the state gave no compensation to civilian victims of the war. The survivors were ashamed of their inability to work and accordingly hid their infirmities. Once back in Tokyo, she and Sartre took part in a meeting organized by the Sobro, Japan's biggest trade union, to protest the American intervention in Vietnam. Sartre and de Beauvoir found this a political issue they could relate to. Each said a few words against war.

Soon after their return to Paris, de Beauvoir participated in a meeting at the Mutualité to protest the Vietnam war. It was November, and *Les Belles Images,* dedicated to Claude Lanzmann, had just appeared. Fifty thousand copies were sold in the first week after publication, and the book remained on the best seller list for three months.

In the USSR the *Literaturnaia Gazeta* of February 14, 1967, declared, "Simone de Beauvoir has written truthfully about the social problems facing us today," then turned the column over to her. "My writing this novel was dictated by the sharp irritation I experience upon seeing the deceptive and illusory universe which surrounds us. The press, television, advertising, and fashion create myths that mask the real world. I think, for example, of today's myth, 'the world of the future.' This 'future world' we're always being told about is a subterfuge employed to avoid facing current problems."

In *Les Belles Images* de Beauvoir made a montage of clichés used in advertising and described the life of the technocratic middle class that revels in all the material goods modern civilization has to offer. "I don't mean to say that I reject out of hand all technological progress. I like jet airplanes, nice radios. I'm against profiteers who use progress to serve their own interests."

Money and the pursuit of success are false values: "Aestheticism, culture, and knowledge are exploited in advertising to conceal poverty, injustice, and social inequality." Catherine, a ten-year-old, painfully discovers that evil and social outcasts exist in the world. "I emphasize that I'm speaking about evil in the social sense of the word. I am not didactic in this novel. My book is not a tendentious book . . . it's a work which reveals the lie of middle-class life."[66]

In condemning the enslavement of human beings to the material world and advertising, de Beauvoir declared herself at the same time the enemy of bourgeois humanism and of the technocrats' antihumanism.

EGYPT

*I*n February 1967, Hassaneim Heykal, a spokesman for Nasser and the editor of the newspaper *El Ahram,* invited Sartre and de Beauvoir to Egypt.[67] *Les Temps modernes* was preparing a report on the Israeli-Arab conflict, and Claude Lanzmann accompanied them. The journey took on overtones of a state visit: The two writers were treated like expert witnesses whom Egypt wished to win over to its cause. Few writers before them had stirred so many passions, bred so many hopes. In Paris the families of eighteen young men imprisoned in Egypt for having tried to reconstitute a Communist Party had asked them to intercede on their behalf, Nasser having by 1967 become reconciled with the left.

Sartre and de Beauvoir held a press conference upon arriving in Cairo. An escort of journalists was constantly at their side. The government put a luxurious small plane at their disposal, and Nasser assigned an archaeologist to guide them. A horse-drawn carriage transported them to the temple at Karnak, in the moonlight. The next day they sailed the Nile in a boat, and a limousine took them to examine the myriad splendors of the Valley of the Kings. They flew over the Aswan Dam, and when they touched down, women presented them with baskets of fresh dates. A civil servant showed them around the construction sight, and that evening they enjoyed a private screening of a film on the inauguration of the dam's construction, which had been presided over by Nasser and Khrushchev.

After the treasures of ancient Egypt came the marvels of modern times. In the company of Egyptian dignitaries, they visited many accomplishments of the new regime, including the great orchards irrigated by spanking new canals tended by the army. Soldiers waving French and Egyptian flags lined both sides of the road. An agronomist suggested cutting the tour short, which made one of the escorting generals furious; he had posted flag-waving soldiers for many miles to come, and Sartre and de Beauvoir were obliged to inspect them. The bus continued on its appointed rounds. A triumphant welcome awaited them at an agricultural workers' center. The workers had been coached to chant "Long live Sartre! Long live Simone!" in French. Following a luncheon for forty, a government minister presented them with medals and asked them to inform the world of the good work the regime was accomplishing. Several days later, in the company of the regional perfect, they made their way through a crowd who held banners proclaiming "Nasser Is a Friend of the People" and shouting "Vive Simone! Vive Sartre!" Off in a corner, an enthusiastic schoolteacher led a group of placid peasant women through the motions of saying "Vive Simone! Vive Simone!"

The organized tours did not satisfy de Beauvoir's curiosity. She had noticed the poverty-stricken villages and their emaciated inhabitants; there were increasing numbers of mouths to feed. Nasser had undertaken a birth control campaign, but the fellahin relied on their children to work the land. De Beauvoir was discovering a poignant aspect of overpopulation: hunger.

The Charter of 1962, on which Nasser based his regime, called for equality between the sexes, but the tradition of Islam overruled man-made decrees. De Beauvoir challenged her audience while giving a speech at the University of Alexandria. She invoked Nasser's charter and pointed out that socialism could not exist as long as women were not equal to men. Male voices hastened to add, "Within the limits of religion!"

De Beauvoir was even more adamant when speaking in Cairo. She accused the Egyptian men of "behaving like feudalists, colonialists, and racists toward women." She told them that the arguments they were using to keep women down were as unjustified as those used by their former colonial rulers against the people they colonized. "I condemned their attitude in the name of the battle that they themselves had fought for their own independence."[68] Only the women applauded. Men approached her after the discussion to attempt to make her understand that the inequality of women is a part of their religion, clearly incorporated in the Koran, and that holy law must be respected above all other laws. In each of her many interviews in Cairo, de Beauvoir emphasized that she condemned all discrimination toward women, particularly from those who claimed that women had an eternal vocation imposed by religion and a specific function imposed by biology. "Woman must not be a copy of man, nor man a copy of woman: equality is not identity." In El Ahram she reaffirmed that work was the sole means of attaining liberation but added, "In many countries work does not necessarily lead to freedom insofar as the property remains in men's hands."[69]

She and Sartre became increasingly involved in discussions of current problems with the minister of culture, the head of the Socialist Union ("the single party to which all Egyptians automatically belong"), the editors of the magazine Al Talia, and other public figures. Toward the end of their stay, Nasser received them at his residence in Heliopolis and spoke with them for three hours, "without haste, weighing his words." He explained to de Beauvoir that during a discussion of the Charter a man had pointed out that since the Koran permitted a man to have four wives, equality meant that every woman would be entitled to four husbands. Nasser had responded that Islam was introduced into an already polygamous society and that the Koran, rather than encourage polygamy, tried to end it through restrictions. Nasser himself believed in God, but he said that religion "had thwarted him at every step."[70]

After the lengthy interview with Nasser, there remained one trip to be made. Sartre and de Beauvoir wanted to see a Palestinian refugee camp. Surrounded by journalists, they arrived in Gaza, where they were given flags of the "Palestinian liberation forces" and taken through the camp by their Egyptian escort and the Palestinian leaders, who invited them to enter the dwellings, talk to the people, and take note of their misery.

De Beauvoir observed that the money sent by the UN Relief and Works Agency for Palestine Refugees was not well utilized. The refugees could have been encouraged to build real homes, for there was plenty of space. Faced with the profusion of food at the banquet given for one hundred guests by the Egyptian governor of Gaza, de Beauvoir lost her appetite. Then they were escorted to the border. De Beauvoir made out the Israeli flag in the distance and looked at the no-man's-land between the two countries guarded by blue-helmeted UN soldiers. At dinner the number of guests and the array of food had increased, along with de Beauvoir's indignation at the discrepancy between the plenty before them and the deprivation outside. Sartre concluded a discussion with the Palestinian leaders: "In Paris I shall give a faithful account of the opinions I have heard here." The insistent propaganda had had the opposite of the intended effect on de Beauvoir. The visit to Gaza had depressed her. When an Egyptian woman friend told her that "the Jews should have stayed in 'their own countries' after the war," de Beauvoir realized that this woman, and by inference her fellow countrymen, "knew nothing whatsoever about the Jewish question as it existed in the West."[71] In Cairo they learned that Nasser had freed the eighteen prisoners whose pardon Sartre had sought, and the gesture touched them.

The farewell dinner was held in a sixteenth-century Arabic building, and Sartre and de Beauvoir were presented with two funerary masks from Al Fayyum.

ISRAEL

After the thousand and one nights of Egypt, Israel's welcome was quite simple. A delegation of intellectuals greeted Sartre and de Beauvoir and got them settled in Tel Aviv. After the luxury of Cairo, de Beauvoir felt as though she had rediscovered the cafés and restaurants of the Latin quarter. Simha Flapan, a member of the Israeli leftist Mapam Party, had arranged their itinerary and preceded them everywhere. Kaddish Louz, president of the Knesset, welcomed them at Degania B, the oldest kibbutz. At a frontier kibbutz de Beauvoir went into the deep trenches that served as shelter in case of danger. She could see the Syrian forward positions atop a nearby hill. They visited the kibbutz where survivors of the Warsaw ghetto lived, and de Beauvoir recalled the images that had stunned her in 1945 when the liberated press published the first photos of Dachau, Treblinka, and Auschwitz.

The tireless writers wanted to see one of Israel's Arab villages, since "one of our chief concerns was the Arab question."[72] They found that every means for gathering information was put at their disposal, and they were able to speak freely with everyone.

De Beauvoir noted the difference between the Jewish villages and the Arab villages. The former, "aseptic and built according to the rules of logic," resembled modern housing developments, while the Arab village they saw "was rooted in the earth—it looked as though it had grown naturally from it." In a municipality that gave them an official reception, they heard Arabs "express their bitterness" about harassment, confiscation of property, and police surveillance. Visiting the almost exclusively Arab city of Nazareth, Sartre and de Beauvoir were driven into the center of town, where a great "spontaneous demonstration" had been organized. Men shouted and waved signs that proclaimed their claims and grievances. At the hotel Sartre "received Arab delegations representing a variety of different tendencies." In Jerusalem they held talks with Arabs and Israelis who "were trying to break the barriers that kept the minority apart and isolated."[73]

The condition of Israeli women was of particular interest to de Beauvoir, and she regretted that for the most part they had given up their pioneer lives and settled for performing unproductive household chores. There were no longer any men in the kitchens or the laundries, work was no longer done in common. De Beauvoir wanted to know whether women benefited from complete economic equality and found out that equality was not respected in the labor market; a hard-won principle had been bent in favor of men. Moreover, women were given the least interesting tasks. The State of Israel had been built by men and women working side by side; women had dug with spades, fired machine guns, and laid down their lives. Now young Israeli women told de Beauvoir that they thought the preceding generation had sacrificed too much of its femininity. They were weary of heavy labor and were less active than the men in politics, but they believed they were serving Israel just as well by filling more traditional roles as they would be in competing with men. De Beauvoir had noted the same evolution in Cuba: No sooner had the revolution been accomplished than the women lost their equal status with men. People conveniently forgot that together they had fought, slept on the floor, prepared ambushes, and been under fire; people forgot that women too had struggled for a cause and risked their lives. In times when everything was at stake, nothing had set women apart from men. Then, once victory had been won, equality was stolen away from them.

De Beauvoir found the point of view of her Israeli women friends disconcerting. They maintained that they had achieved a sufficiently important place in society and contended that the question of feminism was no longer posed in their country. On March 23 de Beauvoir lectured to a packed auditorium at Hebrew University in Jerusalem. The audience had come to hear her speak on the role of women in the world today, but de Beauvoir, persuaded that the subject was no longer vital in Israel, spoke instead about the role of literature.

An authentic writer, she explained, must universalize the individual. "That is obviously to seize tolerance at its roots, to destroy all forms of racism, of sexism, fanaticism of all kinds in order to open the mind on the world and to call on the universal spirit."[74] Throughout her life de Beauvoir had outgrown notions of class, religion, race, sex, nationality.

The Israeli prime minister, Levi Eshkol, received Sartre and de Beauvoir and their visit wound to an end. En route to France they stopped in Athens and, alone at last, analyzed what they had seen. Their influence on public opinion was considerable, and no one could silence them. De Beauvoir and Sartre, seated at the Acropolis, contemplated an Athens where Socrates had taught and democracy had been invented.

During the time of her travels in the Middle East, de Beauvoir finished three tales that she would publish under the title *The Woman Destroyed*. She had found a renewable source of reflections on the female condition. Then she began researching the essay on old age that she intended to write.

Egypt closed the Gulf of Aqaba on May 23. Several French intellectuals joined Sartre and de Beauvoir in signing "an appeal calling upon both Israel and the Arabs not to engage in hostilities."[75] De Beauvoir was overcome by a very personal sense of anguish. She had just been to those cities and villages that were likely to be bombarded, she had left new friends behind in both countries. She believed that Egypt, deeply rooted in millennia of existence, was strong enough to survive an eventual defeat, but she thought the young State of Israel would cease to exist if it were vanquished. She was afraid for Israel.

During the Six-Day War, de Beauvoir was not in agreement with any of her friends. "I did not consider Israel as the aggressor, since by international law the closing of the Gulf of Aqaba constituted a casus belli, as Nasser himself had acknowledged."[76]

In France, the Gaullists were against Israel, and the Communists sided with the USSR, which had furnished arms to Egypt. The Trotskyists, the Marxists, the extreme left, all supported the Arab cause. De Beauvoir proved her independence. She explained herself in *All Said and Done.* "I did not look upon Israel as a bridgehead for imperialism. . . . It is not true that Israel's existence hindered the development of the Arab countries—it neither prevented Algeria from winning its independence, nor Nasser from building the Aswan Dam. . . . It is a capitalist country, and it has committed grave mistakes; but it is not the only one, and the others do not see their existence called into question. For my part, I find the idea that Israel might vanish from the map of the world perfectly hateful." Because of the position she took on the Middle Eastern question, de Beauvoir nearly always found herself on uneasy ground in her relationships with left militants. Although she felt close to the leftists where their activities in France were concerned, she could not accept their monolithic viewpoints. "A left-winger must necessarily admire China without the least reservation, take Nigeria's side against Biafra and the Palestinians' against Israel. I will not bow to these conditions."[77]

12

The Citadels

Freedom is the source from which all meanings and all values arise.

The Ethics of Ambiguity

THE RUSSELL TRIBUNAL

*O*ne of the secretaries of the Russell Foundation, a young American, Ralph Schoenman, called on Simone de Beauvoir in July 1966 to ask her to be part of the tribunal that Bertrand Russell, the English philosopher, wanted to organize to pass judgment on American actions in Vietnam. The foundation had taken it upon itself to send investigative committees into the field and to obtain documents from American opponents to the war. They hoped to reach world opinion and to influence American opinion. International personalities would serve as judges. De Beauvoir liked the idea and agreed to take part along with Sartre, who was elected executive chairman and took it upon himself to establish the statutes for the International Russell Tribunal on U.S. War Crimes in Vietnam. Sartre appointed Claude Lanzmann as his deputy. The meetings were to be held in Paris, but President de Gaulle, in a letter in which he addressed Sartre as *Mon cher Maître,** announced the government's decision to bar the Russell Tribunal from convening on French soil. Sartre replied that, if necessary, the tribunal would conduct its business on a boat anchored outside territorial waters. Finally Sweden agreed to welcome them. The judges came from Yugoslavia, Germany, Turkey, Italy, the United States, and Cuba. Gisèle Halimi, who had campaigned against torture in Algeria and fought for modifications in the abortion laws, figured among the members of the legal commission responsible for assisting the judges. For eight days de Beauvoir, "captivated by this undertaking," was surprised by the vehement dissension among people who opposed American imperialism. De Beauvoir, Sartre, Laurent Schwartz, and Halimi represented the non-Communist French left. From May 2 to 10 they heard reports and testimony from doctors, journalists, historians, and physicists who described the damage inflicted by new weapons being tested in Vietnam. Wounded civilians spoke of the war's hellish reality. Gisèle Halimi, just returned from an on-site inspection tour, painted a harsh picture of the situation.

Every day at the same hour, young people brandishing signs—LONG LIVE THE U.S.A.! WHAT ABOUT BUDAPEST?—marched in front of the House of the People in Stockholm, where the tribunal sat. Counterdemonstrators waved other placards.

De Beauvoir experienced an intense period of commitment during which she felt "totally mobilized." The ordered, assiduous work was to her liking, and she looked forward with interest to the tribunal's resumption in the fall.

The Sartre–de Beauvoir couple became more disconcerting. The Iraqi government prohibited the sale of their books because "these two personalities supported Israel."[1] The steering committee of *Les Temps modernes* signed an article protesting the military coup d'état in Athens, and their works were banned in Greece.[2]

De Beauvoir's play *Who Shall Die?* took on new relevance and was performed as part of the Saint-Germain-des-Prés Festival. The sacrifice of civilian populations continued. The problem of human rights that had been posed in 1945 in the wake of Nazism had not been resolved on a global scale by 1967. De Beauvoir increasingly took part in humanitarian causes. In July she wrote Venezuelan President Raul Leoni to protest the arrest and disappearance of opposition militants and demanded that all cases of human rights violations be brought to light. Then she signed an open letter to Miguel Ángel

---

*A traditional manner of addressing famous and well-respected writers; ironic when applied to Sartre, who saw himself as a political figure.

Asturias, winner of the Nobel Prize for Literature and Guatemalan ambassador in Paris, to protest the kidnapping and assassination of numerous
Guatemalans.

In November the Russell Tribunal resumed its work in Denmark. A
Japanese presented a report on defoliation: Chemical products were poisoning
people and animals. Testimony on tortures and massacres continued to
mount. Was there genocide? The judges were divided on this point. De
Beauvoir and Sartre were doubtful as to whether one could charge the United
States with genocide in Vietnam, and they held to an accusation of war
crimes. The Cuban delegate, "a lovely woman," and the Japanese delegates,
for whom this was a political affair, found their scruples superfluous. Sartre,
who always fell for beautiful women, let himself be convinced by the beautiful Cuban delegate. In his capacity as executive chairman, it fell to him to
write the preamble to the tribunal's verdict. His text, composed in the early-
morning hours, was adopted unanimously. Sartre declared that genocide is
"total war waged with unending determination by one side only and without
the slightest reciprocity." The International Russell Tribunal on U.S. War
Crimes in Vietnam condemned the United States for genocide.

THE WOMAN DESTROYED

*I*n January 1968 *The Woman Destroyed* was released in a deluxe
edition with original engravings by Hélène de Beauvoir. The printing of fifty
thousand copies was sold out in a week. The relationship between de Beauvoir and the critics remained a singular one. Some critics appeared never to
have forgiven her for *The Second Sex.* The new addition to her bibliography set
off a hostile chain reaction: "This isn't literature" was one response; "It's a
mawkish and sentimental novel" was another. When *The Second Sex* was
released, critics had called her frustrated and abnormal and accused her of
every conceivable vice and proclivity toward debauchery. This time around
her book was that of "an aging woman whose looks have faded" (read "a
hag");[3] one critic claimed that Gallimard continued to publish her out of pity.
Feminists reproached her for not having written about a liberated woman.
Bernard Pivot* wrote in *Le Figaro littéraire, "The Woman Destroyed* is a complete

---

*Pivot is now host of the weekly French television program *Apostrophes,* the single most
influential forum for books in France.

women's magazine unto itself. It's *Elle* inside *Elle.* * All that's missing is the horoscope."[4] De Beauvoir had the curious privilege of writing best sellers that were immediately translated throughout the world, and of being detested by numerous critics and an imposing number of her fellow citizens.

In an interview with a Norwegian journalist, de Beauvoir, ever sensitive to critics and criticism, explained, "In *The Woman Destroyed,* the woman is taken in because she believes that by living for her family she is accomplishing a task that justifies her life—a task that her family still demands of her, a sacrifice that her family accepts with pleasure. In reality, it's due to her 'sacrifice,' which has made her dependent on her husband and children, that she becomes a burden to them. As she never tried to develop her personality, she has nothing to offer them and no resources with which to struggle against her difficulties."[5]

People told her she had put marriage on trial; she replied that it was more like putting the wife on trial. Not that the woman who devotes herself to her husband and children is necessarily doomed to failure: "I think she runs a great risk of one day finding herself abandoned and unhappy." For "women who do nothing else, marriage is a sort of career, but an unhappy one. A laborer collects his money at the end of the day, while the housewife works and still finds herself totally dependent. Thus it is a badly chosen career, one which obviously may be very easy and agreeable for women of the well-to-do middle class for whom marriage represents a certain fortune and a great deal of leisure time." She returned again and again to the same conclusion, from interview to interview: Women must work. "I am of the opinion that a woman wants to be a human being like everybody else and that beings are not human except by virtue of their relationship with society, with others. These relationships can have no real effectiveness unless they come about through work, through economic action, through political action. It follows that women absolutely must take an active part in running the world."[6]

Some chose to see this book as an autobiographical portrait and, at the age of sixty, an acknowledgment of failure. No one would have dreamed of speaking of Sartre's sixty-three years. At eighty-three Victor Hugo was a god; at eighty Chateaubriand was a great man. When a male writer's beard turns white, he becomes a sage, a thinker, a prophet, a magus. Hatred and hateful remarks directed against de Beauvoir rebounded from paper to paper, rico-

---

*"I wanted people to know about the existence of this edition . . . so I agreed to let my text, together with my sister's pictures, appear in *Elle* as a serial" (*All Said and Done,* p. 142).

cheting through time. In 1984 a parallel drawn between Germaine de Staël and Simone de Beauvoir prompted one misogynist critic to call the two writers "our two distinguished learned broads."[7]

MAY 1968

On March 23, 1968, de Beauvoir participated in a day-long conference of intellectuals for Vietnam, held at the porte de Versailles. Then she left for Yugoslavia, where, as the guest of the writer Vladimir Dedijer, she gave an interview on women's issues.

Once back in Paris, she learned that four lycée boys, all members of committees against the war in Vietnam, had been arrested in connection with explosive charges that were set off on the night of March 17. Four days later, Daniel Cohn-Bendit, a sociology student, organized the student occupation of the administrative offices at the University of Nanterre. The series of events that would lead to the explosion of May 1968 had begun.

For some time de Beauvoir had been interested in the movements that were shaking up certain sectors of student life. In February 1964 Kravetz, the president of the students' union (UNEF), had written an article for *Les Temps modernes* demanding that the traditional lecture system be abolished, along with all classification by rank. The editorial team was far from unanimously agreed on these views, but Sartre and de Beauvoir approved of the students' claims. They wanted to see knowledge handed down and disseminated by new means that remained to be defined. In America and throughout Europe the student world was seething with unrest. In the United States student action centered on the struggle for civil rights and protest against the war in Vietnam. In France the early demands took a vaudevillian turn. In 1967, when Minister of Youth François Missoffe inaugurated the swimming pool at the University of Nanterre, Daniel Cohn-Bendit gave him a hard time. The minister had recently prepared a report on youth, and Cohn-Bendit reproached him for having ignored the sexual needs of students. The minister replied to the young provocateur that from now on he could avail himself of the new pool to cool his raging hormones. The students roared "Down with sexual ghettos" and demanded men's visitation rights in women's dorms, since the reverse was authorized. That evening the male students invaded the women's quarters.

In March the uprising took on another aspect. Students handed out tracts against the Vietnam war and tracts denouncing the oppression of which they considered themselves victims. Matters continued to escalate. Grappin, the University rector, closed Nanterre for the weekend, prompting the students to meet in the Descartes amphitheatre at the Sorbonne in Paris. In April they demonstrated in the Latin Quarter to show their solidarity with the German student leader Rudi Dutschke, who had been seriously wounded by a fascist. Since Grappin had closed Nanterre, everyone invaded the Sorbonne. Roche, the rector of the University of Paris, called the police, who arrested a large number of demonstrators and closed the Sorbonne. The UNEF immediately organized a demonstration. On May 6 students and police clashed in the streets, and the Latin quarter smelled of tear gas for the first of many times. Barricades were erected along the boulevard Saint-Germain. The students updated the old image of Parisian insurrectionists by digging up paving stones and using them as ammunition against riot police and firehoses. Crowds of reporters and the curious ran a real risk of being clubbed amid the explosions, screams, and clouds of dust and tear gas.

De Beauvoir was delighted by the audacity of this revolt and felt in complete solidarity with the young people. She hoped that the riot would become outright insurrection and bring down the regime. She who had claimed her freedom at twenty, when for lack of barricades the bars had served as the stage for her revolt, she who had dreamed of the surrealist revolution, experienced the days of turmoil with an adolescent's hope and joy.

Twenty thousand—some say fifty thousand—demonstrators brandishing the red flag and the black flag of anarchism assembled at the Lion of Belfort in the place Denfert-Rochereau and marched all the way to l'Etoile singing the Internationale. On May 8 de Beauvoir, Sartre, Colette Audry, Michel Leiris, and Daniel Guérin issued a statement calling on "all workers and intellectuals to support morally and materially the struggle begun by the students and teachers."[8] The following day, another manifesto signed by de Beauvoir, Sartre, Maurice Blanchot, André Gorz, Pierre Klossowski, Jacques Lacan, Henri Lefebvre, Georges Michel, and Maurice Nadeau declared:

> The solidarity that we hereby affirm with the worldwide student movement—this movement which has in the space of dazzling hours abruptly shaken the so-called society of well-being, perfectly incarnated by the French realm—is first of all a response to the lies by which all institutions . . . seek to pervert meaning . . . it is of capital importance that the student movement . . . establish and maintain a power of refusal capable, believe us, of opening up a future.[9]

On May 10 the barricades sprung up in the rue Gay-Lussac. People set fire to cars, the police moved in, and many peaceable passersby and onlookers were beaten and injured. This night of violence terrified the local residents and stirred public indignation. Two days later Radio Luxembourg broadcast an interview in which Sartre spoke about the events in the rue Gay-Lussac: "These young people want nothing to do with a future which will be that of their fathers, that is to say, our future, a future which proved that we were cowardly, burnt out, exhausted men made flabby by a total obedience and completely the victims of a closed system. . . . Violence is the only thing remaining, regardless of the regime, for students who have not yet entered the world their fathers have made for them. . . . The only relationship they can have with this University is to smash it, and the only way to smash it is to take to the streets."[10]

A short time later Sartre congratulated the protestors with the now famous words, "What's interesting about your action is that it puts the imagination in power." He whom Jean Genet called "the brilliant pain in the neck of the bourgeoisie" was expressing de Beauvoir's opinions along with his own. They were experiencing an adventure that seemed capable of meeting their expectations. Are the events of May 1968 spoken of without mention of the incursion of Sartrian freedom in history? Sartre grasped the inner workings of the movement whose process he had already described in 1960 in the *Critique of Dialectical Reason.*[11]

De Beauvoir strolled through insurgent Paris. On May 13 students, leaders of the left, workers' delegations—half a million demonstrators in all—challenged "a lunatic order." They chanted, "Students, teachers, workers, all united." Premier Georges Pompidou, himself *agrégé* in literature, had the Sorbonne reopened. The students occupied it. De Beauvoir marveled at the audacity of the young people: "Neither in my studious youth nor even at the beginning of this year of 1968 could I ever possibly have imagined such a party. The red flag flew over the chapel and the statues of great men."[12] She relished reading the posters, tracts, and slogans that flourished throughout the Latin Quarter, awakening an echo within her. Perhaps the slogan that touched her most was, "It is forbidden to forbid."

The walls spoke out: "Enjoy without restraint"; "I decree the state of permanent happiness"; "Dream is reality"; "Don't liberate me, I can do it myself"; "Be realistic, ask the impossible"; "Long live the city united toward Cythera!"; "Run, comrade, the old world is behind you."

The students knew that they would not succeed in overturning the regime without help from the workers. On May 17 they carried the red flag of the Sorbonne to Boulogne-Billancourt. Another banner proclaimed: "The

working class takes the flag of battle from the frail hands of the students."
On May 24 ten million workers went on strike. France was paralyzed.

On May 15 the place de l'Odéon became a sort of branch of the Sorbonne, and the black flag flew from the National Theatre in the square. Bands
appeared and music contributed to the festivities.

On May 20 the students invited a number of writers to hold discussions
with them at the Sorbonne. The speakers did not position themselves behind
a podium on a stage but sat in the midst of the audience. There was no
microphone, and everyone was free to pose questions as he pleased. De
Beauvoir went to the second floor and found Marguerite Duras, Duvignaud,
and Claude Roy at the "Cultural Agitation Center." Seven thousand people
had invaded the amphitheatre, which was designed to hold four thousand.

The students asked de Beauvoir, Duras, and the other writers who were
putting the weight of their prestige on the students' side to go into the
Sorbonne courtyard and say a few words. The crush of the crowd was so
dense that no one could move in the hallways, let alone reach the courtyard.

Someone grabbed Sartre and got a microphone to him, and he spoke to
the tightly packed crowd from a window, then disappeared. Someone slipped
him inside the amphitheatre, where he fielded questions from the audience
for an hour and declared, "What is taking shape is a new conception of
society based on full democracy, a union of socialism and liberty."[13]

For de Beauvoir the reconciliation of the two leaders of the left, François
Mitterrand and Pierre Mendès-France, during a huge meeting at Charléty
Stadium, seemed "full of promise. . . . It seemed likely that the union of the
left wing might be accomplished, and that this united left might confront the
bourgeoisie with an anticapitalist program and a transitional government."[14]
In fact from that day on the tide began to ebb.

De Gaulle dissolved the Assembly. On May 30 one million people
marched on the Champs-Elysées chanting, "De Gaulle is not alone" and
"Mitterrand, you're not gonna be president."[15] Increasingly violent clashes
frightened the citizens of Paris. Demonstrators hacked down trees, set fire to
cars, smashed store windows. Demonstrations were prohibited and the police
made large gatherings impossible.

De Beauvoir wanted to visit the Sorbonne one last time. The amphi-
theatres reeked of marijuana and hashish, drug dealers peddled their wares
on the premises, and at night "the Sorbonne was filled with beatniks, whores,
and tramps." The sociologist Lapassade, director of the "Cultural Agitation
Center," told her how worried he was to see mercenaries called Katangais
"helmeted and armed with iron bars . . . defending the Sorbonne against
possible attack by the right-wing Occident movement" and the police. La-

passade wanted her to write an article on the decay of the Sorbonne, but de Beauvoir was not interested in denouncing the students whose cause she still shared. For her the May explosion had been original in that "the prime mover in revolutions had always been poverty: The students had replaced this by a fresh requirement, that of sovereignty. In our technocratic society the notion of power had become more important than that of ownership, and it was power that they were claiming,"[16] not the power to govern, but the power to choose their role in society. This aborted revolution reflected a crisis in society as a whole. De Beauvoir and Raymond Aron agreed in their analyses of the immediate motivation for discontent: There were too many young people in the universities, and they feared not being able to find jobs. They were demanding reforms in University policy, in which they wished to participate. The workers presented new demands concerning business structure, self-management, the chain of command, the fight against pollution.

Ideology played a big part in the French student revolt. Some saw the influence of Sartre's *Critique of Dialectical Reason,* with its notion of groups in fusion. People spoke of the revolt of praxis against institutions, of Sartrianism versus structuralism, of leftism versus Communism. The diversity and subtlety of May's ideological discourse took many by surprise; the insurrection was as eloquent as it was sophisticated. The philosopher Herbert Marcuse maintained that the quality of life is more important than the level of material comfort. His ideology of the happy life appeared in the praise of happiness and the slogans that blossomed on the walls. The students popularized themes they had found in the works of leaders in contemporary thought and held on to hope despite failure. This positive attitude, this way of shouldering and accepting failure seduced de Beauvoir, who wanted to open a forum for student views in *Les Temps modernes.*

Once again the tumultuous stream of world events swept de Beauvoir across borders. In August an article written by the editorial committee of *Les Temps modernes* harshly denounced the USSR for its intervention in Czechoslovakia. The Czechoslovakian Writers' Union invited the notorious couple to see the situation for themselves and to attend the premiere of *The Flies.*

At the dress rehearsal their two seats were placed side by side onstage; at home and abroad Sartre and de Beauvoir remained an indivisible institution. The numerous students in the theatre asked them questions. In this rainy November, a distant echo of the Parisian May, they said they considered the Soviet aggression "a war crime." They spoke more cautiously on television, but in an interview article in which once again they were not separated, they insisted on commitment on the part of the intellectual, who must demand, for himself as for all others, "this concrete freedom. The sole thing a writer can do is to point out the paths of the struggle for man's liberation, the risks he runs, the possibilities for change."[17]

In parting, de Beauvoir was more optimistic. How could the Soviets crush such a unanimous resistance? The facts would relieve her of this illusion; the Soviets had discouraged her hopes once and for all.

In France on April 27, the no's carried the day on a referendum concerning the organization of regions and the Senate. De Beauvoir abstained from voting. The following day Charles de Gaulle resigned his office as president of the Republic.

Le Monde published a statement signed by Sartre, de Beauvoir, Colette Audry, Marguerite Duras, Michel Leiris, and Maurice Nadeau supporting Alain Krivine, the leader of a Trotskyist movement, as a candidate for the presidency. "This candidature is the occasion for the new forces revealed in May and June of 1968 to make themselves heard, this time utilizing the means furnished by bourgeois legality."[18] Their support was limited to this formal statement.

That summer de Beauvoir visited Nohant and enjoyed herself in George Sand's house. One hundred years earlier, George Sand had assimilated the quest for personal happiness with moral regeneration, repudiated her class, fought against prejudice, and set herself the task of furthering society's transformation through the written word. De Beauvoir could not be indifferent toward the novelist who had wanted to liberate women and improve the condition of the working class.[19]

De Beauvoir rejoined Sartre in Rome, where they met Cohn-Bendit, Kravetz, and other young leftists who had spent their vacation on the Italian shore. De Beauvoir noted that they had the mentality of combat veterans; they were already the *soixante-huitards*, * nostalgic and embittered, and somewhat hostile to one another. They accused *Les Temps modernes* of having become an institution—the plan for opening up the magazine as a forum for their views had never materialized. Nevertheless neither de Beauvoir nor Sartre lost interest in the extreme leftists and their activities.

---

*The sixty-eighters were the young people marked by the events of May 1968, an experience that shaped lives in the same way that political and social activism (and, nonpolitically, the concert at Woodstock) were meaningful influences for youth in the United States in the 1960s.

"LET'S PULL THE ELDERLY OUT
OF THE GHETTO"

The Coming of Age appeared in 1970. In this book de Beauvoir tore the clichés to pieces and showed old age for what it is. She denounced the gaps and shortcomings in administrative policy, the red tape of regulations, and the selfishness in evidence everywhere. She pulverized the myths and lies that camouflage the shameful treatment society reserves for its own members once they are no longer productive.

As she had done for *The Second Sex*, de Beauvoir did extensive research before synthesizing the data and drawing her conclusions. She examined the statistics, read all the recent gerontological studies, and consulted with researchers in the laboratory of comparative anthropology in the Collège de France, which Claude Lévi-Strauss put at her disposal. She read diaries and memoirs, solicited testimony from social workers, and interviewed the elderly in hospices, retirement facilities, and nursing homes.

In *The Second Sex* she had taken her own situation as a point of departure, then expanded her study to encompass the universal condition of women. On the threshold of old age, drawing once again upon her own experience, she spoke in the name of the elderly to claim an honorable and dignified place for them in society. The conspiracy of silence needed breaking; de Beauvoir set about the task.

Her study sparked enormous and immediate repercussions, particularly abroad. On the right as on the left, the press acknowledged that the problem of the elderly in society had not been resolved.

De Beauvoir told *Newsweek* that "technocratic society advances rapidly and leaves the old behind."[20] She told *The Guardian*, "Old age is a problem in which all of society's failures converge. This is why it's so carefully concealed. Men must remain human beings for as long as they live."[21] She developed the same theme in interviews with Eastern-bloc newspapers. She criticized societies that are supposedly happy and well balanced and accused them of relying on the sacrifice of millions of human beings, the elderly. She wanted to see a well-integrated society in which old people would work in accordance with their abilities and would not be outcasts. She demanded work and independence, dignity and its resulting satisfaction, for all. Unfortunately, at around the age of sixty, a worker is often completely worn out and, lacking the intellectual's cultural resources, has nothing to do but await his death. As de Beauvoir looked for the liberation of women as a consequence of work and their full integration into the very texture of society, so she expected work to render old age a valid and valuable stage of life and to bring about the liberation of the elderly.

For twenty-five years de Beauvoir had been demanding a universal right to work, equality through work, and independence through work. Yet journalists asked her the same old questions, to which she gave the same answers: To be outside the world of productive, remunerative work is to live in limbo; the right to happiness is inalienable and can be accomplished only through contracted, paid, and respected activity.

De Beauvoir spoke with journalists from *Il Giorno* and the *Nouvel Observateur.*

Let's integrate the elderly into the mainstream of the community. We are producing old ages that are only waiting periods for death. Old age is a psychosomatic phenomenon—if you act upon an individual's body by removing all possibility of its behaving normally, you influence the mind at the same time. Money and social standing play an extremely important role. Neither writers nor artists nor statesmen languish in old age; they go right on being what they were, even if they they have to fight illness more and take better care of themselves. These "normal" old ages don't compare to the "social old age" with which technocratic society hits its citizens earlier and earlier. It does not correspond to biological old age. The man of forty who cannot find another job because he is too old takes on an old man's mentality.[22]

De Beauvoir maintained that old age is a cultural phenomenon. The contemporary aged person is the product of a society that does not make him an integral part of itself. In America the message hit home with the elderly, who immediately put a Beauvoirian principle into practice: take action. The Gray Panthers set themselves the goal of making the elderly part of the life of the nation. They created businesses, and they succeeded in raising or abolishing mandatory retirement ages in some professions.

The Coming of Age was a new plea in defense of freedom, a new assault on the citadels of privilege. It called out, "Live and let others live to the fullest!" "Those who reconcile themselves to old age too easily are simply people who don't love life."

FREEDOM OF THE PRESS

After the riots of 1968, Parliament passed a law prohibiting violence in the streets. In the spring of 1970, the Proletarian Left, a Maoist group that advocated global revolution by violent means, was declared illegal and its newspaper *La Cause du peuple* systematically confiscated. Its successive editors, Le Dantec and Le Bris, were arrested. The group got in touch with Jean-Paul Sartre, who, while not sharing all their views, sympathized with the Maoists and "approved of their desire to bring revolutionary violence back to life." He asserted that since legitimate activities were having scant effect, "what had to be done was to move on to illegal action."[23] Sartre agreed to be the official editor of the paper in the hope of being arrested. He was not arrested, but the authorities continued to confiscate *La Cause du peuple.*

On the day of Le Dantec and Le Bris' trial, de Beauvoir accompanied Sartre to the Palais de Justice, where he had been summoned as a witness. The trial was of passionate interest to intellectuals. The court did not rescind the paper's legal existence, but Le Dantec was sentenced to one year in prison, Le Bris received an eight-month term, and the Proletarian Left was dissolved. Fighting broke out in the Latin quarter. The police surrounded the shop where the paper was printed and would have taken away the printer if his employees had not put themselves between him and the police. De Beauvoir held a press conference in her apartment and called attention to the inconsistency of an authority that officially recognized the existence of the paper but wanted to close down its press. With Michel Leiris as copresident, she formed the Friends of *La Cause du peuple,* an association that the Prefecture of Police refused to acknowledge officially. They filed a lawsuit, which was dismissed, but de Beauvoir persisted, and eventually the association received legal recognition. Sartre joined Secours Rouge, an organization that came to the aid of victims of repression.

Thirty vendors of *La Cause du peuple* had been arrested on charges of trying to reconstitute the Proletarian Left. De Beauvoir and the Friends, in order "to put the government in a state of self-contradiction," decided to sell the paper in the rue Daguerre.[24]

People were doing their evening shopping on this pedestrian thoroughfare of fruit, vegetable, cheese, and flower stands. Sartre, de Beauvoir, and their friends pushed through the crowd crying, "Support the freedom of the press! Read *La Cause du peuple*!" Journalists and photographers escorted the two illustrious peddlers.[25]

On the avenue du Général-Leclerc, beneath the gaze of the bronze lion that had seen so many demonstrations of late, the literary notables handed out tracts and papers to flocks of amused and supportive passersby. The atmosphere was festive.

The plot thickened when a young, overzealous police officer stopped Sartre, took his newspapers, and tried to lead him away. People cried out, "You're arresting a Nobel Prize winner!" The cop released Sartre's arm and quickened his pace, nearly breaking into a run. He was followed by Sartre and the journalists. Onlookers shouted, "Stop, thief!" The cop, with the newspapers still under his arm, managed to lose himself in the crowd. At the place d'Alésia, the defenders of freedom of the press settled into a café to draft a communiqué for the press. Radio Luxembourg was already broadcasting a recorded account of the blitz, and de Beauvoir could make out her voice and Sartre's coming from nearby portable radios and mixing with the street noises.

On June 26 they tried again. The participants gathered in front of the offices of *L'Humanité*. This time a police van pulled up, and Sartre, de Beauvoir, and company were politely taken to the police station for an identity check. There the police left Sartre on the sidewalk with his stack of newspapers and told him, "You are free to go, Monsieur Sartre." De Beauvoir was taken inside with the others. A suspicious officer asked, "Aside from Monsieur Sartre, none of you are public figures, are you?" In a chorus they replied, "We're all public figures." The policeman looked them over and failed to recognize anyone. "It's not our fault if you don't know celebrities when you see them," the gathering informed him. The superintendent began examining identity cards. "Bertrand de Beauvoir—that's not the writer. . . ." A smattering of discreet laughter succeeded in unnerving him. The door opened and an incensed police officer brought in Sartre, who had taken advantage of an opportunity to hand out his newspapers. The superintendent telephoned his superiors; he was told to release Sartre and de Beauvoir and detain all the others. Sartre and de Beauvoir announced that they would be the last to leave, and that was what eventually happened. Journalists and photographers crowded outside the police station. François Truffaut was speaking live on the radio, and he reported the news as it was relayed to him. English, German, Italian, and Swiss television treated their viewers to excerpts of the affair. *Combat* devoted a full page to the proceedings, and *Le Monde, Le Figaro,* and *France-Soir* all ran the story.

In the wake of this success, de Beauvoir carried on the fight for freedom of the press by officially taking over the job of editor on another threatened leftist publication, *L'Idiot international,* while Sartre became director of *Tout* and *La Parole du peuple.* De Beauvoir qualified her editorship as Sartre had; she accepted the position but let it be known that she did not necessarily agree with all of the newspaper's views.

Le Monde published a communiqué: "In the face of repression, which is taking on increasingly brutal forms against freedom of expression, Simone de Beauvoir has agreed to assume, as a matter of class justice, the responsibilities of editor of *L'Idiot international.*"

Because the government obstinately continued to confiscate *La Cause de peuple,* de Beauvoir and Sartre organized another demonstration. They called together the association of Friends, including the film director Jean-Luc Godard, the actresses Delphine Seyrig and Marie-France Pisier, and many other celebrities to transport thousands of copies of the paper to the Maspéro publishing house and the bookstore A la Joie de Lire. They stacked some newspapers inside the store and distributed the rest in the street. The police kept an eye on them from a van on the corner but did not interfere. In the Latin Quarter, Godard, Pisier, and Seyrig were picked up for distributing the paper, along with some less well known people. As soon as they learned of this, Sartre and de Beauvoir went to the police station in the place du Panthéon, accompanied by journalists and foreign television crews. A police car followed them. A policeman posted in a window took photos of everyone. Souvenirs? Intimidation? Nothing whatever happened. But when the newly released troublemakers went to a restaurant for lunch, the car went right on following them. "This was such an absurd waste of the taxpayers' money that I could scarcely believe my eyes," de Beauvoir wrote."[26]

Jean-Edern Hallier, the former editor-in-chief of *L'Idiot international,* was arrested on October 19. De Beauvoir had a statement published in *Le Monde:*

The government has just indicted the former director of *L'Idiot international,* while I am in charge of the publication as of issue number 10. ... When I agreed to take on the direction of *L'Idiot international* I knew it to be a paper that is the organ of no organization or political party ... this paper wishes to be the forerunner of a new press that permits increasingly numerous voices to be heard. ... The three comrades who were indicted ... are so arraigned ... for having written ... these truths: that the accidents called "industrial accidents" are legal crimes, that young workers and intellectuals are joining forces to fight, and that their unity is a unifying force for the French people. Let us make no mistake about it: The government tolerates only that information which serves it, it denies the right to inform to those papers that reveal misery and rebellion. In spite of the court convictions and legal harassment, I say, along with my comrades on *L'Idiot international,* that through the fight for freedom of the press we will pursue the fight for freedom.[27]

At sixty-three Simone de Beauvoir was taking to the streets.

On January 26, 1971, she and Michel Leiris presided over a meeting at the Mutualité auditorium. She wished to inform the public of the Friends association's goal, which was to defend the freedom of the press, one of the democratic principles dearest to the French heart. To her way of thinking, an antiestablishment press was useful to a democracy. To demonstrate her sympathy, she agreed to write a feature account of an industrial accident for the newspaper *J'accuse.*

Her attitude became increasingly radical. "In spite of certain reservations" she sympathized with the Maoists because "while the whole of the traditional left wing accepts the system . . . the Maoists stand for a root-and-branch denial of it . . . they arouse public opinion. They try to focus 'fresh forces' in the proletariat—the young, the women, the foreigners, the workers in the small provincial factories . . . whatever the future may bring, I shall never regret whatever I may have done to help them."[28]

But on May 5, in a letter published by *J'accuse* and *Le Monde,* she declared that she was no longer responsible for *L'Idiot international.* "L'Idiot represents nothing more than itself, that is to say, a handful of editors . . . I see nothing in it but negative and disorganized criticisms of current leftism."[29]

On September 24 de Beauvoir was charged with libeling the police in a complaint filed by the minister of the interior concerning articles published in the March 10 and April 7 issues of *L'Idiot international,* during de Beauvoir's tenure as editor. Upon leaving the magistrate's chambers she explained, "I took on the direction of *L'Idiot international* from September 14 through April 27, 1971, in order to show my solidarity with this opposition press whose role I consider necessary in a society that clamps down on freedom of expression and in which the ordinary newspapers camouflage or hush up the truth. I shall provide proof of the facts which the minister of the interior considers libelous if I am brought before the criminal court. Furthermore, I have refused to give the names of the authors of the offending articles."[30]

In February 1972 she and Sartre stepped in on behalf of the militant Maoists dismissed by Renault. Sartre and de Beauvoir entered the factory grounds in a small truck, accompanied by delegates from the Gracem Ali Committee, founded to assure legal representation for the fired workers. They distributed tracts that declared: "The state-owned Renault factory is a national firm, public property. You are not at home here, *monsieur le directeur.* You have accounts to make not to the government in power but to the collective, the group. . . . This action is a first step toward the control of Renault by the population of Boulogne."[31]

The illustrious demonstrators were forcibly thrown off the premises, and a pack of photographers led them to the Boulogne-Billancourt police station to file a complaint in connection with their bruises and injuries. Soon after, New Order, a small group of extreme right-wing militants, conducted an auto-da-fé of Sartre's and de Beauvoir's books in the place Saint-Vincent in the city of Le Mans.

APROPOS OF WOMEN

A new struggle was to mobilize de Beauvoir. Toward the end of October 1970, a group of young feminists resolved to publish a manifesto in support of legalized abortion. Anne Zélinzki and Christine Delphy, who had figured among the movement's feminist leaders in 1968, having come from the Women's Democratic Movement, launched this idea.[32] The signatures of a few famous women on such a manifesto would have a strong impact on public opinion. With two other feminists, Anne Zélinzki went to the rue Schoelcher and presented Simone de Beauvoir with the text they were asking her to sign: "One million women have abortions each year in France. They do this in dangerous conditions because of the clandestine nature of the operation when, performed under proper medical supervision, this procedure is among the most simple. Everyone remains silent about these million women. I declare that I am one of them. I declare that I have had an abortion."

De Beauvoir, looking thoughtful and attentive, listened without interrupting. "Well! I think it's a very good idea. As for me, I'm signing the manifesto. I can try to get in touch with women I know. Let's make a list." Without losing an instant she took pen and paper and wrote a series of names. *Le Nouvel Observateur* made the text of the manifesto and the names of the 343 women who signed it their cover story. *Le Monde* devoted two pages to the event under a headline that indicated its importance: A DATE.[33] The story was widely reported in other countries.

Twenty years earlier, in *The Second Sex,* de Beauvoir had protested the repression of abortion and its tragic consequences. She had never failed to point out that contraception was always preferable, but in the meantime, according to her, the majority of French women had no alternative. On November 20 the Women's Liberation Movement (MLF) marched through Paris. De Beauvoir marched along from the place de la République to the place de la Nation, under placards and banners demanding the freedom to choose maternity, birth control, and abortion. Four thousand militant women brandished lengths of wire decked with dust rags, laundry, and paper dolls and handed out parsley, the symbol of clandestine abortion.

The MLF asked de Beauvoir to take part in an action directed at an institution for young unwed mothers in the Paris suburb of Le Plessis–Robinson. This "college" accommodated girls between the ages of twelve and eighteen who, pregnant for the first time, had been expelled from their schools. Two hundred girls passed through the institution in a given year, and they were treated like delinquents for the length of their stay. Three teachers taught perfunctory classes that were aimed at the younger inmates and were of no scholarly use whatever to the older girls, whose school careers were wrecked as a consequence. There was no library. Eight typewriters was the meager provision for those destined for secretarial work.

Since 1968 a family-planning organization had been offering to conduct free classes on birth control, but the headmistress had refused. The girls asked to be allowed to join a delegation of unwed mothers who were going to see the educational authorities, but the headmistress denied them permission. The girls began a hunger strike, and "the headmistress sent each of their parents a short, imperious telegram, 'Come and fetch your daughters at once,' and announced that she was closing the school."[34] The MLF, informed of the goings-on by one of the college employees, decided to occupy the premises, and de Beauvoir took part in the expedition. She accompanied a group of students to see the regional rector. Invited to state their case, the adolescents demanded to be set free and to be qualified for state aid with which to raise their children. If a girl of fifteen was married, she was free to make her own decisions about her child's welfare; an unwed minor had to answer to her parents' authority, and her parents alone had the right to decide whether the child could be kept or put up for adoption. The law considered that the infant belonged to his grandmother.

In de Beauvoir's estimation, society was the true culprit. There was no sex education in the schools, no contraception; education was based primarily on prohibitions, and adolescents who would more than likely take the necessary precautions if only someone would tell them what those precautions were were deliberately kept in the dark. She found the parental and institutional attitudes, which confused ignorance and innocence, patently absurd.

De Beauvoir gave the rector a start by asking him under what code he judged it a mistake to have sexual relations at thirteen. In the article she wrote for *La Cause du peuple* she denounced the abuses of parental authority and "the dramatic situation imposed upon our society's young people."[35]

De Beauvoir's feminism became more and more radical as she "allowed her name to be used for acts of political provocation."[36] One of the riskiest operations was the establishment of a clandestine network for performing abortions. De Beauvoir put her studio at the militants' disposal in order to give any eventual scandal the maximum amount of publicity. The campaign raised such a fuss and attracted so many new members that the MLF became a political force to be reckoned with.

De Beauvoir and a handful of militant feminists organized the Days of Denunciation of the Crimes Against Women, to be held at the Mutualité auditorium. She was convinced that a dual strategy was in order, one that involved both legal and illegal work. "However, she never wavered in her rejection of all existing political parties and her decision to work only outside them."[37] This particular stand made her both the most admired and the most hated feminist. She would not accept concessions or compromises.

In *The Second Sex* de Beauvoir wrote that she was confident about the future and that the arrival of socialism would bring with it justice and equality for women. In 1972 her opinion had changed; she believed that it was necessary to engage in struggle to achieve equality through action. She separated class struggle from feminist struggle and declared herself ready to fight for "specifically feminine claims, parallel to the class struggle."

De Beauvoir described her perception of the condition of women in France for a woman reporter from Yugoslavia. "Our government is above all a regime of personal power that wants citizens to be as unpoliticized as possible so there won't be any opposition to it. Work implies a political stand. If women cannot work, there will be an entire nonpoliticized sector, and when women are less interested in politics, men take less political action. The women insist that their men stay at home, watch television, play with the kids, spend more time with them." She elaborated: "Political activity can exist only in the context of work. The individual who doesn't work is isolated." The Yugoslavian journalist asked whether she had found the condition of women to be better in the socialist countries she had visited. She replied, disillusioned, "I've visited many socialist countries. In the Soviet Union I was struck by the fact that women who don't work are considered inferior to those who do work, but all the same they are not equal to the men. Even the most capable women reach important positions, positions of responsibility, with difficulty." And, she continued, working women must also take care of their housework and their children, and the day-care centers and laundromats that would make their lives easier are not available in sufficient numbers.

"Women can obtain equal rights only under a socialist regime, but that is not enough. There exist ancient traditions that influence women. These inequalities are passed down from century to century. Women have inferiority complexes, and men have superiority complexes. It will take a lot more time before great progress is made, even under socialism."[38]

In an interview with Alice Schwarzer, de Beauvoir declared that although the men of today did not invent patriarchy, they have interiorized it into their thinking to the extent that they assume it is a fact of nature. "A cultural fact, even an ancient one, can be modified, abolished. A new society remains to be created." De Beauvoir maintained that the family must disappear and be replaced with something else, that women must refuse to marry, and that children must be freed from their parents. The liberation of women cannot come to pass outside the context of a vast revolution and cannot be accomplished without violence because men profit from patriarchal society and intend to hold on to its present structure. Women will be forced to meet violence with violence. Men attack them, insult them in the streets, beat and injure them in their homes, and rape them, and all this is carried on under the protective auspices of timeworn laws that must be questioned.

The idea of responding to violence with violence was new and surprising. De Beauvoir said clearly, "Because men resort to violence against women . . . women should use violence to defend themselves."[39]

In June 1972 de Beauvoir accepted the presidency of the Choisir association, which she had founded along with Gisèle Halimi, Christiane Rochefort, Delphine Seyrig, and Jean Rostand of the Académie Française. The association counted two Nobel Prize winners, in physiology and medicine, among its members: Professor Jacques Monod and Professor François Jacob. The association had three objectives: to make contraception readily available free of charge, to see to it that all legislation pertaining to the illegality of abortion was repealed, and to assume the costs of defending any person accused of having or performing an abortion. On June 15, before two thousand people assembled in the Maison de la Culture in Grenoble, de Beauvoir and Halimi announced that Choisir had developed a proposition for authorizing legal abortion, would assume the legal costs of all trials concerning abortion, and would take it upon itself to publish, despite a law forbidding such publication, the court proceedings of these trials. The proposal for a new law was argued before the National Assembly by the Socialist leader Michel Rocard. The first case selected by the Choisir association to challenge the government took place in November at Bobigny, a suburb of Paris. The mother of Marie-

Claire, a seventeen-year-old who had had an abortion, was tried and found guilty of complicity. Her daughter, being a teenager, was not charged but was called to testify.

Following standard procedure, the courtroom was closed to the public and details of the proceedings were to be kept secret. Choisir published the transcript of the trial in its entirety. In a vigorous preface, Simone de Beauvoir wrote that it was not the accused but the law in whose name they were charged that was on trial, "a law radically divorced from the collective conscience." She accused the penal code of turning the most disadvantaged women into victims of repression and drew particular attention to a glaring contradiction, that to consider the fetus as a human being is a metaphysical attitude grossly belied by common practice: "When a woman miscarries in a hospital, the administration tosses the fetus into the trash and the Church approves."[40] To legalize abortion would be to spare useless suffering, humiliation, fear, and occasionally mutilation and death. Planned parenthood would enable women to give birth in accordance with their educational and professional objectives, which meant that women could claim their autonomy at last.

De Beauvoir's feminism was based on her moral doctrine and philosophy: to take action. Freedom is the primary and essential objective, all else is secondary. In *Pyrrhus et Cinéas* she had written, "The sky belongs to he who knows how to fly, the sea to he who can swim and navigate."[41] If women take action, go to work, they will have a hold over that world and they will possess the freedom that men have and that women are denied. "I have never seen a woman with a job who was in the same state of distress and degradation as that of married women who have been abandoned."[42]

De Beauvoir was not agitating exclusively for women's rights; she had defended basic human rights all her life, and even in the feminist struggle she implicated both sexes. She insisted that women will not be liberated from the cultural oppression of which they are the victims unless men are freed of the weight of the prejudices of which they are at once the authors, beneficiaries, and dupes. "One is not born a woman, one becomes one" has its corollary, "One is not born a man, one becomes one." Virility, with all its social consequences, is also a cultural by-product. Man and woman, manufactured artificially from century to century, need to be reinvented. Only a change implicating both sexes can transform the quality of life for all humankind.

An article that she wrote for *Le Monde* was another milestone in Simone de Beauvoir's commitment to the struggle for human rights. "Syria's Prisoners" is a plea in defense of the exchange of prisoners and a call for the reestablishment of humane reciprocity even in time of war. Israel and Egypt, respecting the Geneva Convention, had agreed to exchange prisoners of war. Syria refused to do so, would not furnish the names of Israelis it held prisoner, and denied the Red Cross authorization to investigate the manner in which the prisoners were being treated. In the article de Beauvoir expressed her indignation at seeing "the anguish of a detention with no guaranteed end in sight" inflicted on young unnamed men and consequently plunging the prisoners' families into "the torments of doubt." The silence of Damascus seemed to her all the more cruel because "this cruelty is gratuitous."[43] There is no political option in this article, only the deep compassion that is the source of her stand against all forms of oppression, whatever their origin.

De Beauvoir's memoirs are an essay on contemporary mores and manners and an account that is sometimes a call to reason, sometimes an indictment. *The Long March,* her essay on China, is a report on the gestation of a society in quest of the common good. In *The Coming of Age* she speaks for those who have been relegated to the fringes of life. *Djamila Boupacha* is a plea against torture, and the preface to *The Bobigny Affair* is an indictment of a law that condemns victims.

Pursuing her campaign for the dignity of women, de Beauvoir instituted a new column in *Les Temps modernes* devoted to denouncing the exploitation of women in advertising, on posters, in articles, and on radio and television programs. The new feature's goal was to bring about a state of awareness in which sexist insults would be seen as an offense of the same degree as racist insults. An individual who, before witnesses, calls someone a "dirty nigger," or causes offensive words to be printed regarding Jews or Arabs, can be taken to court and convicted for "racial insults." But a man who calls a woman a "stupid slut" in public runs no risk whatever; the notion of "sexist insults" is nonexistent.[44]

With several other feminists, de Beauvoir founded a League for Women's Rights whose objective was to rise up against all sexist descrimination. Pursuing her fight, she prepared a special edition of *Les Temps modernes,* "Women Agree," for which she wrote the introduction and in which she tackled the problem of language—a hotly debated feminist topic in 1974. According to some, language and logic are universal values. For others, language—because it was forged by men—is an instrument of women's oppression that needs new vocabulary and new written expression to reflect women's specificity. De Beauvoir saw in language a means of communication and a universal tool, and she warned of the danger of a feminine ghetto of language.[45]

The twenty-fifth anniversary of *The Second Sex* in 1974 gave rise to conferences, colloquiums and symposia, television programs, and countless articles in France and to an even greater extent abroad. The media conducted what amounted to a general consciousness-raising. *Le Figaro* noted that this essay, which had been dragged through the mud when it first appeared, was more topical and more relevant than ever. De Beauvoir accepted Jean-Louis Servan-Schreiber's invitation and appeared on television for the first time. Servan-Schreiber introduced his guest to viewers: "The public knows one of our greatest contemporary authors through her novels. But it is through an essay, *The Second Sex*, published twenty-five years ago, that Simone de Beauvoir played a historic role in the evolution of ideas in our time. These two thick, difficult volumes describe and explain for the first time the secondary spot women occupy in humanity. As *Das Kapital* serves as the ideological reference for Communists, feminists the world over refer to *The Second Sex*."[46]

13

THE FORCE
of WORDS

*It is because there is a real danger, real failures, true
earthly damnation that the words* victory, wisdom,
and joy *have meaning.*

The Ethics of Ambiguity

SYLVIE

All Said and Done, the fourth volume of Simone de Beauvoir's
memoirs, appeared in 1972. Through her accounts of the events, friendships,
and commitments of 1962–1972, she drew up the balance sheet of her life and
her life's work. "I no longer feel that I am moving in the direction of a goal,
but only that I am slipping inevitably toward my grave."[1]

This is the author's farewell to her readers. She will write no more novels,
plays, essays. Her life has been the success she wanted it to be; "I have made
many friends among my readers. I asked no more."[2] But as she wrote these
words announcing a sort of withdrawal if not an outright retirement, Simone
de Beauvoir was joining the outspoken ranks of militant feminism.

If she stopped writing, her life was in no way less active. Sartre, nearly
blind, needed his faithful companion to continue the work that had been

begun. More often than not, staff meetings of *Les Temps modernes* took place in de Beauvoir's studio; she wanted to see the review as a collaborative effort, a sort of intellectual cooperative, but she alone kept the vessel on course and saw to it that *Les Temps modernes* appeared regularly.

The taste for discovery and travel had not lost its fine edge, nor had the desire to live life intensely: "My curiosity is less barbaric than in my youth, but nearly as demanding."

For de Beauvoir the joy of knowledge consisted of an ebb and flow of ideas, opinions, and emotions that conferred fresh life on each new experience, unceasingly renewing her relationship to the world, but de Beauvoir's world was a clannish one from which anyone who disagreed would be rejected. Many friendships were broken: Camus, Koestler, Merleau-Ponty, Raymond Aron, Gisèle Halimi, to quote only the most famous names. One of her friendships took a privileged place in her life. De Beauvoir was fifty-five years old and everything seemed to speak to her of death when, in the autumn of 1963, Sylvie Lebon, a young student at the Ecole Normale de Sèvres, brought her great comfort. "The better I knew Sylvie, the more akin I felt to her . . . I loved her enthusiasms and her anger, her gravity, her gaiety, her horror of the commonplace, her uncalculating generosity . . . day by day I keep her in touch with my life, and I told her about my past in detail. There is no one who could have appreciated as well as she what I was able to bring her, there is no one who could have appreciated more than I what I have received from her."[3]

When, in her collection of interviews *After "The Second Sex,"* Alice Schwarzer asked Simone de Beauvoir whether Sylvie, who was thirty-five years younger than she, was a sort of "substitute daughter," de Beauvoir's reply was unmistakably clear. "Absolutely not! Mother-daughter relationships are generally catastrophic. . . . The mother-daughter relationships I see around me are bearable at best, never really passionate or loving, which is what I think relationships ought to be."

"And your relationship with Sylvie?"

"That is different."[4]

In *All Said and Done* she wrote, "I was wrong in 1962 when I thought nothing significant would happen to me any more, apart from calamities; now once again a great opportunity has been given to me."[5] The same expression signals all the meaningful encounters in de Beauvoir's life. To announce her meeting with Sartre to her reader, she wrote, "And then I had been given a great opportunity; I suddenly didn't have to face this future all on my own."[6] She celebrated the element of luck that brought her Algren and Lanzmann: "When the opportunity arose of coming back to life, I seized it gladly."[7] It was affection, a deep understanding with someone else, the decisive meetings of her life, the happy encounters, fullness and joy, that de Beauvoir spoke of as opportunities.

The friendship with Sylvie Lebon spanned almost twenty-five years and finally she adopted her. She and de Beauvoir saw each other every day. "She is as thoroughly interwoven in my life as I am in hers. . . . We read the same books, we see shows together, and we go for long drives in the car."[8]

De Beauvoir dedicated *All Said and Done* to Sylvie, as she had dedicated *She Came to Stay* to Olga, *The Blood of Others* to Nathalie Sorokine, and *The Ethics of Ambiguity* to Bianca.

Friendships with other women have held a large place in her life.

I have had some very important friendships with women, of course, some very close relationships, sometimes close in a physical sense . . . but they never aroused erotic passion on my part. . . . It is most probably the way my upbringing has conditioned me. . . . Women should not let themselves be conditioned exclusively to male desire anymore. And in any case, I think that these days every woman is a bit . . . a bit homosexual. Quite simply because women are more desirable than men. . . . they are more attractive, softer, their skin is nicer. And generally they have more charm.[9]

When questioned about homosexuality, de Beauvoir told Alice Schwarzer: "In itself, female homosexuality is just as restricting as heterosexuality. The ideal thing would be to be able to love a woman just as well as a man, a human being pure and simple, without fear, without pressure, without obligations."[10]

"COMMITMENT, MORE THAN EVER"

*D*e Beauvoir never quit fighting for individual liberties. She was awarded the Jerusalem Prize in January 1975. The prize honors writers who have promoted the concept of freedom of the individual. Bertrand Russell, Max Frisch, André Schwarz-Bart, Ignazio Silone, and Jorge Luis Borges were recipients before her. And 3500 guests gave de Beauvoir a long ovation. She signed a call to heads of state of member nations of the Helsinki Conference (*Le Monde*, January 12, 1977), reminding them that they recognized every citizen's right to circulate freely, although "Mr. Brezhnev is far from recognizing that Soviet citizens have this right." She drew attention to the case of Dr. Mikhail Stern, deported to a forced labor camp because he had not objected to his two sons' emigrating. But the alleged official reason, she said, was that he had taken bribes—supposedly he had received two ducks, two baskets of apples, one rooster, seven eggs, and 775 rubles over the course of twenty-four years. Sixty-six Nobel Prize winners signed a petition, without result.

She intervened on behalf of rebel militants imprisoned in Barcelona, a Nigerian musician, evictees in the Paris suburb of Saint-Denis, and countless others.

When a journalist asked de Beauvoir whether signing so many appeals was effective, she replied, "It is said that we saved several Greeks' lives. In any event, you cannot not sign. . . . Certainly, out of all the given appeals, some are not effective. But even if only a few make a difference, that's all it takes for one to be obliged to give it a try."

Human solidarity and respect for the liberty of the individual inspired her to enlarge the activity of the League for Women's Rights—of which she had been president since it was founded—by joining an International League for Women's Rights. To mark the occasion on International Women's Day, March 8, 1983, she granted an interview to *Le Monde.* Human rights, she said, "are not as universal as one would like them to be, and within human rights, there is no statement of the specific rights of women." She declared that official bodies do not hear the voices of women demanding that not only their exploitation be brought to an end but their torture as well. She blamed the government: "In France, the minister of foreign relations replied to the League for Women's Rights that we should not get involved in what other countries consider customs—most notably, excision, the ritual sexual mutilation of young girls in African countries."

Beginning in 1972, in order to reach a larger public with her message, she turned to film and the audiovisual realm. She gave her endorsement to the New York Women's Film Festival and agreed to appear in filmed interviews. In the film *Sartre by Himself,* directed by Alexandre Astruc and Michel Contat, she took part in the discussions, and one scene was shot in her apartment. She adapted *The Woman Destroyed* for the screen. To parallel the film on Sartre, she agreed to make an autobiographical film with Josée Dayan and Malka Ribowska. She considered it likely that many of her readers were completely mistaken about her. Through the medium of film she wanted to reach people who, without ever having read her work, had heard about her and had an impression of her that she feared was altogether false. This had been a major concern all her life. She wrote an enormous autobiography in four volumes and *Adieux: Farewell to Sartre,* and her novels are largely autobiographical. The images of herself, Sartre, and the people around her were carefully crafted; a film could only help to reinforce the written word.[11]

She collaborated with the filmmakers Marianne Ahrne and Pepo Angel on a film about old age. De Beauvoir wrote the narration and, as a reporter, conducted interviews. *La Promenade des vieux* is a lengthy documentary report filmed in the inner courtyard of the Nanterre regional nursing home, which serves as both hospital and shelter. It has not changed since the nineteenth century. Simone de Beauvoir calmly dismantled the emasculating and repressive universe of this prisonlike nursing home.[12]

"A voice must be given to all those elderly people who don't have one," she said. "Their right to an economic, social, and cultural existence, to health, reasonable surroundings, and freedom must be defended. It is not death that frightens—it's old age and its parade of injustices."

In 1983 the Danish government awarded de Beauvoir the Sonning Prize for her entire body of work. De Beauvoir made use of the $23,000 that accompanies "this small Nobel Prize" to go incognito to the United States, where for six weeks she and Sylvie crisscrossed the northeast by car. She spent several days with Stépha Gerassi, reminiscing about the distant years of Zaza and the Closerie des Lilas. Their stay finished up with a stop at the farm of the American feminist Kate Millett, where every summer a dozen women artists get together on the vast domain they have restored and tend to raising Christmas trees. During the visit to Poughkeepsie, Josée Dayan filmed a conversation between Simone de Beauvoir and Kate Millett for the television series based on *The Second Sex.*

In 1984, four one-hour programs called *The Second Sex* were broadcast on French television, a joint production of the Ministry of Culture, the Ministry of Women's Rights, the national French television production facility, and T.F.1, one of the three government-owned national television channels. The series is a hybrid; on the one hand it is Simone de Beauvoir herself ("because we use her book as a starting point," according to the director, Josée Dayan), and on the other it is an investigative report on the condition of women throughout the world. On May 14, 1985, a one-hour television program devoted entirely to Simone de Beauvoir was broadcast as part of a series about famous women. But she did not want to be interviewed by herself, so she asked that other feminists be invited to appear, thereby giving them a forum on national television.

Simone de Beauvoir Centers for research, created in the United States and Canada, mark the importance of her ideas. In 1982 in France the Simone de Beauvoir Audiovisual Center was established to give rise to and support the creation of original work by and about women.[13] Films by Agnès Varda, Nelly Kaplan, and Liliane de Kermadec, television programs, video footage, photographs, everything that concerns the feminine condition is on file.

Beauvoirian feminism is never limiting and does not isolate woman in a ghetto—an approach that has made it a target of criticism from some militant feminists. In keeping with her brand of feminism, which is simultaneously radical and sensitive to the human condition, de Beauvoir opposed International Women's Year because "the next thing will be an International Year of the Sea, then an International Year of the Horse, the Dog, and so on. . . . People think of women as objects that are not worth taking seriously for more than a year in this man's world."[14] She wanted to reach women who do not read theoretical treatises but leaf through mass-market magazines and newspapers for answers to their problems. She contributed articles to such popular women's magazines as *Marie-Claire* and *Elle,* and she supported action that might reach a large female audience. "I prefer to have a limited but solid hold over the world through them than to drift and float in the universal."[15]

Her importance today can be measured by the action she inspired at the first Ministry of Women's Rights. The former minister Yvette Roudy paid tribute to de Beauvoir in *Because of Them.*

> If there had not been Simone de Beauvoir's very complete, very solid, and enduringly true theoretical and historical analysis, the effects of the women's movement struggles which sprang up around 1968 would not have been as powerful.
>
> I do not think that any movement, whatever it might be, can thrive unless it is based on a serious, coherent analysis of the situation, and it is the framework furnished by Simone de Beauvoir that permits us to work and advance even today. If I had not read *The Second Sex* and other texts by Simone de Beauvoir, I would not have the self-assurance which I do to continue the task I'm in the process of accomplishing.[16]

She named Simone de Beauvoir spokesperson for the Commission on Women and Culture, which was quickly nicknamed the de Beauvoir Commission, although de Beauvoir herself considered that there is no sound basis for speaking of feminine culture, of feminine language or writing. "It's not a matter of shutting women up in the ghetto of difference which men would like to impose upon us." It is necessary to work at the center of universal culture in a manner "that is particular and personal to us, trying not only to steal the instrument to make this culture our own, but also to change it, to introduce our own values. These changes should be just as valuable for men

as for women. The way women look at the world is different from that of
men because they, the women, were oppressed all through the centuries."[17]
According to her, a feminine outlook could bring social progress, an improvement in living conditions for one and all, a more equitable, more rational
administration of the world's resources. Once a month the minister of
women's rights assembled de Beauvoir and other feminists to discuss
women's business and the business of being women, and a few days before
de Beauvoir was always asked to compose the menu for the cook to prepare.

But her relationship with the feminist groups was chaotic. Many thought
she was no longer in touch with her times. She was a symbol but a faded one.

ADIEUX: A FAREWELL TO SARTRE

*H*er relationship with Sartre was becoming strained. In 1973
Sartre had become blind and took as his secretary a young Maoist who was
one of the directors of the outlawed Proletarian Left. Benny Levy, whose pen
name was Pierre Victor, was a stateless Jew born in Cairo. He emigrated to
France and studied at the ENS, Sartre's alma mater. Because of his militancy
as a Maoist, he had to report once a month to the French authorities. Sartre
personally obtained the naturalization of his protégé from French President
Valéry Giscard d'Estaing. Pierre Victor became more and more important to
Sartre and de Beauvoir acknowledged that he was well versed in Sartrian
philosophy. He wanted Sartre to put aside the monumental essay he was
writing on Flaubert to support the ideologies of the 1968 movement. He also
wanted Sartre to write a popular political novel to reach the new generation.
At sixty-seven, Sartre felt an urgency to finish the fourth volume of his
Flaubert. His health was failing. Little by little the relationship between
Sartre and Pierre Victor grew more intimate. For seven years they worked
every morning on projects they devised in common.

De Beauvoir was aware of the growing influence of this young intellectual on Sartre's life; it paralleled Sylvie's growing influence on her. Each one
had adopted their protégés' small group of friends, and went out and had
lengthy dinners and discussions with them. On the outside de Beauvoir's and
Sartre's lives seemed to go on as usual. Sartre kept his regular vacation
schedule: three weeks with Arlette in their house in the south of France; two
weeks with Wanda in Capri, Venice, or Florence; several weeks on a Greek
island with Helen, his Greek girl friend; and with de Beauvoir a month at their

suite at the Albergo Nazionale. In the summer of 1974 in Rome, de Beauvoir taped a series of conversations with Sartre. These conversations, later published in *Adieux: Farewell to Sartre,* were to be the couple's last work together. In the film *Simone de Beauvoir,* she made it clear that for her and for Sartre all had been said and done. But Sartre wanted to remain abreast, involved in what he perceived as a future revolution; and for that he put his trust in Pierre Victor. He wanted to co-author several projects with Victor and was dreaming of a new intellectual future with him. De Beauvoir felt betrayed; Victor found her unduly possessive. In 1978 the tensions grew worse. Victor had become more and more interested in his own roots, and he started to learn Hebrew and read the Cabbala. He organized a trip to Israel with Sartre and Arlette. He had prepared a text made of conversations with Sartre on the Israeli-Arab conflict, which he sent to the *Nouvel Observateur.* The editor found the text too weak, did not recognize Sartre's philosophy, and alerted Jacques-Laurent Bost, then a journalist for the paper, who immediately telephoned de Beauvoir. She was appalled and told Sartre bluntly that the text was unpublishable. Some witnesses of the scene said Sartre was very angry at this attack on Victor, some said that he did not care if the text was not published. It was not published.[18] There was no truce possible between the two clans: It was Victor, Arlette, and their friends against de Beauvoir, Sylvie, and the old guard of *Le Temps Modernes.*

Victor and de Beauvoir carefully avoided each other. Meanwhile Sartre was pursuing his idea to co-author with Victor *Power and Freedom,* eight hundred pages of taped conversations. Victor delivered the text in person to the newspaper *Le Nouvel Observateur.* De Beauvoir and her friends were alerted and all night long the editor received phone calls asking him not to publish the work. In the morning Sartre himself called requesting that his text be published; if not, he would publish it elsewhere. "I know that my friends have contacted you, but I also know that they are mistaken: They have not grasped the new direction of my philosophy, none of them, the Castor included."[19]

At Sartre's apartment, a violent quarrel exploded between Sartre and de Beauvoir. To Arlette he said later that he did not understand de Beauvoir. When she had read the text, she became furious, burst into tears, and flung the pages around the room. She did not want to listen to his explanation. The relationship between them remained strained. For de Beauvoir Sartre had betrayed Sartrian philosophy, but more than that he had betrayed their lifetime of mutual intellectual endeavor. "He though he had taken a step which I refused to take. He thought I was manipulating the whole thing. . . . He was blind, he no longer had a future, he knew he was condemned to die quite soon."[20]

In March 1980 for three consecutive weeks *Le Nouvel Observateur* ran conversations between Sartre and Pierre Victor. On March 20 Sartre was taken to the hospital. Eighteen months later de Beauvoir published *Adieux: Farewell to Sartre,* a meticulous description of Sartre's last years. She spoke of him in words that pulsed with the essence of life, words through which we feel time slipping away, strength ebbing, words that simply state the daily progression of age, illness, and the dark scandal of death. But it was also an attempt to recapture her unique position as Sartre's alter ego and the sole confidant of his philosophy.

Like so many of her books, *A Farewell to Sartre* was received with hostility by some. She spoke frankly without idealizing the human condition. This book takes its readers right to Sartre and enables them to follow, with a pang of anguish, the difficult path of the final years.

De Beauvoir wrote a dazzling biography of Sartre in her memoirs; she showed the powerful thinking, the teeming genius of the philosopher and the writer. In writing this book of decline, in having us present as twilight falls on Sartre's life, she expressed—as she had in *A Very Easy Death* and *The Coming of Age*—her rebellion in the face of the end of all things for a being who lived fully, who made a success of his life.

Sartre is a man, not a statue. His ideas become blurred and confused, he thinks mistakenly he has an appointment, he sits down at his work table and realizes that he has no ideas to convey. He who was independence itself now depends more and more on others. De Beauvoir explodes into anger when she discovers bottles of alcohol brought in by girl friends when alcohol is lethal for him! In order to transmit them, she gathers his thoughts on a thousand things, making herself nearly invisible, present only so as to pose a question or relaunch an idea. It is an act of love, of fellowship, and the heartrending need to hold on to a mind and its thoughts as it flickers and dims.

Some readers cried, Sacrilege! We must not be shown genius breaking down into dissolution. Yet it is the truth, it is daily life, it is inescapable, and it is all the more moving to find it set down in a clear style that lets life go by unadorned—which is not to say a style bereft of art.

When *Adieux: Farewell to Sartre* was released, another tempest erupted. The quarrels of the two Sartrian clans became public. Arlette Elkaim-Sartre felt personally attacked and answered Simone de Beauvoir in an open letter published by *Libération* on December 3, 1981. She reproached de Beauvoir for not having come to Sartre to discuss the controversial conversations with Benny Levy. Arlette published Sartre's *Les Carnets de la drôle de guerre* in 1982 and *Cahiers pour une morale* in 1983. Legally she alone was now in charge of

Sartre's posthumous publications. But de Beauvoir did not want the image of an undestructible couple to be tarnished. She published the letters Sartre had written to her.

LETTERS TO THE CASTOR AND A FEW OTHERS

*B*y publishing the letters, de Beauvoir destroyed the myth of a certain couple that served as a reference for many lovers determined to live their love outside the rules. The majority of their emulating admirers knew nothing of the operating instructions that made the relationship tick. The model couple disappeared, replaced by a couple inimitable in its singularity.

Free love is a carbon copy of marriage, minus the necessity to divorce in the event things do not work out. The de Beauvoir–Sartre relationship was something else entirely. They never lived together. For fifty years the shatter-proof kinship that linked them so closely served as their common household. For a long time they lived in hotels where each had a room, sometimes on different floors. De Beauvoir then lived in her studio, and Sartre lived with his mother before getting his own apartment. Their love, not free but freeing, detached them from dull chores.

If this sort of existence is not unusual for a man, it is surprising for a woman and unheard of for a couple whose particular understanding was broken only by death. Insofar as they were not held to or held down by anything, they pooled their two free selves for no reason other than the need they had for each other, enabling them to live in a sort of osmosis.

Decisions were made jointly, and "we almost develop our thoughts jointly."[21] Their style of life and their style of travel were de Beauvoir's contribution to the couple. Philosophical theories originated with Sartre, according to de Beauvoir, but thoroughly discussed, gone over in detail, modified and readopted, they bore de Beauvoir's mark all the same. By treating her as an equal whose thoughts and feelings were every bit as valid as his own, Sartre freed de Beauvoir from everything that in education and society hinders a woman's creativity. In living a defiant, revolutionary relationship with Sartre, de Beauvoir voluntarily rid herself of everything that was not herself, of everything that was not genuine, and at the same time enabled Sartre to find the security of relying entirely on her critical judgment and her total understanding.[22] In 1940 Sartre wrote the Castor, "You are like the solidity of my personality. Our relationship is the only thing that is success, perfection, and peace of mind."

There had been this stroke of good fortune, this lucky break: the meeting of two equally gifted writers who together created a relationship that suited them alone. The *Letters to the Castor* reveal, without minimizing the consequences, the effects of the overriding priority of their love above others, which de Beauvoir clarified further in an interview with Alice Schwarzer: "Third parties, in Sartre's life as well as in mine, always knew from the start about our relationship and that it would put pressure on any relationship either of us had with them. . . . So our relationship is not above criticism . . . because it has sometimes meant that we didn't behave very well toward other people."[23]

Voltaire seems to have played a role vis-à-vis Madame du Châtelet that was analagous to that of Sartre vis-à-vis Simone de Beauvoir. Through the intellectual, moral, and emotional understanding he established with her, he contributed to making her available to herself, permitted her to escape the anxieties, the depressing questions, the inferiority complex that always lies in wait for women. "Love, far from being a source of alienation, was the condition of her emancipation and even of her autonomy. Appreciated by the man she admired most, she could finally dare to be herself and devote herself to her own ambition," Elisabeth Badinter wrote in *Emilie . . . Emilie.*[24]

Although no one reproached Sartre for exercising his freedom, many women and men strongly criticized de Beauvoir. According to Elisabeth Badinter, it was necessary "that the image of the all-love-and-devotion mother cease to dominate the collective unconscious and that the opportunity be granted to express the virility which lies dormant in everyone. More openly androgynous than in the past, the women of today . . . because the period of active maternity is shorter and shorter, don't like to be defined as mothers . . . they want to be feminine and virile at the same time."[25]

The couple formed by de Beauvoir and Sartre was above all two people —writers, intellectuals, and creators—who set themselves apart by inventing and living out their own art of loving. De Beauvoir replied without reticence to a question from Alice Schwarzer: "In the first two or three years, sexual relations with Sartre were very important to me because I discovered sexuality with him. Later it declined in importance . . . it wasn't the most important thing."[26]

Sartre described de Beauvoir's attitude from the very start of their alliance: "She found it was better for her to have affairs with several men . . . in her life, and she didn't want her relationship with me to prevent her from having them. . . . She didn't think that sexual life should be exclusively defined by relations with one man." He knew and said as much that nothing shook his absolute certainty about being the most important when someone else came along: "With Simone de Beauvoir I considered that our relationship was such that even an affair with a man like Nelson Algren didn't concern me. Didn't take anything away from me."

"I," de Beauvoir said, "have always spoken my mind as far as I have been able. I have always followed my desires and my impulses. . . . If I had my memoirs to write over, I would give a frank and balanced account of my own sexuality. A truly sincere one, from a feminist point of view; I would like to tell women about my life in terms of my own sexuality because it is not just a personal matter but a political one too.

"I did not write about it at the time because I did not appreciate the importance of this question, or the need for personal honesty."[27]

Their love story was literature's most disconcerting. It was a revolutionary romance, for it relegated to the fringe all traditional morality, codes of conduct, customs, taboos, the bonds and boundaries, shackles and constraints, all the barriers constructed by popular wisdom to stand in the way of this redoubtable force that had the power to sweep everything else aside.[28]

In the Middle Ages people spoke of a magical love potion for which there was no remedy when love wrenched lovers away from the conventions of society, making them rebels in the sight of the king, the Church, and honor itself. No teller of tales, no noter of legends, no observant scribe, be it Béroul, Thomas, or Chrétien de Troyes, missed his mark in recounting this power which says no to laws both human and divine: "The first great romance in the West, Tristan and Isolde, is the story of a rebellion," and in the context of this, our century, it is the story of a freedom.

14

A Day in
May 1985

*I*t is 4:58. We wait two minutes before ringing the bell. We know that Simone de Beauvoir displays exemplary punctuality and that she has a demanding schedule of commitments. Five o'clock. Simone de Beauvoir opens the door herself and smiles. Lively blue eyes, an outstretched hand, very firm but delicate, For ten years she has greeted us with the same warm welcome, the same simplicity. She encourages and facilitates interviews. We are accustomed to the somewhat abrupt tone of her diction. In every one of her gestures, in each of her inflections there is eagerness and impatience. Her face has retained a classic oval, her complexion is fair. She looks frail. During all the years that Sartre's health deteriorated, as he slowly died, she too disintegrated physically. "I took too many tranquilizers and drank too much alcohol while he was ill, to try to hold on, not to break down. I was in very bad shape when he died. My lungs were congested, I could no longer walk. But they cured me at the hospital. They gave me fortifying medication and brought me back to life. When I returned home I was tired and weak, but I was walking, and since then I'm better."

She walks carefully, wrapped up in a cherry-red robe. A turban matches her outfit. She wears a large silver ring on her index finger.

In the white studio, violet, yellow, and green throw pillows lend three notes of color. The large picture windows of an artist's studio flood the room with light. Books climb the walls, up and up until they are out of reach, row upon row, interrupted by a bullfight poster, a memento of Spain. And everywhere eyes look out: Smiles and faces and fleeting moments of joy are captured in the photos that tell an unfolding story from their place on the wall. Souvenirs and memories envelop the room in a network of love and friendship. On a low table sits a petrified tree root, a strange sculpture that was a gift from Violette Leduc. Above the sofa is a small silhouette of Sartre, white on white. The studio still contains the presence of friends now gone. Refusing to take care of herself, Olga died at the beginning of the year. Some weeks earlier Simone de Beauvoir had told us, "Olga has been angry since *Letters to the Castor* came out. She thinks they shouldn't have been published. She's furious because Sartre wrote some unpleasant things about her, she thinks I thought the same way. It's the first time that she will not make up."

The meeting begins with the ritual question, "Should we have something to drink?" She walks slowly to the refrigerator, takes out three icy glasses and a cold bottle of whiskey. She pours the whiskey herself; sometimes she measures it carefully with a pewter jigger, sometimes not. There are boxes and small bottles of pills on the sofa within her reach, as well as an appointment book and her telephone. This is her favorite place, just where the two sofas meet at an angle to make a nook under the soft glow of a lamp designed by Giacometti. Across the coffee table we sit on two small armchairs, one purple, one green, with our notebooks on our laps. In the middle of the table, next to a bonsai tree, we place the tape recorder that is our constant companion. De Beauvoir treats it with friendly patience, allowing us time to change tapes and then picking up carefully the conversation where it left off. It is obvious that she is trusting us to record and keep these conversations for the future, for that distant, we think very distant, time when the rapid, eager voice will no longer be heard in the sunlit studio.

"Today we have accomplished some good work," she says as our two- or even three-hour sessions come to an end. She pours another jigger of whiskey in each of our three glasses and comments briskly on her most recent activities. She sets the appointment for our next working session, speaks of the work of such-and-such scholar who is writing about her. The word "work" seems to have some magic in it, it rings out with a special brilliance, a special tone. It has been her password to life; through work she has always been in gear, cruising at the right speed through the years, riding the right paths to efficiency and to fame.

"I have enjoyed everything as much as I could and as long as I could." She has stopped her long hikes reluctantly, but there is still the car, and she is always available to seek out gastronomic specialties. Every weekend Sylvie takes her on short excursions, and during school vacations the two of them travel Europe, taking as much pleasure in the scenery as they do in happening upon an exceptional restaurant or an unknown wine. To live abundantly and freely appears to be de Beauvoir's special venture.

Simone de Beauvoir is fascinated with the future. "Young girls must learn karate at school, we must support a Tour de France for women cyclists."

At seventy-seven, she is interested in adapting her books to film. She wrote a screenplay for *She Came to Stay*. She is involved with *Les Temps modernes,* and the magazine's editorial team meets in her home every Thursday. She receives countless visitors from throughout the world and carries on an enormous volume of correspondence.

At around five the doorbell rings, the janitor brings the mail—an enormous heap of letters and books fresh from the presses—everything is piled on the sofa, at her elbow, the world comes right into her studio, she measures with obvious delight the size of her correspondence.

Simone de Beauvoir has lost none of her fighting spirit. During her press conference on October 24, 1984, she criticized the government for not conducting its business in the manner of true socialism. Simone de Beauvoir has been received several times at the Elysée Palace, but she turned down the Legion of Honor that President Mitterrand wanted to award her. Small matter if she is not given immediate satisfaction by the minister of culture or if President Mitterrand does not reply to the letters bearing her signature and those of other feminists, letters that call attention to the children born of French mothers and Algerian fathers who are automatically taken from their mothers when the relationship founders. The bell rings again. In walks Hélène de Beauvoir, with laughing blue eyes, tanned and talkative: "I just heard a very fine radio program. You came across quite well. You and the others said intelligent things." She laughs and asks how the biography of Simone is coming along, then slides smoothly onto the subject of her childhood, summoning up the balcony above the Rotonde from which she watched wild scenes of Montparnasse. This café was the most fascinating of forbidden realms for both of them: "Do you remember one night when our parents were out, you were fourteen and I was twelve, you took me to the Rotonde for a *café crème*?"

"I don't remember that."

"Well, I remember it very well. The utter daring! The audacity!"[1]

Audacity. The daring of an adolescent, the daring of the written word, the daring of a life, the daring of a woman. It is with this word that revolutionaries blaze trails.

15

A Day in April 1986

On the first day of April 1986 Simone de Beauvoir had to be taken to the Cochin Hospital. Rumors spread rapidly: She had appendicitis, maybe a tumor in the colon, or it was a recurrence of pneumonia. Finally the news came that she was suffering from complications of pulmonary edema.

Hélène de Beauvoir had been invited to Stanford University in California for a show of her paintings. She was reluctant to leave Paris, but Simone, who was beginning to feel better, urged her to make the trip. She did, and the exhibition opened on April 10. Hélène's paintings and enlarged photographs of the de Beauvoir family hung on the walls of the president's office.

At 7 A.M. on Monday, April 14, the telephone rang and Sylvie Lebon told Hélène that Simone had just died. Hélène flew to France that day. De Beauvoir had been frail, but she had enjoyed life with such a passion that it was hard to imagine that she had lost her hold on the world that meant so much to her. "I have never met anyone in the whole of my life who was so well equipped for happiness as I was, or who labored so stubbornly to achieve it.

No sooner had I caught a glimpse of it than I concentrated upon nothing else."[1]

She had conquered love and fame, wealth and freedom with Sartre. "Together we set forth to explore the world. My trust in him was so complete that he supplied me with the sort of absolute unfailing security that I had once had from my parents, or from God . . . there was nothing left for me to wish, except that this state of triumphant bliss might continue unwaveringly forever."[2]

They had been so strongly bonded to one another that when Sartre died she wanted to lie down at his side and go with him "into that good night."

Now April 14 was slipping away, and April 15 was a heartbreaking anniversary. On that day in 1980 Sartre too had lain with pulmonary edema at the Broussais Hospital.

What memories flew through her mind on that April 14 as she lay dying? The anniversary of Sartre's death would not be hers to live. She passed away in the busy hours of the day, when people are at work, when the world is full of sounds and voices. It was the brink of spring, when life bursts into blossom and love is everywhere. De Beauvoir dreaded death. She was fourteen years old when she "felt with anguish the emptiness of heaven." Death became a terrifying threat. "I realized that I was condemned to death. I was alone in the house and did not attempt to control my despair: I screamed and tore at the red carpet. . . . It seemed to me impossible that I could live all through life with such horror gnawing at my heart. When the reckoning comes, I thought, when you're thirty or forty and you think it'll be tomorrow, how on earth can you bear the thought?"[3]

This concern with death flows through the entirety of her work. In *Memoirs of a Dutiful Daughter* the death of Zaza marks the turning point of Simone's life. "In *The Blood of Others* I had attempted to show death laying siege in vain to the fullness of life. In *Pyrrhus and Cinéas* I wanted to demonstrate that without it there could be neither projects nor values. In *Who Shall Die?* I intended to portray the fearful gulf that yawns between the living and the dead. When I began *All Men Are Mortal* in 1943, I envisaged it in the first place as a sort of protracted wandering around the central theme of death."[4] *A Very Easy Death* is the most pathetic meditation on the subject. "There is no such thing as a natural death: nothing that happens to a man is ever natural since his presence calls the world into question. All men must die: but for every man his death is an accident and, even if he knows it and consents to it, an unjustifiable violation."[5]

The funeral of Sartre took place on April 19, 1980. At his grave reporters photographed Simone de Beauvoir, supported by friends, devastated with grief, as she dropped a rose into the open grave in a pathetic farewell. Six years later, on April 19, 1986, five thousand people gathered for her funeral. For two hours traffic was interrupted as the funeral procession moved along the boulevard Montparnasse. Everyone could not help but wonder at the coincidence: Sartre and de Beauvoir buried on the same date. Behind the slow-moving hearse came women bearing sprays, wreaths, banners sent by feminist groups from five continents. Some women sang a feminist hymn composed in 1971 to the music of a song of the Russian fighters of World War II.

> *Arise, enslaved women,*
> *Break your shackles.*

French political leaders from all parties, celebrities, people from all movements for human rights, from all the movements against racism, sexism, discrimination, and injustice, people who had read de Beauvoir's books and admired her as a writer, all came. The funeral procession stopped at the gates to the Montparnasse cemetery, the family and close friends were allowed in, and the gates clanged shut to keep the crowd out. The grave that had received the ashes of Sartre was open, de Beauvoir was lowered into it, her sister dropped a rose on her coffin. Claude Lauzmann read from her works and ended with the heartbreaking words of Simone's adieu to Sartre. "His death separates us. My death will not reunite us."[6]

The gates were thrown open, and within seconds the gravesite had become a mountain of blossoms. Flowers overflowed into the pathways and tumbled onto the neighboring graves in a springlike celebration of the two writers.

When you visit the Montparnasse cemetery, the guard will indicate a grave with a plain headstone on which you will read:

> *Jean-Paul Sartre 1905–1980*
> *Simone de Beauvoir 1908–1986*

On April 21, two days after the funeral, a preface signed by de Beauvoir came off the press. The preface reveals a concern that had occupied her in her final days, a cause she still wanted to fight for. The three-page essay deals with love, the love of an American art dealer in his fifties for a young Arab worker who makes a living by digging trenches for the telephone company in the streets of Paris.

Once, in an article written for *McCall's,* she had equated love with a revolutionary force. Here she takes up the same topic and presents it in disturbing terms. "Can a love be strong enough to overcome the conflicts of civilizations and cultures? This is the question asked in a heartbreaking manner in this book which blends the audacity of crude realism with a romantic touch seldom to be found today."[7]

Simone de Beauvoir summarizes the autobiography. Alan is the son of Polish immigrants to the United States; he grew up in the Middle West, then roamed from Africa to India, a man from nowhere. "His homosexuality intensifies his loneliness, he describes the rootlessness created by his homosexuality, the distress at finding himself different." He is an expatriate living in Paris, "he criticizes America bitterly but cannot adjust himself to Europe." Mihloud, the young Arab, has also had great difficulties in adapting to the French way of life. He comes from a small Moroccan village, his father has repudiated his mother and denied him the right to bear his name. Yet his own culture is strong enough to pit him against all the values of his American lover. The author's name is absent from the book, for his heirs would not give their permission to print it. In a footnote de Beauvoir writes, "Handsome, disenchanted, but with a great sense of humor, the author, shortly after having finished this manuscript which he so much wished to see published, died of a disease little known in France at that time, AIDS."[8]

Why did de Beauvoir choose to lend to this book by an anonymous American the support of her worldwide renown?

In her final preface she wrote of a tormented, rootless homosexual who "to feel anchored in this world has a pathetic need for a definitive and absolute passion. The failure of his affair with Mihloud is more than the failure of a love, it is the breakdown of his whole being." Once more de Beauvoir was defending the right of an individual to be himself, meditating as she had in *The Second Sex* on the hardships created by cultures. At the end of her life she could still argue that man had to be reinvented.

BIBLIOGRAPHY

Works of Simone de Beauvoir

L'Invitée (novel). Paris: Gallimard, 1943.
She Came to Stay. Cleveland: World Publishing, 1954.

Pyrrhus et Cinéas (essay). Paris: Gallimard, 1944.
"Pyrrhus and Cineas" selections, *Partisan Review* III:3 (1946), pp. 430–437.

Le Sang des autres (novel). Paris: Gallimard, 1945.
The Blood of Others. New York: Knopf, 1948.

Les Bouches inutiles (play). Paris: Gallimard, 1945.
Who Shall Die? Florissant, Missouri: River Press, 1983.

Tous les hommes sont mortels (novel). Paris: Gallimard, 1946.
All Men Are Mortal. Cleveland: World Publishing, 1955.

Pour une morale de l'ambiguité (essay). Paris: Gallimard, 1947.
The Ethics of Ambiguity. New York: Philosophical Library, 1948.

L'Existentialisme et la sagesse des nations (collected essays). Paris: Nagel, 1948.

L'Amérique au jour le jour (essay). Paris: Mohrien, 1948.
America Day by Day. New York: Grove Press, 1953.

Le Deuxième Sexe (essay). Paris: Gallimard, 1949.
The Second Sex. New York: Knopf, 1953.

Les Mandarins (novel). Paris: Gallimard, 1954.
The Mandarins. Cleveland: World Publishing, 1956.

Privilèges (essays: "Faut-il brûler Sade?" "La Pensée de droite aujourd'hui," "Merleau-Ponty et le pseudo-sartrisme"). Paris: Gallimard, 1955.
Must We Burn Sade? New York: Grove Press, 1955.

La Longue Marche (essay). Paris: Gallimard, 1957.
The Long March. Cleveland: World Publishing, 1958.

Mémoires d'une jeune fille rangée (memoirs, 1908–1929). Paris: Gallimard, 1958.
Memoirs of a Dutiful Daughter. Cleveland: World Publishing, 1959.

"Brigitte Bardot and the Lolita Syndrome" (article). *Esquire,* August 1959.

La Force de l'age (memoirs, 1929–1944). Paris: Gallimard, 1960.
The Prime of Life. Cleveland: World Publishing, 1962.

Djamila Boupacha (co-author, Gisèle Halimi). Paris: Gallimard, 1962.

Djamila Boupacha. New York: Macmillan, 1962.

La Force des choses (memoirs, 1944–1962). Paris: Gallimard, 1963.
Force of Circumstance. New York: Putnam, 1965.

"What Love Is—and Isn't" (article). *McCall's,* August 1967.

Une mort très douce (narrative). Paris: Gallimard, 1964.
A Very Easy Death. New York: Putnam, 1966.

Les Belles Images (novel). Paris: Gallimard, 1966.
Les Belles Images. New York: Putnam, 1968.

La Femme rompue (stories). Paris: Gallimard, 1968.
The Woman Destroyed. New York: Putnam, 1969.

La Vieillesse (essay). Paris: Gallimard, 1970.
The Coming of Age. New York: Putnam, 1972.

Tout compte fait (memoirs, 1962–1972). Paris: Gallimard, 1972.
All Said and Done. New York: Putnam, 1974.

La Promenade des vieux (commentary). Short film by Marianne Ahrne and Pepo Angel, 1975.

Les Ecrits de Simone de Beauvoir (unpublished writings). Paris: Gallimard, 1979.

Simone de Beauvoir (dialogue). Film by Malka Ribowska and Josée Dayan, Paris, Gallimard, 1979.

Quand prime le spirituel (stories). Paris: Gallimard, 1980.
When Things of the Spirit Come First. New York: Pantheon, 1982.

La Cérémonie des adieux (essay). Paris: Gallimard, 1981.
Adieux: A Farewell to Sartre. New York: Pantheon, 1984.

Books About Simone de Beauvoir

Alcantara, Maria Beatriz de, *La Révolte positive de Simone de Beauvoir.* Fortaleza: Ceara, 1973.

Armogathe, Daniel, *"Le Deuxième Sexe": Simone de Beauvoir.* Paris: Hatier, 1977.

Ascher, Carole, *Simone de Beauvoir: A Life of Freedom.* Boston: Beacon Press, 1981.

Audet, Jean R., *Simone de Beauvoir face à la mort.* Lausanne: L'Age d'Homme, 1979.

Berghe, Christian Louis van der, *Dictionnaire des idées: Simone de Beauvoir.* Paris and The Hague: Mouton, 1967.

Bieber, Konrad, *Simone de Beauvoir.* Boston: Twayne, 1975.

Cayron, Claire, *La Nature chez Simone de Beauvoir.* Paris: Gallimard, 1973.

Cottrell, Robert D., *Simone de Beauvoir.* New York: Ungar, 1975.

Descubes, Madeleine, *Connaître Simone de Beauvoir.* Paris: Resma, 1976.

Francis, Claude, and Jeanine Niepce, *Simone de Beauvoir et le cours du monde.* Paris: Klincksieck, 1978.

Francis, Claude, and Fernande Gontier, *Les Ecrits de Simone de Beauvoir.* Paris: Gallimard, 1979.

Gagnebin, Laurent, *Simone de Beauvoir ou le refus de l'indifférence.* Preface by Simone de Beauvoir. Paris: Editions Fischbacher, 1968.

Gennari, Geneviève, *Simone de Beauvoir.* Paris: Editions Universitaires, 1959.

Henry, A. M., *Simone de Beauvoir ou l'échec d'une chrétienté.* Paris: Fayard, 1961.

Hourdin, G., *Simone de Beauvoir et la liberté.* Paris: Cerf, 1962.

Jaccard, A. C., *Simone de Beauvoir.* Zurich: Juris Verlag, 1968.

Jeanson, Francis, *Simone de Beauvoir ou l'entreprise de vivre.* With two conversations with Simone de Beauvoir. Paris: Le Seuil, 1966.

Julienne-Caffié, Serge, *Simone de Beauvoir.* Paris: Gallimard, 1966. ("Bibliothèque idéale" series.)

Keefe, Terri, *Simone de Beauvoir: A Study of Her Writings.* Totowa, New Jersey: Barnes & Noble, 1983.

Lasocki, Anne-Marie, *Simone de Beauvoir ou l'entreprise d'écrire.* The Hague: Nijhoff, 1971.

Leighton, Janet, *Simone de Beauvoir on Women.* New Jersey: Associated University Presses, 1975.

Lilar, Simone, *Le Malentendu du "Deuxième Sexe."* Paris: Presses Universitaires de France, 1969.

Madsen, Axel, *Hearts and Minds.* New York: Morrow, 1977.

Marks, Elaine, *Simone de Beauvoir: Encounters with Death.* Rutgers University Press, 1973.

Moubachir, Chantal, *Simone de Beauvoir ou le souci de la différence.* Paris: Pierre Seghers, 1972. ("Philosophes de tous les temps" series.)

Romero, C. Z., *Simone de Beauvoir.* Hamburg: Rowohlt, 1978.

Schwarzer, Alice, *Simone de Beauvoir aujourd'hui.* Six conversations. Paris: Mercure de France, 1983. (*After "The Second Sex": Conversations with Simone de Beauvoir.* Translated by Marianne Howarth. Pantheon Books, 1984.)

Schmalenberg, E., *Das Todesverständnis bei Simone de Beauvoir.* Berlin: De Gruyter, 1972.

Wasmund, D., *Der "Skandal" der Simone de Beauvoir.* Munich: Mac Hüber, 1963.

Whitmarsh, A., *Simone de Beauvoir and the Limits of Commitment.* London: Cambridge University Press, 1981.

Zéphir, Jacques, *Le Néo-feminisme de Simone de Beauvoir.* Paris: Denoël-Gouthier, 1982.

Books Devoted in Part to Simone de Beauvoir

Barnes, H. E., *The Literature of Possibility.* University of Nebraska Press, 1959.

Burnier, Michel Antoine, *Les Existentialistes et la politique.* Paris: Gallimard, 1955.

Fitch, B. T., *Le Sentiment de l'étrangeté chez Malraux, Sartre, Camus, Simone de Beauvoir.* Paris: Minard, 1964.

Merleau-Ponty, Maurice, *Sens et non-sens.* Paris: Nagel, 1968.

Nahas, Hélène, *La femme dans la littérature existentielle.* Paris: Presses Universitaires de France, 1957.

Ophir, Anne, *Regards féminins.* Preface by Simone de Beauvoir. Paris: Denoël-Gonthier, 1975.

Reck, R. D., *Literature and Responsibility.* Louisiana State University Press, 1969.

Other Sources

Sartre, Jean-Paul, complete works.

Contat, Michel, and Michel Rybalka, *Les Ecrits de Sartre.* Paris: Gallimard, 1970.

SOURCE NOTES

Abbreviations of Titles of Frequently Cited Works

MDD: *Memoirs of a Dutiful Daughter* (translated by James Kirkup), Harper Colophon Books, 1974.

POL: *The Prime of Life* (translated by Peter Green), Penguin Books, 1984.

FOC: *Force of Circumstance* (translated by Richard Howard), Penguin Books, 1985.

All Said: All Said and Done (translated by Patrick O'Brian), Penguin Books, 1984.

SS: *The Second Sex* (translated by H. M. Parshley), Penguin Books, 1972.

VED: *A Very Easy Death* (translated by Patrick O'Brian), Pantheon Books, 1985.

Adieux: Adieux: A Farewell to Sartre and *Conversations with Jean-Paul Sartre* (translated by Patrick O'Brian), Pantheon Books, 1985.

America: America Day by Day, Grove Press, 1953.

Ecrits: Les Ecrits de Simone de Beauvoir, Gallimard, 1979.

Letters: Jean-Paul Sartre, *Lettres au Castor et à quelques autres,* Gallimard, 1983.

Carnets: Jean-Paul Sartre, *Les Carnets de la drôle de guerre,* Gallimard, 1983.

Schwarzer: Alice Schwarzer, *After "The Second Sex": Conversations with Simone de Beauvoir* (translated by Marianne Howarth), Pantheon Books, 1984.

Isolde's Gesture
  1. *Adieux,* p. 125.
  2. MDD, p. 345.
  3. *Adieux,* p. 127.
  4. POL, p. 245.
  5. POL, p. 245.
  6. Catherine Chaîne, "Sartre et les femmes," *Le Nouvel Observateur,* January 31, 1977.
  7. VED, p. 105.
  8. *America,* p. 75.
  9. FOC, p. 648.

Chapter 1. The Child and the Others

The Verdun Banker's Bankruptcy

1. De Beauvoir: "No, absolutely not, never any noises" (September 17, 1985). This recollection was contradicted by her sister Hélène and by our research in the 14th arrondissement archives.

2. De Beauvoir: "This is totally false. You say this drama happened in 1909; I was already one year old! I was very happy. My childhood was never affected by this drama. Well, maybe indirectly since it forced me to go to the University and work for a living. Ostracized? No . . . yes, in Verdun. My grandfather was living a very comfortable life in Verdun, that's all—I think he even had a car and horses, too —but they did not go to the beach or to Paris: They were provincial bourgeoisie." F and G: "But your parents met at Houlgate, which was one of the fashionable resorts? And your grandfather's lawyer had been a former minister of justice?" De Beauvoir: "Anyhow, I was not affected by this drama. I had a very happy childhood." We do not deny that Simone's childhood was a happy one, but the facts show that the background in which she grew up was not that of an average provincial bourgeois family. The bankruptcy issue was so sensitive that when *Memoirs of a Dutiful Daughter* was published, Françoise de Beauvoir was upset because Simone mentioned her grandfather's ruin and her father's bankruptcy (September 27, 1985).

3. *L'Illustration,* July 1898.

The Bertrand de Beauvoirs

4. De Beauvoir wrote in MDD that the house and land "he inherited among other properties." She corrected it but was not sure: "No, he bought it with his wife's money."

5. MDD, p. 32.

The Scandal

6. VED, p. 36.

7. *Le Petit Verdunois,* July 30, 1910.

8. *Le Courrier de la Meuse,* July 27, 1910.

9. Simone recalled vividly her grandparents' apartment in the slums around the Montparnasse train station (September 17, 1985), but she did not mention it in MDD.

10. De Beauvoir: "No one ever mentioned the bankruptcy. We, the Beauvoirs, were living a very comfortable life. We still had the large apartment on the boulevard Raspail" (September 17, 1985). In May 1983, when asked to describe it: "I shared one bedroom with the maid, my sister slept in the poorly ventilated corridor. There was a dining room and a kitchen. You had to cross the living room to go into my parents' bedroom. My father's office was a very dark room at the end of

the corridor." "We never had any children's parties. We lived a very thrifty life, my father was totally ruined" (September 20, 1985). MDD, p. 47.

11. De Beauvoir denied this fact, which she had stated in VED, p. 34.

12. De Beauvoir: "He was faithful for at least ten, even fifteen years. He had a few women from the Café de Versailles. It is not the same to have a woman at two o'clock in the morning at the Café de Versailles *(baiser une femme à deux heures du matin),* it is not the same as to abandon his wife" (September 23, 1985).

13. De Beauvoir: "My mother never reacted with anger" (September 17, 1985). See MDD, p. 37. In several interviews she had told us she found her mother's constant shouting *(criailleries)* hard to take.

Harlequin's Cloak

14. De Beauvoir: "He did not coach her, he simply taught her how to perform on a stage. That's all. He did not teach her how to apply makeup, he taught her how to act, simply by taking her with him onstage" (September 17, 1985).

15. De Beauvoir: "No, no, my father never recited plays for us. Sometimes when we had company he would recite comic monologues, which were very popular in those days" (September 17, 1985). See MDD, pp. 35–36 and 106–107.

16. De Beauvoir: "I never recited poems. I have never recited anything. My father never taught me to recite. Not at all, not at all." See MDD, p. 36: "He taught me to read them aloud, putting in the expression."

17. See note 10 above.

18. De Beauvoir: "We did not read *Comœdia* at home. My father glanced through it, and my parents were not interested in backstage gossip" (September 17, 1985). See MDD, p. 35.

19. MDD, p. 277.

The Vines of Montparnasse

20. MDD, p. 54.

21. MDD, p. 13.

22. MDD, p. 18.

23. MDD, p. 17.

24. De Beauvoir: "He always made a scene when asked for money. . . . One day he told a friend that he was a failure. He despised work, thrift, a dutiful life because he thought of himself as an aristocrat, an artist and all that" (September 20, 1985).

25. De Beauvoir: "Tonton Gaston and Tante Marguerite had just one maid in Paris. . . . At La Grillère, Madeleine and Robert had private tutors. Yes, there were several servants, but not real servants, they were men who worked in the fields and in the vegetable gardens" (September 20, 1985). See MDD, p. 77.

26. VED p. 35.

1914–1918

27. De Beauvoir: "The second one, in a book given by Bon Papa" (September 17, 1985).

28. De Beauvoir: "I was just like everybody else. I was never difficult" (September 15, 1985). See MDD, pp. 59, 60: "I even tended to look upon myself at least from the childhood level as the one and only."

29. MDD, p. 22, and interviews.

30. MDD, p. 67.

31. MDD, p. 69.

32. MDD, p. 70.

33. MDD, p. 70.

34. MDD, p. 61.

35. MDD, p. 65.

36. MDD, p. 62.

37. MDD, p. 102.

38. *When Things of the Spirit Come First*, p. 207.

39. MDD, p. 66.

40. MDD, p. 47.

The Alchemist's Dream

41. MDD, p. 64.

42. De Beauvoir: "The cause was not the wounded but the family quarrels" (September 17, 1985).

43. MDD, p. 65.

44. MDD, p. 9.

45. MDD, p. 10.

ADDITIONAL SOURCES, CHAPTER 1
Archives of the Legion of Honor
Archives of the Mairie of the 14th arrondissement
La Revue d'Histoire du XIVe arrondissement
Le Bottin mondain
Le Courrier de la Meuse (1907, 1908, 1909, 1910)
Le Courrier libéral (1908)
Comœdia
Dictionnaire historique de la ville de Paris
L'Illustration
Le Gaulois
Le Petit verdunois (1910)
L'Union verdunoise (1909–1910)
Revue Montparnasse (1911–1931)

Aressy, Lucien, *Nuits et ennui de Montparnasse.* Paris: Jouve, 1944.

Bourquin-Cussenot, *Histoire d'un quartier de Paris.* Chez l'auteur, 1963.

Braudel, Fernand, and Ernest La Brousse, *Histoire économique et sociale de la France,* vol. IV, archives 1880–1914. Paris: P.U.F., 1979.

Crespelle, Jean-Paul, *La Vie quotidienne á Montparnasse à la belle époque, 1905–1930.* Paris: Hachette, 1976.

Chapsal, Madeleine, *Les Ecrivains en personne.* Paris: Julliard, 1930.

Jeanson, Francis, *Simone de Beauvoir ou l'entreprise de vivre.* Paris: Le Seuil, 1966.

Lauwick, Hervé, "Les Cafés de Montparnasse: Le Dôme," in *Le Rire,* 1919.

Pillement, Georges, "Hôtels et folies de Montparnasse," in *Revue de l'Alliance Française,* June 1947.

Salmon, André, *Souvenir sans fin.* Paris: Gallimard, 1961.

CHAPTER 2. 71 RUE DE RENNES

"The Darkest Days"

1. MDD, p. 66.

2. MDD, p. 55.

3. De Beauvoir: "My father's office [which was the room the family used as the living room] faced the wall of the firehouse, and so did the kitchen; the rest of the apartment overlooked the rue de Rennes" (September 17, 1985).

4. Letter to Algren, Folder G.

5. Simone de Beauvoir (May 19, 1984).

6. VED, p. 37.

7. Edmond Rostand, *Cyrano de Bergerac.*

8. MDD, p. 107.

9. MDD, p. 107.

10. MDD, p. 107.

11. MDD, p. 102, and interviews with Simone de Beauvoir.

12. MDD, pp. 176–177, and interviews with Simone de Beauvoir.

Meyrignac

13. De Beauvoir: "We read the indecent couplets in the songbooks" (September 17, 1985).

14. MDD, p. 124.

Elisabeth L.

15. MDD, pp. 94–95.

16. MDD, p. 137.

17. MDD, p. 58.

18. MDD, p. 58.

19. MDD, pp. 58–59.

20. MDD, pp. 58–59.

21. MDD, p. 123.

22. MDD, p. 122.

23. MDD, p. 138.

"My Father Let Me Down"
24. MDD, p. 121.

25. SS, vol. II, p. 199 (Gallimard, Edition Idées, 1975).

26. MDD, p. 141.

27. De Beauvoir: "Above all freedom. I wanted to be free, free to live my life the way I wanted."
F and G: "Is it what you and Sartre call authenticity? To live your life the way you want and assume all your acts, whatever they might be?"
De Beauvoir: "Yes" (September 20, 1985).

1925
28. MDD, p. 171.

"Everything in My Life Must Serve a Purpose"
29. Chrétien de Troyes, *Yvain ou le chevalier au Lion,* edited by Bédier.

30. Sartre, in jest, called Robert Garric "her love" in *Letters,* vol. I, and this led some critics to assume that Garric was her first lover. De Beauvoir denied having had any sexual involvement before Sartre. "I discovered my sexuality with Sartre, it lasted for two or three years, then it was not very important." Interview and Schwarzer, p. 113.

31. MDD, p. 225; see also p. 166.

32. MDD, p. 190.

33. Albistur and Armogathe, *Histoire du féminisme français,* p. 385.

34. SS, p. 295.

35. MDD, p. 191.

36. MDD, p. 188.

Jacques Champigneulles and Surrealism
37. Maurice Nadeau, *Histoire du surréalisme.* p. 107.

38. Maxime Alexandre, *Mémoires d'un surréaliste.* p. 42.

ADDITIONAL SOURCES, CHAPTER 2
La Nouvelle Eve
La Revue française
Le Matin
Albistur, Maïté, and Daniel Armogathe, *Histoire du féminisme français du Moyen Age à nos jours.* Paris: Des Femmes, 1977.

Aragon, Louis, *Anicet ou le panorama.* Paris: Gallimard, 1921.

Aragon, Louis, *Le Paysan de Paris.* Paris: Gallimard, 1978.

Bardette, Gilles, and Michel Carassou, *Paris Gay 1925.* Paris: Presses de la Renaissance, 1964.

Beach, Sylvia, *Shakespeare & Co.* New York: Harcourt Brace Jovanovich, 1959.

Chastenet, Jacques, *Histoire de la Troisième République.* Paris: Hachette, 1957–1963.

Cocteau, Jean, *Journal.* Paris: Gallimard, 1983.

Desanti, Dominique, *La Femme au temps des années folles.* Paris: Stock, 1984.

Flanner, Janet, *Letters from Paris.* New York: Viking Press, 1981.

Guiral, Pierre, and Guy Thuillier, *La Vie quotidienne des professeurs de 1870 à 1940.* Paris: Hachette, 1982.

Thibaudet, Albert, *La République des professeurs.* Paris: Sauret, 1973.

Touchard, Jean, *La Gauche en France depuis 1900.* Paris: Le Seuil, 1977.

CHAPTER 3. THE AGE OF FRIENDSHIP

Students of the Right

1. De Beauvoir denied that she was pretty or attractive: She insisted that she was very plain and that everybody who knew her would say that she was homely. This contradicts MDD, pp. 295–296, and Maurice de Gandillac's recollection. "I was never a star, never" (September 24, 1985).

2. MDD, p. 245.

3. MDD, p. 246.

4. *Le Figaro littéraire,* December 6, 1947.

5. MDD, p. 247.

6. MDD, p. 248.

7. MDD, p. 329.

8. MDD, p. 256.

9. MDD, p. 256.

10. MDD, pp. 260, 264.

11. MDD, p. 261.

12. MDD, p. 265.

13. MDD, p. 244.

Students of the Left

14. MDD, p. 238.

15. MDD, p. 237.

16. MDD, p. 237.

17. De Beauvoir: "My mother used to check the contents of my bag; that is how she found *La Nuit kurde* of J. R. Bloch and many others." MDD p. 226.

18. Raymond Aron, *Mémoires,* pp. 41–42.

One Deceptive Evening

19. De Beauvoir: "Jacques was affectionate, kind. He introduced me to painting and told me which books to read. Thanks to him I read contemporary literature. In my loneliness he was the one and only, but I did not see him often." She denied that Jacques was expected to propose (September 23, 1985). See MDD, pp. 268–270.

The Bars

20. MDD, p. 273. De Beauvoir denied that she thought of herself as a young writer in quest of material.
F and G: "Why did you go to the bars?"
De Beauvoir: "It was sheer debauchery."
F and G: "So the writer was not there."
De Beauvoir: "No, never. I observed, I lived. I was not in quest of the Adventure either. I was there, that was all" (September 23, 1985).
F and G: "How did you get the money?"
De Beauvoir: "Once in a while I stole some, but my mother used to count her pennies. It was not easy, but I managed anyhow" (September 20, 1985).

Living Dangerously

21. MDD, p. 273.

Stépha

22. MDD, p. 277.
23. MDD, p. 307.
24. MDD, p. 307.
25. MDD, pp. 307–308.

The Castor

26. MDD, p. 323.
27. MDD, p. 322. James Kirkup, the translator of MDD, wrote, "You must be a pathological case"; the French text reads, "Ou vous êtes psychologue," which means "a psychologist."
28. MDD, pp. 314, 313.
29. MDD, pp. 324–325.
30. MDD, p. 326.

Love and Death

31. MDD, p. 332.
32. *Letters*, p. 54.
33. De Beauvoir gave us all the details, the names and the sequence of events, which

differ from the account in MDD. She told us that she was happy to be able to give the public the real version of the events that led to Zaza's death.

ADDITIONAL SOURCES, CHAPTER 3

Alexandre, Maxime, *Mémoires d'un surréaliste.* Paris: La Jeune Parque, 1968.

Aron, Raymond, *Mémoires.* Paris: Julliard, 1983.

Aron, Raymond, *Le Spectateur engagé.* Paris: Julliard, 1981.

Aron, Raymond, *D'une sainte famille à l'autre.* Paris: Gallimard, 1969.

Archives of the Jacques Doucet Library.

Brassaï, *The Secret Paris of the Thirties.* New York: Pantheon Books, 1976.

Capdevielle, Jacques, et al., *La France de gauche vote à droite.* Paris: Fondation des Sciences Politiques, 1981.

Estier, Claude, *La Gauche hebdomadaire 1914–1962.* Paris: Armand Colin, 1962.

Gide, André, *Journal 1889–1939.* Paris: Gallimard, 1948.

Kriegel, Annie, *Aux origines du communisme français, 1914–1940.* (2 vols.) Paris: Mouton, 1964.

Lefranc, Georges, *Les Gauches en France, 1789–1972.* Paris: Payot, 1973.

Maitron, J., *Histoire du mouvement anarchiste en France, des origines à nos jours.* (2 vols.) Paris: Maspero, 1975.

Marcel, Jean, *Autobiographie du surréalisme.* Paris: Le Seuil, 1978.

Nadeau, Maurice, *Histoire du surréalisme.* Paris: Le Seuil, 1984.

Nizan, Paul, *Les Chiens de garde.* Paris: Gallimard, 1934.

Nizan, Paul, *La Conspiration.* Paris: Gallimard, 1938.

Nizan, Henriette, and Annie Cohen-Solal, *Paul Nizan.* Paris: Grasset, 1980.

CHAPTER 4. JEAN-PAUL SARTRE

Jean-Paul

1. De Beauvoir: "I did not give a damn about my family. As far as I was concerned, they had not the slightest interest. I felt rejected only by my father. Family did not exist for me" (September 23, 1985). See MDD and VED.

2. MDD, pp. 319, 320.

3. MDD, p. 323.

4. De Beauvoir: "How could it be? I looked so homely." See note 1 in Chapter 3.

5. MDD, p. 325.

6. MDD, p. 326.

7. MDD, p. 339. According to de Beauvoir, Sartre meant: "From now on Maheu is no longer in charge. I'll take you out to play pinball." She insisted that the simple statement in her memoirs, "I'll take you under my wing," had been misunderstood. "No, he did not offer to help me. This is the recurring legend that Sartre is the one who formed me completely." She asked us not to quote his famous words, *Je vous prends en main.*

8. MDD, p. 340.

9. Annie Cohen-Solal, *Sartre,* p. 116.

10. POL, pp. 13–14.

The Sartres and the Schweitzers

11. Sartre, *Les Mots,* pp. 23, 31, 48, 132, 150.

12. Bibliothèque Nationale.

13. Archives of the Legion of Honor.

14. *Adieux,* p. 186.

15. Annie Cohen-Solal, *Paul Nizan,* pp. 12–44.

16. Ibid.

17. *Le Magazine littéraire* 59, p. 29.

18. Raymond Aron, *Mémoires,* pp. 35–36.

19. De Beauvoir: "Maybe he [Sartre] said that to Aron to tease him. But I am convinced Sartre never said it. Aron must have condensed several conversations. Sartre never indulged in long speeches like this one" (September 24, 1985).

20. *Carnets,* p. 97.

21. *Adieux,* pp. 189–190.

22. *Carnets,* pp. 297–298.

23. *Letters,* p. 14. Letter addressed to Simone Jollivet.

24. De Beauvoir: "When Sartre had some money and wanted to go to Toulouse, if Simone said, 'No, don't come,' he would send her raging letters" (September 20, 1985). Catherine Chaîne, "Sartre et les femmes," *Le Nouvel Observateur,* January 31, 1977, p. 68.

25. *Carnets,* p. 98.

26. *Carnets,* p. 325.

27. Interviews with former Rouen students. De Beauvoir: "No, no, I never dazzled anyone" (September 20, 1985). She consistently rejected the notion that people found her "elegant" or "dazzling."

28. Interview and POL, pp. 46–47.

29. Sartre, *Les Mots,* p. 129.

30. MDD, p. 341.

The Carousel Oath

31. MDD, p. 345.

32. POL, p. 27.

33. Chaîne, "Sartre et les femmes," and *Carnets,* p. 339.

34. POL, p. 22, and Chaîne, ibid.

35. *Carnets,* p. 99.

36. Chaîne, "Sartre et les femmes," and interview.

37. POL, p. 28.

38. *Carnets,* pp. 310–333.

39. *Carnets,* p. 112.

40. *Carnets,* p. 331.

41. POL, p. 64.

42. POL, p. 65.

The Other Simone

43. De Beauvoir: "Sartre was no longer having an affair with her, but he did go to bed with her once in a while. It was simply a sort of friendship to which Sartre added a slight touch of magic." De Beauvoir insisted on the difference between a liaison and casual sexual encounters; she emphasized the same distinction where her father was concerned (September 20 and September 17, 1985). See POL, pp. 57–65.

44. De Beauvoir: "No, I was not jealous. . . . Yes, I had one or two fits of jealousy. She had never written anything, she was a second-rate actress, very cold. She did not count very much for Sartre. . . . What got on my nerves is that she paid no attention to me." In her letters to Nelson Algren, de Beauvoir referred to her as "the drunken woman"; she mentioned her fifteen times. In 1950 she wrote Algren, "The drunken woman Toulouse who wanted to sleep with Genet and offered her love to Sartre is now undergoing deintoxication, she said to Sartre: 'In a few years I'll be beautiful again and you'll have to love me.'"

45. Clément Borgal, *Metteurs-en-scènes,* pp. 126–127.

46. POL, p. 70.

47. POL, p. 69.

48. POL, p. 74.

"A We That Is Not Two Yous"

49. *Carnets,* pp. 328–347.

50. Chaîne, "Sartre et les femmes."

51. *Letters,* passim.

52. *Carnets,* p. 331; see also pp. 328–331.

53. Madeleine Gobeil, "Sartre," *Vogue* (France), July 1966.

54. Chaîne, "Sartre et les femmes," p. 85, and MDD, p. 465.

55. Aron, *Mémoires,* pp. 35–38.

56. POL, p. 25, and interview.

57. Aron, *Mémoires,* pp. 45–46.

58. De Beauvoir: "For sure this one wanted only glory. . . . Neither Sartre nor I wanted fame and glory, all we wanted was to write, that's all" (September 20, 1985). See *Carnets,* pp. 101–105.

59. POL, p. 53.

60. De Beauvoir: "Truly I made the best of what we could afford. If I had been offered the Ritz I would have accepted gladly."

61. POL, p. 71.

62. POL, p. 73.

ADDITIONAL SOURCES, CHAPTER 4
Archives of the Bibliothèque Nationale
Archives of the Legion of Honor
Archives of the Ecole Normale Supérieure
Cacerès, Benigno, *Histoire de l'éducation populaire.* Paris: Le Seuil, 1964.
Cohen-Solal, Annie, *Sartre.* Paris: Gallimard, 1985.
Gontard, Maurice, *L'Oeuvre scolaire de la IIIe République.* Paris: Institut Pédagogique National, 1965.
Noguères, Henri, *La Vie quotidienne au temps du Front Populaire.* Paris: Hachette, 1977.
Sauvy, Alfred, *Histoire économique de la France entre les deux guerres.* Paris: Fayard, 1967.
Zay, Jean, *Souvenirs et solitude.* Paris: Julliard, 1948.

CHAPTER 5. THE TEACHERS

Professor of Philosophy
 1. POL, p. 100.
 2. Sartre, *Huis clos,* in *Théâtre,* p. 182.
 3. POL, pp. 101–102.
 4. POL, p. 102.
 5. POL, p. 105.
 6. *Ecrits,* pp. 117–118.
 7. POL, p. 105.

Rouen
 8. Colette Audry, "Portrait de l'écrivain jeune femme," *Biblio,* November 12, 1962; and *Carnets,* pp. 111, 225–226, 329–332.
 9. Audry, ibid.
10. POL, p. 121.
11. POL, pp. 151–152.
12. POL, p. 145.
13. POL, pp. 127, 128.
14. POL, p. 128.
15. POL, p. 131.
16. POL, pp. 131, 132.
17. POL, p. 133.
18. *L'Humanité,* September 6, 1932.

"I Have Been Faithful to Thee, Cynara, in My Fashion"

19. POL, p. 132, and Dossier de Carrière de Beauvoir, Archives of the Ministry of Education.

20. POL, p. 190.

21. De Beauvoir on Marie Ville: "I was not worried, absolutely not. I had received enough letters from Sartre to know what it was all about. She was totally illiterate." Annie Cohen-Solal writes in her biography of Sartre (p. 151) that he had wanted to stay in Berlin for a second year but after Simone's visit did not talk about it anymore.

22. POL, p. 182.

23. *Letters,* pp. 380, 51, 43.

24. POL, p. 181.

25. POL, p. 180.

26. Henri Noguères, *La Vie quotidienne au temps du Front Populaire,* p. 103.

Charles Dullin

27. POL, p. 190.

28. De Beauvoir: "It was Shakespeare that they did not like" (*Action,* May 11, 1945). On Charles Dullin, see Jean Sarment, *Charles Dullin;* Charles Dullin, *Revue d'histoire du théâtre,* numéro special, 1950; and Charles Dullin, *Souvenirs et notes de travail d'un acteur.*

André Malraux's Affair

29. POL, p. 167; and interviews, October 1983.

30. POL, p. 168.

31. POL, p. 167.

32. POL, p. 177.

The Little Russian Girl

33. POL, p. 228. Olga is mentioned 97 times in the letters to Algren, and she is portrayed as Xavière in *She Came to Stay.*

34. POL, p. 231.

35. POL, pp. 230–231.

Taking Stock in Le Havre

36. De Beauvoir: "Absolutely false, he never had an exhibit at the Bonjean Gallery." See POL, p. 207. De Beauvoir contested the statement that she and Sartre were depressed that winter. See *Carnets,* pp. 100–101, and POL, pp. 167–168.

37. POL, p. 208.

38. POL, p. 212.

39. *Carnets,* p. 100.

40. *Carnets,* p. 102.

41. POL, p. 245.

42. *Carnets,* p. 102.

43. De Beauvoir, "Jean-Paul Sartre Strictly Personal," *Harper's Bazaar,* January 1945.

The Petit-Mouton Hotel

44. POL, pp. 233, 234.

45. POL, p. 226.

46. POL, p. 233.

Distractions of the Heart and Mind

47. POL, p. 195; interviews, May 1984 and September 1985; and see POL, chapter 4.

48. POL, p. 195.

49. POL, p. 254.

50. POL, p. 195.

51. POL, pp. 240, 195.

52. POL, pp. 239–240.

53. POL, p. 254.

54. *Carnets,* p. 102.

55. POL, pp. 254–255. De Beauvoir, commenting on her own quote: " 'Losing even more.' I don't know what 'losing' means" (September 23, 1985).

56. POL, p. 260.

57. *Carnets,* p. 102.

58. POL, p. 257.

59. POL, p. 257.

60. De Beauvoir: "On the contrary, I always want to listen to everything."

61. POL, p. 258.

1936: Paris

62. Sarah Hirschman, "Simone de Beauvoir, Professeur de Lycée," *Yale French Studies* 22, 1958–1959, pp. 79–82.

63. Ibid.

64. De Beauvoir denies her student's assertion: "I did not read it. I never read those magazines."

65. POL, p. 279.

66. Interview with a former student of Dullin (October 1983).

67. POL, p. 286.

68. POL, p. 292.

69. *Letters,* pp. 103, 96.

70. *Letters,* pp. 103, 96.

71. *Letters,* p. 122.

ADDITIONAL SOURCES, CHAPTER 5
Archives of the Ministry of National Education.
Histoire 51, December 1982.
Compagnon, Antoine, *La IIIe République des lettres.* Paris: Le Seuil, 1983.
Duroselle, J. B., *Politique étrangère de la France—La Décadence, 1932–1939.* Paris: Le Seuil, 1979.
Rougemont, Denis, *Journal d'une époque, 1925–1945.* Paris: Gallimard, 1968.
Vincent, Raymond, *Le Temps d'apprendre à vivre.* Paris: Julliard, 1982.

CHAPTER 6. CONTINGENT LOVES

All About Love

1. SS, p. 652.

2. SS, p. 653.

3. Catherine Chaîne, "Sartre et les femmes," *Le Nouvel Observateur,* January 31, 1977, p. 68.

4. POL, p. 27.

5. POL, p. 26.

6. POL, p. 27.

7. Chaîne, "Sartre et les femmes," p. 84.

8. Jacques-Laurent Bost: see Gerbert in *She Came to Stay.*

9. De Beauvoir: "It all happened exactly as I tell it in *She Came to Stay*" (May 8, 1984).

10. *Letters* II, pp. 93–94.

11. POL, p. 282.

12. POL, p. 305.

13. POL, p. 308.

14. POL, p. 230.

15. *Letters,* pp. 159–160 and passim.

16. *Letters,* pp. 184–186.

17. *Letters,* p. 187.

18. *Letters,* p. 189.

19. *Letters,* pp. 190–191.

20. *Letters,* p. 247.

21. *Letters,* p. 248.

22. *Carnets,* pp. 144–145.

23. De Beauvoir: "I have always taken care of Olga. I gave her money. I took care of her. That is it" (September 23, 1985).

24. *Letters*, pp. 159–160.

25. *Letters*, pp. 159–160.

26. *Letters*, p. 194.

27. *Letters*, pp. 163–165.

28. *Letters*, p. 193.

29. Letter to Algren, Folder G.

Life Goes On

30. Interview, May 8, 1984.

31. POL, p. 346.

32. POL, p. 355.

Descent into Horror

33. Rita Thalmann, *La Nuit de cristal* (Paris: Laffont, 1972).

34. POL, pp. 357–358.

35. POL, p. 359.

36. POL, p. 359.

The Little Polish Girl

37. *Letters* to Louise Védrine, pp. 228–234, 244–272.

38. *Carnets*, pp. 332–333.

39. *Letters* to Louise Védrine.

40. *Letters* to Louise Védrine.

41. *Letters* to Louise Védrine.

42. *Letters*, pp. 236–237, 317–318.

43. *Letters*, p. 236.

44. *Letters*, p. 243.

"Literary Honesty Is Not What It Is Commonly Taken to Be"

45. POL, p. 479.

46. POL, p. 365.

47. Madeleine Gobeil, "Entrevue avec S. de Beauvoir," *Cité libre* 15, August–September 1964.

48. Letter to Algren. De Beauvoir: "I never collaborated with Sartre, never. . . . This was a lie for Algren, I always told a little white lie to Algren because I wanted to make him feel less resentful when I went back to Paris." In her letter to Algren from Algeria, she said she was working with Sartre and Bost on a film script of *Dirty Hands* and did not like it; she did it for the money.

49. POL, p. 340.

50. POL, p. 338.

ADDITIONAL SOURCES, CHAPTER 6

Audry, Colette, *Léon Blum ou la politique du juste.* Paris: Julliard, 1955.

Falk, André, *Le Roman vrai de la IIIᵉ République: Les Années difficiles.* Paris: Denoël, 1958.

Fohlen, Claude, *La France de l'entre-deux-guerres.* Paris: Casterman, 1966.

Signoret, Simone, *La Nostalgie n'est plus ce qu'elle était.* Paris: Le Seuil, 1975.

CHAPTER 7. THE WAR

The First Days of the End of a World
1. POL, p. 375.

2. De Beauvoir: "We were confident the storm would blow over."

3. POL, p. 375.

4. POL, p. 376.

5. Letters, p. 128.

6. Letters, pp. 272–273.

Time Without Meaning
7. Letters, pp. 273–276.

8. Letters, pp. 329–330.

The Drôle de Guerre, *1939–1940*
9. POL, p. 385.

10. POL, p. 402.

11. Etudes sur la France de 1939 à nos jours (Paris: Le Seuil, 1985), pp. 12–20.

12. Jacques Chastenet, *Histoire de la Troisième République* IV, p. 101.

13. POL, p. 418.

14. POL, p. 420.

15. De Beauvoir: "Only marginally, my father did so poorly" *(c'était minable!).*

16. POL, p. 422.

17. POL, p. 423.

18. POL, p. 423.

1940
19. POL, p. 429.

20. Charles de Gaulle, *Mémoires.* Paris: Plon, 1954–1971.

21. POL, p. 435.

22. POL, p. 437.

23. POL, p. 438.

24. De Beauvoir: "I never lost Sartre's letters, I just published them. Maybe I lost a few." See POL, p. 349. In *Letters*, p. 52, de Beauvoir writes, "Many letters written by Sartre in 1931–1932 when I was in Marseille were lost. Also lost are those he sent me from Germany in 1933–1936." In *Carnets*, p. 40: "The letters written during the summer of 1929 have been lost."

25. POL, p. 444.

26. POL, p. 447.

27. De Beauvoir: "Sometimes I can't help it. I have been crushed by situations I could not control: the German Occupation and the fact that Sartre was taken prisoner."

28. POL, p. 451.

29. POL, p. 452.

30. POL, p. 460.

31. *Letters* I, pp. 282–283. See pp. 200–306.

32. *Letters*, pp. 284–285, 291.

33. *Letters*, pp. 286–288.

34. *Letters*, p. 294.

35. *Letters*, pp. 295–301.

36. *Letters*, p. 301.

37. *Letters*, p. 303.

38. POL, p. 465.

39. POL, p. 468.

40. POL, p. 469.

41. POL, p. 470.

The Blood of Others

42. *Letters*, p. 306.

43. POL, p. 482.

44. POL, p. 494.

45. POL, p. 492.

46. POL, p. 492.

47. POL, p. 496.

48. POL, p. 498.

49. *All Said*, p. 131.

50. POL, p. 490.

51. POL, p. 503.

52. Alfred Fabre-Luce, *L'Epreuve 1930–1945* (Paris, 1963).

53. *Simone de Beauvoir,* dialogue of the film (Paris: Gallimard, 1979), p. 47. See pp. 46–52 on Bost, Sartre, and de Beauvoir.

54. POL, p. 475.

55. *Letters* I, p. 183. For letters on Nathalie Sorokine, see pp. 356, 459, 484–485, 503; II, pp. 44, 236–245. See also POL, pp. 378, 418.

56. Letters, p. 236.

57. Letters, p. 207.

58. Letters, pp. 275–276.

59. Letters, p. 503, and *Simone de Beauvoir,* dialogue of the film, p. 50.

60. Interviews.

61. *Letters* II, p. 312.

62. POL, pp. 558–559.

63. POL, p. 555.

64. POL, p. 555.

65. Herbert Lottman, *La Rive Gauche* (Paris: Le Seuil, 1981), p. 386.

The Fiestas

66. POL, p. 567, and *Simone de Beauvoir,* dialogue of the film, pp. 51–52.

67. POL, p. 575.

68. Dialogue, p. 49.

69. In POL, p. 511, de Beauvoir wrote: "He grabbed it instantly and ran downstairs to deposit it in the dustbin," but in our interviews with her and in the dialogue of the film *Simone de Beauvoir,* pp. 49–50, de Beauvoir said that Sartre tossed the rabbit out of the window.

70. POL, p. 595.

71. FOC, p. 12.

72. POL, p. 607.

Violette Leduc

73. Letter to Algren, 1948. De Beauvoir wrote about Violette Leduc 56 times.

74. Violette Leduc, *La Bâtarde* (New York: Dell, 1966), pp. 6, 10, 18.

ADDITIONAL SOURCES, CHAPTER 7

Amouroux, Henri, *La Vie des français sous l'occupation.* Paris: Fayard, 1961.
Bourget, Pierre, *Paris 1960–1966.* Paris: Plon, 1979.
Aron, Robert, *Histoire de l'épuration,* Paris: Fayard, 1975.
Aron, Robert, *Histoire de la libération de la France.* Paris: Fayard, 1954.
Azéma, Jean-Pierre, *De Munich à la libération.* Paris: Le Seuil, 1979.
Cotta, Michèle, *La Collaboration 1940–1944.* Paris: Armand Collin, 1964.
Heller, Gerhard, *Un allemand à Paris.* Paris: Le Seuil, 1981.

Loiseaux, Gérard, *La Littérature de la défaite et de la collaboration.* Paris: Sorbonne, 1984.

Morgan, Claude, *Les Don Quichotte et les autres.* Paris: Roblot, 1979.

Paulhan, Jean, *Oeuvres complètes,* vol. V. Paris: Gallimard, 1970.

Paxton, Robert, *Vichy France.* New York: Knopf, 1972.

Perrin, Marius, *Avec Sartre au Stalag XIIb.* Paris: Delarge, 1980.

Rougemont, Denis, *Journal d'une époque 1926–1946.* Paris: Gallimard, 1968.

Roy, Claude, *Les Yeux ouverts dans Paris insurgé.* Paris: Julliard, 1944.

Seghers, Pierre, *La Résistance et ses poètes.* Paris: Seghers, 1974.

Sperber, Manès, *Au-delà de l'oubli (Ces Temps-là III).* Paris: Calmann-Lévy, 1979.

Touchard, Jean, *Le Gaullisme 1940–1969.* Paris: Le Seuil, 1978.

CHAPTER 8. EXISTENTIALISM

"It Was Our Turn to Carry the Torch"

1. Interview and Schwarzer, p. 114.
2. FOC, p. 434.
3. FOC, p. 434.
4. Sartre, *Situations II,* p. 45.
5. FOC, p. 46.
6. For a study of *Les Temps modernes,* see Anne Boschetti, *Sartre et "Les Temps modernes"* (Paris: Editions de Minuit, 1985).
7. *Samedi-Soir,* January 15, 1949.
8. Roger Garaudy in *Les Lettres françaises,* November 24 and December 1, 1945.
9. Jean Kanapa, *L'Existentialisme n'est pas un humanisme* (Paris: Les Editions Sociales, 1946).

Daniel Secrétan

10. FOC, p. 30.
11. FOC, pp. 30, 31.
12. FOC, p. 14.
13. FOC, pp. 31, 32.
14. "Quatre jours à Madrid," *Combat,* April 14–15, 1945.
15. "Le Portugal sous le régime de Salazar," *Volontés,* April 23–24, 1945.

Literature and Metaphysics

16. FOC, p. 45.
17. POL, p. 563.
18. POL, p. 588.
19. *Who Shall Die?,* pp. 2–3.
20. Jacques Lemarchand, *L'Arche* 12, December 1945.

21. FOC, p. 71.

22. FOC, p. 75.

The Existentialist Offensive

23. FOC, p. 46.

24. Sartre, *Being and Nothingness,* in which he develops his philosophical theory known as Sartrian existentialism. See *Situations IV.*

25. FOC, p. 47.

26. FOC, p. 47.

27. FOC, p. 47.

28. François Mauriac, *Le Figaro littéraire,* November 14–20, 1963.

29. *Poetry* 69, December 1946.

"People Will Speak of the Existentialist Era"

30. Paul Guth, *Le Figaro littéraire,* August 20, 1949.

31. Jacques Robert, *Samedi-Soir,* May 3, 1947.

32. Ibid.

33. Boris Vian, *Le Manuel de Saint-Germain-des-Prés,* pp. 162–163; Boris Vian, *Chroniques de jazz* (Paris: La Jeune Parque, 1967), and *Chroniques du menteur.*

34. Quoted in *Samedi-Soir,* January 15, 1949.

35. Raymond Las Vergnas, *L'Affaire Sartre; Les Lettres françaises,* November 24 and December 1, 1945.

36. Ibid.

37. Gabriel Marcel, quoted in Christine Cronan, *Le Petit Catéchisme de l'existentialisme pour les profanes.*

38. *Je suis partout,* November 16, 1946.

39. Las Vergnas, *L'Affaire Sartre.*

40. Paul Guth, *Le Figaro,* August 20, 1949.

41. *Samedi-Soir,* November 17, 1945.

42. *Samedi-Soir,* ibid.

43. De Beauvoir, *L'Existentialisme et la sagesse des nations.*

44. Interview by Franco Fortini, "Alcune domande a Jean-Paul Sartre e a Simone de Beauvoir," *Il Politecnico,* July–August 1946, pp. 33–35.

45. Dominique Aury, *Les Lettres françaises,* December 1, 1945.

46. FOC, p. 76.

47. FOC, pp. 116–117.

48. "French Novelist Speaks at Vassar," *Poughkeepsie New Yorker,* February 8, 1947.

49. Ibid.

Additional Sources, Chapter 8

Arts et loisirs 24, "Quelques autochtones authentiques," March 9–15, 1966, pp. 66–68.

Combat, September 8, 1945.

Club maintenant, "Pour l'histoire de l'existentialisme," 1946, pp. 84–86.

Critique 19, Georges Bataille, "De l'existentialisme au primat de l'économie," December 1947, pp. 515–526.

Le Figaro, Avron, "Guillotine et coups d'épées," December 29, 1945.

Le Monde, December 14 and 15, 1945.

Les Lettres françaises 83, Dominique Aury, "Qu'est-ce que l'existentialisme?" November 24 and December 1, 1945.

Les Lettres françaises 81, M. C., "Les Trompettes de l'existentialisme," November 10, 1945.

Les Nouvelles littéraires, November 15, 1945.

Les Temps modernes 2, Maurice Merleau-Ponty, "La Querelle de l'existentialisme," November 2, 1945.

Minerve, Paul Guth, "Haro sur Sartre?" January 11, 1946.

Barnes, Hazel, *Humanistic Existentialism and the Literature of Possibility.* Lincoln: University of Nebraska Press, 1959.

Boutang, Pierre, and Bernard Pingaud, *Sartre: Est-il un possédé?* Paris: La Table Ronde, 1946.

Burnier, Michel Antoine, *Les Existentialistes et la politique.* Paris: Gallimard, 1966.

Camus, Albert, *Oeuvres complètes.* Paris: Gallimard, La Pléiade, 1963.

Casarès, Maria, *Résidente privilégiée.* Paris: Fayard, 1980.

Cau, Jean, *Une nuit à Saint-Germain-des-Prés.* Paris: Julliard, 1977.

Cazalis, Anne Marie, *Les Mémoires d'une Anne.* Paris: Stock, 1976.

Cronan, Christine, *Le Petit Catéchisme de l'existentialisme pour les profanes.* Paris: Dumoulin, 1948.

Doelnitz, Marc, *La Fête à Saint-Germain-des-Prés.* Paris: Laffont, 1976.

Garaudy, Roger, *Une littérature de fossoyeurs: Un faux prophète, Jean-Paul Sartre.* Paris: Editions Sociales, 1948.

Gréco, Juliette, *Jujube.* Paris: Stock, 1982.

Hanoteaux, Guillaume, *Ces nuits qui ont fait Paris* Paris: Tallandier, 1971.

Heller, Gerhard, *Un allemand à Paris.* Paris: Le Seuil, 1981.

Koestler, Arthur, *Hiéroglyphes.* Paris: Calmann-Levy, 1955.

Las Vergnas, Raymond, *L'Affaire Sartre.* Paris: Haumont, 1946.

LeRoy, Jules, *Saint-Germain-des-Prés, capitale des lettres.* Paris: André Bonne, 1952.

Maschino, Maurice, *L'Engagement.* Paris: Maspero, 1961.

Mouloudji, Marcel, *Un garçon sans importance.* Paris: Gallimard, 1971.

La Petite Histoire de l'existentialisme. Paris: *Club maintenant,* 1946.

Pour et contre l'existentialisme. Paris: Atlas, 1948.

Mougin, Henri, *La Sainte Famille existentialiste.* Paris: Editions Sociales, 1947.

Vian, Boris, *Chroniques du menteur.* Paris: Bourgois, 1974.

Vian, Boris, *Manuel de Saint-Germain-des-Prés.* Paris: Le Chêne, 1974.

Wahl, Jean, *Esquisse pour une histoire de l'existentialisme.* Paris: Editions de l'Arche, 1949.

Chapter 9. The American Lover

America! America!

   1. FOC, p. 94.

   2. Janet Flanner, "The Talk of the Town," *The New Yorker,* February 25, 1947.

3. De Beauvoir: "I was not elegant at all."

F and G: "Your elegance is mentioned in several articles."

De Beauvoir: "Don't use articles. You can never trust journalists. . . . Before I left [Paris] I had a pretty dress, deep blue with large green patterns, made by a young couturier [she could not remember the name], and I had a fur coat, a poor little fur coat that I bought in Portugal. It made one of my friends laugh and say, 'Ah! That poor Simone, she is so very proud in *her* fur coat' " (September 20, 1985). "Bost laughed his head off when I told him about my New York elegance. You see, people were saying, 'But what is the matter with Simone, doesn't she have more than one dress?' and Stépha would answer, 'She is lucky enough to have one.' I bought precisely my first nice things in New York. Back in Paris, Raymond Queneau's maid exclaimed, 'How chic you are since you came back from New York.' But Jean Genet told me, 'You look like a sack' " (September 23, 1985). In 1947 she wrote Nelson Algren that at the premiere of a play by Salacrou people told her she looked very elegant: "I wore my mink coat." See *Ecrits,* pp. 144–147.

4. "An Existentialist Looks at America," *The New York Times Magazine,* May 25, 1947.

5. Ibid.

6. De Beauvoir: *"La mère* Knopf had said to me in Paris, 'So you are *still* interested in Faulkner.' "

7. *America,* pp. 29, 75.

Nelson Algren

8. Nelson Algren had an affair with Mary Guggenheim, who would later try to write a novel about it. In 1948 she was to marry Roditi, an editor of *The Partisan Review.*

9. H. E. F. Donahue, *Conversations with Nelson Algren.*

10. FOC, p. 135.

11. W. J. Weatherby, "The Last Interview," in Nelson Algren's *The Devil's Stocking* (New York: Arbor House, 1983).

12. De Beauvoir insisted that he was a Polish Jew and that his real name was Abraham, not Algren. In her letters she told him several times that if he lived in Paris he would assume his Jewishness. "He was Jewish but never wanted to assume it" (September 25, 1985).

13. Donahue, *Conversations,* pp. 30–31. See chapter entitled "The Young Man," pp. 21–66.

"Ma Petite Gauloise"

The quotations in this chapter, unless otherwise identified, are from Simone de Beauvoir's letters to Nelson Algren.

14. FOC, p. 135.

15. De Beauvoir: "After the liberation of Paris, Bost had many girl friends; we had been very close during the war, after that . . ." (February 1985).

16. FOC, pp. 136–137.

17. FOC, p. 142.

18. FOC, p. 144.

Love Letters

19. De Beauvoir: "Cut all that; it looks so silly. I look ridiculous. Even with Sartre we played the game of a married couple."

20. "Too Much Salt on the Pretzels" ("Trop de sel sur les pretzels") is not mentioned in Martha Cox and Wayne Chatterton, *Nelson Algren* (New York: Twayne, 1975), or in Donahue, *Conversations.* It was published in *Les Temps modernes* 35, September 1948.

21. Letter to Algren, Folder H.

22. Letter to Algren, Folder B.

23. Letter to Algren, Folder D.

24. FOC, p. 166.

25. *America,* p. 23.

26. FOC, p. 262.

27. Letter to Algren, July 24–29, 1948, Folder H.

28. Interview with Nelson Algren, *Harper's,* May 1965.

ADDITIONAL SOURCES, CHAPTER 9

Algren, Nelson, *Chicago, City on the Make.* New York: Doubleday, 1951.

Algren, Nelson, *The Last Carousel.* New York: Putnam, 1973.

Algren, Nelson, *Never Come Morning.* (Introduction by Richard Wright.) New York: Harper, 1942.

Algren, Nelson, *Who Lost an American?* New York: Macmillan, 1963.

Algren, Nelson, "Last Rounds in Small Cafés: Remembrance of Jean-Paul Sartre and Simone de Beauvoir," *Chicago,* December 1980.

Algren, Nelson, "The Question of Simone de Beauvoir," *Harper's,* May 1965.

Algren, Nelson, "Les Amours de Simone de Beauvoir dans un miroir à deux faces," *Arts* 937, November 1963.

Algren, Nelson, "Simone de Beauvoir: A New Kind of Nun." Review of *Memoirs of a Dutiful Daughter,* in Martha Cox and Wayne Chatterton, *Nelson Algren.*

Donohue, H. E. F., *Conversations with Nelson Algren.* New York: Hill and Wang, 1964.

Feninger, Andreas, *The Face of New York.* New York: Crown, 1954.

Gunther, John, *Inside U.S.A.* New York: Harper, 1947.

Pringle, Lauren Helen, *An Annotated and Indexed Calendar and Abstract of the Ohio State University Collection of Simone de Beauvoir's Letters to Nelson Algren,* Ph.D. dissertation, Ohio State University, 1985.

CHAPTER 10. PATHS OF GLORY

"One Is Not Born a Woman, One Becomes One"

1. François Mauriac, *Le Figaro littéraire,* June 25, 1949.

2. FOC, p. 197. The translation is our own.

3. Armand Hoog, *Le Figaro littéraire,* August 27, 1949.

4. André Rousseau, *Le Figaro littéraire,* November 12, 1949.

5. *Paris Match,* August 6 and 13, 1949. Certainly one of the best critical articles written on *The Second Sex* in 1949.

6. Ibid.

7. SS, pp. 28–29.

8. SS, p. 295.

The Mandarins

9. FOC, pp. 203, 275.

10. Sartre's press conference, published in *Franc-Tireur,* March 10–14, 1948.

11. FOC, pp. 184, 187.

12. FOC, p. 215.

13. FOC, p. 223.

14. Herbert Lottman, *Camus* (Paris: Le Seuil, 1978).

15. *Les Temps modernes* 79, May 1952.

16. FOC, p. 271.

17. *Samedi-Soir,* September 6, 1952.

18. De Beauvoir: "We supported only the USSR position on peace" (September 25, 1985). For de Beauvoir's position regarding the USSR in 1954, see J. R. Rolland, "Interview de Simone de Beauvoir," *L'Humanité dimanche,* December 19, 1954; *Les Temps modernes* 112–113 and 114–115 (1954), pp. 1539–1575 and 2219–2275; and Sartre, "Les Communistes et la paix," *Situations VI,* 1964, p. 80.

19. Letter to Algren, Folder G.

20. FOC, p. 276.

21. FOC, p. 266.

22. FOC, p. 264.

23. FOC, p. 294.

24. FOC, p. 297.

"Am I Past the Time of Loving?"

25. "The Two Pigeons," a fable by Jean de la Fontaine.

26. FOC, p. 297. "In fact it is because he wanted it" (September 25, 1985).

27. FOC, pp. 298, 279.

28. De Beauvoir: "Lanzmann was working for *France-Dimanche* to earn a living and was not very proud of it."

29. FOC, p. 309.

30. FOC, p. 311.

The Prix Goncourt

31. FOC, p. 326.

32. FOC, p. 326.

33. FOC, p. 280.

34. Letter to Algren, Folder I.

35. Las Vergnas, *L'Affaire Sartre.*

36. FOC, p. 282.

37. Letter to Algren, Folder L.

38. *L'Osservatore romano,* July 13, 1956.

39. FOC, p. 328.

40. Pierre Dubry, *Actualités,* February 1962.

ADDITIONAL SOURCES, CHAPTER 10

Armogathe, Daniel, *"Le Deuxième Sexe": Analyse critique.* Paris: Profil d'une oeuvre, 1977.

Gennari, Geneviève, *Le Dossier de la femme.* Paris: Perrin, 1964.

Lilar, Suzanne, *Le Malentendu du "Deuxième Sexe."* Paris: Presses Universitaires de France, 1969.

Plancard d'Assax, Jacques, *Madame Simone de Beauvoir et* Ses Mandarins. Paris: La Librairie Française, 1954.

Rind, Anita, *"Deuxième Sexe*: Tant qu'il y aura des femmes," *Le Monde,* November 10, 1984.

Viansson-Ponté, Pierre, *Histoire de la République Gaullienne.* Paris: Fayard, 1971.

Les Ecrits de Simone de Beauvoir has a list of articles on *The Second Sex.*

CHAPTER 11. THE TIME OF ACTION

The Trip to China

1. FOC, p. 337; *Ecrits,* pp. 63, 176, 179, 190, 260, 330, 360, 393, 407.

2. FOC, p. 345.

3. FOC, pp. 346, 348.

A Room of One's Own

4. FOC, p. 356.

5. FOC, pp. 368, 369.

The Course of World Events

6. Raymond Aron, *Le Figaro littéraire,* January 21, 1956.

7. FOC, p. 377.

8. FOC, p. 385.

9. FOC, p. 124.

10. FOC, p. 381.

11. FOC, p. 402.

The Demonstrations

12. FOC, p. 401; *Ecrits,* pp. 65–67, 74–75.

13. FOC, p. 417.

14. FOC, p. 420; *Ecrits,* pp. 70, 118, 186, 196, 201, 205–260.

15. FOC, p. 422.

16. FOC, pp. 437, 441, 443.

17. FOC, pp. 449, 454.

18. Sartre, "Les Grenouilles qui demandent un roi," *L'Express,* September 25, 1958.

19. FOC, pp. 461, 460.

20. Sartre, "Les Grenouilles."

21. FOC, p. 461.

22. FOC, pp. 465–466.

"Brigitte Bardot and the Lolita Syndrome"

23. "Brigitte Bardot and the Lolita Syndrome," *Esquire,* August 1959. De Beauvoir's original title for the article was "Brigitte Bardot."

"What Has Become of My Friends?"

24. From "La Complainte Rutebeuf," by the thirteenth-century French poet Rutebeuf.

25. Lottman, *Camus,* p. 329.

26. FOC, p. 497.

27. Lottman, *Camus,* p. 683. See chapters 49 and 50.

28. Sartre, "Albert Camus," *France-Observateur,* January 7, 1960.

Cuba

29. *Lunes de Revolución,* March 21, 1960, and FOC, p. 501.

30. FOC, p. 503; *Ecrits,* pp. 68, 71–72, 190, 194.

31. FOC, p. 504.

"Give Me Back the Age of Love"

32. Voltaire to Mme. du Châtelet: "If you want me to love you, give me back the age of love."

33. De Beauvoir: "After *The Mandarins,* Algren was quite amused because women pursued him and fell into his arms. They thought that he was a fantastic lover" (June 1985).

34. Algren, *Who Lost an American?* p. 96.

35. Algren, "Les Amours de Simone de Beauvoir dans un miroir à deux faces," pp. 20–26.

36. Algren, "The Question of Simone de Beauvoir," *Harper's,* May 1965.

37. FOC, p. 522.

38. Algren, *Who Lost an American?* pp. 96–97.

39. Algren, "The Question of Simone de Beauvoir."

The Trip to Brazil

40. Maria Craipeau, *France-Observateur* 514, March 1960, and *Ecrits,* pp. 70–72, 179, 196–198.

41. Ibid.

42. FOC, p. 525.

43. Letter to Algren, October 28, 1986, from Hotel Nacional, Cuba: "Dearest Beast of my heart, my own Nelson."

The Unindicted Indictables

44. See *Le Procès du réseau Jeanson* (Paris: Maspero), from p. 104.

45. FOC, p. 559.

46. FOC, p. 581.

47. *L'Express,* December 8, 1960.

48. FOC, p. 595.

49. FOC, p. 601.

50. FOC, pp. 602, 612.

51. Preface to Gisèle Halimi, *Djamila Boupacha.*

52. Jean Touchard, *Le Gaullisme 1940–1969,* p. 189.

Back to the USSR

53. *All Said,* pp. 314, 315.

A Very Easy Death

54. Interview with Madeleine Gobeil, *Cité libre* 15, August 1964.

55. *All Said,* p. 326.

56. *All Said,* p. 328.

57. Introduction to Charles Perrault, *Blue Beard and Other Fairy Tales,* translated by Richard Howard (Introduction by Simone de Beauvoir translated by Peter Green), New York: Macmillan, 1964.

58. *Que peut la littérature?* Paris Collection 10/18, no. 249, 1965.

59. Gabriel Marcel, "Prise de Position," *Les Nouvelles littéraires,* October 29, 1964.

"What Love Is—and Isn't"

60. De Beauvoir, "What Love Is—and Isn't," *McCall's,* August 1965, pp. 77, 133.

Human Rights

61. *All Said*, p. 145.

62. "Ils n'étaient pas des lâches: Entretien avec Simone de Beauvoir," *Le Nouvel Observateur*, April 1966, pp. 14–17.

63. Ibid.

"I Shall Never See Moscow Again"

64. Lena Zonina died in Moscow in February 1985. Her last book was *Paths of Our Time: Reflections on the French Novelists in the Sixties and the Seventies*. Sartre dedicated *The Words* to her.

Japan

65. *All Said*, pp. 286, 287, 288. For the complete texts of the lectures given by de Beauvoir, see *Ecrits*, p. 422, "Women Today"; p. 439, "My Experience as a Writer"; and p. 458, "Woman and Creativity."

66. *Literaturnaia Gazeta*, February 14, 1967.

Egypt

67. *El Ahram*, February 26, 1967.

68. *All Said*, p. 407; *Ecrits*, pp. 79, 226.

69. *El Ahram*, February 26, 1967.

70. *All Said*, pp. 406, 408, 409.

71. *All Said*, pp. 411, 412.

Israel

72. *All Said*, p. 420; *Ecrits*, pp. 93–97, 254, 522–526, 528–531.

73. *All Said*, pp. 420–423.

74. *The Jerusalem Post*, March 26, 1967.

75. *All Said*, p. 431.

76. *All Said*, p. 436.

77. *All Said*, pp. 436, 437.

ADDITIONAL SOURCES, CHAPTER 11
Alger Républicain, L'Express, Le Figaro, International Herald Tribune, Le Monde, Les Temps modernes
Mauriac, François, *Nouveaux Blocs-Notes*. Paris: Flammarion, 1965.
Rioux, Jean-Pierre, *La France de la IVᵉ République*. Paris: Le Seuil, 1980.
Servan-Schreiber, Jean-Jacques, *La Guerre d'Algérie*. Paris: Paris-Match, 1980.
Vaisse, Maurice, *Le Putsch d'Alger*. Paris: Editions Complexe, 1983.
Verdes-LeRoux, Jeanine, *Au service du parti: Le P.C.F., les intellectuels et la culture 1944–1956*. Paris: Fayard, 1983.
Vidal-Naquet, Pierre, *La Torture dans la République*. Paris: Editions de Minuit, 1972.

CHAPTER 12. THE CITADELS

The Russell Tribunal
1. *Le Monde,* June 3, 1966.
2. *Les Temps modernes* 261, February 1968, p. 400. See *Ecrits,* pp. 79–82, and *Tribunal Russell, le jugement final* (Paris: Gallimard, 1968).

The Woman Destroyed
3. *Marie Claire,* February 1968. See *Ecrits,* pp. 82, 237, 577–579.
4. *Le Figaro littéraire,* October 30–November 5, 1967.
5. Ved Solveg Saetre, "Intervju med Simone de Beauvoir," *Vinduet* 3, August 22, 1968.
6. Ibid.
7. "La femme," *Penela,* September 1968.

May 1968
8. *Le Monde,* May 8, 1968.
9. *Le Monde,* May 10, 1968, and May 27, 1968.
10. *Les Ecrits de Sartre,* p. 464.
11. *Le Monde,* November 30, 1968.
12. *All Said,* p. 458.
13. In this meeting a shoemaker told Sartre that what he had to offer were only words; he and his friends never had to work for a living.
14. *All Said,* p. 461.
15. Catherine Nay, *François Mitterrand* (Paris, 1983), p. 307.
16. *All Said,* pp. 462, 463.
17. Dagmar Steinova, "Aujourd'hui plus que jamais l'engagement," *La Vie tchéco-slovaque,* May 1969.
18. *Le Monde,* May 10, 1969, and *La Révolte étudiante: Les animateurs parlent.*
19. De Beauvoir: "George Sand did not write well. She refused any type of solidarity with women. She was always giving stupid names to her lovers, 'my child, my little one.' She was a landowner. She settled down and became a conservative."

"Let's Pull the Elderly out of the Ghetto"
20. "The Terrors of Old Age," *Newsweek,* February 9, 1970.
21. Nina Sutton, "Simone de Beauvoir Faces up to Mortality," *The Guardian,* February 16, 1970.
22. "Pourquoi on devient vieux?" *Le Nouvel Observateur,* March 16, 1970; *Il Giorno,* February 16, 1970.

Freedom of the Press

23. *All Said,* p. 465.

24. *All Said,* p. 467.

25. *Ecrits,* pp. 86–89.

26. *All Said,* pp. 470, 471.

27. *Ecrits,* pp. 87–88.

28. *All Said,* p. 478.

29. *Le Monde,* June 25, 1970.

30. *Le Monde,* September 14, 1970; October 9, 26, and 27, 1970.

31. *Le Nouvel Observateur,* February 16, 1972.

Apropos of Women

32. Anne Zélinzki, *Histoires du M.L.F.* (Paris: Calmann-Lévy, 1977). De Beauvoir wrote the preface. The book was published under the pseudonyms Anne Tristan and Annie de Pisan.

33. Ibid.

34. *All Said,* p. 481.

35. *La Cause du peuple,* June 1970.

36. De Beauvoir: "It was to do them a service, not to provoke public opinion" (September 25, 1985).

37. Schwarzer, p. 17.

38. *Vjesnik Zagreb,* May 12, 1968.

39. Schwarzer, p. 46.

40. *Libération,* March 1983.

41. *Pyrrhus et Cinéas,* p. 15.

42. Madeleine Gobeil, "No Exit," *McLean's* (Canada), February 1973.

43. *Le Monde,* December 18, 1973.

44. *Les Temps modernes,* December 1973.

45. "Les Femmes s'entêtent," *Les Temps modernes* 333–334, April–May 1974.

46. Televised interview with Jean-Louis Servan-Schreiber, T.F.1, April 7, 1975.

ADDITIONAL SOURCES, CHAPTER 12

L'Express, Le Nouvel Observateur (from 1967), *Le Monde, Il Giorno, Newsweek, The Washington Post, The Guardian.*

Daniel, Jean, *l'Ere des ruptures.* Paris: Grasset, 1979.

Delale, Alain, and Gilles Ragache, *La France de 68.* Paris: Le Seuil, 1978.

Fontaine, André, *Histoire de la guerre froide.* Paris: Le Seuil, 1967.

Freund, Gisèle, *Mémoires de l'oeil.* Paris: Le Seuil, 1977.

La Révolte étudiante: Les animateurs parlent. Paris: Le Seuil, 1968.

Viansson-Ponté, Pierre, *L'Histoire de la République Gaullienne.* Paris: Fayard, 1971.

Chapter 13. The Force of Words

Sylvie

1. *All Said,* p. 8.

2. *All Said,* p. 500.

3. *All Said,* p. 75. De Beauvoir: "We don't see each other every day but we call each other every day. Let's say 'very often' " (September 25, 1985).

4. Schwarzer, p. 91.

5. *All Said,* p. 69.

6. MDD, p. 345.

7. FOC, p. 291.

8. *All Said,* pp. 75–76.

9. Schwarzer, pp. 112–113.

10. Schwarzer, pp. 112–113. "We asked de Beauvoir if it was true that during her last trip to the United States in 1983, according to an American journalist, she shared the same room with Sylvie at their New York hotel. De Beauvoir answered, 'Yes, but I slept on the box springs and Sylvie on the mattress on the floor.' "

"Commitment, More Than Ever"

11. De Beauvoir on the preceding paragraph: "It is more a desire for truth than for propaganda."

12. For this film de Beauvoir interviewed patients in several nursing homes and spoke with older people. "I have met very happy old folks like [the writer] Jouhandeau."

13. Delphine Seyrig, Carole Roussopoulos, and Joana Wilder were at the head of the center. De Beauvoir: "They fought. There are now two centers. I am with Seyrig, but that has nothing to do with revolution." She added, "You should stop this book after 1980, because today all these people [the feminists] don't stop arguing" (September 27, 1985).

14. Schwarzer, pp. 18, 67. *Cahiers Bernard Lazare* 51, June 1975, pp. 30–37.

15. De Beauvoir: "I keep as far as I can from the magazines for women, they are not feminist magazines."

16. Yvette Roudy, *À cause d'elles* (Paris: Albin Michel, 1985). p. 113.

17. "Les Femmes s'entêtent," *Les Temps modernes* 333–334, April–May 1974.

Adieux: A Farewell to Sartre

18. Annie Cohen-Solal, *Sartre,* pp. 647–649; and de Beauvoir, *Adieux,* pp. 138–142, 149–153.

19. Ibid., p. 652.

20. Ibid., p. 653.

Letters to the Castor and a Few Others

21. Schwarzer, p. 57.

22. De Beauvoir: "All that was so normal for us."

23. Schwarzer, pp. 52–53.

24. De Beauvoir: "I know that is an idea dear to Elisabeth Badinter, but let's drop *Emilie, Emilie.* It is another century, another couple."

25. De Beauvoir on "virility": "Too much machismo. Why don't we write, 'the taste of freedom.' "

26. Schwarzer, p. 108.

27. Schwarzer, pp. 84–85.

28. "Why revolutionary? It was accepted that two brilliant *agrégés* lived together, it was quite accepted by the administration. M. Paraudy [the general academic inspector], who was a close friend of Mme. Morel, gave us two positions not too far from each other, Sartre was appointed to the Lycée du Havre, I was in Rouen."

CHAPTER 14. A DAY IN MAY 1985

1. De Beauvoir: "Don't end the book on my sister, she fantasized about her childhood."

CHAPTER 15. A DAY IN APRIL 1986

1. POL, p. 28.

2. POL, p. 27.

3. MDD, pp. 137, 138.

4. POL, p. 478.

5. VED, p. 106.

6. *Adieux,* preface.

7. Anonymous, *Mihloud* (Paris: Alinea, 1986), preface by Simone de Beauvoir.

INDEX